D1598199

Resurrection Logic

Resurrection Logic

How Jesus' First Followers Believed
God Raised Him from the Dead

Bruce D. Chilton

BAYLOR UNIVERSITY PRESS

Printed in the United States of America on acid-free paper with a minimum of
thirty percent recycled content.

Contents Overview

Contents

Preface

When New Testament texts speak of the resurrection, they are much more interesting than might be imagined from recent debates regarding whether God raised Jesus from the dead. When I read the original texts, they do not seem to me to line up with any of the many theories that have been devised to answer the question, "What really happened?"

Perhaps the question in itself is the problem. It encourages attempts to claim that a single cause explains all the texts at once, and so it forces them into a single homogenous category. They lose their individuality.

Homogenizing the texts produces another problem as well. When I work through the texts, their individuality is such that a family resemblance among them emerges. This commonality, as well as their individual character, is hidden when it is assumed that the texts' intent is to provide a single answer to the question of what happened.

At base, I have no interest in debunking a given view of the resurrection in favor of another. Nor would I discount any account of the resurrection, wherever it appears in the development of the New Testament traditions. Yet they make quite a few different and sometimes contradictory statements, so choices have always been involved in reading them. If a given interpreter prefers one account over another, that is to be noted, but it is hardly cause for disapproval. My principal concern is not to argue with colleagues in my discipline, although, when they fall into the habit of homogenizing the texts, criticism is in order.

My focus is to understand how those of Jesus' disciples who claimed God had raised him from the dead explained their conviction and related his resurrection to the hope of their own. The interpretative itinerary I follow was originally set out in the earliest list there is of the apostles by whom Jesus "was seen," which also gives the order of their visions. The introduction explains why that list (in Paul's First Letter to the Corinthians 15:5-8) has not featured as it should in understanding the resurrection. Then, against a contextual analysis of the setting in which Jesus' followers claimed he had been raised from the dead (part 1, "Crucibles of Hope"), the extraordinary range of texts in the New Testament and related literature are interpreted on the basis of Paul's list (part 2, "Catalyst of Transformation"). This is where their individuality is brought out more clearly than in previous discussion.

The family resemblance in the midst of variety concerns part 3, "Reasoning with the Resurrection." My reading of the sources in the order of their development has shown me that those who composed the New Testament themselves sought out the coherence among the individual witnesses whom they valued. They discovered a principle applicable within the sciences of their time, and I show that the same principle might be applied today within the sciences of a new time.

Asking about the *how* of belief, rather than about the *what* of alleged happenings in the past, opens the resurrection to analysis. On the basis of the revised question, I can see the ground of those who have believed in the past and the present. The disciples who shaped the accounts of Jesus' resurrection understood that his continuing presence made sense in terms of their sciences of how the world works.

Because the issue of belief is concerned, I should also situate my own faith for the benefit of readers. A member of a congregation (that I once served as priest) said to me one day, "You have to believe in the resurrection, because it is in the creed." I explained to him that I would reverse the causality: the resurrection has made me a priest who happily uses the creed. The conviction that God raised Jesus from the dead has been with me as long as I can remember; it is not even a matter of deciding to believe. (I have tried not believing, and I found the experiment interesting. But the stance involved was incommensurate with my understanding of how God encounters the world.) I would be neither a believer nor a historian without a sense of Christ alive in our midst, shaping hearts and guiding judgments and actions.

For that reason, because the resurrection is a conviction, not merely an element in a series of doctrines, seeing how others have believed that God raised Jesus from the dead and how that belief might live today is for me an existential concern. Yet the issue is always one of belief. Some people will believe passionately, some to the point of conviction, some with an element of doubt, and some not at all. Overt denial of the resurrection, as we will see, has also featured in modern controversy. I do not think that the range of responses can be pared down by a single, provable scenario of what really happened. Were that possible, broad agreement would have been achieved long ago. My aim is more modest but it is also more in keeping with the inner coherence of the texts: to uncover the resurrection as a belief rooted within the sciences of its time and applicable within the sciences of our time.

B.D.C.
Pentecost 2018

Introduction

Jesus' resurrection, a litmus test for whether a person is a believing Christian, also provokes wonderment, disbelief, and controversy. The familiar Easter announcement of victory over the grave is culturally ingrained and yet foreign, because ordinary experience tells us that death has the last word in human life.

When "after-death experiences" are reported, they are understood as exceptions. A person who has seemed to die and yet recovers, or the sometimes-reported experience that a dead person visits as a living presence, does not overturn the consensus that death imposes irrevocable closure on every human life. Jesus' resurrection, however, insists that his living presence supplants death. In "Death Be Not Proud," John Donne concluded his poem with the stark warning, "Death, thou shalt die." He captured the deep incongruity between common sense and the resurrection. When God raised Jesus—Donne says with the apostle Paul (1 Cor 15:26)—he destroyed death itself.

Since the Enlightenment, arguments over *what* people should believe have buried the resurrection beneath normative claims, allegedly universal rules of the workings of God and the world. Instead of explaining how Jesus was raised in the faith of early Christians, they have reduced it to the terms of their own preferred theologies or worldviews.[1] Protestants have made the issue that of coming to have faith in Jesus despite not only his own death but also the mortal nature of human life. From this perspective, the resurrection presents itself less to be understood than to be embraced by means

1

of a personal decision that is the gateway to an all-sufficient faith.[2] Catholics have portrayed the crux of the matter as being the *magisterium*, the teaching authority of the church, so that by living under the rule of love within the body of Christ, one comes to know him as risen. On this view, Christ directly confers an infallible authority on bishops, and especially the pope, to state the content of faith, including the resurrection.[3] In contrast, a vibrant tradition of revisionism has argued that Jesus died at the time of the crucifixion; his followers, sometimes guilt ridden, deluded themselves into thinking he had not really died.[4] Another revisionist interpretation simply empties his tomb by having Jesus survive the crucifixion.[5]

However well worked out these positions might be, they are more concerned with apologetics than anything else, designed to promote one perspective or another (that of faith, the *magisterium*, or revisionism). The perspective that is propagated covers over the resurrection. Often, the results say something helpful about the texts concerned, but that is almost by the way. The real aim is to argue for the particular view of what should be believed. The most efficient way to do that is to aggregate all the texts, despite their obvious diversity, into a manageable package.

In modern discussion, the need for a manageable amalgam has been supplied by the supposed "empty tomb." As a rule, Gospels on Easter Day, no matter which one is read, center on Jesus' disciples going to the place where he was buried. But the fact is that there is a description of entry into the tomb *only in the last two canonical Gospels* to be written. Luke (24:1-3, 10) has Mary Magdalene and her companions go in, while John (20:3-10) assigns that action to Peter and the beloved disciple. Both Luke and John go out of their way to say the tomb was not empty, since grave clothing was identified. But "the empty tomb," a stock phrase in modern discussion,[6] appeals strongly to the demand for belief in spite of doubt, as it does to the claim of the magisterial authority of the witnesses who visited the tomb, and to the contention that the disciples were mistaken in their belief.

In any case, the earliest gospel (Mark 16:1-5) has women disciples approach the tomb, but they are turned away by a young man who announces the resurrection to them. Matthew (28:1-2), on the other hand, presents a smashed tomb, destroyed by an earthquake and left as rubble, where an angel sits to explain the significance of the scene. The aggregate reading of the Gospels does not produce the monolithic narrative of "the empty tomb" that is often presupposed. Yet "the empty tomb" persists as if the phrase were necessary to refer to the resurrection; sometimes, those words appear in printed Bibles as a heading to passages in which disciples do not enter the burial cave.

When interpreters insist on repeating what they must know is not quite accurate, something other than exegesis is at issue, something like a myth. In this case, the myth ignores or contradicts the earliest of the sources, composed well prior to the Gospels. Paul—who produced the first known written evidence of belief in Jesus' resurrection and was the only person to write of his own experience in that regard—says nothing whatever of Jesus' tomb, referring only (1 Cor 15:4) to a burial after his death.

The conventional presentation has become so prevalent that it needs to be mentioned in this introduction, despite the fact that "the empty tomb" is a latecomer to the traditions regarding how God raised Jesus from the dead. The concluding chapters of this book analyze the texts and examine some distortions caused by the jejune convention of treating a late tradition as if it were primal. That analysis deliberately comes late in consideration, to reflect the chronological trajectory of the traditions about the resurrection and the recent pedigree of attempts to push "the empty tomb" further back in time than is plausible.

This book follows the unfolding of traditions and texts over time, rather than attempting to arrive at or to impose a single view of the resurrection. All the viewpoints in the New Testament (and related literature) are to be assessed, without attempting to collapse the variants into a single, allegedly dominant perspective. The range of the disciples' experience proves startling, when their testimony is not forced into conformity to one normative claim or another of what the resurrection has to have been.

The variety of the disciples' views of the resurrection presses the issue of not what, but *how*, the disciples believed. Their belief, of course, emerged within a setting quite different from the modern period. The ancient world shared views of resurrection and immortality, as well as considerations of how possible they might be, long before Jesus lived. Claims that individuals had escaped death appear sporadically, sometimes in ways that invite comparison with Jesus' resurrection. Part 1, "Crucibles of Hope," investigates that rich background with particular reference to the science that was articulated by those who asserted that death need not be the last word on human life.

"Science" in antiquity did not mean that all investigation had to be conducted by experimental method. That Enlightenment definition of science has not proven easily applicable to the issue of what happens to a person after death (although it has been attempted).[7] Long before programmatic experimentation, there was "knowledge" (*scientia* in Latin) of the natural world. That knowledge could also be systematized into a cosmology, a comprehensive account of the world or universe (*kosmos* in Greek). Resurrection and related concepts were worked out in cosmologies that exerted an influence on the New Testament within its accounts of how God raised Jesus from the dead. Ancient Near Eastern cosmologies are often complex, and their accounts of what awaits human beings beyond the span of their lives offers surprising similarities to current views, as well as some startling departures. These ancient sciences of resurrection are sometimes comparable to one another and are better understood when taken together, because the sources involved are nothing like comprehensive. Nonetheless, what does remain, even when fragmentary, reveals an array of views in constellations of cosmology, religion, philosophy, and ritual.

The New Testament did *not* break new ground in addressing the hope that God would raise the dead. Even the inclusion of humanity at large in the anticipated resurrection, with a committed refusal to restrict its scope to a few select religious heroes, finds a precedent in Second Temple Judaism. The surge of expectation during the Maccabean period—producing competing views of how exactly people were to be raised from the dead—changed the shape of the religion of Israel and influenced the character of those religions that inherited its legacy. From a system of belief that barely toyed with the boldest expectations of life after death in the ancient Near East during the period of the First Temple, Second Temple Judaism addressed the profound challenges of its time with an entire series of expectations for how God would raise the dead. These hopes were not systematized, and in some cases they provoked resistance within Judaism. But in each case a science of how God would act to vindicate the righteous has left a trace in a vivid literature across several genres. Resurrection hopes of remarkable diversity are a permanent inheritance from ancient Judaic texts.

Christianity distinguished itself, not by means of inventing hope in afterlife, but in making a dual assertion—emblematic for its adherents and its detractors alike. Believers claimed (1) that God had raised Jesus from the dead and (2) that his resurrection swept up humanity as a whole within the process of resurrection. This change—from hope to a conviction that God had raised one person from the dead to signal his raising of people globally— made Christianity distinctive in its time. Jesus' resurrection was taken as the catalyst of existential transformation.

Part 2, "Catalyst of Transformation," maps that process by following the list of disciples identified by the apostle Paul as those by whom Jesus "was seen" (1 Cor 15:1-9) after his death. In the past, Paul's standing as the earliest of all writers on the resurrection has been substantially overlooked in favor of the Gospels, which were produced later. In addition to his own perspective, Paul presents a list of apostolic witnesses before him that has not been accorded the chronological priority it naturally deserves. Paul presents this list as a stemma, the sequence of accounts of the resurrection, set out according to the principal disciples involved in shaping the accounts: Peter, the Twelve, more than five hundred "brethren," James (the brother of Jesus), "all the apostles," and Paul himself.

Paul relates his own experience only in part, and yet he indicates how he came to know Jesus as raised from the dead, and he details the cosmological implications of that encounter. He does not provide any details concerning the sciences of others on the list, whom he acknowledges all came before him. The Gospels, however, do provide accounts of the resurrection that involve some of those named on the list, most obviously Peter and the Twelve. Although James is not associated with accounts in the canonical Gospels, the Gospel of the Hebrews and Hegesippus fortunately help in characterizing his perspective.

No reference outside of Paul to the "more than five hundred brethren" has been discovered, yet it has proven possible to associate them with materials in the book of Acts as well as the Gospel according to Matthew. Mary Magdalene and her associates (variously named) appear in all the gospel accounts, so that her apparent absence from Paul's list requires explanation. Her place within the Gospels corresponds to the role of "all the apostles" in Paul's stemma. She joins others in the apostolic community named in the New Testament, including Barnabas and Silas. All their influences as sources of resurrection accounts with their sciences are traced in part 2.

Differing accounts of the resurrection, derived from different sources, are presented in the New Testament and related literatures, and the exegesis of this book details that variety. Variations appear not only in the details and the very nature of experiences related but also in the worldview or cosmology that frames each account. To address that variety and at the same time to understand how Jesus' followers claimed they were speaking of the same reality, part 3, "Reasoning with the Resurrection," identifies how the traditions came to be coordinated within the New Testament.

Paul's list identifies the principal witnesses of the resurrection, and each of those witnesses developed an account that centers on the imperative given by the risen Jesus. In every case the imperative is disruptive, an evident break from the practices and attitudes of the past, even within the movement of Jesus. The rationale for the disruption imposed by the imperative has to do with the cosmologies that the resurrection involved. Again, these are not a single worldview, but they nonetheless share a remarkable trait: each of the cosmologies portrays the risen Jesus as the basis on which God refashions the world. The social disruption of the risen Jesus' imperative corresponds to the disruptive cosmology that his resurrection signals.

Two lines of reasoning are deployed within the New Testament in order to coordinate these accounts. In one, the characteristic idiom is that of prophecy, so that those who see Jesus are empowered by a spiritual vision that enables them to pursue their own resurrection sciences. In the other, an arc of narrative, including the various descriptions of disciples visiting Jesus' tomb, grounds the resurrection more in the Jesus who is seen than in the disciples whose gift is to see.

Accounts of how God raised Jesus from the dead deliberately portray the disruption of stable convictions concerning how the world works, socially and ontologically. The imperatives of the risen Christ defied the received wisdom of how to behave, while his very presence breached the order of history as reflecting finite, finished human life. The ancient sciences that his disciples framed do not agree with modern sciences, and yet they also correspond to questions raised within all cosmologies—no matter what their age—concerning the relationship of humanity to the transcendence that is part of the human project to conceive and aspire to.

I
Crucibles of Hope

1

Resurrection and Immortality before Jesus

Introduction

Influential and compelling literary sources from antiquity explore resurrection and related topics from long before the time of the New Testament. They represent widespread traditions of thought and practice. At their points of origin, these sources unfold by means of narrative and ritual: stories and ceremonies about people and gods who crossed the line between mortal and immortal, human and divine. Philosophical discourses exploring those boundaries arrive later on the scene, although still well prior to the New Testament. Across a broad range of writings and a wealth of cosmological thinking, ancient views of afterlife—including the resurrection of the dead—provided a foundation for the distinctive teachings of Judaism and Christianity.

Four ancient myth cycles shaped views of resurrection in their times, influencing discussion for millennia: Gilgamesh and Utnapishtim, Isis and Osiris, Semele and Dionysos, and Ishtar and Tammuz. Each cycle represents a literary and ritual tradition that was well known in antiquity. They reflect cosmologies that are well defined, and sometimes specific indications of a technical knowledge that allegedly conquers death. Those outside the traditions—ancient and modern—have tended to call this knowledge "magic," but, within the mythic cycle, cosmology functioned as a science and ritual amounted to a technology that was crucial to master. In every case, the cycles concerned originated in a time well before the Hebrew Bible emerged, and even prior to recorded history.

Epic and poetry, originally created for oral performance, were the usual style of the literature concerned, so that a narrative mode of speaking of resurrection came naturally. But the form of story also provided the opportunity to use plot in order to negotiate a boundary that could seem strangely porous: the dividing line between mortals and the divine world. Yet in each case, the tantalizing similarities between people and their gods run into the ultimate conviction that humanity as such remains under the power of death, however spectacular sporadic exceptions to that rule might seem.

In the conception of the most ancient peoples, the difference between gods and humans was a matter more of degree than of kind. In their sharing of traits, the obvious line of demarcation was that people die, while divine beings do not. Yet that line was not only thin but wavy. Some gods were subject to death, while fascination with the possibility of human life after death was expressed within ancient mythology. Variations in the fate that might befall a god were standard, because the gods of antiquity were as varied, and just about as numerous, as people. They were also as unpredictable as human beings.

Stories provided an opportunity to investigate just what resurrection might mean, and whether it was possible in individual cases, with plot lines that made gods more human and people more divine. These four mythic cycles relate some of the dominant traditions of the ancient Near East and Mediterranean. The worldviews concerned vary, so that what it means to avoid death involves something distinctive in each case. Yet in them all, several common traits emerge. They agree, first of all, that resurrection is rare to the point of being a bare possibility, and then only for certain elite practitioners of the religion involved. Severe limitation on any hope of being raised from the dead followed from the underlying premise that death is an ordering principle in all life, even the life of the gods.

Ancient sources are also quite explicit in a second common trait. They are clear that resurrection is not the same as the descent into an underworld, where the body is consumed by corruption while some remnant of personality persists. That conception, most familiar to readers today in the "Sheol" of the Hebrew Bible, offers an afterlife that is not quite a life, because it is disembodied. Embodiment distinguishes the aspiration to cheat death from assurances that some shadow of mortal life survives. For this reason, the most ancient of the relevant sources do not make a broad distinction between resurrection and immortality. In both cases, embodied life is at stake, but with the substance of the gods rather than of people.

Gilgamesh and Utnapishtim in Sumeria

The *Epic of Gilgamesh* exerted a widespread influence within the ancient world, and it burst upon the modern world in the nineteenth century as a result of archaeological discovery.[1] Within the epic, Utnapishtim features as the exceptional case of a human being who cheated death permanently. Gilgamesh and Utnapishtim were originally Sumerian heroes. Gilgamesh was king of Uruk in Mesopotamia, who ruled during the third millennium BCE. Utnapishtim was a mythic figure, a sage who—warned by a god of a coming deluge—rescued his family, his community, and the animals of the field by putting them on a giant vessel. The story of Noah in Genesis 6–9 bears obvious comparison with that of Utnapishtim.[2] But from the perspective of the *Epic of Gilgamesh*, the cataclysmic flood is not the focal point of the narrative. Rather, both Gilgamesh and Utnapishtim, each by means of his personal chronicle, address whether human beings can escape their mortality.

The attraction of that existential question helps explains the appeal of the *Epic*. A unique style—blending myth, fantasy, drama, and suspense—makes for a compelling narrative. It addresses matters of the afterlife in story form, with a plot that crackles through the widespread versions of the *Epic*. After the eclipse of Sumerian power, the Old Babylonian and Assyrian periods saw new versions, until by 1000 BCE an entire epic had emerged, with Gilgamesh now a partially divine figure, "two thirds god and one third man."[3] His story led into Utnapishtim's.

Gilgamesh's strange pedigree gave him extraordinary size and power, which he deployed in contests against another semidivine figure, named Enkidu. Enkidu had been sent by the gods to tame Gilgamesh's appetite for plundering his own people. Enkidu joined Gilgamesh in combat, when the king of Uruk was in the midst of taking the virgins of his city as his own sexual possessions. The two demigods fought ferociously, and, at the end of their battle, they emerged as friends.

Gilgamesh and Enkidu partnered in quest of fame and fortune. They ventured out from Uruk in order to defeat Humbaba, the god of a cedar forest. Their victory netted them cedar for building, which Humbaba offered in exchange for his life, but the two friends killed the god in any case. The goddess Ishtar proposed marriage to Gilgamesh, but he spurned her, knowing her history of torturing her cast-off lovers. Ishtar demanded that her father, the god Anu, take revenge by sending the bull of heaven against Uruk; the whole city was to suffer for what its king had done. After all, Ishtar was a goddess, while Gilgamesh was only partly divine: honor was to be restored by means of collective punishment.

Gilgamesh and Enkidu slay the cosmic bull, but Enkidu has a dream in which one of the two heroes must die for their having slain Humbaba and the bull, both divine figures. The gods decide to take Enkidu's life, and he dies of illness. Despairing the loss of his friend, and appalled at the prospect of death that he realizes must also await him, Gilgamesh sets out to find Utnapishtim, the one person who has escaped death and entered into the assembly of the gods. To find Utnapishtim, Gilgamesh has to depart from the realm of ordinary mortal life. He travels to the western edge of the earth, traversing the passage the sun itself takes in its course, and enters the garden of the gods. He still is only part way to his journey's end, because gods themselves are subject to death in the cosmology of the *Epic*. Gilgamesh must also cross the waters of death, and then at last he meets Utnapishtim and his wife.

Utnapishtim's story is as primordial as Gilgamesh's and comparable in some ways; a Sumerian tablet identifies him as king of Shuruppak and calls him Ziusudra. That name means "life of long days," and Utnapishtim means "he who found life." But he is also called Atrahasis, "exceedingly wise,"⁴ and in that regard he is in a class apart from the king of Uruk. He relates to Gilgamesh that, prompted by Enlil, the great gods decided to engulf the world in a flood. But the god Ea warned Utnapishtim to tear down his house and build a giant boat in order to preserve his family, his wealth, the craftsmen of the city, and the animals of the field. The flood killed all other living things; even the gods fled to heaven. Ea, Ishtar, and other gods mourn the destruction, and they show their approval of Utnapishtim by swarming around his sacrifice like flies when he arrives back on dry land and offers the appropriate worship.

Ishtar and Ea in particular condemn Enlil for the arbitrary and impetuous destruction of the flood. The original reason for the deluge, and the justification for blaming Enlil once it is over, are not given. The point of the *Epic* is rather that the gods can take and give life and that their actions are often arbitrary. In this case, Enlil relents. He grants Utnapishtim and his wife immortality, sending them far from the company of ordinary people. How far becomes plain in what happens next.

Gilgamesh seeks the gift of immortality from Utnapishtim. Utnapishtim tells him to stay awake for six days and seven nights. The understanding is that sleep is akin to death, and the length of time is comparable to the flood that Utnapishtim and his company survived. But Gilgamesh, exhausted by his heroic efforts, falls dead asleep for the days Utnapishtim had prescribed. As Gilgamesh departs in disappointed failure, Utnapishtim's wife prevails on her husband to offer him at least a cure for getting old, if not categorical immortality.

Utnapishtim relents, identifying a thorn plant at the bottom of the sea as the curative agent against aging. Gilgamesh ties stones to his feet in order to explore for the plant under water, and he harvests some of the thorn plant. On his way back to Uruk, however, he decides to bathe, and a serpent comes and eats the plant. The serpent immediately sloughed off its skin, so the plant indeed produced something akin to immortality—in the molting of snakes. But it is too late for Gilgamesh to search for the plant again, because by then he had already crossed back into the land of the living (which is also by definition where death reigns).

On his disconsolate return to Uruk, Gilgamesh takes pleasure at the sight of the mammoth walls he has built around the city, his enduring legacy. In Gilgamesh's case, then, despite his heroic efforts, the only victory over death he can enjoy is royal architecture (and the *Epic* itself). The buildings can aspire to a future that the king himself can never see. In that way, the *Epic* explains how kings' boundless ambition relates to their passion to erect monuments to themselves. But alongside that cautionary treatment of the mythic king, Utnapishtim achieves what Gilgamesh does not, by means of wise and timely obedience to Ea.

Utnapishtim's wisdom is an evident feature of the whole tradition about him, reflected in his various names. But as the *Epic of Gilgamesh* unfolds, he also functions as a way for the gods to secure a claim on behalf of their own justice: their reward of Utnapishtim's wisdom compensates for their arbitrary injustice. The scale of the compensation relates to the truly exceptional blessing of triumph over death. Death in the *Epic* is an ambient reality for gods as well as men. Gods and demigods can be killed and injured and, like Enkidu, can succumb to illness. In the garden of the gods, the river of death is an obstacle Gilgamesh must cross to meet Utnapishtim. Even the gods answer to death.

The assumption of the *Epic* is that death is an ordering principle for all things living—animal, human, and divine. A breach of that principle threatens chaos. It is notable that the first mention of overcoming death comes when Ishtar demands that Anu unleash the bull of heaven against Uruk. If he does not, she says, she will *raise* the dead in order to crowd out the living. Resurrection is not a hope in this case but opens a terrifying prospect of instability and destruction. This accounts for why—in this instance, as in many treatments of the theme in ancient literature—the rarity of any triumph over death, and its limitation to highly selective elites, is taken as a matter of course.

Ishtar demands a return to the status quo and threatens Anu with unleashing a breach of order whose consequences could only be catastrophic. Anu, then, releases the cosmic bull to avoid an even more dreadful result. Death's role as an ordering principle also helps account for Utnapishtim's refusal simply to give away the secret of how to deny its power. When death itself is denied in the *Epic*, it is to rectify Enlil's injustice in the arbitrary destruction of people and living beings. His cruel arrogance is denounced by Ishtar, who will go on to propose overturning death in a different case, and by Ea, who has opened the path of Utnapishtim's wisdom. But the blessing by definition must be limited, in order to avoid the chaos of a massive restoration to life, and the proliferation of conflicting interests and revived schemes of vengeance that would imply.

The linkage of justice with triumph over death is a feature of the *Epic* that is echoed in much later sources, including the Scriptures of Israel at a much later time. In addition, its carefully constructed plot serves to explain a feature of ancient thought that otherwise might seem difficult to grasp: if death is to be denied, that can be on only a very limited basis for any sort of order to prevail in the world.

Because the *Epic* addresses death and overcoming death in the course of a consistent narrative, it also shows that the line of demarcation between resurrection and immortality was not clearly drawn. At a later time, by the period of the New Testament, that distinction is sensible. But Gilgamesh himself, while seeking immortality, passes through what would have been resurrection, had he succeeded. He leaves the realm of the living to arrive at the garden of the gods, and bodily he crosses the river of death, eventually returning to Uruk. When he arrives back, of course, he has only the metaphorical triumph over death of architecture to show for his efforts, but he missed his aim only because of a long nap and a short bath. Even Utnapishtim—although residing in the garden of the gods with his wife, and on the side of the river of death that puts him at an advantage over some gods—is nonetheless a bodily being. Gilgamesh, with characteristic arrogance, remarks that Utnapishtim looks somewhat feeble, as one would expect a human to appear in comparison to gods and demigods like Gilgamesh himself.

The description of Utnapishtim shows that immortality and resurrection are so closely related that they can be difficult to disentangle. But his status is globally different from that of the dead as a whole. Their bodies have become dust, or "clay," as the *Epic* describes the scene when Utnapishtim sees the results of the flood, so that only some disembodied form of existence can be imagined. What remains is a house "where dust is their food and clay their sustenance." That afterlife, the *Epic* makes clear, is not a consummation to be wished, because it is not a consummation at all but absence compared to what can be enjoyed in this life. The thirst that Gilgamesh tries and fails to quench is for a different satisfaction. The rediscovery of the *Epic*, as a result of the nineteenth-century excavation of Nineveh, permits modern readers to understand how, in the ancient world, resurrection was less a hope than it was a bare possibility likely to lead to disappointment. Power cannot force the prospect of triumph over death; only wise obedience to the gods, combined with the gods' own desire to right the wrongs that their kind have contributed to, secures Utnapishtim the blessing that eluded Gilgamesh and is likely to elude all who come after him.

Isis and Osiris in Egypt

Unlike the case of Gilgamesh, no rediscovery was required for Osiris' narrative to be appreciated in the West. In the ancient world, the ritual reenactment of how the goddess Isis brought her brother and husband Osiris back from death—and even from dismemberment—was famous far beyond Egypt. The myth that accompanied the ritual evolved over millennia and passed through many adaptations. A particular, formative moment of the ritual provides access to the cosmology and accompanying science that claimed Osiris as victor over death itself. He did what Gilgamesh could not accomplish, because Osiris was divine at the beginning and end of the myth. Even then, death appeared in the myth and ritual to have gained the upper hand, until Isis with the aid of other gods (especially Anubis) found the means to reconstitute Osiris' body and help him to make the journey to eternal life.

During the modern period, the dying and rising of Osiris has been cited as a precedent for the resurrection of Jesus.[5] In superficial terms, the argument for a similarity with Jesus makes some sense: after all, Osiris comes back from death (and does so twice) in the course of his myth. On both occasions, however, Isis—Osiris' sister and his wife—is the agent of his restoration to life; she is a vital element within the Egyptian tradition. For that reason, the modern tendency to focus on Osiris to the exclusion of Isis needs to be resisted if we are to appreciate how Osiris was raised to life again in the understanding of the thousands of people who enacted the story every year.

The robust character of the tradition is proven by the Greco-Roman author Plutarch at the close of the first century CE. He was not appreciative of the baroque Egyptian myth, remarking that anyone tempted to repeat it for the purpose of encouraging belief by others should rather spit and rinse out his mouth.[6] Plutarch is an early example of a rationalizing and dismissive approach to the study of others' religions; as a lifelong resident of Greece (and priest at Delphi), he appears especially suspicious of Egyptian influence.

It was easy for Plutarch to ridicule convoluted schemes—and all the more so when he himself contributed some of the convolutions he dismissed. Plutarch also typifies rationalistic critiques of religion because he ignores how traditions concerning Isis and Osiris were put into practice. They were not myths in isolation but scripts for public and very popular rituals in which the drama of death and regeneration was acted out, with thousands of practitioners joining in. Understanding the myth involves appreciating its ritual, and vice versa.

Archaeological work in the ancient city of Abydos in Egypt, which accommodated a vast temple and ceremonial complex in honor of Osiris and Isis, illuminates both the myth and its ritual.[7] Decades-long excavations uncovered a formative moment of the tradition, targeting remains from the thirteenth century BCE. Worship of Osiris and Isis long predates that time, but the Abydos complex provides a full picture of its character. The tradition clearly continued to grow from that moment, providing interesting variants. But the architecture of Abydos offers insight into the application of the entire tradition. The materials have been carefully analyzed and come from the time of the exodus from Egypt. In fact, Ramesses II, plausibly the pharaoh of the story of Moses,[8] brought the complex of Abydos to completion.

The reason for the remains at Abydos is that pharaohs saw themselves as the descendants of Osiris, who—according to the myth—fathered Horus by the remarkable means the story relates. Isis reconstituted her dismembered husband's corpse, consummated a last conjugal embrace by means of a penis she herself had to provide, and brought a son into the world who would rule Egypt. Horus, a falcon-headed god, unified Egypt as the country's patron deity, much as Isis had brought her husband's hacked-apart body together again. Each living pharaoh was regarded as the embodiment of Horus, while dead pharaohs were identified with Osiris. Osiris' act of procreation, engineered by Isis, meant that every pharaoh could legitimate his rule by means of the myth. Acting out the death, regeneration, and procreation of Osiris confirmed the authority of each pharaoh and anticipated a progeny that would govern with unbroken succession. The famed stability of Egyptian power, a unique achievement of governance over several millennia, is to some extent attributable to the attraction exerted by the myth and ritual of Osiris and Isis.

Yet Osiris' appeal was by no means limited to the political realm. As is often the case in religious discourse, his myth saw in him an explanatory force that accounted not only for the social world but also for patterns of nature and the forces that shaped nature. Among those patterns, none was more vital to Egyptian civilization than the cycle of the Nile River. Its flooding between June and September (a time called *Akhet*) watered and silted lands on both sides of the river. That permitted planting of wheat, flax, and papyrus during the months of sowing (*Peret*) and then harvest (*Shemu*) at the close of the year.[9] Cosmologically, Osiris accounted for the myriad ways in which death might appear to be the end of all prospects of life but then proves to be life's gateway. Attraction to his ritual functioned as a vital aspect of being an Egyptian.

Within this tapestry of meaning, ritual reenactment of the life, death, resurrection, and enthronement of Osiris in the netherworld accounted for the cycle that permitted Egyptian life to prosper in its agricultural substance and durable government. In Abydos, the acts of the drama were ritually repeated in a procession. Participants bore the images of Osiris and Isis and other deities from the temple of Osiris at the edge of the floodplain to his traditional tomb in the desert just over a mile away.[10] The procession then returned to its origin. Like the stations of the cross and reenactments of the crucifixion in later Christian tradition, the passion and vindication of Osiris unfolded during the ritual.

Osiris begins the story as king but is deposed by his brother, the god named Seth. Seth drowns Osiris in the Nile, but, by means of herbs of which Isis has knowledge, she brings her brother/husband back to life. Enraged, Seth returns and cuts up Osiris' body, scattering the pieces about Egypt. Isis persists, and, in the climax of the myth, she gathers the dismembered parts of Osiris' body with the aid of her sister Nephthys. One member remains missing, and Isis' desperation to find it ultimately discloses her power. For the purpose of their search for the scattered body parts, the two women transform themselves into birds of prey. In that shape, Isis prepares Osiris' body for burial with the jackal-headed god Anubis, but prior to interment she triumphantly mates with Osiris, whom she has brought to life again and provided with a new penis, the missing member. From her, Horus—the falcon-headed god and progenitor of pharaohs—is born, and he enters into combat with Seth.

From the moment of his death, Osiris is much more acted upon than acting. Even his procreation of his son is possible only because Isis manages to produce a penis for him. Horus emerges as the hero of the narrative, once the transition through Isis' mating with Osiris has taken place. That shift to the agency of Horus as the triumphant pharaonic successor, who defeats Seth after epic combat, no doubt drew the focus of ritual attention as the procession unfolded from Abydos to the desert and back again.

Yet in this myth, as in many others in antiquity, the unspoken is as central to the action as what is openly stated. Osiris steps out of the action of the drama of the succession, because he has also been removed from the affairs of the earth. He becomes king of the realm of the dead, and in that rule he exercised authority on a truly cosmic scale. He is the precedent for the immortality of all the pharaohs, and the model of a physical body preserved by Isis' actions, which amount to a proto-mummification.

Dying and rising from the Nile, Osiris embodies that natural pattern that gave all Egypt agricultural life, and, dismembered so as to be gathered again, he typifies the funeral preparations of his culture.[11] As in the understanding of Egyptian religion as a whole, the physical body is cared for, not to preserve what has eventually to decay, but in order to allow the *ba*—the embodied personality, the metaphysical substance of the deceased person—to make its way whole into the life beyond this life. Having been physically preserved by Isis, Osiris rules as the supreme judge of the dead. Every pharaoh after death appeared before him, and Osiris weighed the heart of the deceased on the scales of justice (*maat*) to determine whether or not the *ba* could enter into the world of the spirit (*akh*). Osiris passed through these stages primordially, and he opened the way to the pharaohs and eventually to those associated with the pharaohs.

In the earliest representations, deceased pharaohs were visible in their immortal *akh* in the stars arranged around the polar circle.[12] Over time, however, two related features developed in Egyptian cosmology, and they are apparent in the ritual of Osiris by the time of the period of Abydos. First, the potential for joining the journey of Osiris and reaching an ideal world among the dead was opened to a circle not limited to pharaohs. As that happened, the old, astral conception of the dead becoming stars was supplanted by locating the dead in a netherworld, beneath the earth.[13] Both refinements contributed to one of the most elegant and powerful cosmologies in antiquity.

Osiris was the "Foremost of the Westerners," because the sun (identified as the god Ra) disappeared from view at the end of the day in the west. As in the *Epic of Gilgamesh*, associating death with the direction of the sun's setting opened up possibilities. In the Egyptian conception, Ra then proceeded on a ship beneath the earth, to emerge again in the east at dawn. As the sun passed beneath the earth, Ra bestowed his life on all the beings of *akh*, as he did for the earth during daylight. The difference was that, in the netherworld, the sun's passing was not measured in the earth's time. Each hour that Ra illuminates beneath the earth represents an entire lifetime for the blessed dead. They plant the Field of Reeds eternally, an ideal image of the process of sowing and tending and harvesting that was the Egyptian paradigm of full life. In the depth of the night, this perfect world is consummated when Ra encounters Osiris. The former king is raised to life all over again, and the sun realizes the radiant power that is Ra's very purpose in being. The whole process rejuvenates the power of the sun for the coming day above the earth.[14]

Osiris embodies death and regeneration at every level: agricultural, sexual, personal, social, and cosmic. He brings all these forces of renewal because he was a god to begin with, and in that role he can also offer them to those who observe his rituals correctly. The extension of life in *akh* to the pharaohs opened the possibility to its further broadening, first of all to members of his household, but then in principle even beyond that.[15] Nonetheless, both knowledge of the journey to the mythical west and reliance on rituals that were both elaborate and expensive were intrinsic to following the path of Osiris.

The famous *Book of the Dead* (better translated as *Spells for Going Forth by Day*) was current throughout the New Kingdom and until the Ptolemaic period. It details the specialist knowledge of the postmortem world and rituals that needed to be followed for living a blessed death. After all, the corpse needed to be prepared and carried in procession to its tomb, its mouth then reopened so that the *ka*—the living energy that makes life possible—might be fed.[16] Offerings of goods and sustenance were served to the *ka*, the memory of its name preserved, even as the mobile attribute of a dead person, the *ba*, made its way from clinging to the earth to proceeding to the underworld.[17] There, Osiris would measure the heart against justice, and one was either made *akh* or destroyed after punishment.

Even without baroque convolutions of the sort Plutarch added to the scheme (some of which did in fact emerge over the course of time), the path to Egyptian resurrection was complex and expensive. Any prospect of following the path required the kind of education and resources normally associated with royalty, and was distributable only to a limited extent. The degree of expectation of living in the Field of Reeds mapped symmetrically over the privileges of class. Even among those of *akh*, some worked and others enjoyed the fruits of others' labor.

The achievement of the Isis-Osiris cycle was neither to provide the template of belief in Jesus nor to generalize the expectation of victory over death. Both of those claims, still sometimes made today, project the theology of the Gospels upon Egyptian theology, imposing the standards of a much later time on a millennial tradition that deserves assessment in its own terms. The pharaoh, as embodying Horus and destined to be identified with Osiris, united not only Upper and Lower Egypt but the living and the dead. The seamless cosmology in which Osiris featured also meant that those who served the dead within the rituals prescribed took part in cyclical eternity, quite apart from the ultimate fate of any particular individual who joined in the ritual triumph of life over death.

The tombs of pharaohs, and those fortunate enough to enjoy interment in a pharaonic manner, were temples of sacrifice, where offerings to the departed mimicked gifts presented to gods. After all, gods and the blessed dead all lived in the realm of *akh*, whether above or below the earth. For this reason, the New Kingdom's Ramesside tombs mirrored temples in their design.[18] Those who entered needed to be ritually pure, because this was a gateway to the realm beyond the west and was a place where the cosmogonic cycle that made the world and Egypt possible was not only recognized but also nurtured in the intimate intercourse between gods and persons.

Semele and Dionysos in Greece

Dionysos (also known under his Latinized name, Dionysius) is perhaps now the most popular of the divinities to be considered under the widely used category of "divinities symbolic of a resurrection beyond death."[19] But although there is a family resemblance among Gilgamesh, Osiris, Dionysos, and on to Tammuz, each of them is distinctive, the cosmology in which each was worshipped is unique, and the science of what it means to come back from the dead differs markedly from myth to myth.

As in the case of Osiris, the tradition concerning Dionysos endured for such a long time that variation is a factor that makes generalization difficult. In addition to that complexity, sources of the religion are difficult to pin down, not least because the worship of Dionysos in the Bacchanalia was outlawed by the Roman Senate in 186 BCE. By that time, Dionysos had been identified with gods such as the Egyptian Osiris and the Greek Orpheus as well as the Latin Liber.[20] Every permutation and combination brought shifts in the story, ritual, and expectation involved in any given local cult of the divinity.

These factors have complicated study of Dionysos. Yet the Greek god needs attention, because he was even better known in antiquity than he is now, and, during the first century CE, traditions concerning him were incorporated within practices such as "the Mysteries," in which initiates were ritually identified with gods. Fortunately, a productive baseline of investigation does survive among the ancient sources.

Baselines are always crucial in the analysis of any religion in terms of myth, ritual, or ethical content. They provide points of reference against which a tradition may be measured at any given time within its development. The *Epic of Gilgamesh* provides a baseline for Utnapishtim, while the excavations at Abydos offer a rich resource for understanding the worship of Osiris. Of course, a baseline is not the same thing as the original form of the religion, which often cannot be known; the point of departure for the traditions of Utnapishtim, Osiris, Dionysos, and Tammuz will in all likelihood remain a mystery to scholarship.

A baseline also does not function as any sort of canonical standard for the rest of the tradition. But a baseline does provide evidence of how a religion functioned in a definable time and place that was known to be influential within the culture concerned with the myth. In the case of Dionysos, worship at a festival named after him was the setting for a play by Euripides, called *The Bakkhantes*. (The term refers to Dionysos' frenzied followers, a usage from which the Latin *bacchanalia* derived.) When a play (or any work of fiction) is the best evidence available for a classic form of a religion, particular questions of how to go about a critical interpretation emerge. Understanding the context of the evidence is, as ever, the first task.

The Great Dionysia by the end of the fifth century BCE was the principal festival of Athens.[21] The city was by that time an imperial hub (although only a few years away from its defeat by Sparta), and pilgrims joined with the local population in a procession honoring Dionysos. As they paraded from outside the city into the god's urban precincts, sacrifice, dance, and festivity drew popular enthusiasm, and all the more so since Dionysos was the god of wine. The festival was also the annual setting of a competition among playwrights. Contenders included Aeschylus, Sophocles, and Euripides, who was awarded first place under the category of tragedy for *The Bakkhantes* in 405 BCE, shortly after his death.

Those who took part in this huge civic and international festival were aware of the underlying story of the god and his gift of wine to humanity. Euripides takes a sample of the tissue of the myth in order to investigate the nature of Dionysos and of the human qualities that both worshipped and resisted the god. The larger narrative that Euripides assumes, but does not detail, began with Dionysos' mother, Semele, a maiden from the nearby city of Thebes. The god Zeus seduced her, taking human form in order to have intercourse with her, since the sight of his divine being would kill her.

When Semele became pregnant, Hera (Zeus' Olympian wife) plotted to destroy both mother and child. She did that by coaxing Semele to have Zeus grant her any wish she might ask and then to demand that he reveal himself to her in his true form. The ruse worked, and, against his own will yet bound by his oath, the storm god showed himself to Semele as lightning, and she died in the immolation that resulted. Before her death, however, Zeus sliced open his own thigh and planted Semele's fetus in this artificial womb, from which Dionysos was born.

Zeus still had to hide the child after its strange birth from Hera's wrath, and so he sent Dionysos into the woodlands to be nurtured and educated by nymphs and the satyr god Seilênos. Dionysos traveled in the east with a fertility band of nymphs and satyrs, dispensing his gift of wine. His ecstasy and that of his followers made them *bakkhantes*, "delirious," and the god himself was known as Bakkhus. His female followers could also be called "maniacs," *mainades.*[22]

The ecstasy of Dionysos and his entourage was much more than simple revelry. Linked to more than fertility, a dark element permeated Dionysian delirium. Hera had not left her lethal jealousy behind. She actively *drove* Dionysos mad and also prompted the Titans, the competitors of the Olympian gods, to attack and dismember Dionysos. Zeus, however, brought him back to life from his heart, the last of his remains, which Athena retrieved.[23] As in the case of Osiris, there is a passive dimension in Dionysos' identity. Likewise, dismemberment signals a death that is followed by life-giving reconstitution. Dionysos' followers, consequently, were known not only for their enjoyment of wine and fertility but for performing the drama of slaying and being slain with animals that represented Dionysos and his antagonists. It is persistently reported that they, dressing in animal skins, killed and tore apart beasts with their bare hands and ate raw flesh.

Dionysian ecstasy was an evident source of violence as well as a celebration of how enthusiasm, having the god within one's midst, could bring the blessings of the spring. Indeed, that power was such that Dionysos would descend into Hades' in order to rescue his mortal mother, Semele, and join her to the gods of Olympus. Being on his right side was crucial, although being anywhere near him was dangerous.

Euripides mentions or alludes to the main lines of the myth of Dionysos and can assume his spectators' familiarity with basic forms of worship, since the Great Dionysia was the setting of the play.[24] He develops an understanding of the god and his significance, which his play articulates with savage clarity. The play opens with Dionysos coming to Thebes, Semele's city. He travels with an entourage of *bakkhantes*, claiming his due as the god of wine and fertility. He arrives in Thebes disguised in human form, changing to mortal nature,[25] in order to determine the level of recognition the city accords him. But what he finds insults him.

Semele's sister, named Agauê, bore a son named Pentheus, who became king of Thebes. Pentheus, Agauê, and most of their kin denied the whole story about Semele and Zeus: they alleged it covered up Semele's sexual escapade with an ordinary human, and in doing so they implied that Dionysos was no god. Only Pentheus, in the view of his surviving family, had the right to rule Thebes.

Dionysos exacts his revenge throughout the play, which pits his vengeance against Pentheus' arrogance. Dionysos' opening gambit is to drive the women of Thebes, including Agauê, into a frenzy. They dance and cavort on a mountain, pounding a fennel staff topped with ivy—the symbol of Dionysos—into the ground. Witnesses claim that milk, wine, honey, and water flow out of the earth as a result. Arrested by Pentheus, Dionysos releases himself from shackles and shakes the royal palace. The play treats such incidents as examples of Dionysos' capacity to invoke a reality for those he influences that may or may not be objectively true.[26] Yet Pentheus persists in his desire to crush the worship of Dionysos, and this unbridled jealousy drives him to the point that Dionysos can use that rage to destroy his adversary.

The god, still disguised despite his supernatural feats, asks the king whether he would like to witness personally the Dionysian frenzy of the women. Eager to spy on what he sees as disloyal subjects, Pentheus consents to dress up as one of the *bakkhantes* himself, turning himself into what he says he despises. Little does he know that, under the god's influence, he is driving himself and his house into oblivion, governed by an impulse no longer under his control.[27] So Dionysos tricks him into exposing himself to the real *bakkhantes*, and—led by Agauê—they tear Pentheus apart alive. Agauê herself puts her son's head on a pike and brings it back to the city, believing it is a lion's, the beast that is one of Dionysos' symbols.

Hubris characterizes Pentheus and his family, but that does not diminish the ruthless violence that Euripides attributes to Dionysos. The play sees the traditional recognition of the god as necessary, but in the not always well-founded hope that the *bakkhantes* themselves will be guided by their own virtues, even in their frenzy. So resistance is lethal, but even cooperation carries its risks. The need to skirt danger comes with the renewal that Dionysos offers, and the assumption of the play is that the god's own triumph over death, delivered by Zeus by surreal means, is not generalized to his worshippers but establishes the honor that is his own as a god. People join in festivity to take on the fresh identities of the new year, but immortality belongs to the gods alone. Dionysos and Semele join that circle only by way of their exceptional myths.

Only a year after *The Bakkhantes* was first produced, Aristophanes' comedy, *The Frogs*, parodied Euripides' argument. Aristophanes has Dionysos descend to Hades' in order to bring Euripides himself back to life, since Athens is in desperate need of a tragedian. The parody is brilliant, because Aristophanes has Dionysos engage in the reverse of the destruction that he wreaks in *The Bakkhantes*. The power of coming back to life implies the capacity to inflict death, and *The Frogs* plays with a reversal of that equation. The later Mysteries would invoke Dionysos to promise a victory over death to initiates, but Euripides' fame was such that the god remained known for his terrible vengeance.

Plutarch reports that, when the Roman general Crassus was killed by the Parthians in 53 BCE, his head was brought to King Orodes II, who made sport of it during a drunken banquet.[28] A local actor used the occasion to stage scenes from *The Bakkhantes*, seizing Crassus' head as if it were Pentheus', and played the role of Agauê. Dionysos might be god of festivity and miraculous life, but he was also known as a master of deception whose victory over death was his alone. Bestowal of that victory on others was theoretically possible but far from his purpose. Mere mortals could enjoy revivified life, alcoholic revelry, and deep sleep thanks to him. Resistance was simply insane, even if acceptance brought its own madness. For all the texture of a myth in which Dionysos cheated death, his worshippers could be assured of rewards only in this life, where they might be diverted and refreshed by their worship, even as their mortality remained unchanged.

Ishtar and Tammuz in Syria

All the gods mentioned to this point, together with their association with motifs of defeating death, were celebrated in antiquity. Myths about them were put into ritual practice and also exerted influence outside their spheres of worship. For all their renown, however, none of them is mentioned in the Hebrew Bible.

The stunning exception to the silence of the Hebrew Bible is Ezekiel 8:14: the prophet is brought in divine vision to the north gate of the temple, where he sees women mourning for Tammuz. The next verse, however, shows that this is truly an exception that proves the rule, because the practice is called an "abomination," one among the many specified in this chapter of Ezekiel.[29] The Babylonian connection of the prophet and his book brought contact with the ritual of Tammuz and elicited a response. Tammuz gave his name to a month, the time when mourning practice was taken up. By the time of Ezekiel, the myth of Tammuz had been developed over millennia, and both Sumerian and Akkadian texts[30] show the background of the practice that Ezekiel referred to.

The story begins with Ishtar, a goddess who combined love and war in her purview and was filled with ambition. Already a mighty presence on the earth, she also desired to rule over the underworld. The epic behind the practice Ezekiel refers to has Ishtar carefully apparel herself for the journey and then make her way to the place of the dead, which is under the authority of her sister. Her sister insists that her netherworldly domain is simply a place of dust and decay, a one-way road to oblivion, but has a servant admit Ishtar when the apparent attempt to dissuade her fails.

As Ishtar proceeds through the gates of death, the gatekeeper strips her of power. She is herself literally stripped, forced progressively to remove every decoration and garment from her body. At last, completely naked, her sister Ereshkigal strikes her with disease all over her body, hangs her lifeless corpse on a hook, and holds her for ransom.

Other gods of the Mesopotamian pantheon see little reason to intervene in the case, since Ishtar has brought about her own fate. But while she, the goddess of love, is in the underworld, all breeding—among people and animals—ceases over the face of the earth. For life to continue, means must be found to give a hostage for Ishtar, and that is the role of Tammuz. He is Ishtar's lover, a shepherd god (or perhaps a human king) who features in cycles of erotic poems along with Ishtar.[31] Now, however, the favored lover must descend to the dead, in order to release the beloved. When the Song of Songs declares that love is as strong as death (Song of Songs 8:6), audiences familiar with the story of Ishtar and Tammuz might well have thought of their tragic tale. During the time Tammuz is in the underworld, Ishtar is released, and vice versa, so that the change of the seasons[32] marked the epic of capture and liberation from the underworld.

Conclusion

Tammuz is a passive victim, even more than Osiris and Dionysos. Tammuz no more defeats death than does the Greek Persephone (who it was said was released temporarily from Hades' every year), while Osiris and Dionysos enjoy a status not of their own making. Even Utnapishtim, whose wisdom won him immortality, is wholly dependent upon the gods. They reward him as they do in order to restore their own honor, not to make a global change in the status of humanity. At base, these heroes of afterlife cannot accurately be described as dying and rising gods. Some in the stories are by parentage partial gods (Gilgamesh and Dionysos), and some are not gods at all (Utnapishtim and perhaps Tammuz). More crucially, none of them, not even Osiris, is described as rising to human life again. They live on in a way that means they part company with the generality of human beings, and this substantial difference is conveyed plainly by all the myths involved. Indeed, the cosmological significance of each hero turns on his difference from humanity.

Each hero of the four great mythic cycles traces a journey across a distinctive cosmology. Death evidently features in each case, but the epics reinforce the finality of dying for the vast majority of human beings. In contrast to the semidivine Gilgamesh, Utnapishtim's wisdom puts him among the gods, and in a sector of their garden that is beyond death. His existence is more bodily translation into heaven than revival to life. Although Osiris' physical body is carefully curated by Isis and Anubis—and Isis wrests her pregnancy from her brother/husband after he has been slain—his rule *in the underworld* assumes a pattern of cosmogonic regeneration. Dionysos, for all his similarity to Osiris, exerts an impact limited to the rejuvenation of the world of nature by fertility and the human world by means of wine and dance. Like Tammuz, but without the constraint to die and return to the underworld year after year, Dionysos' power refreshes life without altering its intrinsic mortality.

These differing cosmologies reinforce death's inevitability. Utnapishtim is an exception, which not even Gilgamesh can imitate, since he must resign himself to his royal legacy as a form of afterlife. Osiris, for all the miraculous power wrought on his corpse by the loving Isis, rules the underworld, not in this life. Dionysos injects his divine gifts of wine and ecstasy into a world that needs renewal but will never last forever, however many times it is made new. Tammuz descends and returns, descends and returns, so that the cycle of rainfall and heat might afford his worshippers a margin of survival. Insofar as they invoke examples of coming to life after death, that is marked as a realm belonging to the gods and the willingness of the gods to let others participate in what is constitutionally theirs alone. Such a gift appears conceivable, although not to be anticipated by the audiences of these ornate myths, whose heroes are as remote from the normally human as their capacities are beyond the reach of most people's imagination. They offer a tantalizing prospect of resurrection in idioms that anticipate the categorical hopes of a later time, but they are also jealous guards of an immortality that keeps its prerogatives for its own.

2

Israel's Revolution of Hope

Introduction

The extent of ancient traditions in regard to resurrection and afterlife can make Israelite religion seem impoverished by comparison.[1] Except for Tammuz, the Scriptures of Israel managed to ignore heroes of literally immortal fame. Utnapishtim, Osiris, and Dionysos go unnoticed, while the single explicit reference to Tammuz (in Ezek 8:14-15) comes by way of dismissal.

When the broad story line concerning Utnapishtim from the *Epic of Gilgamesh* is found, directly or indirectly, reflected in Genesis (6:1–9:17), the narrative unfolds in relation to the primordial flood, not the reward of immortality.[2] Noah wins a fresh covenant for all the world from God, but not personal afterlife. It is interesting that Noah is also credited with the invention of wine (Gen 9:18-28),[3] and this removes the possibility of praise for Dionysos for that discovery. Like Dionysos, Noah in the same story is implicated in drunkenness and its consequences, although at a higher personal cost for himself and his progeny than the Greek god ever had to pay. Read in a comparative fashion, the Hebrew Bible demythologizes a millennial tradition with which it was in contact, shifting the reference from a divine or semidivine being to a human figure in the history of Israel. The result is to collectivize the significance of the narrative, to humanize the hero, all the while distancing the potential for human immortality.

29

Comparative observations make it tempting to see the story of Jephthah's daughter in the book of Judges (chapter 11) as a replacement of the ritual of annual mourning for Tammuz in the spring. In Jephthah's case, however, the story has been shaped to militate against child sacrifice,[4] and the child's role is so reduced that she does not even bear a name. No specific mythic point of departure remains identifiable, although some such myth might conceivably have been in play. It is much more feasible to see the influence of Tammuz' paramour Ishtar in reverence for the "Queen of heaven," which Jeremiah condemns.[5] Read in that way, the condemnation reflects the preeminent place of the goddess in the story of Tammuz. If she and her lover have left a positive, albeit demythologized artifact in the Scriptures, it is likely to be in the Song of Songs (8:6), although that trace would be most indirect.

While comparison with other Near Eastern religions makes the earliest phases of the Hebrew Bible appear relatively unconcerned about afterlife and resurrection, comparison *within* the Israelite Scriptures produces a more startling contrast. During the period of the Second Temple, Judaism became the first documented religion in history to make the general assertion that God would raise the dead in order both to vindicate and to punish human behavior. Once Judaism set that precedent, Christianity and Islam embraced and extended the expectation.

Today, it is commonly supposed that religions generally make personal immortality their central concern, but most traditions in most of their histories until Judaism's assertion of a general resurrection of the dead were content to leave the vast majority of their postmortem practitioners in Sheol, Hades', or a netherworld under some other designation. Stories of exceptions to the rule only reinforced the application of that rule to all but an extremely selective elite. To this extent, the Hebrew Bible aligns well with the expectations of ancient Near Eastern culture. Even the Egyptian veneration of Osiris, which in the past has been held to have "democratized" hope for life after death, in fact reinforced a rigid class and caste structure by giving only the pharaonic aristocracy access to immortality. Until the period of the Second Temple, biblical literature dispenses with the gods and much of the cosmology of surrounding cultures but shares their elitist assumptions in regard to afterlife. Then that pattern was turned inside out.

What happened during the period between the beginning of the Hebrew Bible and the opening of the Common Era represents a fateful and perhaps irreversible religious change. After this key transformation, not only Abrahamic religions, but religions as such, altered their character and took on issues of afterlife in a systematic way as a matter of routine. The shift from notable reticence to speak of the ongoing lives of the dead in the period of the First Temple, to a vigorous assertion that God would raise the dead as a whole, not only a few notable individuals, in the period of the Second Temple, is one of the most significant developments in the long unfolding process of religious history.

Periodizing the history of Israel in terms of the First Temple, built by Solomon, and the Second Temple, restored with Persian permission by the end of the fifth century BCE, has become a standard reference among historians. But fierce debate surrounds the issue of whether sources and books of the Hebrew Bible that refer to the First Temple in fact derive from that time or are really retrospective legends by later writers, from well after the time of the Second Temple.[6]

For the purposes of this discussion, that question need not be settled in order to proceed. However the texts were shaped, there is no doubt but that some *refer* to the First Temple and some to the Second Temple. As they associate with the one or the other, they also trace the epochal change from making bodily afterlife an extremely rare exception, as in most of the religions of the ancient Near East, to making it central to a hope of general resurrection. Allowance should always be made for the influence that later writers have on earlier traditions that they relate, but that strong pattern makes it unlikely that the whole of the biblical corpus was composed by a single generation after the restoration of the Second Temple.[7] Although other judgments are possible, whatever one's opinion, the fact of the dramatic change in regard to resurrection is palpable.

Specific texts map the change from a highly restrictive view of afterlife to a general hope of resurrection. An encounter with them provides insight into dramatic developments within the Hebrew Bible and into a remarkable transformation of the hopes that Israelites had largely embraced by the dawn of the Common Era.

Scriptures of Israel Relating to the First Temple

Reticence regarding the potential to deny death its triumph is dominant within the Scriptures of Israel associated with the period prior to the destruction of First Temple. But it is just that: reticence, rather than neglect or outright denial. Two key prophetic figures, Samuel and Elijah, emerge as exceptions to the rule that the grave ends the effective life and agency of every human being.

The background that makes both of these prophets exceptional needs first to be appreciated. Sheol, a well-known term from the Hebrew Bible, conveys the conception of the fate of the dead. Alternative language, of being gathered to one's fathers, or going to the grave, or simply dying, coheres with the notion of Sheol as a netherworld or underworld that the dead inhabit. However much an honorable death was preferable to the premature obliteration of name, memory, and reputation, Sheol remained Sheol.

Loss of life brought regret, and death's prospect brought sadness. Psalms include the prayer not to be brought to Sheol before one had lived fully (Ps 102:23-24), and a frequently repeated refrain insists that the living, rather than the dead, are the source of God's praise (see Pss 6:5; 30:9; 88:9-12; 115:17; Isa 38:18-19). Still, the fact of death remains inexorable. No distinction in what the dead experience in Sheol by way of reward or punishment is specified, because their reputations are worked out *upon* the earth, not beneath it. What Ishtar learns about the underworld—as a place of dust, shadowy existence, and remnants of mourning—correlates well to how First Temple writers conceive of Sheol.

The description of Sheol (and like designations) offered by the Psalms and other early Hebrew literature is not a matter of great debate. Agreement in this regard is quite striking. Less attention has been devoted, however, to the way that the myths of Ishtar and Tammuz, and Gilgamesh and Utnap-ishtim, *correlate* with the view of an underworld that is an inferior copy of ordinary life, in effect a dark imitation of living on earth. The impression that Israelites were less concerned with afterlife than their neighbors is only an impression.[8] Within the prevalent perspective that most people find their common destiny in the grave, the Israelite Sheol is by no means an aberration.

The great exception to this general pattern of views of death is not Israel but Egypt. The myth and ritual of Osiris involved a mature conception of the netherworld in its linkage to the divine powers that rule the living, with the pharaoh's physical remains in the tomb connected inextricably to his vital soul (the *ba*) beneath the earth. Although the claim of a broad inclusion of Egyptians in this hope has been exaggerated, the scale of participation of the pharaonic dead in the total cosmology nonetheless remains impressive and unusual.

Israelite practice and belief intersected in several ways with its Egyptian counterparts.[9] Ritual circumcision of males (Gen 17:14), the cosmological role of the sun (Ps 19:4-6), and the veneration of the female counterpart to a central male god (Prov 8:22-31) are prominent examples. Yet, when it comes to naming a hero who will continue after their deaths, Ezekiel refers to Tammuz rather than Osiris, and then only to ridicule the pretension of Tammuz. Sheol, it seems clear, did not continue to express the central conception of the abode of the dead because those who composed the Scriptures of Israel knew of nothing more optimistic. The story of Osiris might have been demythologized in the way the story of Utnapishtim probably was, but that did not happen.

Yet a culture's use of an inert model of the place of the dead does not indicate that it is hopeless in regard to human destiny. Achilles' statement that he would choose to be a servant on the earth rather than rule the dead does not reflect any sense of purposelessness on his part.[10] Rather, Achilles expresses his longing for the renown brought by living alone. Similarly, when the psalmist points out that it is the living, rather than the dead, who praise God (Ps 115:16-18),[11] that is a plea for continued life that at the same time expresses the view that the dead have no influential role in shaping Israelite society, as they did in Egypt. Living Israel is accorded a unique destiny, such that Abraham, Isaac, and Jacob are the irreplaceable ancestors, but their legacy is worked out in the communal life of their people, not in their continued personal existence. The deaths of each of those patriarchs is a carefully marked event, such that living Israelites alone can carry their promise to fruition. When the central focus of cosmology is this world, attention to the dead amounts to a distraction rather than a reassurance.

That distraction is illustrated and reprimanded in the story of King Saul's decision to consult the dead; the narrative maintains Sheol's place at the margin of the hope of Israel and also investigates a powerful exception to the rule that the dead do not return to life (1 Sam 28:3-25). Saul despairs because, fearful of an impending battle with the Philistines, he can find no source of divine guidance by means of prophecy or divination. Samuel has died, and in any case that prophet had long since spurned Saul and supported David as the LORD's anointed. Despite the fact that he has outlawed the practice of consulting the dead, Saul (in disguise) seeks out a woman who is a well-known medium. Only his insistence prompts the woman to "bring up" Samuel (1 Sam 28:11-12) over her own objections. When he names Samuel as the aim of the inquiry, she realizes the disguised man must be Saul and panics. But Saul's desperate determination makes her proceed.

What happens next conveys the powerful ambivalence of the story, which condemns necromancy and yet presents the prophet Samuel as literally godlike after his death. Despite the medium's fear to engage further with the invocation, Saul has her describe what she sees. She says that she sees "gods coming up from the earth." When asked for the particular appearance, she describes an old man wrapped in a robe; at that moment Saul bows in reverence to the prophet that had brought him to power (1 Sam

28:13-15). The term "gods" might be intended as a generic comparison of Samuel to God (who characteristically is referred to in the majestic plural of the singular term *'El*, hence *'Elohim*, as here). On the other hand, it is also conceivable that in the imagination of the story, Samuel is coming up with other figures from Sheol who are also described as divine.[12] In either case, the language amounts to a powerful exception to the usual language associated with Sheol. That place, routinely translated as "Hades'" in the Septuagint, is not only for the dead, rather than the living, but also for the *mortal* dead, not for any divine being. *'Elohim* (however defined) had no more place in Sheol than the Olympian gods generally had in Hades'.

Within the encounter between Saul and the medium, her reactions serve as a commentary on this disruptive intervention of an unexpected figure from Sheol. She did not wish to engage in necromancy at all, in view of Saul's edict, and she realizes in horror that her visitor *is* Saul when he demands that she bring up Samuel. Then under pressure she admits she sees *'Elohim* coming up, and she admits the form is of an old man wrapped in his robe. She did not wish to see anything, and apparently she is the only person who can see Samuel. If, as the Septuagint's translation would suggest, she spoke on behalf of the dead,[13] she then is the instrument of Samuel's words in what follows.

Samuel's first response is a complaint: "Why have you bothered me, bringing me up?" (1 Sam 28:15). Here the prophet speaks on behalf of the general understanding that Sheol is not to be inserted into the affairs of the living. But once he has started speaking, Samuel's perspective is consistent with his prophetic role when he was alive (vv. 16-19), intimating knowledge that he is dealing with Saul. He insists that Saul's real complaint is with the LORD, who took the kingdom and gave it to David. He points in particular to Saul's failure to execute Amalek as the disobedience that caused divine disfavor. This repeats what Samuel said to Saul at the time (see 1 Sam 15), but it is notable that in the encounter at Endor, Samuel refers only to that incident and not to the first occasion that had prompted prophetic rebuke.[14] Finally, Samuel also engages in a fresh prophecy, that Saul and his sons will be with Samuel: that is, among the dead, on the next day, and that the army of Israel will be defeated.

The richness of the account of how Saul consulted a medium serves a dual function, reinforcing the view that Sheol has no proper role among the living and at the same time making Samuel a continuing prophetic force, even after death. In his postmortem appearance, he interprets and condenses his prophecies during life and provides new prophecy. But his very first words express resistance to being invoked at all, portraying necromancy as disturbing the dead.

Yet Samuel provides a precedent for a prophetic exception to the clearly demarked boundary between the living and the dead. Just as Utnapishtim represents an exception by means of wisdom, Osiris by means of pharaonic authority, Dionysos by means of ecstasy, and Tammuz by erotic means, Samuel disrupts the anticipated pattern because he continued to prophesy. This exception was picked up during the period of the First Temple in traditions concerning Elijah, and the Second Temple period would see the exception flourish to the point that it became the new rule.

Elijah presents the most famous exception within First Temple Judaism to the rule that the dead inhabit Sheol. The narrative of his removal by means of a tempest from the sight of his disciple Elisha proved pivotal, not only within conceptions of how life is possible despite death, but also in disciplines of meditation. Mystical traditions of Judaism, in which God's chariot (above all as described in Ezek 1) became a master symbol, show the influence of reference to the chariot and horses of fire that accompany Elijah's ascent. Yet the opening of the narrative refers to the event as the LORD bringing Elijah up to heaven by a tempest, not a chariot (2 Kgs 2:1), and starts with a journey by foot that Elijah takes with Elisha from Gilgal to Bethel, Jericho, and then the Jordan River.

Elijah repeatedly attempts to leave his disciple's company, but Elisha insists on remaining by his master. Even Elisha's fellow prophets are aware that Elijah is about to be removed. They say to Elisha, "Don't you know that today the LORD will take your master from over your head?" (2 Kgs 2:2-6). Fifty of the prophets then see Elijah and Elisha standing by the Jordan. Elijah strikes the water with his rolled mantle, and the two cross on dry ground (vv. 7-8). That crossing, in the reverse direction of Joshua's entry into the land of promise,[15] brings the climax of the narrative.

Elijah understands that his disciple is with him for a purpose, and he asks what he can do for Elisha before being taken. Elisha asks for twice the Spirit that Elijah had. Hard though that request is, Elijah says, "If you see me taken from you, it shall be so for you." As they walk along and speak, a chariot of fire and horses of fire separate them, and Elijah goes up into heaven in the tempest. Elisha reacts by crying out, "My father, my father, the chariot of Israel and its horsemen," and sees Elijah no more (2 Kgs 2:9-12).

From then the narrative simply reinforces its message as it closes. Elisha returns to the prophetic company on the other side of the Jordan, using Elijah's mantle, which had fallen from him, to part the waters again. The other prophets recognize that "Elijah's Spirit rests upon Elisha," but the assumption appears to be that the double portion that Elisha asked for had not been given. The chariot and the horsemen had broken his visual contact with his master. They were not the means of Elijah's transport to heaven but marked the descent of the heavenly realm to the point that the wind could transfer Elijah from this world to the home of the Spirit that inhabited him. "The chariot of Israel and its horsemen" are the angelic counterpart of the people of God on the earth; they serve among the hosts around the divine throne. The prophets make a search for Elijah, supposing that the LORD's Spirit might have taken and cast him nearby. Elisha does not agree with their plan, but they persist, and their search confirms the point of the narrative (2 Kgs 2:13-18): Elijah was taken bodily into heaven.

How this ascent or translation into heaven was achieved is not explained, nor is there any indication that Elijah's removal is a pattern for anyone else. When the normal expectation of death is defied, the fact of the anomaly is registered without the suggestion that it might be repeated. Elijah is presented as an exception to an even stronger extent than Samuel is, and in the end he shares Samuel's severe attitude toward a living follower. At this First Temple stage in the tradition, Samuel specifically complains that Saul has disturbed him. Although Elijah promises an enhancement of how Spirit rests on him, the intervening chariot and horsemen prevent the vision that would realize the promise. Like Utnapishtim, he holds out a prospect that then does not eventuate, and so he remains an extreme exception. What Elisha does see at the crucial moment of Elijah's being taken into heaven is not that ascent but the chariot and horses that mark heaven's support of living Israel, where Elisha's attention belongs.

Elijah is presented in a way that at least intimates why he became exceptional. The prophets to whom Elisha returns after the ascent suggest that the Spirit might have taken the master and put him down elsewhere. Interestingly, the Septuagint has them wonder whether Elijah might have been deposited, not only on a mountain or valley, but even in the Jordan (2 Kgs 2:16). The suggestion that the prophet might have been set down in an obscure place accords with a strand in earlier traditions concerning Elijah.

The signs associated with Elijah are more densely packed in the narrative about him than is the case of any other prophet (Moses included). Almost buried by references to his miraculous provision of food, resuscitation of a dead child, and calling down fire from heaven, mention is made earlier to the Spirit removing Elijah from one place to another. The prospect of this happening frightens the manager of King Ahab's household, named Obadiah.

Obadiah is as loyal to the prophets of the LORD as he can possibly be in his position, and he has even hidden a hundred of them from the persecution of Ahab's wife Jezebel. But he dreads the result if, as Elijah asks him to do, he tells Ahab that Elijah will meet him. (The meeting itself is fateful because it is the preamble to the contest between Elijah and the prophets of Baal on Mount Carmel.) Obadiah fears that the commission to invite Ahab to meet Elijah will put him in peril; he says to Elijah, "As soon as I have gone from you, the Spirit will carry you to where I don't know; I will come to declare to Ahab, he will not find you, and he will kill me, your servant who has feared the LORD from my youth" (1 Kgs 18:12).

Because Obadiah is afraid, his statement might be considered hyperbolic. Elijah did travel a great deal. At the time of his being taken up in a tempest, he is not only on a journey but actually walking and talking with Elisha. At one point, after the contest on Mount Carmel, Elijah is said to *outrun* Ahab and his chariot to the city of Jezreel (1 Kgs 18:46). But any thought that Obadiah's statement might express his understandable fear more than a genuine possibility is contradicted by the tempest that actually does take Elijah. Because it does not even return him to earth, Elijah's ascent makes Obadiah's statement a foretaste rather than a forecast of events, and an understatement rather than an exaggeration. The prophet, who has been empowered by Spirit during his activity, is now taken by the tempest into heaven itself. Elisha's sight of the chariot of fire and its horsemen obscures a clear view of Elijah but serves to identify his master's location as with the angelic host of Israel, their defense in times of greatest need.

Elisha's prophetic powers were similar to Elijah's but scarcely a multiple of them. When Elisha himself died, Joash, king of Israel, called out, "My father, my father: the chariot of Israel and its horsemen." That indicated respect for a legacy, but not any duplication of Elijah's ascent. Elisha perished from an illness and was buried, although his bones were reputed to have healing power (2 Kgs 13:14-21). Such a key difference between Elijah and his successor might be embedded in a taunt that Elisha heard just after the ascent of his master. Young men jeered at him, "Go up, Baldhead!" (2 Kgs 2:23), a sneering comparison to what his master had done in going up to God's presence, and he could not.[16] The logic of the narrative makes Elijah an exception that could not be followed, not even by Elisha. The prophet who had been guided by the Spirit is removed by the Spirit in the form of tempest and taken to heaven, whose edge is marked by the appearance of Israel's chariot and horsemen. He is taken bodily into heaven rather than entering into Sheol at his death. His unique status is guarded within Israelite cosmology as carefully as Utnapishtim's, Osiris', Dionysos', and Tammuz' were within their cosmologies. Only a profound change could make Elijah's exceptional stature into a new rule concerning humanity as a whole.

Visionary and Philosophical Judaism

Strong elements of contrast between the literatures of the First Temple and those of the Second Temple have long been apparent. Prominent among them is the emphasis accorded to eschatology. The close of the book of Isaiah conceives of God acting to create "new heavens and a new earth" (Isa 65:17-23; 66:18-23) such that Israel's seed shall remain forever and "all flesh shall worship" in Jerusalem. The categorical hope offered by Isaiah invokes God's primordial activity in creation to restore Jerusalem, the temple, and the fortunes of Israel. Although the original Isaiah lived during the eighth century BCE, large swathes of prophecy developed in his name were added during the Second Temple period.[17]

This promise is linked to vindication: the triumphant descendants of Israel will "look on the corpses of the men that have rebelled against me, because their worm shall not die and their fire shall not be quenched and they shall be an abhorrence to all flesh" (Isa 66:24). That final image of the book of Isaiah portrays death as a punishment for the wicked and the sight of their corpses as a solace for the righteous. But that eschatological judgment does not yet openly promise resurrection, and the extent to which it might be implied is open to debate.[18] Those who see the dead bodies of the wicked are not the righteous people who were once victims but their descendants. The clear line of separation between the living and the abode of the dead, characteristic of First Temple literature, appears strained—but not yet explicitly breached.

Still, so many boundaries are wiped away by eschatological hope that death itself is challenged. A passage from Isaiah also reflecting Second Temple eschatology depicts a feast on the holy mountain for all peoples, where God will "swallow up death forever" and defeat Moab, an enemy of Israel (Isa 25:6-12). Context shows that this a promise for those who survive to that time rather than an assurance of resurrection, but the possibility of vindication even for the dead is suggested at least as a possibility by the eschatological prospect the book of Isaiah offers.

While Isaiah's eschatological promises challenge the finality of death, Ezekiel's vision in the valley of dry bones explores resurrection as a promise for the people of Israel in exile in Babylonia (Ezek 37:1-14). God promises through the prophet that, just as he sees bones that have been clothed in flesh and animated, "I will open your graves and raise you from your graves, my people, and bring you into the land of Israel" (Ezek 37:12). Because God identifies the bones as "the whole house of Israel" (37:11), it is evident that Ezekiel, along the lines of the Second Temple sections of Isaiah, conceives of this resurrection hope as communal, for the living population in exile, rather than as a prediction for what happens postmortem to literally dead people.

Yet although Ezekiel is contextually a vision of collective restoration rather than of the bodily immortality of individuals, the degree of its detail exceeds what would be necessary to express a promise of purely national renewal. The vision could reflect expectations that are unstated, but none-theless in the background, that resurrection might be possible.[19] The promise in Isaiah 25:6-12 might be taken in a similar way, especially in view of the stunning imagery that is associated with it in the following chapter: "Your dead shall live, their corpses shall arise! Awake and sing, those who dwell in the dust, because your dew is a dew of light and the earth shall birth the shades" (Isa 26:19). Taken together with Ezekiel's vision, a movement toward an explicit, nonmetaphorical hope in resurrection exerts a palpable force, even if that stage has not explicitly been reached.

The period of the Second Temple, when the additions to Isaiah and the book of Ezekiel as a whole emerged, also saw stirrings of similar develop-ments toward hope for life after death in other Mediterranean cultures. Pla-to's *Republic*, from the fourth century BCE, closes with a visionary account of what lies beyond death. The reasons for placing the "Vision of Er," as it is known, at this point in the work remain disputed, and it is unclear how straightforwardly to take the vision. In that Plato argued against having poets in his ideal state, it is not obvious why he would complete his work with an account of mythic proportions. Affinities with Ezekiel's vision of the chariot and throne of God have been explored.[20] The suggestion that the "Vision of Er" is a secondary addition to the treatise is understandable but unproven. Yet however interpreted, the vision's presence at the end of the *Republic* assured it a long afterlife.

Socrates presents Er's vision as the *Republic* concludes.[21] Er was a soldier slain in battle; yet after ten days, his body was found without decay, and the corpse was removed to his home for burial. On the twelfth day, he revived on his funeral bier and reported what he had seen while he had been deceased. The journey of his soul is quite involved, and each detail need not be reviewed here. Prominent features include travel in a large group to a divine meadow where there were two openings into the earth and two into heaven. Judges determined who was just (who ascend to heaven) and who was unjust (who descend under the earth). After a thousand years, the souls returned to the meadow from heaven or from beneath the earth. (That reentry is by means of the second opening to heaven or into the earth.) The just recount their joys, and those punished relate their suffering. Some souls, however, are too evil ever to be returned; their lot is perpetual torment and the tantalizing prospect of a release that never comes.

But most souls continue their journey after ascending from under the earth or descending from heaven. They trek to the "Spindle of Necessity," the whirling framework of the entire universe. There they are allotted a new cycle of life, but not by chance: they choose their fates. As they pass beneath Necessity's throne, however, they traverse the Plain of Oblivion and the River of Forgetfulness, the explanation of humans' ignorance of both where they have come from and where they are going. Socrates ends his tale, and the *Republic*, with the remark that the story shows that people should live their lives in pursuit of righteousness with intelligence, so that they become "friends to one another and the gods." Their actions and decisions are consequential "both while remaining here and when we obtain the prizes" after death, just like athletes on their victory laps.

The continuing influence of this vision within Greek literature includes Hellenistic romances written through the first century CE and well beyond, which tell of similar near-death and actual-death experiences. Their affinities with some of the stories of Jesus in the New Testament have been discussed,[22] but, beyond any episodic interest they might have, they show that the combination of vision and philosophy that the myth of Er achieves proved an enduring accomplishment. The very fact that, given its setting within the *Republic*, the line between symbol and reality in Er's vision is difficult to draw is an advantage from the point of view of its continuing reception. What is said might be interpreted with varying degrees of abstraction or literal denotation, depending on the interpreter's point of view. Part of the effective craft of the text, in fact, is that the interpretative task is built into it. When the souls choose their lives after the millennial journey upward or downward, the figure who permits them a choice among options of living is called the "prophet." Prophetic interpretation is portrayed as the key to one's life choices as well as to the understanding of what happens after death.

Within the Judaic tradition, Philo of Alexandria (whose life unfolded during the first centuries BCE and CE) embraced a Platonic reading of afterlife, but not before key changes had already occurred within the broad range of Judaism. Two works in particular, the book of Enoch (now in the Pseudepigrapha) and the book of Wisdom (now in the Apocrypha), signal a fundamental shift in expectations of what lies beyond death. These works, considered together with Philo, demonstrate that, by the first century, immortality had entered the language of Judaism as a feasible hope, not only for a select few heroes of the religion but for all those committed to righteousness. Platonic abstraction was the preference in interpreting life after death for Wisdom and Philo, but Enoch maintained a visionary engagement with the issue.

The book of Enoch appeared within the third century BCE and went through a process of considerable expansion over later centuries. The delineation of which sections belong to what period has been thoroughly debated, and, especially since the discovery of Aramaic portions of the work at Qumran, a consensus has it that the earliest phase of the book has been identified.[23] Attention has usefully focused on how the work portrays Enoch as a heavenly voyager. The tradition takes off from the last biblical reference to Enoch, the enigmatic statement, "Enoch walked with God, and he was not, because God took him" (Gen 5:24). Whatever precisely Genesis meant by that remark, Enoch's walking, his disappearance, and the reference to God taking him all could be interpreted to align with the story of Elijah.

By the time of the author of Enoch, the similarity was taken to mean that Enoch traveled much as Elijah did—into the heavens. In Enoch's case, however, the point is the heavenly travel after being taken up rather than what leads up to the moment. His journey is a prelude to Dante's *Divine Comedy* and a majestic counterpart to the *Epic of Gilgamesh*. Within the trajectory traced in the early section of Enoch, the vision of the divine throne (chapter 14) is a worthy successor to biblical visions involving Moses, Elijah, Isaiah, Ezekiel, and Zechariah, but in Enoch the seer is *in* heaven, not merely looking into heaven.

Prophetic throne visions (grouped in antiquity and by scholarship today within the tradition of the *Merkhabah*—the "Chariot" of Ezekiel in particular but with resonance with Elijah, as well) have absorbed considerable attention.[24] But Enoch also shows that, by the third century BCE, Judaism lived in a mythic environment enriched not only with Utnapishtim, Osiris, Dionysos, and Tammuz but also with the "Vision of Er." Enoch describes a place beyond heaven and earth, where "the spirits of the souls of the dead" are gathered (1 En. 22:3-13) until final judgment. The righteous dwell by a light-filled spring of water, while sinners receive the pain of retribution. The voice of Abel reaches up to God, demanding justice by means of the extermination of Cain's seed. Retribution is meted out according to the severity of wrongdoing, just as righteousness is rewarded. The breadth of the vision of postmortem experience, targeted not on the transmigration of souls (as in the "Vision of Er") but on their experience until final judgment, is an unexpected departure from the clear precedent of texts related to the First Temple.

No direct contact of any kind between the "Vision of Er" and Enoch's description of the place beyond the gates of the dead need be posited. It appears clear that Hellenistic culture encouraged forms of blending that can be observed by comparison, even though the precise influences among texts is not always traceable. The great innovation from the point of view of Judaism is the inclusive breadth of Enoch's expectation of life after death, although its precise conception of that life (for example, in terms of immortality or resurrection) is not specified.

Breadth is also the hallmark of the Wisdom of Solomon, a text contemporaneous with the work of Philo of Alexandria, and perhaps to be associated with the same city. In this case, a less visionary, more philosophical perspective than Enoch's is apparent. The fate of the righteous person is described as one of being persecuted by the wicked (Wis 2:10–3:10). The depiction tracks closely along the lines of the righteous and beleaguered servant of the LORD in the book of Isaiah (53). Initial acquaintance with the passage in Wisdom speaks so specifically of the persecution and killing of the just victim that modern readers often think immediately of Jesus,[25] but he is not the reference of this pre-Christian text. Rather, the Gospels helped to make sense of Jesus' suffering, death, and vindication by embedding his last days within a pattern that the Wisdom of Solomon previously represented. The vindication of righteous persons is marked by the assertion that "they seemed to the eyes of the foolish to have died" (3:2), but they shall "light up" and "judge nations" (3:7-8). The souls of the righteous are in God's hand, and he accepts them as he accepts sacrifice (Wis 3:1, 5-6). Plainly, Enoch's broadening of the vision of afterlife was not unique or aberrant. Judaic texts reflect a seismic religious shift in their expectations by the dawn of the Common Era.

Philo of Alexandria represents a confident expectation of the immortality of the righteous. As in Enoch, Philo portrays Abel—as the just person slain by his brother—as a key figure; for Philo he represents love of God rather than love of self,[26] the principle of immortality (*That the Worse Attacks the Better* 32, 48–56; cf. *On the Sacrifices of Cain and Abel* 2–4). In Philo's view, figures such as Abraham, Isaac, Jacob, and Moses also represent exceptional journeys of immortal souls. Each achieves a distinctive state, with Moses beside God (*On the Sacrifices of Cain and Abel* 5–10; *Questions and Answers on Genesis* 3.11). Their existence after death may be described as equal to angels, because they are "unbodied and happy souls." Yet the "unbodied" existence of angels apparently refers only to the extent to which they are not associated with physical substance. When he describes Moses' transformation at death, Philo says that God changed him from "a double being, having a soul and body, into the nature of a single body, transforming him wholly and entirely into a most sun-like mind" (*Moses* 2.288). Indeed, Philo speaks in several different ways in his discussion in *On the Sacrifices of Cain and Abel* of how the patriarchs were transformed at death and so did not really die.[27] The logic accords with the statement in the Wisdom of Solomon that such only "seemed" to be the case.

Philo of Alexandria is evidently a creative, philosophical, and sometimes experimental thinker. Not every statement he makes in regard to life after death can be taken to reflect a common view in the Judaism of his time. Still, it is striking that he compares the righteous dead to angels, since that comparison is the point of departure for Jesus' teaching of the resurrection (see Mark 12:25). Yet Philo is of concern here, not for any one particular view of life after death he defends, but for the clear fact of his confidence that death need not be the end of truly human life.

Within the first century, Josephus could refer—without elaborate argument—not only to Enoch, but also to Moses and Elijah (just the two prophets who appear with Jesus in the transfiguration; Mark 9:4) as those who disappeared rather than died.[28] Part of Jesus' argument for the resurrection (Mark 12:26-27), as well as the comparison of those raised from the dead with angels, is the confidence that Abraham, Isaac, and Jacob must have been raised, since the LORD of Israel is "God of the living, not of the dead." What is notable about Jesus' and Josephus' assertions of the continuing lives of past figures is that they are taken as a matter of course, marking the fundamental change between First and Second Temple Judaism.

Taken together, sources such as Enoch, the Wisdom of Solomon, Philo of Alexandria, the Gospels, and Josephus show incontrovertibly that Second Temple Judaism had made a profound shift. Afterlife, and sometimes a bodily afterlife, consequent on the action of God was held out as a prospect for the righteous. The movement of other literature from the Hellenistic world appears to be one factor in this development. The surprising "Vision of Er," with its encouragement of visionary and novelistic as well as philosophical successors, suggests that one consequence of the emergence of a truly global culture in the ancient world was an experimental investigation of the ultimate ends of human life.

Yet the influence of cognate hopes in the Hellenistic world upon Judaic literature is not a satisfactory explanation for why Judaism went through its seismic transformation, so that figures such as Enoch and Abraham and Isaac and Jacob and Moses were seen to be alive with God along with Elijah. For many centuries prior to Enoch, Judaism had not only resisted mythic cycles centered on Utnapishtim, Osiris, Dionysos, and Tammuz but also defined itself by that resistance. For what reason did the Hellenistic tendency toward what might be called optimism about life after death, represented by the "Vision of Er," find resonance in Second Temple Judaism?

That question seems best answered on the basis of literature related to the Maccabean movement. The Maccabees' engagement with the threat to Judaism in their time included both an embrace of a hope for life after death and an emphasis on the distinction between immortality and resurrection that differentiated their hope from that of Plato and related thinkers. The common aspiration to understand the nature of life after death—already emergent in the Hellenistic world—became a dominant religious theme because the Maccabees took it up and at the same time insisted on reshaping it. That revolutionary development altered the shape of belief in the resurrection and went hand in hand with a dislocation of the prevalent reserve regarding afterlife that was dominant in earlier periods.

Maccabean martyrs—as described by the literature of the time—pursued their destiny, not in a fixed *kosmos* where resurrection could only be rare, but within a cosmology that conceived of God as setting aside the world that can be seen to produce a world that is coming. A key feature of that eschatological hope included permanent, living embodiment for those who follow God's will. Crucial to the entire perspective was the insistence that real death and substantial destruction were the necessary condition of entry into the new world. Immortality, conceived of as on a continuous spectrum with daily life, was eclipsed by the new hope of disruptive resurrection for large segments of humanity.

The particular history of the period played a vital role in that epochal change. In addition, by the time of the Maccabees and their revolt against the Seleucid regime, resurrection *and* human immortality both had become the topic of widespread speculative discussion throughout the Mediterranean world. Those developments provided models of thought that were available to Jesus, Paul, and those who shaped the New Testament, precedents that are crucial to appreciate the options embraced, and the roads not taken, during the emergence of Christianity.

The Maccabean catalyst for this profound change, the true democratization of afterlife in antiquity, provided the impetus for altering Judaism, and many religions followed suit.

3

Bodies Raised in Israel's Vindication

Introduction

The Maccabees bear the name of the leader of a group of priestly revolution-
aries: Judas, called "the Hammer" (*Makkaba'* in Aramaic). At first under the
direction of his father, but then increasingly at the head of the movement,
Judas produced a surprisingly successful uprising against the Seleucid occu-
piers of Jerusalem and Judea. The way that the Maccabees won proved as
influential as their victory itself, producing a literature that occupies a crucial
position within the pattern of how resurrection and afterlife were viewed
within Judaism.

While First Temple Judaism maintained a collective, this-worldly hope
for Israel disinclined to embrace patterns of resurrection that neighboring
cultures offered, by the close of the Second Temple period a robust and varied
set of afterlife expectations were articulated in Judaic literature. That shift
raises the question of why the contrast is as marked as it is and of how it came
to happen that, as Second Temple Judaism took up hopes of resurrection, it
applied them much more generally than had been the case among its cultural
neighbors. Although not all Judaism's expectations from this period could be
described as truly global in their scope, some of them were, and none of them
were limited to a strictly exclusive elite of Israel.

Precisely during the second century BCE, from just after the initial version of the book of Enoch, the Maccabees and their supporters found the means to mobilize tactical assaults on their enemies. Belief in resurrection was part of their weaponry. The Maccabees called on their compatriots, not as trained soldiers (which the majority of them were not), but as loyal Israelites who were willing to serve as "witnesses" to the truth of God against a tyrannical regime. Each witness was willing to die, and that gave the term *martus* ("witness") in Greek—which emerged as the preferred language of Maccabean literature—the connotation that the word "martyrdom" bears in English.

Ancient martyrdom, defined within its own terms of reference, has become prominent in public awareness—an especially welcome development. An uninformed tendency in recent popular discussion had portrayed Islam as the sole bearer of the tradition, although the praise of martyrs was a well-established genre of literature and thought well before the Qur'an and related sources.[1] Side by side with their call to martyrdom, the Maccabees set out the hope of resurrection, not only for leaders and exceptional elites, but for those Israelites willing to resist to the end in their loyalty to the torah. The Maccabean program and its surprising success is central to answering the question of how resurrection became central within Judaism, and through Judaism within the Abrahamic religions as a whole.

Because Maccabean theology was deeply influential, there has been a tendency to overrate the Maccabees' political and military importance in their time. They came to power during an exceptional moment, when the Seleucid king attempted to suborn the temple in Jerusalem to Hellenistic religion. He tried to repress Judaism as such, so that a resistance movement could draw on far more support than would have been available had Seleucid policy proved more judicious. Because it did not, Judas Maccabeus became the spearhead of cultural revulsion against persecution, and his family came to power. The determined heroism, indeed fanaticism, of the Maccabees was key to their success. But so, too, was the incompetence of the Seleucid King Antiochus IV and the breakup of his power base into a squabbling group of factions and royal pretenders. What had been territorial Israel, under foreign domination from the time of the Assyrians and Babylonians, offered a vacuum of power with the decline of the Seleucids. Yet the Maccabees' propaganda portrayed them not only as master soldiers but also as divinely sanctioned rulers.

Once they restored the temple to the torah's demands and beat back Seleucid occupation, the Maccabees set themselves up as high priests (although their claim to derive from the hereditary family of Zadok[2] may have been questioned) and, by the end of the second century BCE, as kings, although they boasted no David genealogy. They faced real religious opposition within their territory, and their recourse to the Greek language in administration and their hiring of mercenary armies did not endear them to their Jewish subjects. When, in 63 BCE, two Maccabean brothers squabbled over who should rule, they appealed to the Roman general Pompey as a diplomatic and military referee. Pompey took the opportunity to invade; he then entered the temple personally and claimed Jerusalem and Judea for Rome. As a political experiment, the Maccabees' dominance had lasted only a century, a temporary if ostentatious regime that provided transition to the much longer dominion of the Romans.

By contrast to Maccabean power, their literature—taken together with that of their allies and associates—is timeless. Principal examples include biblical and apocryphal works: the book of Daniel, the first book of Maccabees, and the second book of Maccabees. They gave rise to a postbiblical progeny, contemporaneous with or slightly later than the New Testament, that includes the fourth book of Maccabees. Owing to when these works were produced, they found their way into the Bible and its outskirts only with difficulty. Daniel, although a prophetic figure, is not included among the Latter Prophets in the Hebrew canon; instead, the work features among the Writings (together with works such as Psalms and Proverbs). First and Second Maccabees, found within the Septuagint but not the Hebrew Bible, are part of the Apocrypha. Fourth Maccabees is generally considered to belong to pseudepigraphal literature. That is also the designation of the book of Jubilees, an older work (from the second century BCE), which reflects the growing belief in resurrection in much the same way as other materials also found at Qumran. Jubilees shows that the appeal to hope of life after death was not limited to Maccabean literature, although the Maccabees masterfully harnessed that hope to the needs of opposing the Seleucids.

In most of these cases, the works are explicitly designed to motivate resistance, and the prospect of resurrection is central to the argument of their martyrs' theology. In the way of propaganda, the claim of widespread support for the resistance is overstated, and there is little account taken of those who did not endorse the Maccabean cause on religious grounds. Further, even by the time of the New Testament, it is clear that resurrection was by no means a settled expectation within Judaism; differing conceptions competed with one another, and—following the precedent of First Temple Judaism—it was perfectly possible to relativize the importance of resurrection and even to deny some of its formulations (see, for example, Mark 12:18-23). No agreed doctrine of resurrection can be mapped within Second Temple Judaism, but waves of hope emanated from the Maccabees, their allies, other contemporaries, and their predecessors; the contours of those expectations are depicted in the literature of the period. The struggle first to supplant the Seleucids and then to maintain a hegemony of the torah against regimes that, many Jews believed, pursued their own will at the expense of God's served to crystallize clearly defined expectations of how God would give life to the dead within cosmologies that are well articulated.

Martyrdom and Its Victory

The book of Daniel labels the horror that prompted its apocalyptic visions: "the appalling abomination" (Dan 9:27; 11:31; vocabulary that coincides with 1 Macc 1:54). The reference is to the decision of Antiochus IV, the Seleucid ruler, to mandate that Hellenistic worship be conducted in the temple in Jerusalem. Judaism was repressed, copies of the Torah burned, and circumcision prohibited, with atrocities committed against mothers and children alike in reprisal for resistance. To the seer or seers who spoke in Daniel's name, God could not and would not let those abhorrent acts stand. In three and a half years, Daniel 12:11-12 predicts, the sacrifice authorized by God would be offered again by the people of God.

The message of Daniel was consistent with that of prophets before the second century BCE. Jeremiah, Ezekiel, the Second and Third Isaiah, Haggai, and Zechariah were passionate advocates of the restoration of the temple after its destruction by the Babylonians in 586 BCE. Daniel's production of a prophecy of restoration for a temple that had been defiled by the Seleucids, rather than destroyed by the Babylonians, renewed a well-established prophetic mandate. Daniel's method, however, took him from the genre of prophecy into apocalyptic. The book of Daniel speaks in the name of a figure who lived long before the work was written, recounts divine visions that require interpretation from an angelic mediator, and provides heavenly authorization for the particular calendar of salvation that it outlines. Precisely these traits mark the apocalyptic genre as a fresh development of Judaic literature.

The individual characteristics that are usually present in apocalyptic writing[3] resulted in a combination that is transformative. Unlike prophecy, which sets out repentance as an alternative to the threats envisaged, in the apocalyptic universe the envisioned end is to come, whatever people might do.[4] Predestination provides history, however hopeless the prospect might seem to Israel, the pledge of a just and definitive outcome. Daniel's famous vision in chapter 7—when "one like a son of man," the angelic counterpart of Israel (Dan 7:13-14), presents himself before God to receive an everlasting kingdom—assures the result of the confrontation with Antiochus IV. Daniel is promised that the animal-shaped angels of the oppressive empires of the past and present are to be swept away when the Son of Man takes his place, so that "the saints of the most high will possess the kingdom forever" (Dan 7:18).

Because the seer speaks for God's definitive purpose in human events, the inevitability of this outcome is assured. Moreover, the vision is comprehensive, spoken from the perspective of Daniel centuries earlier, during the Babylonian period. For that reason, events between then and the time of writing can be confidently described in order to lay out an apparently inexorable scheme. But Daniel's determinism is the opposite of pessimistic; the vindication of the just and the punishment of the unjust are part of God's judgment, effected by his angelic agent Michael (Dan 12:1-3):

> In that time Michael the great prince who stands over the sons of your people shall stand and there shall be a time of distress, such as has not been since there was a nation until that time. And in that time everyone found written in the book shall be delivered. Many of those who sleep in the dust of the earth shall awake, some to eternal life, and some to shame and eternal contempt. Those who teach insight shall shine like the brightness of the firmament, and those who make many righteous, like the stars—eternal and forever.

Although the statement is compressed, it is also finely calibrated. A distinction is made among those who "awake," "those who make wise," and "those who make righteous." Resurrection involves different statuses among those raised who escape "eternal contempt": they might awake to "eternal life," while those who make wise are shining "like the brightness," and those who make righteous are "like stars." Those gradations are defined within the group of "everyone written in the book of life" under Michael's watchful presence. Daniel is routinely, and rightly, acknowledged as the work within the Hebrew canon that explicitly asserts the resurrection of the dead. But it is also striking that Daniel reflects not a general assertion but a carefully coordinated adjustment of the hope to the particular circumstances of Israel in its time. The fact that the book does so by way of bare statement, rather than argument, suggests that its original environment was one in which the hope in resurrection was already prevalent.

A vital element of Daniel's adjustment of an evidently more common expectation is its bold insistence upon theodicy. Given the condition of Israel—and particularly the temple—under Seleucid oppression, Daniel presents the resurrection as resolving the fate of the righteous and the wicked. Both the promise to Israel and the adjudication of human behavior are crucial, if God's essential justice is to be maintained. Vindication in the final judgment is not only for the righteous but also for God himself. Because that is the case, this judgment is indeed as final as it is inevitable, the last adjudication. Whatever distant echoes of the "Vision of Er" might be detected in Daniel, reincarnation is not among them. Plato's vision had been designed not for a time of persecution but for a symposium that wishes to stress the importance of human choice in destiny. Daniel's vision is thoroughly eschatological in its insistence that its contents are ultimate, because the moment concerned is that of the realization of divine justice.

By the time of the book of Daniel, it appears clear that Zoroastrian sources had regularized a view of rewards and punishments after death. Unfortunately, manuscript attestation of the texts only begins in the medieval period, so that controversy surrounds almost any statement one might make about Zoroastrianism during the Second Temple period. But the actual language in which its texts have been transmitted varies even in currently accessible sources, reflecting chronological development. Analysis of sources permits of a plausible, if very general and approximate, dating. The eschatology of texts comprising what is called "The Younger Avesta"[5] seems a precedent for the motif of the combination of rewards and punishments that appears in Judaism during this time.

Daniel's forecast of victory in the temple after three and a half years corresponds to the length of the Maccabean campaign. Their victory brought them extraordinary power but also involved them in setting themselves up as high priests and ultimately as kings. Their pretension to a priestly office that belonged to the descendants of Zadok and to a royal authority that belonged to a descendant of David brought opposition from many Israelites, including some groups such as the Essenes. The Essenes may well be part of a breakaway group that parted company with the Maccabees at an early stage. Although not all of them lived in communities such as Qumran, some of them did, and they deployed their distinctive hope of resurrection in setting themselves apart, as the "Sons of Light," from every competitor. All adversaries—Israelites included—were the "Sons of Darkness," against whom God would help the Essenes with his angels in a final, eschatological war.[6]

As they crafted not only hopes for their vindication but also the ethos of their entire community on the basis of that expectation, the Essenes built the Danielic language of resurrection into their daily lives. The Rule of the Community promises "endless joy in everlasting life, with a crown of glory together with resplendent attire in eternal light" (1QS 4.7–8) to those within the community, while "eternal perdition by the fury of God's vengeful wrath, everlasting terror and endless shame, together with disgrace of annihilation in the fire of the dark region" await those who follow the spirit of darkness and deceit (QS 4.12–13).[7] The hope was that one might become "as an Angel of the Presence in the Abode of Holiness to the Glory of God," joining in the angelic liturgy of God in the temple of his kingdom (1QSb 4.24–25).

The pseudepigraphal book of Jubilees, probably written just after the book of Daniel, presents a view of the resurrection that combines the Danielic comparison to heavenly brightness and to stars into the single category of "spirits." Although the servants of God "will rise up and see great peace," their "bones will rest in the earth, and their spirits will have much joy" (Jub. 23:30-31). This evidently makes the common distinction between Greek immortality and Semitic resurrection difficult to discern in this case.[8]

But a distinction between immortality and resurrection does apply, albeit not to the issue of the medium in which afterlife unfolds, but to the relationship between life before and life after death. Failure to observe it would be an exercise in straining out the gnat and swallowing the camel. Although Jubilees' wording makes the resurrection spiritual and distances itself from a physical conception, somewhat as in the case of Daniel, both of those texts (as well as Enoch) distance themselves much more emphatically from any conception of reincarnation, which is of pivotal importance in Plato's "Vision of Er." The emphasis upon final judgment in the new life means that any continuation of existence along the same lines as now is out of the question. The formulation in Jubilees is taken up at Qumran (4Q176, fragment 21),[9] joining the ferment of expectation in which Daniel seems to have been the yeast.

The paradigm of resurrection that Daniel represents proved resilient in periods far beyond the Maccabean era, culminating in its influence within the New Testament and related literatures. Given that pattern, there is an irony to be confronted. The clearest example of Maccabean literature proper, called the first book of Maccabees, does not overtly mention resurrection. Yet it would have been natural for the author to bring that perspective in at several points—for example, at the death scene of Mattathias (2:42-69), the father of Judas Maccabeus.[10]

The lack of explicit reference may have to do with the Sadducees, a priestly group with which the Maccabees needed to contend.[11] The New Testament, Josephus, and the Mishnah all claim that the Sadducees did not hold with the teaching of the resurrection.[12] Might that position explain the silence of 1 Maccabees?

Caution needs to be shown in evaluating the position of the Sadducees, since they do not express their own theology in any known source. Moreover, those who reported on their position were biased against them. Josephus found them boorish (*Jewish War* 2.166), the Pharisees believed the Sadducees had no part in the resurrection they denied (Mishnah Sanhedrin 10.1), and the book of Acts portrays them as taking the part of persecutors of those who believed in Jesus and his resurrection (Acts 23:6-10). In any case, examples can be cited—from the ancient period until today—of those who are said to deny the resurrection but who in fact simply believe in it in a different way or on a different basis from their accusers.[13] As a priestly group, the Sadducees took their guidance from the Torah proper, rather than from the Prophets and the Writings within the Hebrew Scriptures. Such a hermeneutical orientation left little occasion to make any robust assertion of the resurrection. The Sadducean position was perhaps more one of reserve than of denial.

First Maccabees does not, it is true, formally set out a teaching of resurrection, and yet the wording of the text provides allusion to that hope. Confronting the Sadducean reserve in regard to resurrection, 1 Maccabees provides an illustration of how a belief can be promoted without spelling it out in detail. When Mattathias tells his children they will be "glorified" if they remain loyal to the torah (1 Macc 2:64), that invokes the promise of being like the servant in Isaiah 52:13. Since the emphasis is on how the living should press on in their loyalty and dedication to those who have gone before them, the promise of what happens after death is not explicitly the issue, yet it could be understood in that way.[14] That is why there is reference to the "eternal name" of the patriarchs, just what Eleazar Avaran wins when he dies in an attack on the enemy (2:51; 6:44). Elijah's ascent to heaven also features (1 Macc 2:58). The brief way in which resurrection can sometimes be invoked when it is assumed, for example in Daniel, supports the finding of allusion to the resurrection in 1 Maccabees.

First Maccabees is in any case an unlikely text for finding theology in any detail, since the work pursues the genre of a court history. In this regard, the strong contrast with the work known as 3 Maccabees might be instructive:[15] it deals with a pre-Maccabean setting and appears to work out a theology of vindication by means of miraculous, divine intervention in this world, rather than by eschatology. All the literature styled "Maccabean," in titles that are in any case later attributions, involves experimental applications of Hellenistic genres of writing to conditions before, during, and after rule by the Maccabees. Silence or reserve on the part of any of the texts in relation to any particular event or belief can scarcely be taken to amount to a denial.

In any case, 2 Maccabees contrasts globally with 1 Maccabees, in setting out a bold conception of how and why God raises righteous Israelites from the dead. The martyrdom of Eleazar, a venerable scribe, and of seven brothers with their mother provides the narrative setting of a carefully articulated conception. The impact of its model became so strong that there has been a tendency to suppose that 2 Maccabees articulated the only belief in resurrection that Jews believed, when other views in fact competed. After a generation of research,[16] the daring creativity of 2 Maccabees has become plain.

Two theological ideas are closely related within 2 Maccabees' creative perspective; resurrection is the second, consequent on the first. The first concerns suffering. The authors (Jason of Cyrene and his epitomist; cf. 2 Macc 2:19-23) take God's immediate punishment for sin to be a sign of his kindness: instead of waiting to inflict retribution for "the full measure of their sins," he chastises his people early on (2 Macc 6:14-17). The example of Eleazar's refusal to eat pork, and his acceptance of torture and death instead, is then provided. His motivation instantiates what the people as a whole confront, because he realizes, "Even if I avoid the punishment of men, yet whether I live or die I shall not escape the hands of the Almighty" (2 Macc 6:26). That is, his willingness to die for the "revered and holy laws" (v. 27) unfolds as part of his being true to himself, his real self or soul (v. 30). At the same time, he also wishes to provide an example to the young (v. 27), potential martyrs his behavior is designed to inspire.

Some of the young people to whom Eleazar consciously left an example then make their appearance in the next chapter. Seven brothers, together with their mother, provide a classic paradigm of resurrection that 2 Maccabees conveyed to its posterity: Jewish, Christian, and eventually Muslim. Rhetorically, the authors concentrate attention on the scenes of torture in order to address the issue of suffering and the promise of resurrection (2 Macc 7:42). In that way, they establish a theological framework within which they can take up the narrative of the revolt of Judas Maccabeus in what follows. Because Eleazar had provided the model of suffering (self-consciously, according to his speech; 2 Macc 6:28), the seven brothers and their mother literally exemplify the pattern. In addition, they provide a commentary on their own grisly torture and deaths that consistently sets out—from brother to brother and then brother to mother—a coherent hope of resurrection, completing the theological framework with its second element.

The statements the martyred family make set out a coherent theology of resurrection, beginning with the confidence that "the King of the universe will raise us up who have died for his laws to an everlasting renewal of life" (2 Macc 7:9). Subsequent speakers spell out their expectation, presented as uniformly held. One brother extended his tongue and his hands to be cut off, stating, "I obtained these from heaven and because of his laws I discount them, and from him I hope to acquire them back again" (2 Macc 7:10-11). In contrast to martyrs who can be confident of this restoration, the fourth brother tells the king, "For you there will be no resurrection to life!" (2 Macc 7:14).

The mother expresses the family's motivating faith most fully of all in her address to her sons (2 Macc 7:22-23):

> I do not know how you appeared in my womb. It was not I who bestowed spirit and life on you, nor I who arranged the elemental order of each of you. So the Creator of the world, who shaped the generation of man and devised the generation of all things, will in his mercy give life and breath back to you again, since you now discount yourselves for the sake of his laws.

In a summary of this theology that appears by way of coda in the symphonic suffering and hope of the chapter, the mother urges her last son to accept death by torture: "so that in God's mercy I may get you back again with your brothers" (2 Macc 7:27-29).

The Maccabean surge of teaching in regard to resurrection involved both intensity and scope. The vivid focus on the palpable sense in which suffering would be vindicated, and how it was to be vindicated, joined with a global link between obedience to the torah and being raised from the dead. The influence of the literature associated with the Maccabees has proved pervasive, to the extent that alternative views of the medium of resurrection are sometimes dismissed as inauthentic.[17] Still, the Danielic insistence that the resurrection leads to punishment for some and vindication for others proved more durable than the conception in 2 Maccabees that the wicked simply have no part in the resurrection to life.

Eschatological punishment became a prominent expectation, and works within the Pseudepigrapha richly illustrate this feature of Second Temple Judaism. In the first-century BCE Psalms of Solomon, the eternal destruction of sinners is contrasted with the eternal life of the righteous (3:3-10; 13:11; 14:9-10; 15:10, 12-13). At this point, the sinners are assigned to Sheol or Hades' (Pss. Sol. 14:9), and "Solomon's" psalms mark the transition into a conception of hell. That is even more pronounced by the end of the first century CE in 4 Ezra, where the "furnace of *Gehenna*" makes its appearance alongside the vindication of the righteous (4 Ezra 7:35-37).

Yet unlike Daniel, and in line with 2 Maccabees, an increasing tendency from the end of the first century CE to portray the resurrection as the restoration of flesh is also apparent. After a cosmic conflagration, Sibylline Oracles 4:180 imagines that God will restore people as they were before from the bone and ash that remains, an evident application of the imagery of Ezekiel 37 at a literal level.[18] While the Pharisees of the first century conceived of resurrection in terms of God's provision of new flesh, by the time of the Mishnah a hundred years later, resurrection is portrayed in terms of "a paradise based on the land of Israel, which the living and the dead share."[19] Subsequent teachings describe how rabbis demonstrated that one bone at the base of the spine, the *luz*, is indestructible. That, they concluded, was the physical kernel from which God would raise the righteous dead.[20]

Alongside these emphatically physical conceptions of what it meant to be raised from the dead, Maccabean literature also took up a categorically different direction; 4 Maccabees presents a philosophical argument, in which pious obedience to the torah of Moses leads to the immortality that only the torah can convey.[21] A person's choice of piety (*eusebeia*) realizes "reason" (*logismos*; 4 Macc 1:14-17), an attribute that comes from God as the eternal component of humanity. That philosophical and ethical orientation corresponded to a drastic correction of the view of 2 Maccabees in 4 Maccabees, by endorsing the view that the pure and immortal soul, *not* the mortal limbs, entered into incorruptible life (9:22; 14:4; 16:3; 17:12; 18:23). Where 2 Maccabees anticipates aspects of Evangelical Christianity today, 4 Maccabees is reminiscent of views of afterlife during the Middle Ages still characteristic of Roman Catholicism.

What is most striking about this perspective in 4 Maccabees is that it is worked out with the same examples of martyrdom earlier introduced in 2 Maccabees. The martyr Eleazar is said to have been guided by reason and thereby to have shielded his "sacred soul" (4 Macc 7:4). Unlike in 2 Maccabees, he believes that all who conquer the passions of the flesh "live to God," as do Abraham, Isaac, and David (4 Macc 7:18-19). Like Philo of Alexandria and Jesus, 4 Maccabees involves the patriarchs in the hope of resurrection to eternal life, a counterpoint to the position of the Sadducees.

Fourth Maccabees then introduces the seven brothers and their mother as exemplars of the hope in resurrection. They portray their conviction that they "will be with God" (4 Macc 9:8). Guided by reason, one son—described in terms of "Abraham's youth," Isaac[22]—overcomes his pain "as if transformed by fire into incorruption" (4 Macc 9:21-22). As a group, the brothers describe themselves as willing to "use bodies for guarding the law," to preserve their souls from eternal torment (4 Macc 13:13-15). This hope involves a recognizable existence, so that "Abraham, Isaac, and Jacob will welcome us, and the fathers will praise us" (v. 17). Each brother, in the analysis of 4 Maccabees, hastened to death in order to run into immortality (4 Macc 14:2-5). The mother of seven also receives her praise (4 Macc 14:11–17:6), as 4 Maccabees extends the panegyrics of 2 Maccabees, all the while assuring that the register of resurrection is changed from the restoration of limbs to the triumph of the soul. Even she knew that she was "bringing the count of sons to birth again for immortality" (4 Macc 16:13).

The conception of how these dead are raised, although focused on the soul, also reflects language related to Daniel. The final praise of the woman addresses her directly by saying, "The moon in heaven with the stars does not stand as holy as you, guiding with light your seven starlike children" (4 Macc 17:5). Clearly, the physicality apparent in 2 Maccabees is comprehensively revised in 4 Maccabees, and yet the basic pattern of resurrection hope is apparent: the righteous dead are vindicated with new lives.[23] The medium of those lives varies, and the shift in idiom from fleshly limbs to starlike souls, illustrated in the relationship between 2 Maccabees and 4 Maccabees, undermines any claim of uniformity within the texts of early Judaism; 2 Maccabees itself instantiates that claim by presenting the seven brothers and their mother in harmonious agreement. But exactly the same brothers and mother then, in 4 Maccabees, vigorously revise the earlier view with a conception that is incompatible with that of 2 Maccabees.

Three features of Judaic resurrection appear consistent, for all the contradictions among the texts: (1) God raises people (2) to recognizable life again, and (3) he does so definitively. Because God is consistently involved, even when the language of immortality is deployed, use of that language does not indicate that people are immortal on the basis of a natural transition after death in which God plays no role (or only a distant or ancillary role). Resurrection is conceived of as a divine act rather than as an inherent endowment. In particular, the role of judgment is evident, as God awakens some to eternal life, while others are either consigned to eternal punishment or literally left in the dust. The recognizability of lives, once people are raised again or awakened by God, implies some principle of the continuity of life before and after resurrection. Being raised from the dead is an exceptional mode of human existence, and yet both identifiably human and a matter of existence.

Finally, resurrection is to a definitive life, and this makes it both exceptional and a break with conceptions of cyclical lives, from one existence to another. The last contrast, as well as its general application beyond a few heroic individuals, marks Judaic resurrection as a distinctive perspective within Near Eastern and Mediterranean views of the afterlife.

Strong though the contrast between Judaic resurrection and Hellenistic immortality appears, it does not vindicate the argument that immortality of the soul and resurrection of the body are irreconcilable.[24] The facts of what the relevant texts have to say cannot be refuted by sweeping away conceptions that are inconvenient to claims that only one view was normative. Judaic texts posit resurrection with a clear family resemblance of hopes, and yet they differ markedly where it concerns the medium in which resurrection to eternal life is to occur. Those differences articulate the distinctive sciences of resurrection they deploy and the cosmologies within which they are articulated.

Ancient Sciences of Resurrection

Clearly, differing conceptions of how the dead were raised coexisted within a broad hope whose family resemblances are striking within a pattern of variation. The dichotomy between "bodily resurrection" and "immortality" is helpful only to the degree that it calls attention to variety in the beliefs of Second Temple Judaism.[25] An attempt to expunge one category or the other can only result in a distorted impression of the expectations current in the first century. In addition, those expectations do not resolve themselves into the simple choice between two alternatives. The picture is more complex and more interesting than that. The portrait of resurrection by a given text varied from others in a way that complemented the entire cosmology of judgment. Raising the dead, God also reframed or remade the world, so that any science of resurrection needed to make sense within the cosmology of the new world that prevailed.

The complexity of the views involved arises from the deployment not of the reductive alternative of only two views (resurrection of the physical body contrasted with triumph of the soul) but of five conceptions of how the dead live again. These five views are straightforward in themselves, but allowance must be made for the intermingling of conceptions that have been described as "immortality," "assumption," "bodily resurrection," and the like. Even in texts that are allusive, what is said addresses the issue of how and in what medium of existence resurrection was anticipated. Their sciences of what God does by means of his definitive judgment to raise some people to recognizable life commonly held the goal of explaining how God would achieve that, but in different idioms.

Resurrected Spirits

First Enoch 22:3-14 describes the differentiated treatment of the "spirits of the souls" of the dead. The vision is comprehensive but calibrated within the epoch *previous* to final judgment. While these spirits are gathered (vv. 9-11) either by a fountain and light (for the righteous) or for retribution within the earth (for sinners), the lead-up to the eschatological climax includes a punishing fire directed against the very stars of heaven (23:4). What endures is a mountain range of fire, whose seventh mountain in the midst of the others is shaped like a throne. Fragrant trees surrounded this form, and one of them exceeded all the others (24:5). The angel Michael explains that this tree shall be given to the righteous, so that "they shall live a long time on earth, such as their fathers lived" (25:6, within 24:6-25:7).[26] An accursed land, described in chapter 27, depicts what is in store for those who are not righteous.

Taken in context, the reference to the "spirits" of the dead in 1 Enoch 22 relates to a conception of interim eschatology rather than eternal life. The visionary journey of Enoch includes sightings of what is in store up to the end and all the way through the end. The conception of life following judgment from the throne appears to be localized in Jerusalem, since the fragrant tree is transplanted to the temple, and that fragrance enters the very bones of the righteous so that they live (1 En. 25:6). Clearly, the spirits are depicted as leading an embodied existence, even prior to the definitive moment of judgment, but full vindication is depicted in the visceral terms of bone (and by implication flesh) enjoying the new life. This new existence is comparable with that of the ancestors, but in a completely changed cosmological and historical order.

Enoch's reference to the bones of the righteous makes an apparent contrast with Jubilees 23:31, where the righteous' bones rest in the earth, while their spirits rejoice. Conceptually, Jubilees offers an alternative to Enoch, but an alternative that also portrays resurrection within an elaborate process.[27]

Jubilees introduces its eschatological scenario by means of a comment following the death of Abraham. The comment remarks on the long life of the patriarch—and the even longer lives of those prior to the flood (Jub. 23:8-10). Ever-shortened life and ever-increasing ignorance, disease, and disaster are portrayed as the consequence of sin (vv. 11-15). A time is to come when children will rise against their parents and elders, opening a period of strife, famine, war, and plague (vv. 16-25). At last, however, as people seek the law again and return to righteousness, lifetimes will increase, evil will no longer prevail, Satan will be no more, and God will heal his servants (vv. 26-30). That is the context in which their bones are said to rest in the earth as their spirits rejoice (v. 31). Although there is a deep affinity between Jubilees and Enoch, in Jubilees "spirits" enjoy God's final vindication, rather than serving as an interim state prior to that judgment.

However much Jubilees and Enoch share a conception of spirits surviving death and God's reward for the righteous and punishment for the wicked, their differing cosmologies correspond to different views of how those spirits factor in resurrection. For Enoch, they are the medium of survival, embodied but of interim standing, prior to definitive judgment in a substantially new earth, while in Jubilees the current earth is restored in order to host the joys of the righteous. In both cases, resurrection of the spirit unfolds in a way that challenges the usual understanding of what immortality and physical resurrection mean.[28]

Resurrection like the Stars

The brief but vivid description of the resurrection in Daniel makes a comparison between those who are raised and the stars. The statement is made by means of parallelism (Dan 12:3):

Those who teach insight shall shine like the brightness of the firmament,
Those who make many righteous like the stars, forever and ever.

In each case, the heavenly status of those raised in this way is stressed, yet the assertion is made on the basis of similarity, rather than identity, with stars. A gradation is also implied, such that "those who make many righteous" shine out more brightly than "those who teach insight."

Comparison is also at play in a succinct but laconic statement in the "Vision of Er." There, Er sees some souls "darting like stars" (Plato, *Republic* 10.621B), presumably a reference to their escape from the cycle of death and return to life. As in Daniel, comparison with heavenly luminaries concerns a select group within the larger whole of those who are judged after death, either to return to mortal life ("Vision of Er") or to awake to the stark and permanent alternative: eternal life or eternal contempt (Dan 12:2). Another example of the imagery might be discerned in the Rule of the Community's reference to "endless joy in everlasting life, with a crown of glory together with resplendent attire in eternal light" (1QS 4.7–8), although the dominant conception appears to be angelic at Qumran. Josephus refers to souls released from flesh on the field of battle as placed among the stars (*Jewish War* 6.47). Similarly, although the emphatic focus in 4 Maccabees falls on the fate of the human soul, the mother is praised for a holiness above that of the moon as she lights the way for her starlike sons (17:5).

These comparative statements in regard to stars do not quite amount to "astral immortality," as is sometimes claimed.[29] Rather, they articulate, in the words of Philo of Alexandria, "sharing in the eternal life of the sun and the moon and the whole universe" (*On the Creation of the World* 144). From Philo's perspective, the universe is a continuing whole in constant relationship to God; his emphasis on divine immanence in creation is a prominent feature of his theology. That is unlike the clear-edged eschatology of Daniel and related texts. Daniel's promise of definitive life comparable to the life of stars participates in Isaiah's prediction of new heavens, as well as a new earth, and as in that case definitive judgment is key to the conception (Isa 65:6-25). Reference to the stars and their light, even as metaphorical or qualified, serves to stress the comprehensively creative action required for God's justice to be vindicated. In that fundamental reordering, astral imagery distinguishes those people who, in their resurrection, stand out for the wisdom and righteousness they have communicated.

Resurrection to Angelic Status

The imagery of stars has sometimes been understood as a metaphor for an angelic conception.[30] At times angels and stars are indeed identified, both in the Hebrew Bible (Judg 5:20; Job 38:7) and in the New Testament (Rev 1:20). In particular, reference to the angelic court gathered around God might easily be conceived of in astral imagery. But in the book of Daniel, where angels frequently appear, the conception of stars and heavenly light, rather than angels, is used to describe the most favored of those who are awakened from the dead. Some angelic beings, possessed of a human form like the "one like a son of man" in Daniel 7:13-14, perform an intermediary role with people, rather than serving constantly in the heavenly court. Perhaps for this reason, kinship between the righteous dead and angels became a prominent motif.

When the prophet Samuel, called up from the grave, appeared to the medium of Endor, she described him both as a distinctively human form and as *'Elohim*, God (1 Sam 28:13-14).[31] In effect, an angelic conception is deployed without the term "angel" being used. Similarly, Elijah occupies angelic space once he is taken up by the whirlwind, and his position is implicitly above the celestial chariot and horsemen of Israel, which blocks

Elisha's vision of his departing master (2 Kgs 2:11-12). Such implicitly angelic usages provided a precedent for the robust view at Qumran that the members of the community are to become as angels when they join in the angelic liturgy (1QSb 4.24–25), while the wicked are consigned to the dark region (1QS 4.12–13).

Philo of Alexandria presents the patriarchs as alive in the divine presence and as enjoying an angelic existence. As in the case of biblical descriptions, this existence includes a union within a single body of "sun-like mind" (*On the Life of Moses* 2.288). Although 1 Maccabees is notoriously reserved in relating to the resurrection of the righteous, its promise of glorification for those who remain loyal to the law (1 Macc 2:64) may allude to a hope of angelic status. Sharing a conception of the angelic status that awaits the righteous by no means implies a shared eschatology. Philo, in his Platonic approach, apparently conceives of a relatively seamless transition into the new order, while the War Scroll from Qumran makes it plain that one reason for the comparison of people with angels is that angels, too, are to engage in the final forty-year battle of the sons of light against the sons of darkness. People and angels are consistently portrayed as in affinity; along what lines they are compared varies greatly.

Resurrection with Flesh

The direct statement of the third son in 2 Maccabees 7:10-11 that he offered his tongue and hands in the service of the divine laws in the hope he would receive them back emphasizes the direct vindication God provides in raising the righteous from the dead. His mother likewise expresses confidence that God will give "spirit and life" to her sons again (2 Macc 7:23). She provides a classic argument of *creatio ex nihilo* in order to explain confidence in the resurrection. As God made the earth out of that which had no existence, so the human species comes to be purely out of divine creativity (2 Macc 7:28). That divine capacity means that God can restore anything that a tyrant takes away.

How this restoration is accomplished is not stated in 2 Maccabees. The Sibylline Oracles 4:80 visualizes an enormous conflagration, and restoration of flesh from bone and ash, while Josephus speaks fleetingly of the Pharisaic belief that God would provide "another body" (*Jewish War* 2.163; 3.374), and some teachers sought for the physiological bone from which the dead could be raised (Genesis Rabbah 18). The prospect, in any case, was so glorious that the ultimate threat is that wrongdoers would have no part in "resurrection to life" (2 Macc 7:14). Following the contrastive judgment on the just and the unjust in both Enoch and Daniel, Psalms of Solomon develops a more explicit threat of eternal destruction (Pss. Sol. 3:9-11; 13:11; 14:9-10; 15:10-13). The emphasis of 2 Maccabees—the classic statement of the hope of the resurrection of the flesh—falls unmistakably on the life to be enjoyed by the righteous. Indeed, so immediate is this hope, the last surviving son accepts suffering in his mother's presence by saying, "Our brothers, having endured brief affliction, have fallen into everlasting life" (2 Macc 7:36). How that life is related to the hope of the restoration of the lost and mangled limbs the martyrs have given is not stated. Conceivably, an interim moment akin to that described in 1 Enoch 22 is assumed, but not stated, in 2 Maccabees.

Resurrection of the Immortal Soul

"The souls of the dead" in 1 Enoch 22:3-14, discussed above, is a phrase that appears in connection with "spirit," as part of a scheme of embodied but interim life until ultimate judgment. That is a reminder that the types of belief in resurrection, and their concomitant cosmologies, sometimes influence one another, sharing language as well as conceptions. "Soul" also, and perhaps surprisingly, emerges as a key term in 2 Maccabees, where we have just seen that the dominant conception is of God's re-creation of flesh to replace what was expended in witness to his law. There, the scribe Eleazar explains his own martyrdom for God: "I endure cruel pains in my body as I am beaten, but in my soul I gladly suffer them for fear of him" (2 Macc 6:30). "Soul," it seems clear, was an available way of speaking of a person's identity beyond death, even as the conceptions of spirit and restoration of flesh were developed.

But the Wisdom of Solomon classically represents the conviction that "the souls of the righteous are in God's hand," so that torment will not touch them (Wis 3:1). The similarity of that assertion to Eleazar's confidence is striking, but Wisdom speaks of the hope of "immortality" (v. 4) rather than restoration of the flesh. Yet the righteous also rise to governance (v. 8), after being tried as if in a furnace (vv. 5-6).

That trial, however, in the unique cosmology of Wisdom is *not* of God's making. God did not even create death (Wis 1:13). Hades, whose dominion is not on earth, was summoned by the unrighteous, who made a covenant with death[32] and used death to attack the righteous (1:14–2:20). Their onslaught is fruitless, however, since "God created man for incorruption and made him an image of his own eternity" (2:23). The righteous realize this divine legacy, while those who afflicted them are to repent (chapter 5).

The souls that are vindicated are to "light up" (Wis 3:7)—imagery that overlaps with the promise of the righteous' status in terms of angels or stars. Similarly, despite Philo's predilection for comparing the patriarchs to angels, he also describes them in terms of souls (see *That the Worse Attacks the Better* 32, 48–56; cf. *On the Sacrifices of Cain and Abel* 2–4, 5–10), perhaps accommodating to Platonist language.

Accommodation of a writer's language to the surrounding culture is a natural phenomenon, but the tendency to see such adjustments as less authentic expressions of a given religion than its allegedly indigenous forms should be approached with caution. In particular, global contrasts between "Greek" and "Hebrew" thought have not fared well in critical discussion.[33] In any case there can be no doubt about the vibrancy of the hope expressed in 4 Maccabees, where the hope of incorruption—linked to the fire of torture[34]— motivates martyrs to preserve their souls and expend their bodies rather than face eternal torment (4 Macc 13:13-15). The stated aim of immortality does not reduce their resistance to torture, and reason is depicted as the instrument of maintaining the soul's discipline (14:2-5; 16:13; 17:12; 18:23).

Conclusion

Variation in conceptions of how the dead are raised is not attributable simply to a preference for different images, or the characteristic usage of distinctive language by the authors, although those factors are involved. More profoundly, the types of resurrection identified here correspond to the setting in which God will have the dead live. The cosmology of how this world becomes the next—usually by eschatological transformation but sometimes not—corresponds to the conception of how the dead live in that new environment. Within these cosmologies, the science of resurrection represents how the transformation was conceived to occur.

1) Cosmologically, "spirits" see the righteous through death and either to new life on a substantially new earth (Enoch) or to the rejoicing of those spirits on a restored earth (Jubilees).

2) Comparison with stars makes the locus of new life heavenly (Daniel, with traces in the Rule of the Community, Josephus, Philo, and 4 Maccabees). Although Philo of Alexandria deploys this view in the sense of God's continuing presence in the world, generally the eschatological link to Isaiah 65:6-25 appears dominant.

3) Angelic status, when attributed to the righteous dead, portrays them in fellowship with the angels. They are glorified in a manner comparable to

Samuel and Elijah, whether eschatologically (the Community Rule and 1 Maccabees) or ontologically (Philo).

4) Resurrection of the flesh provides direct vindication for martyrs. The restoration comes as part and parcel of God's sovereign creativity. Within this type of hope, eschatology is most emphatically maintained, with a variety of views of God's intervention: providing another body (Josephus' Pharisees), apocalyptic conflagration (Sibylline Oracles), and direct restitution (2 Maccabees).

5) The conception of an immortal soul offers the greatest sense of continuity before and after death, but at the price of dualism with the body. The Wisdom of Solomon commits to that dualism, removing responsibility for death itself from God. The result is readily embraced by Philo, but 4 Maccabees shows that eschatological judgment can be consistent with this view.

At no discernible moment do these types of Judaic belief in resurrection melt into earlier views available by means of contact with surrounding cultures. The earlier attitude of separation from the beliefs of the "nations," which resulted in a relative dearth of references to life after death during the period of the First Temple, was not jettisoned during the period of the Second Temple. Some of the pertinent texts but not others embrace the concept of a double resurrection, to eternal life or eternal punishment. Although such an expectation obviously serves the interests of theodicy, one of the motivating concerns of the period, knowledge of the Zoroastrian pedigree of the motif may have generated reserve. The five types of hope in resurrection are also not cyclical, in the manner of Plato; they all envisage definitive judgment in which justice (both God's and Israel's) is vindicated. Crucially, they all extend far beyond the suspicion that a few noble people might escape the ultimate fate of death, and instead they conceive of an entire cosmological environment in which God will accommodate the righteous.

II
Catalyst of Transformation

4

Paul on How Jesus "Was Seen"

Introduction

The sciences of resurrection during the period of Second Temple Judaism related to particular cosmologies. Usually eschatological in expression, each cosmology involved a concept of what the world (or universe) was prior to resurrection and of what it was to be after resurrection. As the transition from one *kosmos* (or *aiôn*, "age") to another, the conception of how God raised the dead expressed the science of just what that change involved.

These types of science resolve into five expectations within early Judaism: resurrected beings that are spirits, or like stars, or angelic, or flesh, or immortal soul. In God's own economy, transformation into those states was the ultimate destination. One conception did not exclude another, and the language of expectation could be transferred from one type to another. Any given expectation related not simply to what would happen to a particular person but anticipated that the universe moved from its present state to a comprehensive and final version. In the end, therefore, the views went their different ways when it came to the goal of resurrection. All that existed would be spiritual or astral or angelic or restored flesh or soul, depending upon the perspective.

In philosophical discussion generally—for example, with regard to whether human beings are free—positions may vary, and yet borrow from one another. That includes debates in natural philosophy (generally called science since the Enlightenment), where arguments concerning the origin of the universe and the reasons species change over time are far from settled. At the same time, positions are defended fiercely when, say, determinism, the "Big Bang" theory, and creationism are discussed. Categorical findings oppose one another, even as debate continues and language is borrowed from one position to another. In a comparable way, New Testament accounts of how Jesus was raised from the dead are consistent with patterns of Judaic expectations, but they also adapt and reformulate the traditions that went before, so that the fluidity of the earlier sciences continued—and grew stronger, more emphatic, and sometimes fiercely categorical.

Indeed, perhaps the most remarkable feature of the New Testament texts that involve resurrection in comparison to their Near Eastern forebearers is their relative specificity in regard to how the dead are to be raised, and to what kind of existence. The reason for that innovative specificity, of course, lies in the conviction that God had actually raised Jesus from the dead. Referring to his being raised required an assertion of how he had been raised, a science that referred both to his particular case and to the new reality he initiated. Resurrection shifted from the realm of hope to an assertion of a precedent available here and now. That catalyzed his followers' expectations of what was to happen into descriptions of what God *had in fact done* in the case of Jesus and was in the process of doing for those faithful to Jesus. For that reason, resurrection science was not only the instrument of a cosmological conception, as is true in many texts of the ancient Near East, but also the assertion of a present reality: that Jesus lives after death and actively involves himself in the transformation of humanity as such into a resurrected state.

The texts involving Jesus' resurrection reflect this relative specificity, which derives from a catalytic encounter with him that each relates. All of them deserve analysis; every one requires assessment if the resurrection is to be understood. Yet as in the case of the sciences of resurrection current in Judaism, and in the surrounding cultural world for millennia before the first century, New Testament texts often allude to more than what they say, and suppose settings of ritual and practice that are left unspoken. Although they are relatively precise in explaining how Jesus was raised, say in comparison to the cases of Tammuz or Eleazar the scribe, they also take for granted a wider world of instruction that their intended audiences could consult.

For several reasons Paul provides the best mode of access to the range of materials that involve Jesus' resurrection. First, Paul wrote the earliest extant written account, well prior to the composition of the Gospels, of what Jesus' resurrection entailed. Moreover, he offers an interpretation of what it means for Jesus to be raised from the dead within a cosmological statement that is more clearly explained than any other account in the New Testament. That is, Paul gives us not only the earliest written description of resurrection science but also the most detailed scientific explanation in the New Testament.[1] To begin with his presentation in his First Letter to the Corinthians, written from Ephesus in 56 CE,[2] is therefore only sensible, although Paul does not (there or elsewhere) offer a full narrative account of the resurrection.

Paul's view of Jesus' resurrection is, of course, by no means the only one available in the New Testament. Any claim of normativity for it would be misleading, even in Paul's own time (when his disagreements with other authoritative teachers were notorious). Each of the Gospels, Acts, and the Revelation to John go their separate ways; there are competing views evident *within* many of those texts, and noncanonical sources articulate yet other conceptions. Resurrection sciences in the New Testament and related sources exhibit another characteristic that is as prominent as their specificity. Although each is detailed as compared to the predecessor conceptions within early Judaism, no account simply repeats the conceptions of the others. Differences that go far beyond matters of circumstantial detail emerge in the wake of specificity.

At times these differences are startling and have troubled generations of readers (and especially preachers); the risen Jesus might be said to disappear (Luke 24:31) and yet to be of flesh and bone, demanding and consuming food in the presence of his followers (Luke 24:39-43). He passes into a locked room (John 20:26) but offers his wounds to be touched (John 20:27). Although at first he is unrecognized when those who know him sight him after his death (John 20:14-15), an evidently visual awareness of him forms the basis of the announcement, "I have seen the Lord" (John 20:18). These and other differences have perplexed readers more than any other factor and have tended to obscure the insight that, although discrepancies and contradictions remain puzzling, they are also a function of the specificity already mentioned. Specificity and variation go hand in hand; both characteristics need to be understood if the New Testament's presentation of how Jesus was raised from the dead is to be assessed.

Fortunately, Paul also offers crucial evidence in regard to the issue of variation. Although 1 Corinthians was written in 56 CE, Paul explicitly sets out the tradition he himself had been taught decades earlier.[3] That tradition was an ordered statement of those by whom Jesus "was seen" after his death (1 Cor 15:3-8). The list gives names, and also the sequence in which Jesus was seen, from Peter to Paul himself. Properly understood, Paul's statement provides a method for organizing, comparing, and identifying the different views and accounts of Jesus' resurrection in the New Testament. Paul not only sets out his own science of resurrection but also gives us the identities of those who taught differing sciences elsewhere in the New Testament.

Anthropology and Resurrection

Paul's thinking is exceptional where it concerns the global question of what makes a person human. He develops his anthropology in his First Letter to the Corinthians, chiefly by means of reflection on the issue of how Jesus' resurrection relates to the life of humanity—after death but also before-hand. His resurrection science is an anthropology, unique within the New Testament in its perspective as well as in its details. In Paul's mind, when God raised Jesus from the dead, that uncovered the prospective nature of all humanity, not yet fully realized and yet perceptible.

Paul's views have often been confused with the theology of later periods, when Christianity was strongly influenced by Stoicism. By the fourth century of the Common Era, Augustine referred to the pre-Christian Roman orator Cicero as "our Cicero," and Stoicism in a Ciceronian idiom became an ambient language for using philosophy to conceive of the faith. That resulted in the now-familiar conception of the soul as eternal and of the body as a passing appearance in the flesh.[4] The presupposition of that dichotomy as part of the normative Christian creed remains current among Christians and non-Christians alike—despite the fact that it does not feature at all in the principal ecumenical creeds.

Paul's anthropology was in any case quite different in this regard from later teachings of the church. Unfortunately, his position has been distorted, sometimes to the point that his writing has not been accurately translated, to make it agree with a Stoicized teaching of an immortal soul or with the later presentation of some Gospels that Jesus' resurrection was essentially physical. But Paul went out of his way to insist that he did *not* believe the soul was immortal and that he did *not* believe that the resurrection body (Jesus' or believers') was essentially physical. The first part of this idiosyncrasy should endear Paul to modern atheists but does not. The second part should make modern Fundamentalists, who see Jesus as raised in the same flesh with which he died,[5] contradict Paul. Instead, they ignore what he says or conflate his teaching with other views in the New Testament.

Learning to let Paul explain himself is one of the most difficult challenges in appreciating the resurrection in the New Testament. Paul thought that a body could be spiritual. In fact he taught that when God raised Jesus from the dead, the Anointed (the meaning of the term *khristos* or "Christ") was a "spiritual body" (1 Cor 15:44-45). Paul developed his perspective as one of the apostolic witnesses who could say on the basis of firsthand experience what the resurrection involved, and so his conception deserves better treatment than to be superseded by the later views of Christian theology.

Paul's science of resurrection was unusual enough in its own time that it demanded the close argument in its defense that he offers in 1 Corinthians 15. It also clashes with conventional assumptions, Stoic conceptions among them. Paul does not presuppose that the soul survives death, and he goes out of his way to refute that idea. In addition, he does not accord with perhaps the best known of all the gospel passages concerning Easter, familiar to believers and nonbelievers alike from innumerable artistic representations. Paul does not—at any point in 1 Corinthians 15 or in his other letters—refer to a visit to Jesus' tomb by his followers after his death. In Paul, there can be no story of an "empty tomb," because there is not a reference to a tomb in the first place.

Any thought that Paul speaks of Jesus' resurrection as physical[6] is unequivocally denied by Paul himself in his discussion in 1 Corinthians. Both of the ideas that Paul does not use—the soul's immortality and the emptiness of the tomb—are without question basic to *other* sciences of resurrection. They deserve attention in their own right. But in exactly the same way, Paul deserves attention in the terms he developed in order to explain himself.

Those terms are developed with regard to the makeup of humanity as created by God. When Paul thinks of human beings, he consistently conceives of every person as a body (*sôma*). Bodies that can be perceived by the senses are physical, composed of flesh (*sarx*). Flesh in his definition is physical substance, which varies from one created being to another (for example, people, animals, birds, and fish; 1 Cor 15:35-39). On this view, bodies are palpable in the flesh that they inhabit. Paul supposes that flesh is a basic physical substance and reflects the conception that there is a taxonomy of kinds of flesh as one moves from one living entity to another.[7] Bodies are composed of their characteristic and elemental flesh, such that one body can become physically tangible to another body.

When the configuration or form that we call body is in flesh, it can be perceived by others with their senses. One kind of animal's body can even perceive another kind of bodily animal as a result. But Paul does not think that the body is only a material entity, simply identical with the flesh in which it is configured. That is where he parts company with the frequently found modern assumption that bodies are to be identified simply and completely with flesh.[8]

Paul develops his perspective out of the insight that people, after all, perceive of their own bodies in quite a different way from those who look at them from outside. They are flesh, but not only flesh. While they are alive, self-awareness characterizes people's lives, such that each of them is aware of one's body as a *being*—in Paul's language a "soul" (*psukhê*). So in addition to being physical bodies, each person is also what Paul calls "psychic body" (*sôma psukhikon*), by which he means bodies with souls, or what we might call ensouled beings (1 Cor 15:44). When it comes to the body, in common experience what you see is not all that you get. Perceiving another's body is not the same order of experience as being in one's own body. Ensoulment is a characteristically human feature (1 Cor 15:45): "The first man, Adam, became a living soul."

The phrase "psychic body" (*sôma psukhikon*) is badly misconstrued in many English versions, but its dependence on the noun for "soul" (*psukhê*) points to its substantial sense. The adjective does not mean "physical" as we use that word; the corresponding Greek usage to the English term "physical" in Paul's thought is *sarkikos*,[9] meaning "fleshly" or "carnal." Although that is a simple point, it requires emphasis in light of common misconceptions and mistranslations. Widely used renderings of *sôma psukhikon* in 1 Corinthians 15:44 include "natural body" (KJV, ASB, BBE, ESV), "physical body" (RSV, GNT, NCV, NRSV), and "earthly body" (NIV).[10] Evidently, the Stoic view of later Christianity, which separated "soul" (*psukhê*) from both "body" (*sôma*) and "flesh" (*sarx*)—and treated the latter two as if they were the same—has influenced translators to the point that they could not permit Paul's adjective *psukhikon* to have its natural relationship to *psukhê*.

In differing ways, none of these renderings does justice to Paul's view that *sôma sarkikon* and *sôma psukhikon* are distinct. In his translation, James Moffatt evoked the Latin correspondent of *psukhê*, which is *anima*, resulting in "animate body," a helpful step forward. People as bodies are not just aggregations of flesh in Paul's conception, but they are self-aware and capable of deliberate action. That deliberative self-awareness is precisely what makes them "psychic body." Although in general discourse, "psychic" is easily confused with allegedly paranormal phenomena, for our purposes it is still more accurate than other adjectives. Moffatt's use of "animate" is defensible, as well, but the term is also not ideal,[11] since it might apply to various forms of life in which self-awareness or consciousness is not at issue.

Paul's "fleshly body" (*sôma sarkikon*, as he would have said) is physical, a carnal entity that any other person or living entity can see and touch. Paul's "psychic body" (*sôma psukhikon*) is the body people are conscious of when they act on the basis of their human agency. The physical body that can be measured and assessed is a fact of biology, while the patterns of activity we learn and follow, as well as the innovative undertakings we might engage in, are facts of history and social life. To Paul's mind, people act with their agency as psychic bodies, in the realm of soul; only their physical bodies can be perceived in the realm of flesh. In both realms, however, flesh and soul, people have perceptions and act in ways characteristic of their personalities because they are bodies. Without a body, an unengaged soul would be as inert as a lifeless corpse. Paul's conception that the body is *not* synonymous with physical substance is among the most challenging aspects of his perspective, but he plainly set it out.

Paul's thought in regard to the physical body and the conscious body has been obscured by the dominance of later Christian doctrine, current from the time of the Middle Ages, which conceives of "body" as purely physical and mortal and of "soul" as ethereal and (at least potentially) immortal. This view is comparable to that of 4 Maccabees. But for Paul, it is impossible to conceive of a human being, in the flesh or psychic, *except* as "body." That is the case whether the person is treated physically or the person acts in society as an agent. Paul cannot and does not define a person apart from a body, whether it is "fleshly" (*sarkikon*) or "psychic" (*psukhikon*). He conceives of human beings as both reflexive (*sarkikon*) and deliberative (*psukhikon*), and only capable of action, whether reactive or conscious, insofar as they are bodies.

Yet although the distinction between *sôma sarkikon* and *sôma psukhikon* is vital for an understanding of Paul, his "psychic" or conscious body is nonetheless *not* immortal—far from it, because Paul conceives of the soul itself, like the act of breathing, as subject to death. Death for Paul is when living existence ceases both as a breathing physical entity (the initial sense of the Hebrew noun *nephesh* and the Greek *psukhê*) and as an agent capable of deliberative action (1 Cor 15:42-44). The psychical body disappears in the "weakness" of mortality (v. 43). Immortality does not continue directly from either physical or social life. Immortality derives rather from "body" in yet a third medium. This is where Paul thinks characteristically about the resurrection.

In addition to being physical body and psychic body, Paul believes a person is (or can become) "spiritual body" (*sôma pneumatikon*; 1 Cor 15:44). That is, people are not only *self*-aware; they can empathetically relate thoughts, feelings, and actions *to one another and to God*. Paul deploys this sense of what is "spiritual" early on in his First Letter to the Corinthians, preparing the way for his account of Jesus' resurrection. Within a larger discussion of how it is possible for people to know God by means of God's Spirit (1 Cor 2:9-16), he comes to a conclusion (vv. 14-15) that previews the distinction between *sôma psukhikon* and *sôma pneumatikon*:

> Psychic man does not receive things of the Spirit of God, for they are foolishness to him, and he is not able to know, because they are judged spiritually. But the spiritual man judges everything, but is himself judged by no one.

Self-awareness has its limits. But just as a person as physical body can become deliberative, so that person can receive, know, and judge spiritually. At all three levels, material, psychic, and spiritual, for a person to engage in perception and action requires a body, the sine qua non of functioning as a human.

A body with operational intelligence, a "mind," is in a position to know God's mind and so to "receive things of the Spirit of God." Paul explains this line of thought by means of a biblical riddle. Quoting Isaiah, he asks, "Who has known Lord's mind?"[12] (Isa 40:13; cited in 1 Cor 2:16). The answer comes in a dramatic claim of access to the "Lord's mind" (*nous Kuriou*): Paul says that he and his audience have "Anointed's mind" (*nous Khristou*), which mirrors the mind of God.

The mind of the "Anointed" (the straightforward meaning of the term *khristos*), embedded within each believer, permits one to know God's mind. In ethical terms, such a person can define purpose in a way that transcends physical or personal interest. But Paul also insists that this transcendence involves a body, which can know and act on the basis of its knowledge in a way that is not restricted to either physical needs or moral wants. Jesus provides the model of the process of becoming *sôma pneumatikon* with a body as well as a mind comparable to his own, a process that Paul goes on to detail in chapter 15 of First Corinthians.

Paul's understanding of Jesus' resurrection is that, having died as people do, in respect of both his flesh and his soul, Jesus became "spiritual body" in a way that reveals human destiny as a whole. Jesus is in that sense the last Adam, a "life-giving Spirit" (1 Cor 15:45) just as the first Adam was a "living being" or "soul" (mortal *psukhê*). The directionality of the progression is necessary for Paul (1 Cor 15:46-50):

> But the spiritual body is not first, but the psychic, thereafter the spiritual. The first man was from the earth, of dust, the second man from heaven. As the man of dust, such also are those of dust; and as the man of heaven, such also are those of heaven. And just as we bore the image of the man of dust, we shall also bear the image of the man of heaven. But this I state,

brothers, that flesh and blood cannot inherit God's Kingdom, neither does decay inherit incorruptibility.

Bearing the divine image so as to inherit God's kingdom requires a spiritual body, so that it would be farcical to claim that one had somehow already come into the final legacy (1 Cor 4:8).[13] Crucially, people can be physical and psychic and spiritual, all at the same time: these modes of living are characteristic of being human.[14] In each mode, it is the distinctive reality of a person, a body, that is at issue: reflexive (*sarkikon*), deliberative (*psukhikon*), and engaged with transcendence (*pneumatikon*). But of those three ways of living, only the third participates in God's being, so as to escape mortality.

For Paul, Jesus is the basis on which people can realize a destiny already intimated in their experience, but only actualized by the power of the resurrection in their own bodies. Jesus' bodily—but at the same time spiritual—resurrection is the premise of human destiny. "Flesh" and "soul" become not ends in themselves but way stations on the course to "Spirit," to which Jesus' resurrection provides access. Just as sin for Paul marks out the necessity of human transformation in the realm of ethics, so physical death marks out the necessity of human transformation in the realm of its medium of existence.

Indeed, the characteristically Pauline tendency to associate death and sin (1 Cor 15:56) derives from his conception of how the human body subsists in parallel media. What death is for the physical body corresponds to what sin is for the psychic body. Because sin on Paul's understanding is implicated with the mortality of the flesh (see Rom 7:14-25), overcoming that ethical obstacle is all of a piece with transcending flesh on the way to becoming a spiritual body. His conclusion insists that God's kingdom ultimately is a matter not of flesh and blood (v. 50) but of change into the realm of immortal Spirit (vv. 51-53).[15]

This, for Paul, is the substance of the resurrection: Christophany, the appearance of God's Anointed, signals a definitive transformation of the world. This is more than the warrant that Jesus himself had been raised, for example in the angelic assurance that the women at the tomb experienced (Mark 16:1-8). It is more even than an encounter with the risen Jesus, because Paul makes Jesus' resurrection the pivot of a cosmological shift. The resurrection is the "primal offering" (*aparkhê*)[16] within the full harvest of humanity (1 Cor 15:20).

Transcendence characterizes Paul's perspective on Spirit, much as agency explains what he means by "soul," and physicality corresponds to his thinking on "flesh." A person lives by means of body physically and as an agent, but also in relation to purposes beyond considerations of self-interest. That transcendent, "spiritual" body is the only one that Paul conceives of as immortal, and, for him, Jesus' resurrection realizes immortality in that sense, not as a continuation of physical or social existence. Indeed, the conception of a survival of flesh or soul would contradict Paul's resurrection science. The contrast of Paul's science of anthropology with that of 4 Maccabees is obvious. A certain overlap is detectable between Paul's reference to the "mind" (*nous*) that can be shared with the Anointed in the process of knowing God (1 Cor 2:16) and 4 Maccabees' recourse to "reason" (*logismos*) as what protects the immortal soul (4 Macc 14:2-5), but Paul's "spiritual body" is defined in contradiction to a conception of the soul as deathless.

Insistence upon the term "spirit," on the other hand, is reminiscent of the usage of Jubilees 23:31, where the bones of the righteous are said to rest in the earth as their spirits rejoice. But Paul's specification of a "spiritual *body*" represents a difference that looms larger than a nuance. The language seems initially more like that of 1 Enoch 22:3-14, where "the spirits of the souls" of the dead pass through differential experiences that presuppose some bodily existence. But Enoch here refers to an interim existence, not to the finality that it is Paul's concern to emphasize.

Paul is familiar with at least some of the language of his predecessors, which is deployed to frame his view of Jesus' resurrection, the cosmological change it signaled, and the science of human participation in a new, heavenly reality by means of a "spiritual body." His precision in arguing for this conception opens the possibility that, with thinkers such as Philo of Alexandria, he also thinks of the resurrected dead in angelic terms, in that—like Moses—they may be said to enjoy a single body of "sun-like mind" (*On the Life of Moses* 2.288) or a "spiritual body" with "Anointed's mind" (1 Cor 15:42-48; 2:16). In this regard, Paul might even presuppose Jesus' teaching that those who are raised from the dead are "like angels" (Mark 12:25; Matt 22:30) or "angelic" (Luke 20:36). In that case, his development of the concept of "spiritual body" would be an attempt to specify what is meant by a comparison with angels in Jesus' statement.

Paul, too, can compare people with angels, and he even says the Galatians had received *him* "as God's angel" and "as Jesus Anointed" (Gal 4:14). His expression implies that the risen Jesus as well as the apostolic Paul bear angelic traits. But Paul's natural tendency is to affiliate angels with God in heaven (Gal 1:8; 3:19); their function of representing God takes over from the sense of angels exerting their own identities. In resurrection, however, Paul sees identity as crucial, so that "spiritual body" expresses both the reality of the Anointed and the prospect of believers better than comparison to angels does.

Elsewhere in 1 Corinthians, Paul cites or alludes to dominical tradition in regard to marriage (1 Cor 7:12) and the Lord's Supper (1 Cor 11:23-25); perhaps Paul's exposition of the resurrection reflects Jesus' teaching, as well. That possibility cannot be ignored, although it is beyond present knowledge to confirm it. But even if Jesus' own articulation of the angelic expectation of how the dead are to be raised was not implicit within Paul's language of resurrection, features of the angelic type of conception remain detectible in 1 Corinthians 15. Still, the emphasis upon Spirit and spiritual body remains crucial to appreciate.

For all the antecedents that appear in his explanation of how Jesus and therefore the dead are raised, Paul's science remains an original and comprehensive account. Its emergence in the year 56 CE reflects confidence in Jesus' resurrection and suggests that Paul was not alone in his categorical assertion, even if the content of his science *was* all his own. Indeed, as Paul developed his account, he also provided the earliest list there is of those by whom Jesus was seen after his death, teachers who had their own views of how God raised Jesus from the dead.

Apostolic Dataset

By detailing those before him among the company of apostles, each commissioned by the risen Jesus, Paul intimates that other sciences of the resurrection circulated in his time. Within the list he does not provide any narrative treatment of an encounter with the risen Jesus—not even his own. Yet he insists that the tradition of Jesus' resurrection was formally bequeathed to him, and he makes a clear distinction between that tradition and the science he defends in the course of replying to the concerns, objections, and questions that the Corinthians had set out to him (1 Cor 15:12-58). His science of resurrection, then, proceeds from the dataset of tradition, but the data are enumerated without their being articulated in terms of their content.

Elsewhere in 1 Corinthians, Paul described himself as without a "commandment of the Lord"—that is, a clear, dominical tradition—and yet as teaching on the basis of his own possession of God's Spirit (1 Cor 7:25, 40). The issue in that case was the advisability of marriage for unmarried people. The Lord does have a teaching that those married should remain so (1 Cor 7:12), but, when it comes to those who had never been married, extrapolation became necessary. The situation is similar—although also more complex—in respect of the resurrection.

Paul acknowledges that everyone on the list prior to him had seen the Lord, implying that they, too, had accounts to give. He insisted that he also was an apostle who had "seen the Lord" (1 Cor 9:1), and that was the basis of his science, as well as of his personal authority. Other accounts obviously circulated with their own characteristic sciences, and the Gospels present some of them. Yet even with that competition, it remains striking that Paul's science, the earliest that was written and the most complete in the New Testament, is not the most prominent in current discussion. That suggests that apostles earlier in the list have exerted an influence disproportionate to Paul's. For that reason, appreciating their views is crucial. It is no more appropriate to distort their views to agree with Paul's than it is to distort his to agree with theirs.

Paul articulates his science of the resurrection on the basis of his own experience, but an experience that he deliberately contextualizes within the experiences of apostles before him. He lists those predecessors and affirms that the dataset belonged to a tradition that was divulged to him and that he "received" as authoritative (1 Cor 15:1-5):

> But I remind you, brothers, of the message (*euanggelion*)[17] that I messaged to you—that you also received, in which you indeed stand, and through which you are saved—by what word I messaged to you—if you hold fast, unless somehow you believed in vain. Because I delivered to you at the first what I also received, that Anointed died for our sins according to the Scriptures. And that he was buried and that he was raised on the third day according to the Scriptures, and that he was seen by *Kêpha'*, then the Twelve, then he was seen by more than five hundred brothers at once (of whom most remain until now, although some sleep), then he was seen by James, then by all the apostles, but last of all as if to the preterm birth, he was seen also by me.

As a general statement, Paul asserts that this was part of his grounding message to the Corinthians, and that the *credo* itself, as regards the death and resurrection of the Anointed, was all "according to the Scriptures."

Both Jesus' death and his resurrection are related as traditional assertions, supported and contexted by the Scriptures of Israel. The recourse to tradition here is somewhat curious, because, in writing three years earlier to the Galatians, Paul had spoken quite differently about tradition and its relationship to his *euanggelion*: "Because I make known to you, brothers, the *euanggelion* messaged by me is not according to man, because neither did I received it from man nor was I taught, but through an apocalypse of Anointed Jesus" (Gal 1:11-12).

The terms used are so similar that the cross-reference between Galatians and 1 Corinthians is not likely to be altogether inadvertent, even if during the intervening period Paul might have better clarified the relationship between revelation and tradition in his experience and thought. In this regard, it is appropriate to note that Paul in Galatians 3:1 makes explicit reference to his graphic portrayal of Anointed Jesus' crucifixion in his preaching, the form of death assumed in 1 Corinthians 15:3. Since Paul did not personally witness the crucifixion,[18] the content of that preaching had to have been traditional.

Taken together, Galatians and 1 Corinthians provide insight into how Paul saw the derivation of the message he announced. The actual moment of disclosure of Jesus as God's Son comes about by pure revelation (*apokalupsis*; Gal 1:12),[19] and Paul goes on in Galatians to explain what that means. When God "revealed his Son in me" (Gal 1:15-17), Paul had no recourse to "flesh and blood." He did not go to Jerusalem to those who were apostles before him, but went away to Arabia for three years. Arabia is also identified in Galatians as the place of Sinai, where Moses received the law (Gal 4:25). Paul's time there focused on the relationship between the torah and Anointed Jesus.

When those three years were over, Paul went back to Jerusalem to take counsel with Peter, whom Paul identified by the Aramaic form of his nickname, *Kêpha'* (Gal 1:18-20). (Like *petros* in Greek, *keypha'* is the Aramaic term for "rock.") Paul insists that he then saw only Peter and no other apostle apart from James, the Lord's brother, during his fifteen days in Jerusalem. If the substance of the apostolic gospel came directly from God in revelation, its content came from Peter and James (v. 19).

For this reason, in 1 Corinthians 15:3, the precise statement that Christ died for our sins according to the Scriptures involves several levels of authorization, Paul's and Peter's together with James'. For Paul, his experience, the Scriptures, and the tradition of apostles before him amount to apocalypse.

This raises the question whether Paul combined the named apostles on the list, as well as adding his name to theirs.[20] The addition of his own name is palpable. Paul calls himself the "preterm birth," a likely reference to a dismissive nickname used for him in Corinth, and goes on to speak of himself as the least of the apostles (1 Cor 15:8-9).[21] Both the nickname and his statement about himself reflect Paul's status as a latecomer among the apostles. The possibility of Paul being familiar with more than one list cannot be excluded, and, in Galatians 1:18, 19, he makes it clear that he met both Peter *and* James after his conversion in Jerusalem. But Paul's own chronology puts him in Jerusalem in 35 CE, with little occasion to have canvassed apostolic traditions beforehand.[22] Although Paul might conceivably have combined two lists, it seems unlikely. He says at the outset of the passage (1 Cor 15:1) that the full list is part of the message he has already promulgated with the Aramaic form of Peter's name.[23]

Substantiation by the Scriptures of Israel for the database as a whole also suggests the list was coherent by the time of Paul's meeting in Jerusalem in 35 CE. But what "Scriptures" are in mind? Reference to the last of the servant poems in Second Isaiah (Isa 53:5, 8) is appropriate, since the servant is said to have been "wounded for our transgressions," "struck for our iniquities," and ultimately "cut off from the land of the living." But precise quotation is lacking, so that the relevance of this passage continues to be a matter of dispute.[24]

Yet the assertion that the Anointed died for our sins according to the Scriptures demands some textual explanation. Even if the general assertion of Scriptural fulfillment appears more emphatic than the citation of any specific text, it seems unreasonable to deny the place of a passage that conforms to the pattern. In the Aramaic version of Isaiah, the Targum, the present text makes the servant of chapter 53 into an exalted figure and applies statements of humiliation to the people he saves, rather than to the Anointed.[25] The servant is in fact identified with the Anointed in the Targum, where he is said to have "handed his life to the death" (Isa 53:12).

The last phrase might be taken of the Anointed's death or of the Anointed's willingness to risk his life. When the ancient Christian gospel that Paul cites refers to the Anointed dying for our sins according to the Scripture, it may well be invoking the pattern of martyrdom. Martyrs were understood to be agents of removing sin and pleasing God, and the image of Isaiah's servant found its place within that language, along with that of Isaac's experience on Mount Moriah (Gen 22). Paul shows no sign of allusion here to the latter passage, although in Romans 3:25, when he speaks of the Anointed as a place of pleasing God by sacrifice, there is virtually no doubt that Paul speaks the language of martyrdom.[26] Martyrdom is the probable sense, for him as well as for those before and after him, of the Anointed dying for our sins *kata tas graphes* ("according to the Scriptures"). The usage conveys a pattern of the martyr's sacrifice, rather than specified passages.

Because Paul makes this statement on the basis of what he "received," it is a legitimate question how far the tradition he learned extends into the passage. It might be, for example, that after he says "that he was raised on the third day according to the Scriptures" (v. 4), Paul then begins a new thought with the statement, "And that he was seen by *Kêpha*'"(v. 5). It is more straightforward, however, to observe that, in specifying the tradition he received and then delivered to his hearers, Paul persistently introduces the authoritative assertion with "that" (*hoti*). By repeating that term, Paul emphasizes that his *euanggelion* proclaimed *that* Jesus died and *that* he was buried and *that* he was raised and *that* he was seen by *Kêpha'*, then by the Twelve, then by the More Than Five Hundred, then by James, and then by All the Apostles. At the end of the list, Paul uses not "that" or "then" but "last of all." That is, he steps out of the series of grammatical indicators of his tradition, in order to refer to himself. He inserts his own experience into an existing dataset.

The total list of six entries, then, is based on a traditional list of five entries (*Kêpha'*, the Twelve, the More Than Five Hundred, James, and All the Apostles). Three years after his own commissioning as an apostle, when Paul explains that Jesus was revealed in him as God's Son, he personally met both *Kêpha'* and James, the brother of Jesus, in Jerusalem (Gal 1:15-20). This meeting, which occurred in 35 CE, is the most plausible occasion for Paul's learning his list and any attendant material that he does not cite here but was nonetheless familiar with.

Paul's use of the name *Kêpha'* (Rock) for the apostle typically called Simon Peter in English is a possible allusion to the significance of the resurrection for Peter, since the experience designated him as the "Rock" of forgiveness. The only extant account of Peter's encounter with the risen Jesus turns on the issue of forgiveness and places the commission to Peter in Galilee (John 21:1-19). Galilee also appears to be the locus where Jesus "was seen" by the Twelve and the More Than Five Hundred brothers. The reference to James, however, along with the undifferentiated group of "all the apostles," seems to assume that Jerusalem is the place where Jesus was encountered, since that is where James and other apostles exerted authority. The issue of the geography of where Jesus was seen, however, has proven complicated.

The debate over whether the resurrection should be placed in Galilee or Jerusalem has long caused dispute. Mark's Gospel anticipates Jesus' being seen in Galilee by the disciples and Peter (Mark 16:7); Matthew fills out that expectation (Matt 28:7, 16-20) but also refers to an appearance in Jerusalem (Matt 28:8-10). Luke's scenes are all concentrated in Jerusalem (apart from in the book of Acts), while John focuses on Jerusalem (chapter 20) until an addendum (chapter 21). Paul's list does not resolve the matter directly, but it opens the perspective of differing teachers, speaking of encounters with the risen Jesus from their respective locations. At the same time, the aggregation of the different names and implicitly different places attests the sense among the apostles that their experiences were coherent with one another.

The teachers named are for the most part well known to readers of the New Testament: *Kêpha'*, the Twelve, and James (apart from Paul himself). Even the generalized reference to "all the apostles," although it obviously involves people beyond the Twelve, concerns a circumscribed set within the New Testament. The "more than five hundred brothers" does not correspond to an obvious grouping, but on the whole the list relates to recognized authorities within the period.

In most cases, named figures also appear within the narratives of the resurrection in the gospels (both canonical and not), so that lines of connection may be drawn between those on Paul's list and the materials presented in the New Testament and related literature. Those lines are not direct; it is obvious that the Gospels do not provide a clearly identified or complete account of the teaching of *Kêpha* or the Twelve, for example. But the dataset Paul presents provides an itinerary for analysis.

By paying attention to the apostles he names, in the order in which he names them, access is opened to traditions prior to Paul, which were then incorporated within the New Testament. His list establishes that there were such traditions, and, by associating them with particular teachers, he offers the prospect of identifying not only the disciples behind the traditions but also the sciences of the resurrection that they developed. Although a precise mapping of Paul's list onto the narrative of the Gospels is not feasible,[27] his identification of key apostolic sources can be applied within an analysis of how those sources developed. Recent study of the Aramaic language can deepen appreciation of such sources and even provides an explanation of how being "seen" is the medium of encounter with Jesus that permeates Paul's dataset.[28]

The Greek usage *ôphthê* is widely acknowledged to be unusual for Paul, along with the possible allusion to Isaiah 53 in 1 Cor 15:3-8, the use of "Anointed" without an article, the formal parallelism of the passage, and the use of the adjective "third" in the last position possible. All of these may indicate an underlying Aramaic tradition.

Yet *ôphthê* need not be taken as a passive; many translators render the usage as "he appeared." Without question, this is a possible rendering, but the true passive with a dative, as here, has been attested in Greek since Euripides (*Bacchanals* 914). What motivates translators to favor the reading as deponent is the theological consideration that Jesus should "appear" actively rather than "be seen."[29] But since many witnesses are named in the passage, commentators should not assume that they all shared exactly the same conception of how Jesus was present to them, nor should that assumption form the basis for translation.

It is Paul's own usage, however, that suggests that the passive rendering here is to be preferred. Within the same letter, Paul insists, "Am I not free?

Am I not an apostle? Have I not seen (*heoraka*) our Lord Jesus? Are you not my work in the Lord?" (1 Cor 9:1). Paul's seeing the Lord and his apostolic status are linked inextricably here, as they are in 1 Corinthians 15:8-9, and he applies the same verb to apostolic experience of the risen Jesus generally.[30] Paul's list makes "seeing" the means by which the resurrection was known by all witnesses known to him.

Pauline Apocalypse

Paul's usage of "seeing Jesus" was commensurate with this description of his own experience of the resurrection (Gal 1:15-16):

> But when it pleased the one who called me in my mother's belly and called me through his grace to uncover his Son in me, so that I might message him triumphant among the gentiles, immediately I did not confer with flesh and blood.

Although Paul does not give a precise geographical indication of where the revelation of God's Son in him occurred, he remarks that afterward he departed to "Arabia" and that then he "returned to Damascus" (Gal 1:17), so that proximity to that city is implied. The whole emphasis—and perhaps the content—of the scene is different from the more familiar stories of Jesus' appearance to Paul in the book of Acts.

Paul describes this revelation as prophetic—like a prophet he felt he had been predestined to this moment from his "mother's belly."[31] The unveiling of God's Son within took priority over any human contact or circumstance. Here the veil or cover is removed from God's Son, who is "in" (*en*) Paul, within his consciousness in an experience uniquely his that constitutes the basis of his apostolic authority.[32]

Paul's experience was not of an empirical event that other people witnessed with him, even partially (as in Acts). He alone was converted that day. His brief reference in Galatians relates to a personal moment of disclosure, an unveiling of the divine (the root meaning of the term *apocalypse*). He conceived of his mystical breakthrough in ways rooted in his mixed background, pagan and Jewish.[33]

The phrase "Son of God" had a life of its own before it was applied to Jesus, referring to angels (Gen 6:2), the whole people called Israel (Hos 11:1), and the king in David's line (Ps 2:7). Direct revelation extends God's favor to people and angels; each is "the Son," "the beloved," as Jesus became in his vision at his baptism (Mark 1:11). When Paul felt the divine "Son" uncovered within himself, the reality was personal and interior. That is the source of his reference to the Anointed "living in" him (see Gal 2:20): the Son was revealed "in me" (*en emoi*; Gal 1:16) so that he lived "in me" (*en emoi*; Gal 2:20). These are coordinated expressions and articulate a coherent understanding.

Paul at the moment of this revelation was a persecutor of the church (Gal 1:13; 1 Cor 15:9; Phil 3:6), who had once considered Jesus as accursed (Gal 3:13; cf. 1 Cor 12:3). A painful dissonance, between knowing the divine Son within him and a profound conviction of his personal unworthiness, never left Paul. This tension powered his ceaseless activity—he might not be worthy to be called an apostle, "but I labored more than all of them" (1 Cor 15:10). He strove to work off his unintended blasphemy, his zealous campaign against what proved to be the way of God's Son, by turning his life over to the guidance of his prophetic vision. This divine Son could become the holy center of God within every person, as Jesus had within Paul: Paul's vision gave him the theme of his thought and of his life.

God disclosed the divine Son in Paul for a specific purpose: "so that I should message him triumphant among the gentiles" (Gal 1:16). The apocalyptic vision of the prophet Zechariah 14—embraced by Jesus when he fulfilled Zechariah's prophecy by expelling traders from the temple[34]—predicted that the gentile world would one day come to Mount Zion *through* its worship in the temple.

But in Paul's experience, the divine Son broke through within him, arcing over the whole fraught issue of correct sacrifice in Jerusalem. Jesus was uncovered within Paul the persecutor, a man as alien to God as a person could be. That showed that God also wanted to uncover the divine Son within gentiles,[35] whose alienation from God was unintentional.

Within this global focus on Jesus as God's "Son," it is interesting that Paul does not deploy the model of the Wisdom of Solomon, where the righteous man is proven as God's Son and so lives in the sight of God, not men (Wis 2:12-3:8). Paul achieves a similar conception with his idea of "spiritual body" but does not deploy the notion of an immortal soul at all. This may be a function of a concern about the "human wisdom" that he criticizes in 1 Corinthians (2:5, for example), but perhaps also it is intended to compete with an alternative science among his apostolic rivals. One of them, Apollos (1 Cor 1:12; 3:4-6, 22; 4:6), was noted for his rhetoric (Acts 18:24); Paul might deliberately leave him unnamed in the general reference to "all the apostles" in the database. Like all databases, the apostolic list could be selectively detailed to favor one result over another; that dynamic only grew stronger as the Gospels developed.

Whatever disagreements he was aware of, Paul asserted that the resurrection grounded all apostolic witness. The particular occasion of his teaching is the apparently general denial of resurrection on the part of some people in Corinth (1 Cor 15:12b). Paul was probably dealing with people who did not agree with his own emphatic teaching of a *bodily* resurrection, although his hyperbolic language makes the denial appear global.[36]

His address of this disagreement is first of all on the basis of the integrity of apostolic preaching. Paul expands on this argument in what follows (1 Cor 15:15-19), but the argument is basically as simple as what he says at first: faith in Jesus' resurrection logically requires affirmation of the reality of resurrection generally. That may seem to be an argument entirely from hypothesis, except that Paul sees the moment when belief in Jesus occurs as the occasion of the reception of the Spirit of God (so Gal 4:4-6):

> When the fullness of time came, God sent forth his Son, born from woman, born under law, so that he might redeem those under law, in order that we might obtain Sonship. And because you are sons, God sent the Spirit of his Son into your hearts, crying, "Abba! Father!"

Because the Spirit in baptism is nothing other than the Spirit of God's *living* Son,[37] Jesus' resurrection is attested by the very fact of the primordially Christian experience of faith.

The availability of Jesus' Spirit shows—according to Paul—that he has been raised from the dead. In addition, the preaching in his name formally claims his resurrection, so that to deny resurrection as a whole is to make the apostolic preaching into a lie: empty preaching, as Paul says, and therefore empty faith, with no recourse to forgiveness of sins (1 Cor 15:14, 17).

Paul's emphasis in this context on the spiritual integrity of the apostolic preaching, attested in baptismal experience, is consistent with Jesus' earlier claim that the Scriptures warrant the resurrection (since God is God of the living rather than of the dead; Mark 12:26-27). Implicitly, Paul accords the apostolic preaching the same sort of authority that Jesus attributed to the Scriptures of Israel. Paul also proceeds—in a manner comparable to Jesus' argument—to an argument on the basis of *the category of humanity* that the resurrection involves: he portrays Jesus as the first of those raised from the dead (1 Cor 15:20). Where Jesus himself had compared those to be resurrected to angels (Mark 12:25), Paul compares them to Jesus. Paul's classic discussion represents his continuing commitment to the categorical understanding of the resurrection as angelic that Jesus initiated. His view of Jesus' resurrection is what provides hope for the resurrection of the dead as a whole (1 Cor 15:20-28).

Just as Paul had presented the catalog of those by whom Jesus was seen in 1 Corinthians 15:5-8 in a definite sequence, so in verses 23-28 he stresses the "order" (*tagma*) of the resurrection's unfolding. The presentation makes Jesus' resurrection the template of the whole, but the Anointed alone is the *aparkhê*, followed by "those of Anointed in his arrival," his parousia (v. 23).

That is a much briefer reference than Paul's insistence earlier, when he wrote with his principal coauthor Silas in 1 Thessalonians 4:15-18:

> This we say by a word of the Lord, that we who are alive, remaining until the *parousia* of the Lord will not precede those who have slept. Because the Lord himself by a command, with the sound of an archangel and with God's trumpet, will descend from heaven, and the dead in Anointed will arise first, then we who are alive, remaining, will be snatched up together with them in clouds to meet the Lord in the air, and so will we always be with the Lord. So reassure one another with these words.

Although Paul's more succinct statement in 1 Corinthians 15 does not contradict Thessalonians 4, he does not choose to defend hope in the resurrection in the same way he does in the earlier letter. The ground of hope for believers who doubt is no longer, as in 1 Thessalonians, "a word of the Lord" but rather the comprehensive arc of divine events beginning with the resurrection. Similarly, the hope "to meet the Lord in the air" seems an early, provisional statement of what will later be called the hope of a "spiritual body." Silas was prominent among "all the apostles," in the language of Paul's list, and fortunately his distinctive teaching is also identifiably reflected in the New Testament. His influence is palpable within Paul's thought, but Paul also went his own way.

Hope, Paul goes on to argue, is what permits the Corinthians themselves to engage in the practice of being baptized on behalf of the dead (15:29).[38] The practice assumes that, when the dead come to be raised, even if they have not been baptized during life, baptism on their behalf after their death will confer benefit. The Anointed as the "primal offering" (v. 20) offers a salvation that reaches back as well as forward in time.[39] Similarly, Paul takes his own courage as an example of the hopeful attitude that must assume the resurrection of the dead as its ground (15:30-32a). Whether in existential or cosmic terms, Paul takes the bodily resurrection to be the fulcrum of human experience.

5

Seen "by *Kêpha'*," Then "by the Twelve"

Kêpha' in Paul's List and the Gospels

Paul's database emphasized the priority of Simon Peter, *Kêpha'*, within the order of Jesus' disclosure (1 Cor 15:5). The Gospels both agree and disagree with that presentation; any claim of their concord (whether with Paul or with one another) is far from straightforward. Two Evangelists, Luke and John, were explicitly aware of a tradition of Peter's priority, although their connection with Paul's list cannot be established. By taking those indications into account alongside the very different presentations of Mark and Matthew, it becomes evident that the Gospels do not catalog in the way Paul does. He sets out his database, and then he explains his science. Gospels embed their sciences within their narratives; they do not list traditions that they did not follow, although they are capable of alluding to them. That is what makes for their complex relationship to one another and to Paul when it comes to the resurrection.

Each Gospel's literary order of presenting its distinctive group of traditions of Jesus' appearance after his death emerges as a function of its view of the resurrection. Gospels articulate their conceptions of how Jesus was raised from the dead by their citation of traditions, some that are connected to those that Paul names, but also by their displacement of, allusion to, and omission of traditions available to them. That is why not even *Kêpha'*, the first to see Jesus on Paul's understanding, enjoys a stable position within the presentation of the Gospels. For this reason, the connection with Paul's list can be investigated only by means of an awareness of the autonomy of each gospel in presenting not a comprehensive database but the governing conception within the circumstances of composition. The texts convey both traditions available to the Evangelist[1] and views of the resurrection that the Evangelist develops by means of aggregating those traditions.

Mark, the first of the Gospels to be written, closes with the young man at the tomb instructing Mary Magdalene and her companions that they are to tell Jesus' "students and Simon that he goes before you into Galilee; there you shall see him" (Mark 16:7). Simon is uniquely singled out, so it would be ingenuous to insist that he is second on the list; had Mark's narrative continued, it might have referred to Peter in a position of preeminence.[2] Still, one could not say that Mark designates *Kêpha'* as the first in the way that Paul does. Matthew's Gospel agrees almost entirely with Mark's, except that the angel (as the young man becomes in Matthew) refers *not* to Simon Peter but only to Jesus' students (Matt 28:7). In any case, Matthew's narrative then has Jesus encounter Mary Magdalene and her companion, directing them to instruct Jesus' "brothers" about meeting him in Galilee (Matt 28:9-10). On any plausible reading, Matthew and Paul contradict one another by this point, because Mary Magdalene precedes Peter in encountering Jesus in Matthew. Peter is only involved as one among Jesus' students who see Jesus after Mary's encounter.[3]

Luke, on the other hand, confirms Peter's preeminence. Yet his confirmation raises an oddity in regard to the Lukan presentation. In Luke's narrative, Jesus after his death engages with two students as they travel on their way to Emmaus (Luke 24:13-35). The story in itself derives from a circle of tradition independent of Peter; its conclusion, however, immediately concerns the issue of the order of Jesus' disclosure as raised from the dead. The Emmaus narrative carries its own summary, when the two students explain that Jesus "was made known to them in the breaking of the bread" (Luke 24:35). In Luke (where there is no appearance of Jesus to Mary Magdalene), that is the first time that Jesus was seen,[4] judged from the point of view of the sequence of the text.

Until the Emmaus narrative, Luke's characteristic concern—for the first time in the Synoptic Gospels' tradition—has been the provable, physical absence of Jesus' corpse from the tomb (see 24:3 in particular, an assertion not shared by Mark or Matthew). The two students on the way to Emmaus provide perspective on the meaning of that absence by what they say. By not being in the tomb, Jesus can be present in the breaking of bread. The Lukan presentation is masterful, but that mastery seems to come at the cost of reducing Peter's importance and contradicting Paul's dataset in a way comparable to what Matthew does.

But then, as the two students return from near Emmaus to Jerusalem—and before they relate their experience—"the Eleven and those with them" declare that "the Lord has been raised, and was seen by Simon" (Luke 24:33-34). At the climactic point of conveying the meaning of the disclosure near Emmaus, its importance is relativized, by portraying Simon as the prior source of Jesus' being seen after his death.

Luke winds up calling even more attention to this oddity, because nowhere in his Gospel (or Acts) is there a scene that corresponds to the statement that Jesus was initially seen by Simon. The assertion is simply made—without the benefit of accompanying narrative. To a formal but limited extent, Luke compensates for the absence, by making Peter visit the tomb after Mary Magdalene and her colleagues found it empty. Peter sees what is not mentioned in connection with the women: linen dressings (Luke 24:12). In Luke's presentation, Peter's seeing that sign of Jesus' absence takes the place of his seeing the Lord in Paul's list. Peter does not actually see Jesus, and he is bewildered at the sight of the grave clothes in the otherwise empty tomb. His stature is elevated by his being named but then relegated because he does not understand the significance of what he sees. The moment when Jesus was seen by Peter is passed over in silence, although the fact of that moment is explicitly endorsed. Luke hears and echoes the sound of a tradition that is not explicitly repeated.[5]

John's Gospel repeats a fuller version of the narrative of Peter's visit to the tomb as compared to Luke's, weaving in reference to the beloved disciple and to the kerchief that covered Jesus' head as well as the dressings (John 20:4-9). This gives Peter a special place in the discovery of the empty tomb but still robs him of being the first to look in and the first to believe that Jesus had risen (since that status goes to the beloved disciple). Instead, he is simply the first person into the tomb (and he therefore displaces the women in Luke's account). Yet Mary still says, "I have seen the Lord," before any appearance involving Peter (John 20:18) in the literary order of John.

The means of compensation for not mentioning Peter vary from Luke to John, but in both cases the compensation is only partial, in that a narrative when Jesus is first "seen by *Kêpha*'," as in Paul's list, is not provided (1 Cor 15:5). These variations provide a guide to the traditions the Evangelists prefer, but they also allude to traces of traditions concerning Peter. Those traces demand attention, especially in light of the claim of Peter's prominence, and they convey a science of the resurrection that differs from Paul's.

Restitution by the Sea

John's Gospel seems to come to a conclusion at the end of chapter 20. Following Jesus' appearance to his twelve students and Mary Magdalene in Jerusalem or its immediate vicinity, the Evangelist refers to many "signs" that might be recounted, with those chosen having been selected in order to encourage belief (John 20:30-31). To this point, there is no narrative in which Jesus singles out Peter, although his membership of the Twelve is of course presupposed. Then chapter 21, an apparent addendum, states that "Jesus manifested himself again to the students by the Sea of Tiberias" (John 21:1). This narrative, consisting of two scenes, is the only one in the canonical Gospels where Peter personally engages with Jesus after the crucifixion. A later work, the Gospel of Peter, also shows knowledge of the story. There, the setting is after Passover, when Jesus' followers went back "to their homes, with the feast over"; the Twelve are described as grieving (Gos. Pet. 14:58-59).

The story is unusual in its circumstantial details. In John, Simon Peter is said to go fishing with Thomas, Nathaniel, the sons of Zebedee, and two other disciples (one of whom is the beloved disciple; John 21:2). The Gospel of Peter identifies those involved as Peter with his brother Andrew, and "Levi of Alphaeus" (Gos. Pet. 14:60), treated as a close follower of Jesus.[6] After that point, however, the manuscript of Peter, a fifth-century papyrus buried with a monk in Egypt and discovered in 1886, breaks off. It seems to offer a version of the same narrative as John's but from the second century.[7] It would be useful to know how this noncanonical version continued, but only John 21 provides the story as a whole. Once named, the students fish during the night in John but catch nothing. At morning, Jesus stands by the shore "although the students did not know that it was Jesus" (John 21:3-4).

This reference to the mystery surrounding Jesus' presence contributes a liturgical tenor to the narrative. The action refers to the preparation of an impromptu meal but with increasingly eucharistic overtones (John 21:5-12). Jesus commands his students to cast their nets to the right, and they haul in a huge number of fish. The beloved student recognizes Jesus, and Simon leaps into the water to get to land. Jesus prepares a fire, and he has fish and bread arranged *even before* the big catch of fish is dragged in by the students in the boat. Jesus is the personal host of the meal, and his students dare not ask who he is.[8] The meal occurs when he "takes the bread and gives to them, and the fish similarly" (v. 13)—an echo of Paul's language in the most ancient reference to the Eucharist (1 Cor 11:23-24).

By referring to fish within the meal, a tight correspondence to Jesus' Feeding of the Five Thousand is achieved (John 6:1-14), and this for John had provided the setting when Jesus explained that he himself was the "bread that came down from heaven" (John 6:41). Although chapter 21 gives the structural appearance of being an addendum, because it belatedly adds the Galilean appearance of Jesus, in fact it coordinates with the Gospel as a whole. Already, in John 6:1, the Sea of Galilee is identified with the Sea of Tiberias, its alternative name and the usage in 21:1. The story of the feeding is placed near Passover uniquely in John (6:4), which accords with the timing of what is described in John 21 (a correspondence that the Gospel of Peter stresses). Allusion to the story of the wedding at Cana, which occurs only in John (2:1-11), features in the naming of Nathaniel in John 21:2. He is identified as "from Cana of Galilee," where, for John, Jesus "made water wine" (John 4:46): so the wine that is notable for its absence in the action of John 21 has found its true source in Jesus all along. These connections serve the climactic assertion, that by the Sea of Tiberias,[9] for "the third time Jesus was manifested to the students, raised from the dead" (John 21:14).

John 21 does not address random or unexpected concerns but elements prepared carefully in the body of the Gospel. The deliberate emphasis upon climactic meaning provides the best explanation for a familiar puzzle within the Gospel: John's specification that the haul from the miraculous catch brought in 153 fish (John 21:11). Why that number in particular?

The specification of 153 fish has occasioned an enormous amount of comment[10] but no consensus apart from the observation that it is a considerable catch. In general terms, however, the specification of the large number of fish is reminiscent of the miraculous feedings associated with Jesus, of five thousand (Mark 6:32-44; Matt 14:13-21; Luke 9:10b-17; John 6:1-15) and of four thousand (Matt 15:32-39; Mark 8:1-10). The integer 153 itself attracted Augustine's attention, who noted that this "triangular" number (that is, counting objects that can form an equilateral triangle) is the sum of the integers between one and seventeen.[11] Augustine anachronistically explained the number seventeen in terms of the Ten Commandments and the sevenfold gift of the Spirit.

John's Gospel itself provides a more likely key, the equivalent of the question in the Synoptic Gospels that Jesus poses to his disciples in regard to the meaning of the numbers of loaves and containers of fragments when he provided food to multitudes (Mark 8:19-20; Matt 16:9-10). John presents the

Feeding of the Five Thousand (John 6:1-15), but not of the four thousand, and the overt riddle about the meaning of the numbers also does not appear in John. But within the story of the Feeding of the Five Thousand, John uniquely explains that the twelve bushels of fragments contained fragments of the five loaves (John 6:13). The latter number had been specified before (v. 9; cf. Matt 14:17; Mark 6:38; Luke 9:13), but John repeats it without reference to the fish involved and pairs it with the number of bushels. The source of the triangular number seventeen, whose sum is 153, lies within John in the specification of the twelve bushels and five loaves and makes the resurrection story into a fulfillment of the promise of the earlier passage with its eucharistic explanation (John 6:26-59).

This rich development becomes the premise of Jesus' engagement with Peter in particular (John 21:15-19),[12] the second scene within the narrative of chapter 21. The scene pivots around Jesus' threefold question, "Do you love me?" (vv. 15, 16, 17). Variations in that query, as well as in Peter's response, need attention in understanding the exchange in detail, but the structure of the interaction is telling in itself. As in the case of the previous scene, linkage with the body of the Gospel drives the intended meaning. The threefold question to Peter, the spine of the dialogue that follows, echoes Peter's denial of his association with Jesus, which also occurs three times (John 18:13-27).[13] Having denied his association with Jesus, Peter requires both rehabilitation and renewed commission as an apostle.[14]

Neither is possible without forgiveness, and for that reason the close of Jesus' appearance to the Twelve (see John 20:23) appears pivotal, because Jesus' forgiveness—his gift to his students—makes the restitution of Peter possible. The restoration of Peter's role is so complete, the image of shepherding ("herd my lambs," "shepherd my young sheep," "herd my sheep"; 21:15-17) puts Peter into the role of Jesus himself, the Good Shepherd caring for his sheep (John 10:1-18). Despite his denial of Jesus, then, Peter's role at the close of the Gospel is greater and more comparable to Jesus' than at any time within the previous narrative; this restitution goes beyond regaining earlier status. The proof of Jesus' identity as the Good Shepherd is that he lays down his life (10:17), and so the scene continues with a prophecy of Peter's death (John 20:18-19). Jesus, having forgiven Peter, now indicates Peter will also fulfill the promise to lay his own life down that earlier resulted in disappointment (cf. John 13:37-38).

Peter's death lies over the literary horizon of John's Gospel, but a famous scene in the Acts of Peter 35 attempts to give Jesus' prophecy narrative fulfilment. Prior to Peter's crucifixion head down, the Acts of Peter portrays him as departing from Rome in disguise. But the risen Jesus, entering the city, meets Peter and tells him that he goes to Rome to be crucified again. Peter then sees the Lord ascending into heaven and understands that it is he himself who is to be crucified. A relationship between this vignette and John 21:18-19 is apparent, with the second-century Acts of Peter appearing to presuppose a dialogue such as John represents.[15] Peter is executed on an inverted cross by his own desire in the Acts of Peter. That is quite unlike the situation forecast in John 21:18, where Peter is told, "You will stretch out your hand, and another will gird and carry you where you do not wish." At every measurable point, the Acts of Peter seems dependent on canonical (and other noncanonical) materials that extend the principle of Peter's restitution to heroic proportions.[16]

At the same time, comparison with the Acts of Peter highlights by contrast how much John focuses not on Peter's eventual death but on his overall purpose, in life as well as in his death, as a result of his exchange with Jesus. Peter in John receives a threefold commission, to take up the function of shepherding Jesus' community in ages that range from "lambs" to "sheep," with particular emphasis on herding them to pasture.[17] Simon Peter is to take up his restored and enhanced status with an intensified concern for the lambs (v. 15), young sheep (v. 16, following the usage of *probatia* in Vaticanus),[18] and sheep (v. 17) of the community after the resurrection.

The repetition forges the link to Peter's denial of Jesus but also permits an evocative variation of the language on which the meaning of the commission turns: whether Peter truly loves Jesus. Jesus' first question is whether Peter "loves" Jesus "more than these" (John 21:15). The verb for "love" (*agapaô*) is just what is used in Jesus' "new commandment," given after he washed the feet of the students and ate with them for the last time in his ordinary life. There (13:34-35), Jesus instructs them to love one another just as he has loved them.

John provides other indications that the new commandment is key to understanding Jesus' question to Peter, "Do you love me more than these?" (John 21:15). Immediately after the instruction to love one another is given, Peter says he will lay down his life for Jesus, and Jesus replies with the prediction of the threefold denial (John 13:36-38). And before the commandment is spoken, Peter has first refused to have his feet washed by Jesus and then asked for his hands and head to be included (John 13:8-9). Jesus replies that one who is washed is pure, except for the feet, and yet he limits the statement "you are all pure" out of awareness of who would deliver him over (John 13:10-11). The text explicitly designates Judas Iscariot in that connection

(13:2), but denial implicitly tarnishes Peter's purity. For that reason, his leap into the Sea of Tiberias in John 21:7—notably putting on a garment in the process, as if taking on a new identity in baptism, instead of removing clothes—amounts to a fresh purification that anticipates what will happen in his encounter with Jesus.

Given Peter's denial, Jesus' question ("Do you love me?") is understandable. The additional probe ("Do you love me more than these?") makes sense in terms of the Gospel's previous narrative, as well. Jesus had known, after all, that the students would scatter off home and leave him alone when the time to suffer came (John 16:32). The question "Do you love me more than these?" presses the issue, whether self-preservation will again prove a governing concern. That helps explain why the exchange between Peter and the risen Jesus moves seamlessly from shepherding the community to Peter's eventual martyrdom.

But for that transition to be possible, Jesus needs to be satisfied with Peter's answer to the direct question. Initially, Peter's response—"Yes, Lord: you know that I love you" (John 21:15)—seems categorical. Yet the verb for love has changed compared to Jesus' usage. Jesus has asked using *agapaô*, and Peter replies using *phileô*. The latter verb, redolent of becoming a friend (*philos*), expresses affection as well as the ethical dedication implied in Jesus' new commandment. "No one has greater love (*agapê*) than this, so that someone lay down his life on behalf of his friends (*philôn*)" (John 15:13). The verbal alternation in John 21:15 corresponds to how Jesus characterizes love, but Peter's behavior to this point has *not* fulfilled the paradigm. That is the underlying drama of his encounter with Jesus.

When Jesus tells Peter, "Herd my lambs," that seems to imply that he has accepted Peter's answer. But then he asks again, "Simon of John, do you love me?" (John 21:16). Here, the comparison ("more than these") is dropped, and the issue focuses on loving Jesus in itself, denoted with the verb *agapaô*, as in the new commandment. Peter's response is identical to his first answer, so that Jesus accepts his pledge of affection (*phileô*) as the equivalent of loving (*agapaô*) and commissions Peter again to shepherd his young sheep. The third time of asking, however, challenges Peter in his own terms (21:17). Jesus asks, "Simon Peter, do you love me?" And this time the verb *phileô* appears. The issue emerges: Is the pledge of affection sincere, and will it go deep—deeper than in the past? That is why Peter's response at the third question protests his integrity: Jesus' repetition is not the only challenge; the issue of sincere affection is paramount, and Peter addresses that directly. This time, when the commission to herd Jesus' sheep follows, there are no further questions.

Although John's presentation is simple, by means of back reference the commission of Peter is mounted in terms that give him a fresh role, as a pastor of Jesus' followers and taking up the place of Jesus himself. For that reason, Peter is not merely restored to a previous position: he is afforded new status within the community. Johannine language develops symbolism as it unfolds through the Gospel, and a principal meaning of the narrative in the final scene turns on the power of repentance and forgiveness.

In Luke's Gospel, Jesus also forecasts Simon Peter's behavior in terms that allude to repentance (Luke 22:31-34), while John's narrative conveys remorse and restitution: Peter protests his loving affection for Jesus despite his earlier actions, and Jesus accepts his love, commissioning Peter in his pastoral role. Because the occasion of Peter's restoration is that he has personally denied Jesus, in John 21 the resurrection is the moment when Jesus—the one person who can forgive the wrong—extends forgiveness after his death and by that restitution makes Peter pastor of the Good Shepherd's flock.

The implicit means of the care that Peter is to extend to Jesus' sheep must include the forgiveness that makes Peter's role possible. In John 21, that meaning remains at an underlying level as a result of the power of Spirit that Jesus breathed into his followers in John 20:22-23.[19] The close association in the Gospels between the resurrection and forgiveness, and between Peter and forgiveness, shows that this is the medium in which the Petrine tradition understood that Jesus had been raised from the dead. Resurrection provided an occasion not only for Peter to be restored to his role but for an enhancement of that role on the basis of a dedicated practice, a *halakhah*, of forgiveness.

Halakhah of Forgiveness

The setting of Peter's restitution in John 21 enables the scene of his commissioning to weave together themes and motifs from earlier in the Gospel. Forgiveness features prominently among them. In fact, the resurrection in John's Gospel has already been identified as the principal source of forgiveness within its community by the time Jesus appears by the Sea of Tiberias. Jesus' students see him after his death within a locked room (John 20:19-23); the purpose of the epiphany is an apostolic commission: "Just as the Father has delegated me, I also send you" (v. 21). The substance of that charge comes when Jesus "breathed into and says to them, Take Holy Spirit: whose sins you release have been released them, whose you hold have been held." This view of how the Spirit is received—and for what purpose—contrasts with the familiar scene that the book of Acts places at Pentecost. In John 20:22-23, forgiveness is specifically empowered by Jesus as he is raised from the dead and on that basis infuses Holy Spirit directly and personally into his students. They are to forgive as he did, and on the basis of the same divine authority.

The substance of the imperative is that *intentional* forgiveness is to be offered. The issue is not limited to responding to bad behavior and then pardoning harm that has been done. Forgiveness acquires a preemptive character, because it seeks to offer itself, rather than accepting a reactive role. That programmatic element emerges as an aspect of the resurrection outside of John, in particular in Luke 24:47; Acts 5:31. The last reference, within a speech attributed to Peter before the Sanhedrin (Acts 5:27-32), presents the focus of forgiveness emanating from the risen Jesus as Israel, particularly in view of the involvement of Israelites in the crucifixion. A strand of tradition associated with Peter portrays forgiveness as a power commissioned by Jesus at his resurrection that rises above responsibility or complicity in the death of Jesus.

This connection between forgiveness and the resurrection has influenced the presentation of Matthew 16:17-19, the promise to Peter of the keys of the kingdom of heaven so as to enable forgiveness. The language of the promise—which is unique to Matthew—is cosmological, without reference to the setting near to Caesarea Philippi. The occasion is Peter's recognition (v. 16) that Jesus is the Anointed, the Son of the living God:

> Jesus replied and said to him, "You are favored, Simon bar Jonah, because flesh and blood did not uncover this for you, but my father who is in heavens! And I say to you that you are Rock, and upon this rock I shall build my congregation, and Hades' gates will not prevail over it. I will give you the keys of the Kingdom of the heavens, and whatever you bind upon the earth shall have been bound in the heavens, and whatever you loose upon the earth shall have been loosed in the heavens."

A vigorous strand of commentary has taken this commission as originally coming from a narrative of the resurrection akin to John 21 and then transposed to the middle of the Gospel.[20]

Whenever arguments of that kind, involving a transposition of material, are invoked, some explanation is owed for why it would have occurred. In the case of Matthew, the majestic ending of the appearance of Jesus to the Twelve, with a commission that differs from the commission to Peter, might account for the shift. Nonetheless, the linkage of the promise in Matthew's text to the disclosure at Caesarea Philippi seems deliberate and strong, so that treating it as a transposed resurrection account would seem strained,[21] unless the promise to Peter shows signs of a setting within the resurrection.

Several features do, in fact, naturally associate Matthew 16:17-19 with the resurrection. The strongest of those features is the assertion that God, not "flesh and blood," revealed Jesus' identity to Peter (v. 17, language reminiscent of resurrection texts such as Gal 1:15; 1 Cor 15:50), along with the reference to the gates of Hades, a metonym for death in Aramaic (v. 18),[22] and the implicit comparison of those gates to the gates of the kingdom of heaven (v. 19; cf. 1 En. 9:2). In view of the high density of Semitisms in the promise, the existence of an Aramaic tradition at the base of the promise has been proposed.[23] Simon here is even called "bar Jonah" ("son of Jonah"; compare "Simon of John" in John 21:16), an obvious Aramaism.

Although Matthew's localization of Peter's confession at Caesarea Philippi (which after all also appears in Mark and Luke) seems secure,[24] the wording of the promise itself (the Matthean addition to the scene) does seem to reflect a different setting. The imagery of the keys, used to speak of definitively opening and closing, alludes to Isaiah 22:22. In the Aramaic version of Isaiah, the Targum, the issue is not the Davidic palace but the temple.[25] That is the locum, linked to heaven, from which the forgiveness of sins is possible (see, for example, 1 Kgs 8:33). That association of ideas is evidently active in the promise to Peter, and it includes the defiance of death, under the figure of the gates of Hades' (cf. Acts 2:25-32, which includes Davidic themes in line with Isa 22).

All those connections assume a knowledge of Jesus' deadly confrontation in Jerusalem in regard to the temple, rather than simply the themes and events of his earlier period in Galilee. The donation of the power of the keys to Peter assumes not only a setting in the resurrection of Jesus but also the cosmological perspective in which sin is no longer a durable power on the earth but must yield to the authority to dissolve sin that derives from heaven. At issue is not just the episodic pardon, overlooking, or forgetting of bad behavior but the dissolution of its consequences. The promise to Peter not only empowers forgiveness, as he himself was forgiven, but presents that power as commensurate with the authority of the temple. The Johannine presentation of this power to forgive sins in association with the resurrection is more plausible than the presentation in Matthew's Gospel.

The story in Luke 5:1-11 of Jesus instructing Simon how to fish, and then making him into a man-catcher, has also attracted attention for its similarity to John 21. The sons of Zebedee are involved, as in John 21, and Peter's identification of himself as a sinner (Luke 5:8) seems to presuppose a dramatic event such as Peter's denial of Jesus.[26] Luke's Gospel places all appearances of the risen Jesus within Jerusalem and its environs, so that a motivation for retrojecting the Galilean narrative of the miraculous draught of fish into the early period of Jesus' activity can easily be supplied. Still, forgiveness is so persistently associated with Peter that it would seem mechanical to presume that each and every pericope in which he is forgiven, or is called to forgive, must be seen as an account of the resurrection. Matthew 18:21-35, for example, shows the tight relationship between Peter and the *halakhah* of forgiveness, without demanding a context in the renewed commission at the resurrection.

At times the Gospels speak in ways that show that the perspective of Peter's forgiveness at the time of the resurrection influences the presentation of instruction given to him before that time. Following the renewal of the promise of binding and loosing (this time to the students as a whole; Matt 18:15-18), Matthew has Jesus state, "Because where two or three are gathered together in my own name, there I am in their midst" (Matt 18:19-20). The perspective of the resurrection is manifest within this discourse, set on the way to Jerusalem. That does not mean that every reference to forgiveness must be located within a narrative of resurrection, but it does suggest that an awareness that the risen Jesus forgave Peter and gave him the imperative to convey forgiveness programmatically permeated the sensibility of those who framed the Gospels.

Jesus' statement "Your sins are released" features as an aspect of his healing others that provoked scandal, since God was understood to be the source of forgiveness (Mark 2:5-7; Matt 9:2-3; Luke 5:20-21; cf. 7:48-49). The extension of the release of sins by means of those acting on Jesus' behalf during his life is plausible, so that forgiveness cannot be considered a theme unique to the resurrection. But the Petrine narrative in chapter 21, describing what it meant for Jesus to give the student who had denied him an enhanced role, portrays forgiveness as the power and the direct continuation of Jesus' risen presence. The narrative so focuses on that issue that little energy is devoted to the description of Jesus' presence; he is eventually (21:7) but not immediately (21:4, 12) recognizable as the host of the meal, and where he goes after the final scene is an open question. Jesus' capacity to forgive and to imbue Holy Spirit for the purpose of forgiving is portrayed as the active content of the resurrection. And because he associated forgiveness with restoration to health[27]—a connection that the Scriptures of Israel claim and clinical literature supports[28]—in the case of Peter's science of the resurrection, a therapeutic component is palpable. When the apparently iron law that sin's consequences perdure (see, for example, Deut 5:9) is broken, the result is a change in the principles that govern the world.

Counting on the Twelve

Matthew relates no scene in which Simon Peter saw the risen Jesus in a personal encounter. Yet despite the Evangelist's silence, the Gospel reflects knowledge of such an encounter, which it retrojects into the earlier narrative of Peter's commission to forgive sin (Matt 16:17-19). But the wording shows that the resurrection was the context in which *Kêpha'*—the first person on Paul's list—received forgiveness, as well as a commission to forgive others, because the risen Jesus forgave his denial. Awareness of the tradition that Matthew deflected heightens appreciation for the tradition that Matthew preferred: Jesus' commission of the Twelve (or Eleven, as Matthew calls them after Judas' death).

The scene in Matthew (28:16-20) is brief, so succinct as to frustrate those interpreters interested in knowing the details of Jesus' appearance after his death. Yet its conception of how Jesus continues to live and direct his followers after death is a model of clarity:

> Yet the eleven students proceeded into Galilee, to the mountain where Jesus directed them; they saw him and worshiped, yet they doubted. Jesus came forward and spoke to them, saying, "All authority has been given to me in heaven and upon earth. Proceed, then, make students of all the nations, immersing them in the name of the Father and of the Son and of the Holy Spirit, teaching them to keep everything, whatever I decreed to you. And look: I am with you all days, until the completion of the age."

Connections with the Matthean narrative that precedes enhance the clarity of the conception, which proves also to surface in connection with the Twelve in the Gospel according to John.

The key term of reference within the tradition of the Twelve is the imperative given as *mathêteusate* in Greek, traditionally interpreted "make disciples." The followers of Jesus who learned from and kept company with him called him their rabbi,[29] and they were known as his students (in Aramaic the plural is *talmidin*; *mathêtai* in Greek). The English term "disciple" comes from the Latin equivalent, *discipulus*. Today it is applied to Jesus' students but also to people whose attachment to a teacher is considered excessive. For example, recent coverage of followers of Rajneesh in popular culture uses the term "disciple" to refer to them and "cult" to describe the movement.[30] The word is used so restrictively in a religious sense today (whether with positive or negative connotations) that it seems wiser to render *talmid* and *mathêtês* as "student." The purpose of a rabbi in gathering *talmidin* was to teach them his *halakhah*—that is, a "way" of enacting his own view of serving the God of Israel. For example, in his appearance after his death, Jesus was seen by *Kêpha'* in a way that produced a *halakhah* of forgiveness.

Just that death, however, produced a crisis among Jesus' students that went beyond their personal loss, and even beyond the shame that came of knowing that he had been executed by crucifixion. Ordinarily, a rabbi crafted his teaching during the course of his activity, instructing his *talmidin* to memorize the principles and parables and illustrations that he set out. Formulating that body of work represented the rabbi's aim. When he reached that goal, he had composed a *mishnah*, material to be repeated within oral tradition. A *talmid* who had mastered that *mishnah*, who knew how to "speak in the words of his master,"[31] was in a position himself to take up the task of producing *halakhah*. When the Roman ruler ordered Jesus' death, however, that stopped the usual process, so that there was not a complete *mishnah* of the body of teaching he wished to see under the control of all his disciples.

The incomplete arc of Jesus' production of a *mishnah* is one reason for variation among the Gospels. From the outset, different informants of Jesus' teaching had heard him say different words at different times. There is no cause to ignore other factors, such as the particular theologies of Evangelists and the special interests and social settings of the informants who passed on materials to the Evangelists, but the underlying instability of the initial teaching also needs to be taken into account. That factor should feature today, of course, in any exegesis of the Gospels. But for those who framed the Gospels, Jesus' premature death was not just a factor but a genuine crisis. The resources needed to be found that would articulate the *halakhah* of an absent rabbi.

Even during his life, Jesus had authorized some of his students, the group he constituted as the Twelve, to represent him. During the period when Herod Antipas sought to eliminate Jesus, he sent these delegates in his place to continue his own activity: promulgating God's kingdom and exorcising unclean spirits. That demanded a commission, and the authorization of the Twelve is a key scene within the Synoptic Gospels (Mark 3:13-19; 6:7-11; Matt 10:1-16; Luke 6:12-16; 9:1-5). Central though it is, variations within the scene from Gospel to Gospel are evident, illustrating the underlying volatility of even relatively stable traditions. Absent a settled understanding of what their rabbi's *mishnah* had been, the students whom Jesus had chosen to represent him when he was alive emerged after his death as arbiters of his *halakhah*. They conveyed their authorization in that role by means of their narration of how he was raised from the dead. The Twelve's status as purveyors and interpreters of the rabbi's teaching came with their conception of Jesus' resurrection.

Commission on the Mountain

The final scene in the Gospel according to Matthew delineates a clearly marked and epochal change, which comparison with the previous narrative makes unmistakable. Jesus' perspective prior to this scene, articulated in Matthew as it is nowhere else in the New Testament, is that he was sent only "to the lost sheep of Israel's house" (15:24) and that the Twelve were only to address that public (10:5-6). Gentiles are excluded, and any sporadic inclusion is both exceptional and awkward (as in the case of the centurion from Capernaum and the Canaanite woman; Matt 8:5-10; 15:21-28). The pivot that turns the outreach to "all nations" occurs only at the close of the Gospel, complete with the command to baptize gentiles "in the name of the Father and of the Son and of the Holy Spirit" (28:19).

Matthew is written more with the church in mind than the other canonical Gospels; the term *ekklêsia* appears only here (16:18; 18:17) among them. The Evangelist relies on his hearers' knowledge from experience of characteristic practices such as prayer (6:5-8), fasting (6:16-18), and excommunication (18:15-18) that set them apart—by means of distinctive adjustments—from their Jewish contemporaries. For them, even the term *rabbi* is to be reserved for their master alone and not to be applied to anyone else (23:8). In the same vein, the Gospel's climax completes the picture of a community that now expressly includes gentiles and turns the practice of immersion into an identity-changing moment of initiation rather than the ritual of purification that had made it standard within Judaism.

Matthew delivers its powerful understanding of the resurrection with a direct but elegant presentation of Jesus' encounter with the Eleven. The manner of his appearance, for all its brief description, is decisive because it signals that "all authority," as he gives his command, has passed to Jesus (Matt 28:18).

Nonetheless, the famous qualifier, that the students "doubted" (v. 17), follows the statement that they "saw" Jesus. In Matthew's presentation uniquely, the narrative of the guard at the tomb (27:62-66; 28:11-15) has occurred prior to the mention of doubt, and so the students' reaction seems unreasonable. But the reference to the guard derives not from the Twelve (or Eleven) but from another source with its own conception of the resurrection. Within the narrative of the Eleven, a reaction that includes doubt is presented as straightforward and sincere, for all the brevity of the presentation. Another uniquely Matthean passage presents doubt in the same way (14:28-33) and with the same verb.[32]

In no sense, however, is the doubt of the Eleven the point of Matthew's statement; it is not even clear what is doubted—might it be there is some question whether it is Jesus, or does the matter turn on whether he is truly present? In any case, the meaning of the encounter lies in what follows. The authority that Jesus has secured, with its concomitant commission of the Twelve, represents the effective force of his resurrection. For the Evangelist, seeing Jesus after his death does not in itself represent the purpose of his resurrection. Rather, within the setting of that sighting, Jesus brings his aim to fruition by what he says.[33]

The statement itself, with its claim of "all authority," whether in heaven or on earth, is key to all that follows in the scene—and to the life of the Matthean community thereafter. Authority, *exousia*, has been carefully developed as a theme in Matthew by this point. Jesus teaches with authority (and not as the scribes; 7:29 and Mark 1:22), is described by the centurion as a man under authority (8:9 and Luke 7:8), asserts the Son of Man has authority to forgive sins (9:6, 8; Mark 2:10; Luke 5:24), gives authority to the Twelve (10:1; Mark 6:7; Luke 9:1), and answers a challenge in regard to his own authority with a question about John the Baptist's (Matt 21:23-27; Mark 11:27-33; Luke 20:1-8). He has also stated, "Everything (*panta*) has been delivered over to me by my father" (11:27; Luke 10:22). These elements are shared with Mark and Luke in aggregate, but *only* Matthew brings them all together, so that the reference to "all (*pasa*) authority" in 28:18 builds on the established theme and brings it to a climactic conclusion. Jesus as raised from the dead becomes comparable to the depiction of the "one like a son of man" in Daniel 7:13-14.[34] Further, this and any further meanings of the resurrection are explained as generated from the continual presence of Jesus: "And look: I am with you all days, until the completion of the age" (28:20).

The means by which the new derogation of authority to Jesus links his students to him until the completion of the age lies at the heart of his commission to Matthew's Eleven. They do what he once did, specifically enlisting *talmidin* on the basis of Jesus' teaching, and with the enhanced sanction that derives from his resurrection. That function uniquely belongs to the Twelve, as distinctive a factor as the focus upon forgiveness is within the Petrine tradition. The Twelve assume guardianship of a teaching that is about to become a *mishnah* as they pursue their own role as *talmidin* in Jesus' continuing presence by recruiting new *talmidin*.

Two elements, present in the text of Matthew but representing the influence of a different tradition, have tended to obscure the compelling result of what it meant for Jesus to be "seen" by the Twelve (to follow Paul's language and counting). Thematically, both the pivot to the gentiles and the command to immerse in the name of the Father, Son, and Spirit relate to the ecclesial ethos of Matthew, and they are crucial to appreciate within the literary structure of the Gospel. But those instructions do not derive directly from anything that is said within Jesus' announcement that he has "all authority." They are justified not by the contents of the final scene of the Gospel but by familiarity within the Matthean community that acceptance of gentiles and baptism have become characteristic of belief in Jesus, even though they had not featured in Jesus' program of activity prior to the crucifixion. Both of those traits *are* explained by means of what the "More Than Five Hundred" understood to be the imperative behind their seeing Jesus after his death. Those themes need to be taken up in their own terms (as in the next chapter) in the strand of tradition that produced them. Matthew can incorporate those crucial elements here because he builds on the principle of the Twelve's authorization, which in his mind makes such revolutionary changes possible and necessary.

Because Jesus now has "all authority," he enhances the commission of the Twelve, who had earlier been sent to represent him (10:1). Now they are to proceed to make *talmidin themselves*, which assumes that they have mastered Jesus' teaching, since they are to teach others "to keep everything, whatever I decreed to you" (28:20). That memory, together with Jesus' own persistent presence, becomes the basis on which the Twelve enlist the students that Jesus himself can no longer recruit. Their facility in his teaching makes them instruments of his own manifestation.

The location of this commission in Matthew is an index of its importance. The Eleven go in Galilee to "the mountain where Jesus directed them" (28:16). No instruction in regard to place, apart from the general reference to Galilee (28:7, 10), has featured within Matthew's resurrection narrative prior to this scene. Earlier, however, a mountain features in the transfiguration (17:1), and Matthew refers to it as "the mountain" (17:9), a usage shared with Mark (9:9) and Luke (9:37). Sometimes, all the Evangelists—with Matthew in the lead and John a distant fourth—refer to "the mountain," as if the location were understood (Matt 5:1; 8:1; 14:23; 15:29; Mark 3:13; 6:46; Luke 6:12; 9:28; John 6:3). In origin, the use of the definite article in Greek might be explained as reflecting the determined state in Aramaic, which specifies less than the Greek definite article does but makes a less general reference than the indefinite usage. But even if that lies behind the appearance of the definite article on some occasions, once repeated as frequently as in Matthew it is clear that "the mountain" becomes the place of Jesus' normative disclosure, and the affinity with Moses seems evident.[35]

The degree of uncertainty regarding the location of "the mountain" and the reference to the unspecified doubt of the students who saw Jesus leave the impression that further explanation, once available, has been lost. The account seems to have been brought into the conclusion of the Gospel with some preliminary narrative removed. This tells against an analysis that attempts to explain Matthew 28:16-20 as a construction of the Evangelist,[36] and it suggests rather that the Gospel weaves traditions together, such that the Twelve speak in the command on the mountain to make *talmidin*, and the "More Than Five Hundred" are heard in the reference to "all nations" and baptism.

Because Matthew's procedure is to weave traditions together, the thread of "the mountain" articulates a theme of authorization that is then capped in the resurrection. Even in the case of the transfiguration, Jesus instructs Peter, James, and John to speak of "the vision to no one until when the Son of Man is raised from the dead" (Matt 17:9 cf. Mark 9:9-10). What they see on that mountain can only truly be known and spoken of when Jesus is raised, because then he is continuously in the company of Moses and Elijah, the two prophets who speak with him as he is transformed. Elijah had been taken up to heaven, and, by the first century, both he and Moses could be portrayed as living figures who would never taste death.[37] Moses and Elijah each came into authoritative status upon their mountains (Exod 24; 1 Kgs 19); the same is true for Jesus, especially in the transfiguration but definitively—in Matthew alone—in his resurrection. In the final scene of Matthew's Gospel, the Eleven achieve commensurate status, because Jesus—to whom "all authority" has been provided—gives them the task of using their familiarity with him to extend the circle of his *talmidin*.

The relationship between the commission of the Eleven and Jesus' transfiguration assures that in speaking of one scene, the other is invoked. The resonance between the two by means of the mountain occurs only in Matthew, of course, which enables this Gospel to view Jesus *and his students* in the overt lineage and continuing presence of Moses and Elijah. Within the final scene itself, however, the Eleven are put uniquely in Jesus' enduring presence, on the understanding that they shall teach what he has instructed. The final verse of the Gospel in fact balances a command to teach people to keep everything Jesus commended during his life with an assurance that he is with them until the close of time itself (v. 20). Past, remembered teaching together with present, corrective discernment[38] combine to focus the full authority of Jesus.[39] This strong ending of Matthew casts all that precedes it in a new light. The risen Jesus articulates the perspective of the whole work for the first time and casts himself as a figure comparable to Moses and Elijah but endowed with "all authority." Within the prophetic exception that makes victory over death possible within Judaic theology, he secures a place as the most authoritative exception.

Teaching Jesus' Directives

The wording of Jesus' imperative, to teach others "to keep everything, whatever I decreed (*eneteilamên*) you" (Matt 28:20), puts what he earlier taught in a new light. After he is raised from the dead, his statements, parables, and occasional teaching become occasions of command, as they are conveyed by the Eleven within their commissioned role of enlisting *talmidin*.

The means by which Jesus' teachings become directives, authorized by God and embedded within the resurrection, are delineated in the Gospel according to John. John's depiction of the resurrection itself focuses by the end of the work on Simon Peter (chapter 21) and therefore on the underlying issue of forgiveness. Even when John presents narrative in relation to Jesus' students more broadly (in 20:19-23), forgiveness remains a focal concern. But then, another narrative involving the students presents the story of Thomas, "one of the Twelve," and this story marks the transition to a statement of the purpose of the entire Gospel (20:24-31). This famous vignette bears a meaning that has been prepared by the Evangelist by means of the presentation of Jesus' teaching in the body of the Gospel. The force of the narrative concerning Thomas becomes plain in the context of that preparation, which explains how Jesus' teaching becomes divine direction.

Set within the uniquely Johannine depiction of Jesus' last meal with his students prior to his death, a discourse of Jesus assumes the perspective of what is to follow his life. That is, John here—as elsewhere in the Gospel—presents events during Jesus' life from the standpoint of his resurrection: "If I proceed and will prepare a place for you, I come again and shall take you along to myself" (14:3). He responds to students' questions, including Thomas' (14:5), because they do not grasp that he refers to his continuing care for them. In death and beyond death, he is the Good Shepherd (10:1-18) whose sheep know his voice (v. 4), as they know him (v. 14). Their continuing link to him lies within his teaching. "If you love me, you will keep my commandments" (14:15) is a signature concern of the discourse, also expressed in terms of Jesus' "word(s)" (14:23-24), echoing Jesus' command to the Twelve in Matthew 28:20 to teach *talmidin* to keep everything Jesus decreed.

But John does more than echo Matthew: the Fourth Gospel also explains how Jesus' students can keep the teaching of their rabbi after his premature death and how that means they are not left orphaned after his execution (John 14:18). He promises "another advocate," identified as the "Spirit of truth," to be given by God at Jesus' request to the students even as the world ignores that Spirit (14:15-17). They will know the Spirit, even as they know Jesus, and that Spirit is to remain with them. By means of Spirit and keeping Jesus' word, Jesus manifests himself to each of his students, yet not to the world (14:21-23). The function of Spirit in this case is not forgiveness, as in the tradition identified with Peter singly. Rather, the collective of students receives "the advocate, the Holy Spirit," such that the Spirit attests to Jesus, joining the memory of the students (15:26) but also guiding them into "all truth" (16:7-15). Even those things that Jesus did *not* say, as well as events beyond the horizon, are within the purview of that advocate, because Spirit shares all with Jesus and the Father (vv. 12-15). Implicitly and yet emphatically, prophecy sees a new age with the resurrection,[40] since the Spirit is provided to Jesus' students.

Because Jesus' long discourse in John has prepared a theology of the Spirit, when Jesus breathes on his students at the close of the Gospel, the hearer (or reader) sees a significance that goes beyond the words that are stated. As he breathes into his students and tells them to take Holy Spirit, that is explicitly an authorization to forgive or confirm sins (20:22-23). At the same time, however, his act fulfills his assurance of the advocate, the Holy Spirit, which is to teach his words and more than his words. The overlay of the fulfilled promise of the Spirit of truth that brings Jesus' personal presence after his death and the authorization of forgiveness by means of the Spirit permits John to do justice to two streams of tradition, derived from the Twelve and Peter, respectively.

The source of the resurrection derived from the Twelve, as in Matthew's Gospel, treats of how Jesus' teachings become words of command. At the same time, John goes much further than Matthew's bare reference to the Spirit, explaining how the advocate extends Jesus' teaching, so that accurate memory is combined with creative assertion. Those new statements, however, derive from Jesus and together with the preservation of teaching combine to put the hearer into his living presence. "Because I live, you also will live" (John 14:19) conveys both emotional reassurance and empowerment for innovation.

The power of that presence is the theme of the narrative concerning Thomas, which turns so precisely on the issue of belief in the risen Jesus that it serves as the transition to the Evangelist's statement of belief that is the very purpose of his entire work (John 20:24-30):

> Yet Thomas, one from the Twelve, called the Twin, was not with them when Jesus came. Then the other students were saying to him, "We have seen the Lord." But he said to them, "Unless I see in his hands the mark of the nails and thrust my finger in the mark of the nails and thrust my hand into his side, I shall not believe." And after eight days again his students were inside, and Thomas with them. Jesus comes while the doors were shut and stood in the midst and said, "Peace to you." So he says to Thomas, "Bring your finger here, and see my hands, and bring your hand and thrust it into my side, and do not become disbelieving but believing." Thomas answered and said to him, "My Lord and my God." Jesus says to him, "Because you saw me have you believed? Favored are those who did not see and have believed." Then Jesus did many other signs before the students that are not written in this scroll; but these are written so that you might believe that Jesus is the Anointed, the Son of God, and so that believing you might have life in his name.

Belief within this encounter is, in the end, not produced by touching. The other students have reported to Thomas, "We have seen the Lord" (v. 25), and that has occurred—as Jesus earlier promised—not to the world but only to Jesus' followers, and within a locked room (v. 19).

John's elegant presentation calibrates with the previous scene. Thomas demands to touch just the wounds Jesus had previously shown (v. 25; cf. v. 20); the eighth day echoes the meeting on the first day of the week, with doors shut again (v. 26; cf. v. 19); Jesus offers his peace and then proof of his presence (vv. 26d-27; cf. vv. 19d-20); acknowledgment is the result (v. 28; cf. 20b). The whole is articulated to bring out the significance of belief. Specification of the eighth day not only calibrates to the earlier scene but also invokes the conception of a sequence beyond the seven days of creation, a new eighth day of new creation.[41]

Although Jesus breathes on the students (v. 22), they do not touch him, just what Thomas demands to be able to do in order to believe. (Thomas' attitude echoes his statement in the discourse in which Jesus explains how he manifests himself to the students but not to the world [14:5].) But confronted with the offer to touch Jesus, Thomas does not do so. Instead, he recognizes Jesus as "my Lord and my God" (v. 28). Belief is produced, not by touch, but by the recognition of who Jesus is.

John—unlike later traditions—portrays Jesus' offer to be touched without claiming Thomas or others did touch him.[42] One result of John's presentation is that, until this moment in the Gospel, Jesus is known as risen from the dead by means of Mary Magdalene's announcement: "I have seen the Lord" (20:18). She makes this statement after Jesus has cautioned her not to touch him (20:17). Likewise, the disciples rejoice "having seen the Lord" (20:20), and they echo Mary when they tell Thomas, "We have seen the Lord" (v. 25). Thomas breaks that pattern when he demands to touch Jesus, but in Jesus' presence he also acknowledges him as "my Lord and my God" (v. 28), and Jesus asks, "Because you saw me have you believed?" (v. 29).

The terms of that recognition have been prepared by the earlier discourse. Jesus has already indicated that he and the Spirit and the Father together dwell within the students. "Those who did not see and have believed" (v. 29)—including those who hear the Gospel—are offered the same promise of this indwelling as those who have seen. In effect, the risen Jesus first criticizes the need to touch as a condition of belief, and then he criticizes the need to see. This articulated criticism in John corresponds to Matthew's notice of doubt in the scene with the Eleven. In both cases, the content of the resurrection is the application of Jesus' teaching as commands that are to be kept.

Calling Jesus "Lord" (John 20:28) acknowledges his living, magisterial presence after his death; calling him "God" is, as when Moses stands for God,[43] to understand Jesus as at one with the divine. Thomas realizes what Jesus has already said, that he and the Father are one (John 10:30). The more precise acknowledgment of Jesus is as "the Anointed, the Son of God" (20:31), the true christological climax of the Gospel (cf. 11:25-27).

These terms realize the promise of the Prologue (John 1:17-18), which claims that those who "believe in the name" of the light that came into the world receive authority to become God's children, to be begotten of God (John 1:12-13). That is the sense in which Jesus says at the close of the Gospel, "Favored are those who did not see and have believed" (20:29). In the end, Thomas' demand for an extra sign of Jesus' presence is rebuked, even as it is accommodated, because belief, rather than vision or anything like vision, is what yields "life in his name" (v. 31). The Apocryphon of James from Nag Hammadi puts the point more robustly: "You have seen the Son of Man and have spoken with him and have heard him. Woe to those who have only seen the Son of Man. Favored shall they be who have not seen the man, have not had contact with him, have not spoken with him, and have not heard anything from him" (Ap. Jas. 3:13-24).[44]

When Jesus' words are guarded and extended in order to produce *talmidin*, the result is his living presence, warranted by the Spirit but not the equivalent of tangible or even of optic evidence for the vast majority of believers. For John, believers are afforded the remembrance of "signs" (vv. 30-31) rather than proofs. Signs point to a reality beyond this world; knowing what they indicate demands insight. They may lead to unbelief (John 12:37), although their purpose is to occasion belief (2:11). John weaves the signs recorded within and around the words and commandments of Jesus. They serve from the point of view of the believer to occasion love for Jesus, which is why the commandments are kept. At the same time, from the point of view of Spirit, they occasion the presence of Jesus. Everything he taught, according to Matthew, or in John's presentation everything he taught in addition to new extensions that the advocacy of Spirit attests, represents the living presence of Jesus as mediated by the Eleven or the Twelve. Where Peter's resurrection breaks the form of this world by means of the forgiveness it conveys and commands, for the Twelve the resurrection compensates for the absence of Jesus by means of the directives he articulates in teaching that promises to outlast the world.

6

Seen "by More Than Five Hundred," Then "by James"

Identifying the "More Than Five Hundred"

Paul's list—read within the context of the development of the Gospels—offers insight into how *Kêpha'* and the Twelve advanced characteristic views of the resurrection. Forgiveness lies at the center of the Petrine tradition, while the Twelve's conception is anchored in extending the *mishnah* of Jesus. In both cases, Holy Spirit, imbued by Jesus, is the source of the activity. The two traditions have another striking commonality: originally, they derived from Galilee; yet as the Gospels evolved, Jerusalem played an increasing role and became more prominent than Galilee as the locus of the resurrection.

Luke's Gospel, especially as compared to Mark and Matthew, plays a major role in the growing association with Jerusalem. Although Luke provides no explicit report of how Jesus was seen by Peter personally, the Evangelist puts Peter in Jerusalem (Luke 24:12) and attributes familiarity with Peter's vision to the Twelve, whom he also locates specifically—and exclusively—in Jerusalem (Luke 24:36). That is where John places the Twelve, as well, assigning them the power of forgiveness (John 20:19-23) and the mandate to promote belief on the basis of Jesus' words and signs (John 20:24-31). The trenchant localization of all the narratives in Jerusalem by Luke, the reference to Galilee alone in Mark, and the uneasy hybrid of geographies in

Matthew and John make it seem apparent that different constituencies vied for geographical ownership of the resurrection. In the order of Paul's list, *Kêpha'* is immediately followed by the Twelve and "more than five hundred brothers" (1 Cor 15:5-6). Explicit reference to the last group occurs only in Paul's accounting; literal reference to the More Than Five Hundred does not appear in any of the Gospels. That absence is much more striking than the problem of the paucity of material relating to Peter's seeing Jesus.

The only narrative in the New Testament that relates to the resurrection in terms of large numbers of people "at once," as Paul says the More Than Five Hundred saw Jesus (*ephapax*; 1 Cor 15:6), is the story of Pentecost. That account as it stands serves the overarching purpose of Luke as expressed both in the Gospel and in Acts. The whole sweep of salvation's unfolding is marked by the Spirit's presence: with Jesus from before his birth (Luke 1:35), Spirit comes to his students at Pentecost (Acts 1:5, 8; 2:4) as a result of his own action in being raised from the dead (2:32-33) so that they preach repentance, baptism in Jesus' name for forgiveness, and the gift of the Holy Spirit (Acts 2:38). The steady outworking of that theme during the course of the book of Acts is skillful and programmatic, so that there is a broadening and at the same time an intensification of the conception of God's Spirit as released by the resurrection.

The elegance of Luke's presentation can give the impression that the Pentecost scene is a literary construct.[1] Certain features of the text seem at least as symbolic as they are circumstantial: the sound of wind that fills the house parallels the Spirit that fills those gathered in it (Acts 2:2, 4); the tongues of fire correspond to the tongues that the upward of 120 "brothers"[2] gathered there speak (2:3-4); Jews and proselytes in Jerusalem drawn to the sound come from the four points of the compass (2:5-11); fully three thousand are baptized (2:41). Presumably, they represent a fraction of the several thousand that would have clustered around the "house," a much larger installation than one can easily imagine Jesus' followers commanding in Jerusalem at this time. All of this is punctuated with a well-crafted speech from Peter (2:14-36), complete with two thorough interpretations of Scripture.

Other features of the chapter, however, suggest that the material incorporated had a background prior to Luke's composition. Some of those features are matters of detail that are difficult to explain on the supposition that the entire account was composed by the author of Acts. Geographically, the orientation of the passage sometimes seems odd, if Jerusalem is taken to be the generative point throughout. First, the gathering crowd poses the question, "Are not all these who speak Galileans?" (Acts 2:7). Since, by this time,

Luke counts the "brothers" as a growing group of already 120 people in the previous scene (1:15), a limitation to Galileans probably does not feature at this point in the imagination of Acts.

That sizeable number and the echo of Paul's reference to the "more than five hundred brothers" in Luke's usage of the term "brothers," taken together with the seemingly gratuitous reference to Galileans, is evocative. Similarly, within the list of the regions that those who hear the sound of the wind and the speaking in tongues come from, the term "Judea" appears (v. 9). That, of course, *is* the region of Jerusalem, so the reference is useless if the setting were originally Jerusalem. The usage is so odd that commentators have been known to eliminate the reference as a mistake, but there is no textual warrant for doing so.[3] What is anomalous from the perspective of Jerusalem, however, makes sense from the perspective of Galilee, and the reference seems to be an artifact of the account's origin.

The triumphant climax of Peter's explanation of the events at Pentecost in Acts 2:36 is that "the whole house of Israel shall know certainly, then, that God has made him Lord and Anointed: this Jesus whom you crucified." The messianic significance of the whole complex of events, as in 1 Corinthians 15:3-7, remains explicit: it is as *Khristos* that Jesus is raised from the dead. Indeed, the speech in Acts portrays God as *making* Jesus both Lord (*kurios*) and Anointed (*khristos*) by means of the resurrection.

Two interlocking assertions come out of this narrative; although crucial to Luke, they are hardly Lukan innovations. First, Spirit is held to be available as a result of Jesus' resurrection, as Peter's speech explains (Acts 2:32-33):

This Jesus God stood up,[4] of which we are all witnesses. Exalted, then, to God's right, and taking the promise of the Holy Spirit from the Father, he has poured out this, which you see and hear.

This revolution in the availability of Spirit also means that Peter can go on to urge his hearers in the second major claim (v. 38): "Repent, and be immersed every one of you in the name of Anointed Jesus for the forgiveness of your sins, and you shall take the gift of the Holy Spirit." Spirit, poured out by Jesus, can be apprehended in baptism.

The central importance of Spirit also comes to expression in Paul's explanation of what occurs in baptism, when he asserts, "Because you are sons, God sent out his Spirit[5] into your hearts, crying: *Abba*, Father" (Gal 4:6). The assumption here, in a letter written circa 53 CE, is that Paul's hearers know that this is the practice they followed, and that they received the Spirit in baptism and cried out "*Abba*," using a language that was not native to most of them.

Both the sending of the Spirit and baptism are Lukan concerns, without amounting to Lukan inventions. They are a part of the underlying tradition incorporated in Acts 2 within the Pentecost scene, associated with how Jesus was seen—in Paul's words—by "more than five hundred brothers." Paul's own understanding of Spirit and baptism buttresses the impression that the More Than Five Hundred exerted a profound influence on practice as well as on the understanding of the resurrection long before the writing of Luke–Acts.

The force of this tradition from the More Than Five Hundred is also felt in Matthew 28:19[6] where the setting in Galilee is emphatic in the mandate to baptize in the name of the Father and of the Son and of the Holy Spirit, *and* to baptize "all nations"—that is, gentiles. Luke–Acts, of course, develops that theme in detail, but that development shows in its convolutions that it came on the basis of evolving vision and insight rather than as a single commandment simultaneous with the resurrection. Similarly, in John 20:21-22, when Jesus sends his students as he was sent and breathes Spirit into them, telling them to "take Holy Spirit," the empowering theme also evident at Pentecost comes to expression. These passages are governed with the concerns of the Twelve (to extend Jesus' *mishnah*) and of Peter (to promulgate forgiveness), but they also incorporate elements of the characteristic issues embedded in the tradition of the More Than Five Hundred. The force of that conception took the activity of Jesus' students far outside Jerusalem.

Pentecost and the Household of Cornelius

Pentecost bore meanings within the practice of Judaism that contribute to the sense of the scene in Acts. The feast is named for the fifty days or seven Sabbaths[7] (Lev 23:15) following Passover. The biblical command to remember Israel's slavery in Egypt during Pentecost (Deut 16:10-12) led to an association with covenantal moments. By the time of the book of Jubilees, covenants involving Noah (Jub. 6:1-22), Abraham (Jub. 15:1-10), and Moses (Jub. 1:1-26) were brought to mind in association with the feast. The last association led to the rabbinic commemoration of the giving of the torah at *Shavuot* (b. Pesachim 68b; b. Megillah 31a), and its offer in the seventy languages of the nations (b. Shabbath 88b). None of the postbiblical dimensions of meaning can be taken to be a controlling influence on the presentation of Acts, because contact between Luke and circles remote from him in terms of cultural location or time cannot be assumed. But the wide range of the application of Pentecost, before and after Luke, remains striking.

Luke in any case shows which meanings of the feast are in control from his point of view. By quoting Peter's citation of Scripture (Joel 2:28-32),[8] Luke centers the meaning of the entire passage and locates it as the pivot of his work (Acts 2:14-43). The Spirit once particularly upon Jesus (Luke 4:18) now comes upon his over 120 followers, and they are to extend baptism[9] in his name so that others may also receive the Spirit, because God has resolved to "pour out my Spirit upon all flesh" (Acts 2:17; Joel 2:28). Pentecost marks an epochal change, predicted in Joel and realized according to Peter's speech. "All flesh," of course, is an immense expansion of the Spirit's extension, far beyond a usual understanding of its focus on particular figures such as prophets, kings, or Jesus himself. No single idea differentiates early Christianity as clearly as this from other religions, before or after its time.

Yet even here, at an evidently crucial juncture in the resurrection's impact on the emergence of a new faith, a degree of continuity with the first-century meaning of Pentecost remains evident. After he receives the torah, the book of Numbers depicts Moses as setting out into the wilderness near the end of the second month (Num 10:11-12). After an unstated time, but within range of the observation of Pentecost during the third month, the people provoke God to anger, and fire breaks out in the camp. Their complaints about provisions lead to Moses' choice of seventy elders; they receive God's Spirit at the tabernacle and prophesy. Even two people who had been left behind in the camp, Eldad and Medad, also prophesy, but Moses does not object; he would prefer that all God's people were prophets (Num 11:1-30). The association in this passage of fire, Spirit, and prophecy is striking on comparison with Acts 2, as is the reference to seventy elders—the number of the nations of the earth.[10] In effect, the Pentecost scene both reverses the trajectory of Babel (Gen 11:1-9), by moving from incomprehension to mutual understanding, and endorses the promise of Moses with seventy elders, by extending the range of God's Spirit.

The fact remains, however, that the Pentecost scene does not literally endorse an extension to the gentiles, whatever the symbolism employed. Just as Jesus sent the seventy (or seventy-two) within territorial Israel (Luke 10:1-2), those gathered at Pentecost are the Jewish *residents* of Jerusalem.[11] Overwhelmingly, they come from the diaspora, and their numbers include proselytes, but the dramatic scene is limited in its extension. Acts documents the move to the gentiles after Pentecost; it does so by reference to the same principle identified in the Pentecost account but within conditions unimagined in that story.

When Peter is speaking in the house of Cornelius in Caesarea (in Acts 10), the Spirit falls upon those who are listening, and Peter's companions who were circumcised are astounded "that the gift of the Holy Spirit has been poured out even upon the nations" (10:44-45). The choice of the verb "to pour out" is no coincidence: it is resonant with the quotation of Joel in Acts 2:17. Cornelius, a Roman centurion, is also described together with his household as a fearer of God and a worshiper of God. Although not of Israel, they recognize Israel's God, falling into the category of sympathizers with Judaism in the Greco-Roman world. When God's Spirit comes to this household, it becomes a place of divine presence.[12]

Peter himself concludes that those in the household are to be baptized, since they "took the Holy Spirit as we also did" (Acts 10:47). In crafting the account in Acts, Luke devotes considerable space to Peter's call by the Spirit to travel from Joppa to Caesarea, the coming of the Spirit to those hearing Peter in Cornelius' house, and Peter's resolve to baptize them. Peter also recounts the whole narrative when "the apostles and the brothers who were in Judaea heard that the nations received the word of God" (Acts 11:1-18). He then repeats the story at the time that controversy breaks out over the baptism, not of God-fearing gentiles, but of gentiles whose background had nothing to do with the God of Israel (Acts 11:20-26; 15:1-5). Altogether, Acts devotes more space to this incident than to Paul's conversion, and throughout the focus is not on Cornelius as an individual but on his household as the pivot of the narrative as a whole.[13]

Luke's Peter presents the gift of the Holy Spirit to the gentiles of Caesarea as equivalent to the experience of the community in Jerusalem,[14] and he does so repeatedly (10:47; 11:15; 15:8). He is also clear that what happened in Caesarea compares directly to Pentecost, and Peter states: "The Holy Spirit fell upon them just as upon us in the beginning (*en arkhê*)" (11:15). That "beginning" can refer back only to Pentecost, but it is striking that Peter here calls it that. Empowerment by Spirit is the *outset* of Luke's story in Acts. Just as in the case of the over 120 followers of Jesus in Jerusalem (not the larger crowd that gathers), those in Cornelius' house praise God "in tongues" (10:46). The assumption here and in Acts 2 is that Spirit makes people more articulate than they normally are. That is also the way Paul believes tongues are properly to be conceived (1 Cor 14), as opposed to those who see the gift of tongues as resulting in incoherence.

Baptism cannot be withheld, in the logic of Peter's defense, where God's Spirit is present, especially since the gift of the Spirit has been defined as the very purpose of the immersion (Acts 2:37-38). This immersion is not for the general purpose of purification, as in the common practice of Judaism; it is baptism into Jesus' name, his presence that mediates the Holy Spirit. This was the contribution of the Galilean "brothers," more than five hundred of them, for whom Peter serves as the advocate in the narrative of Acts.

Taken together, the relationship between the descriptions of what happened at Pentecost and what happened in the house of Cornelius do not suggest any real dispute as to whether the gift of the Spirit followed or preceded baptism into Jesus' name. The point is rather that belief in and baptism into him are connected directly by the outpouring of God's Spirit. The apparent disruption of the usual model in Acts 10 is intended to call attention to the artificiality of attempting to withhold baptism from those who believe (as Peter says in so many words; 10:47).[15]

Still, two questions immediately arise at this point. First, why would it have been natural for Peter to extend baptism to non-Jews on the basis of the outpouring of Spirit, when he was still sensitive to the scruples of Judaism? (And that sensitivity is recorded by Paul, a contemporary witness; see Gal 2:11-14.)[16] Second, where did Peter understand the new, radicalizing infusion of Spirit to have derived from?

Those two questions have a single answer. Spirit's source proves to revise the understanding of the people and places that can host Spirit. The specificity of this answer relies on the resurrection science of the More Than Five Hundred, for whom the risen Jesus *is* the source of Spirit.

The Source and Influence of the Spirit

In Peter's speech at Pentecost, Jesus, having been exalted to the right hand of God, receives the promise of the Holy Spirit from the Father and pours it out on his followers (2:33). The Spirit that is poured out, then, comes directly from the majesty of God, from his rule over creation as a whole. This is the Spirit as it hovered over the waters at the beginning of creation (Gen 1:2) and not as limited to Israel. Because the Spirit is of God, who creates people in the divine image, its presence marks God's own activity, in which *all* those who adhere to Jesus are to be included.

Jesus' program prior to the crucifixion had involved proclaiming God's kingdom on the authority of his own possession of God's Spirit (see Matt 12:28). Now, as a consequence of the resurrection, Jesus had poured out that same Spirit upon those who follow him. Baptism in the Spirit (see Acts 1:4-5) and baptism into the name of Jesus were one and the same thing for that reason, distinguishing this immersion from John's and from Judaic practices of purification. That was why believing that Jesus was God's Son and calling upon his name were the occasions on which the Spirit was to be received.[17] In the new environment of God's Spirit that the resurrection signaled, baptism was indeed, as Matthew 28:19 indicates, an activity and an experience that involved God in God's fullness: Father, Son, and Holy Spirit.

Acts has Peter specify this understanding of the resurrection, as when Jesus was not merely raised but "exalted at God's right" (Acts 2:33). As in the book of Jubilees (23:30-31), the Rule of the Community (1QS 4.7–8), and the book of Daniel (12:1-3)—but unlike the second book of Maccabees (7:10-11, 22-23, 29)—the movement is less from death back to physical life than from death to a vivified presence with God.[18] The absence of Jesus, because he is with the Father and in a position to broadcast Holy Spirit, is necessary for him to effectuate the presence of that Spirit, but that absence is his resurrection, when God stood him up (Acts 2:32-39):

> "This Jesus God stood up, of that we are all witness. Exalted to God's right, he took the warrant of the Holy Spirit from the Father and has poured out this, which you both see and hear. Because David did not ascend into the heavens. He says himself, 'The Lord said to my Lord, Sit at my right, until I make your enemies a footstool for your feet.' All the house of Israel shall therefore know that God made him Lord and Anointed, this Jesus whom you crucified." They heard this and were stabbed to the heart; they said to Peter and the rest of the delegates, "What shall we do, brother men?" Peter said to them, "Repent, and each of you be immersed in the name of Anointed Jesus for release of your sins, and you shall receive the gift of the Holy Spirit, because the warrant is for you and your children and all those far off, as many as the Lord our God summons."

The exaltation of Jesus here is not a discrete entity, subsequent to the resurrection, but an understanding of what it fundamentally meant for God to have countermanded his death. Alive in the presence of the Father, Jesus directs God's Spirit in new and unexpected ways.

This conception of Jesus' living, resurrected presence as the source of God's Spirit, animating all believers, survived among those who preserved the spirituality of Paul. The Epistle to the Ephesians, composed after Paul's death, reflects the linkage between Jesus' location in relation to God and his donation of the Spirit (Eph 4:7-8):

> To each one of us the grace has been given according to the measure of the bounty of the Anointed. Therefore it says, "When he ascended on high he took captivity captive, he gave gifts to men."

The quotation is an adaptation from Psalm 68:19, adjusted so that Jesus gives gifts, rather than receiving them.[19] The result links Pentecost with just the model of resurrection as exaltation that has been identified in Acts 2:32-33.

Similarly, the Pauline reading of what it means for Jesus to have been taken up to God corresponds to the insistence that the Spirit he bestows is available to humanity at large. The single Spirit animates the single body of the Anointed (Eph 4:4), in which "there is not one Jew or Greek, not one slave or free, not one male or female, because you are all one in Jesus Anointed" (Gal 3:28). The context of this statement, in what precedes and follows (Gal 3:26–4:7), sets out human identity in terms of its relationship to God's Spirit, which Paul believed was established in baptism. Paul's logic is that God sends the Spirit of his Son into the heart of each person, so that he or she becomes a "son" of God who is no longer governed by well-established and often divisive distinctions within the Roman Empire.

At the end of Luke's Gospel, despite the gradual, often painful expansion to include gentiles unassociated with Israel that is depicted in the book of Acts, the Evangelist also makes the program of the resurrection inclusive (Luke 24:44-53):

> But he said to them, "These were my words that I spoke to you when I was still with you: that it was necessary for all the writings in the Law of Moses and Prophets and Psalms concerning me to be fulfilled." Then he opened up their mind to understand the writings. And he said to them that: "So it was written, for the Anointed to suffer and to arise from the dead on the third day, and for repentance on his name to be proclaimed, for release of sins to all the nations—beginning from Jerusalem. You are witnesses of these things. And look: I dispatch the promise of my Father upon you, but you remain in the city until when you are clothed with power from on high." Yet he led them out to Bethany, and lifting up his hands, he blessed them. And it happened while he blessed them, he stood apart from them and was carried up into the heaven. They themselves worshipped him and returned to Jerusalem with great joy, and they were always in the sacred space blessing God.

Emphasis on scriptural interpretation (Luke 24:44-47) features as an important element of continuity between the scene of the Eleven (v. 33) in Jerusalem and the Emmaus narrative. The differences between them are to some extent minimized, because the Eleven are a nucleus that includes "those with them" (v. 33)—disciples such as Cleopas and his companion.

Now this group has their "mind" (*nous*; Luke 24:45)—no longer their eyes, as in the Emmaus narrative (v. 31)—opened to understand the Anointed's suffering, arising on the third day, and a new element: preaching of repentance in his name for the release of sins to all the nations. This is the commission the Eleven and those with them receive, to start from Jerusalem, waiting until Jesus sends the promise of his father on them, so that they will be clothed with power (vv. 44-49).

They bless God, the final note of the Gospel (v. 53), but they can do so because Jesus takes them out to Bethany to be blessed. There he parts from them and is taken up (*anaphereto*; v. 51) to heaven. Just as this concluding narrative answers the question of why Jesus appeared to these students, so it addresses why he disappears: he is on his ascent to God to bring the "promise of my father" (v. 49), only to be realized at Pentecost and beyond.

The Gentile Crisis

Within the presentation of Luke–Acts, the trajectory of Jesus' resurrection/ exaltation heads inexorably to the inclusion of gentiles by baptism into the destiny of salvation. Luke has Paul articulate this arc in the speech at Pisidian Antioch (Acts 13:13-43). The sequel describes believing gentiles in terms of "as many as were appointed to eternal life" (v. 48),[20] language that addresses the relationship between Israel (a key term in Paul's speech) and the new range of those saved.

Even before the story of Peter in the house of Cornelius, a conventional view of Israel as the people of God has been strained in the book of Acts, notably in the interactions between Philip and the Samaritans and Philip and the Ethiopian eunuch (Acts 8:4-25, 26-40).[21] But the three key moments that define the arc of salvation are (1) the Spirit's coming at Pentecost, said to fulfill Joel's prophecy of the pouring out over "all flesh" (Acts 2:33); (2) the Spirit's falling on the God-fearing gentiles in the house of Cornelius (Acts 10:44-47); and (3) the decision of "the apostles and the elders" gathered in Jerusalem that immersion in Jesus' name alone, apart from the acceptance of circumcision, was God's vehicle for including gentiles in salvation (Acts 15:1-29).

The first of these moments is a promise. The mention of proselytes (2:10) and the stress that those gathered came from "every nation under heaven" (2:5) clearly point ahead to the inclusion of non-Jews by means of baptism within Acts.[22] Yet those who are baptized at Pentecost are described as Jewish and proselyte residents of Jerusalem itself, so the promise is spoken without being fulfilled.

The second moment might have been taken to have fulfilled the promise. Those "from the circumcision" (Acts 10:45) with Peter in the house of Cornelius are amazed that the gift of the Spirit was bestowed on gentiles.

Still, Godfearers were understood to represent a version of faithfulness to God that was not the same as the standard of Israel but did not challenge that standard.

The Sibyl—the premiere prophetess of Greco-Roman culture—is Noah's daughter-in-law in the Sibylline Oracles 3:823-827. She makes a triumphant forecast (Sib. Or. 4:24-34):[23]

> Happy will be those of earthly men who will cherish the great God, bless-ing before eating and drinking and having confidence in piety. They will deny all temples and altars they see: purposeless transports of dumb stones, defiled by animates' blood and sacrifices of four-footed animals. But they will behold the great renown of the one God, neither breaking into reckless murder, nor transacting what is stolen for gain, which are cold happenings. They do not have shameful desire for another's bed, nor hateful and repul-sive abuse of a male.

What is especially striking about this prophecy is that it is directed to the people of Asia and Europe (Sib. Or. 4:1) through the mouth of the Sibyl (Sib. Or. 4:22-23), the legendary oracle of mantic counsel. Her utterance here is explicitly backed up by the threat of eschatological judgment for all (Sib. Or. 4:40-48). A version of Acts' arc of salvation that had stopped with the story of the household of Cornelius would have accorded with this model.

But Acts, of course, presses on to the fateful claim that gentiles as such, not only those who had previously demonstrated their faith in the God of Israel, were among those "appointed to eternal life." Antioch was the initial site of including "Greeks" (Acts 11:19-26) and became the headquarters of "prophets and teachers" whom the Spirit commanded to send Barnabas and Paul deliberately to recruit gentiles (13:1-3). Inevitably, this programmatic inclusion of gentiles as gentiles produced a crisis, since the issue of their rela-tionship to Israel and Israelites needed to be addressed.

Peter's role in the controversy is anchored in what happened in the house of Cornelius (Acts 15:7-11) and in his climactic repetition of those pivotal events during his meeting with key leaders in Jerusalem. The resolution of the conflict is of obvious and crucial importance, but, prior to the conten-tion, there was the reason for the contention. The prophets and teachers in Antioch, named in Acts 13:1-3, are instructed by the Holy Spirit to separate Barnabas and Paul for the work that the Spirit called them to. This is a direct command and, at the same time, the realization of the program of Luke–Acts, the third and final moment of the arc that defines the work as a whole. The Spirit speaks while the prophets and teachers "were engaged in the priestly service[24] of the Lord and fasting." The "Lord" here is none other than Jesus, whom Paul has repeatedly addressed as Lord in the conversion narrative (Acts 9). The pattern has been established by this juncture that turning to the Lord Jesus in his heavenly presence quickens the activity of the Holy Spirit that Jesus has poured out. The Pentecostal resurrection/exaltation demanded the inclusion of gentiles.

That inclusion, however, raised the issues whether "Israel" (and under what definition) was in fact the people God chose, whether the lines of purity and impurity that are engraved in the torah and embedded in Judaism needed to be observed, and how a group guided by a risen Lord who sent his Spirit to a variety of people could maintain enough coherence to survive. When that Spirit was poured upon all flesh, the consequence was conflict, and an arbiter was required who could resolve the issues of Israel, purity, and leadership. That arbiter was not Paul—who only helped provoke the dispute. Rather, it was James, the brother of Jesus.

Why Purity? And Why James?

Until recently, purity as a concept has been treated as if it were foreign to Christianity. That is a problem, especially in dealing with James' view of the resurrection, in which the risen Jesus declares the achievement of purity and commands its recognition.

When Jesus in Luke disagrees with a Pharisee named Simon in regard to contact with a woman described as sinful (Luke 7:36-50), that is sometimes taken to mean that bodily contact with uncleanness is beside the point. Similarly, Mark makes a parenthetical remark, saying that Jesus was "cleansing all foods" when he disagreed with Pharisees about ritual cleansing (Mark 7:19). Is that not the equivalent of invalidating ritual considerations as such?

Yet this is not the direction in which the passages take the hearer (or reader). The point about the woman in Luke is that her love produced forgiveness (Luke 7:47) and that her faith had saved her (Luke 7:50). Contact with her is warranted, not because such contact does not matter, but because love and faith purify. In Mark, the fundamental principle is not that purity is beside the point but that purity moves from the inside out rather than from the outside in (Mark 7:18-20). Jesus and his followers disagreed with many of their contemporaries in regard to the achievement of purity, but they did not deny the importance of purity.[25] The rhetoric of disagreement has been exaggerated and misunderstood in those forms of Christianity that claim Jesus superseded purity and ritual and set them aside.

Yet because Christian theologians from the Enlightenment and later have asserted that, unlike other religions, theirs does not deal with purity, so secular thought in the West has taken up the perspective that purity is not a relevant concern. That makes the study of purity challenging, but it is a challenge that needs to be faced for anyone interested in religion, since purity features centrally in all known religious systems. Fortunately, considerable interest in what Jesus and early Christianity taught in regard to purity has taken up an increased role in critical discussion.[26]

The most influential figure in the early church in regard to the topic was James, called "the Just" since the first century.[27] He was not only Jesus' brother and the leader of a community of believers in Jerusalem but a practitioner of sacrifice in the temple who won the admiration of the population as a whole. Most important, James adjudicated the most consequential ritual issue of his time (and, for that matter, most times in Christian history): whether those who accepted immersion into Jesus' name also needed to keep the practice of male circumcision. That single question provoked a deep dispute, which combined in itself the definition of believers in relation to Israel and the place of ritual practices of purity within the faith.

No religion, in antiquity or today, could reasonably claim that purity is of no concern, because the range of concerns of what is clean and unclean permeates social life. What foods are eaten and how they are prepared, the definition of genders as well as the selection of sexual partners and practices, attitudes toward those who do not accord with practices of cleanness— these are among the basic social norms and personal attitudes that purity addresses. In contemporary discussion, the category might seem at first to be moot, but experience proves it is far from that. Questions of what we put in our mouths, how gender and sexual relations are to be conducted, and appropriate policies toward those who deny community norms are among the most contentious of our time. All societies maintain standards of purity; the question is only what they are. When a teacher such as Jesus violates convention, the result is to redefine purity rather than to obliterate it or—as he says in Matthew—to fulfil rather than to destroy (Matt 5:17).

The underlying relationship between Israel and the nations, the gentiles, turns on the issue of purity. The difference between Israel and others was the covenant, a covenant that included precise rules of purity that were well known in the ancient world, and the mark of that covenant was male circumcision on the eighth day (Gen 17:10-14). For that reason, the amazement of those with Peter who were "from circumcision" when the Spirit was poured out on the gentiles (Acts 10:45) is perfectly natural. Peter himself had to be prepared to accept the event. He says that God had shown him not to call a person "defiled or unclean" (Acts 10:28).

The moment of that showing was Peter's vision, when he was instructed to "kill and eat" unclean animals lowered from above in a linen cloth (Acts 10:9-16); he resisted, but the voice in the vision insisted a total of three times: "What God has cleansed, you do not defile" (Acts 10:15). The dense symbolism of the narrative depends on appreciating that purity is a complete system, linking dietary practice, ritual circumcision, and the definition of Israel. Only then can a story about animals in a sheet be related to the cleanness of uncircumcised males and their contact with Israelites.

Peter's own activities take him into the house of Cornelius, a God-fearing alien, but an alien for all that. The Samaritan and Ethiopian contacts of Philip (Acts 8) as well as Peter's with Godfearers (Acts 10, 11) are vital precedents for inclusion, but they do not prompt the crisis that the community in Antioch provoked. Experience in Antioch went beyond possible exceptions to the rule that the covenant with Israel was normative.

In Antioch, some of those who had been with the community in Jerusalem (from Cyprus and Cyrene originally; Acts 11:20) incorporated gentiles, without the qualification that they were Godfearers (Acts 11:19-26). This innovation was strong enough that, "for the first time," the students of Jesus were referred to as "Christians" (11:26). Although that might seem a matter of course, the neologism reflects the awareness of observers in Antioch that they were dealing with a strange religious phenomenon. The city already had a population of "Jews" (that is, descendants of Israel) and "Godfearers" (sympathizers with Judaism), but how could one describe a gentile who devoted himself to Jesus without a previous connection to Judaism? *Khristianos* came to be used, a term such as one would apply to political partisans of a leader, in this case the Anointed (*khristos*), as believers called Jesus. In a single word, the observers in Antioch summarized perplexity at what seemed a new and untraditional religion, what Roman law called a *superstitio*.

The reaction of perplexity was by no means limited to the general population in Antioch. In the book of Acts, Luke signals awareness at an early stage that the inclusion of non-Jews by baptism and without circumcision was deeply contentious. When Peter was in the house of Cornelius, believers "from circumcision" (Acts 10:45) were beside themselves (*exestesan*) at the coming of Spirit upon gentiles. That usage probably reflects Paul's usage of "those from circumcision" as a united front against his own outreach to the uncircumcised (Gal 2:12, for example). The reason for the language is that circumcision became a metonym for the central issue: whether gentiles who were immersed in Jesus' name and took upon themselves God's Spirit were also to be incorporated within Israel.

First in Antioch, and then at a meeting of apostles and elders in Jerusalem, a group of believers—identified as Pharisees during the meeting—insisted in regard to baptized gentiles, "It is necessary to circumcise them and to command them to keep the law of Moses" (Acts 15:5). This becomes the third occasion on which Peter relates his visit to the house of Cornelius in Acts (15:6-11), but it is notable that his account does not resolve the issue. Resolution only comes with the intervention of James, who sets out both why and how purity is to be kept, even as gentiles are immersed in the name of Jesus.

James explains his finding on the basis of Scripture, which he cites in a way that is unusual within the New Testament.[28] James claims that Peter's baptism of non-Jews is to be accepted because "the words of the prophets agree, just as it is written" (Acts 15:15), and he goes on to cite from the book of Amos. The passage cited will concern us in a moment; the form of James' interpretation is an immediate indication of a distinctive approach. As James has it, there is actual agreement between "Symeon" (the transliterated Aramaic form of Simon Peter's name) and the words of the prophets, as two people might agree: the use of the verb *sumphôneô* is used nowhere else in the New Testament in respect of Scripture. The continuity of Christian experience with Scripture is marked as a greater concern than within Paul's interpretation (for example), and James expects that continuity to be verbal, a matter of agreement with the prophets' words, not merely with possible ways of looking at what they mean. Exegesis on the basis of the meaning of precise words is reminiscent of the approach of *pesher* interpretation at Qumran.[29]

The citation from Amos (9:11-12, from the version of the Septuagint, which was the Bible of Luke–Acts) comports well with James' concern that the position of the church agree with the principal vocabulary of the prophets (Acts 15:16-17):

> After this I will come back and restore the tent of David which has fallen, and rebuild its ruins and set it up anew, that the rest of men may seek the Lord, and all the Gentiles upon whom my name is called.

In the argument of James as represented here, what the belief of gentiles achieves is not the redefinition of Israel (as in Paul's thought) but the restoration of the house of David, with gentile recognition of the torah as it impinged upon them.[30] The argument is possible because a Davidic genealogy of Jesus—and, therefore, of his brother James[31]—is assumed.

Gentile belief in Jesus was therefore in James' understanding a vindication of his Davidic triumph, but it did not involve a fundamental change in the status of gentiles vis-à-vis Israel. That characterization of the gentiles, developed by means of the reference to Amos, enables James to proceed to his requirement of their recognition of purity. He first states, "I determine not to trouble those of the Gentiles who turn to God" (15:19), as if he were simply repeating the policy of Peter in regard to circumcision. The implicit authority of that "I" (in James' case, an episcopal "I") contrasts sharply with the portrayal in Acts of apostolic decision as communal. But he then continues that his determination is also "to write to them to abstain from the pollutions of the idols, and from fornication, and from what is strangled, and from blood" (15:20).

The rules set out by James tend naturally to separate believing gentiles from their ambient environment. They are to refrain from feasts in honor of the gods and from foods sacrificed to idols in the course of being butchered and sold. (The notional devotion of animals in the market to one god or another was a common practice in the Hellenistic world.)[32] They are to observe stricter limits than usual on the type of sexual activity they might engage in, and with whom. (Gross promiscuity need not be at issue here; marriage with cousins is also included within the likely area of concern. That was fashionable in the Hellenistic world and proscribed in the book of Leviticus [see chapter 18 and 20:17-21].) They are to avoid the flesh of animals that had been strangled instead of bled, and they are not to consume blood itself. The proscription of blood, of course, was basic within Judaism; and strangling an animal (as distinct from cutting its throat) increased the availability of blood in the meat. Such strictures are consistent with James' initial observation, that God had taken a people from the gentiles (15:14); they were to be similar to Israel and supportive of Israel in their distinction from the Hellenistic world at large.

The motive behind the rules is not separation in itself, however. James links them to the fact that the Mosaic legislation regarding purity is well and widely known (15:21):

> For Moses from early generations has had those preaching him city by city, being read in the synagogues every Sabbath.

Because the law is well known, James insists that believers, including gentile believers, are not to give even the impression of violating what Moses enjoined. In the words of Amos, they are to behave as "all the Gentiles upon whom my name is called." As a result of James' insistence, the meeting in Jerusalem decides to send envoys and a letter to Antioch, in order to require gentiles to honor the prohibitions set out by James (Acts 15:22-35).

The same chapter of Leviticus that commands "love your neighbor as yourself" (19:18) also forbids blood to be eaten (19:26) and fornication (19:29; see also 18:6-30). The canonical (but secondhand) letter of James calls the commandment of love "the royal law" (Jas 2:8), acknowledging that Jesus had accorded it privilege by citing it alongside the commandment to love God as the two greatest commandments (see Mark 12:28-32). In Acts, James himself, while accepting that gentiles cannot be required to keep the whole law, insists that they should acknowledge it, by observing basic requirements concerning fornication and blood and idolatry.

It is of interest that Leviticus forbids the eating of blood by sojourners as well as Israelites and associates that prohibition with how animals are to be killed for the purpose of eating (17:10-16). Moreover, a principle of exclusivity in sacrifice is trenchantly maintained: anyone, whether of Israel or a sojourner dwelling among them, who offers a sacrifice that is not brought to the LORD's honor in the temple is to be cut off from the people (17:8-9). In other words, the prohibitions of James—involving sacrifice, fornication, strangled meat produce, and blood—all derive easily from the very context in Leviticus from which the commandment to love is derived. They are elementary and involve interest in what gentiles as well as Israelites do. The position of James as reflected in Acts upholds the integrity of Scripture in the discipline of the church in a way that recalls the authority of both the *mebaqqar* from Qumran and the *episkopos* from the Pastoral Epistles.[33]

James' prohibitions as presented in Acts are designed to show that believing gentiles honor the law that is commonly read, without in any way changing their status as gentiles. Thereby, the tent of David is erected again, in the midst of gentiles who show their awareness of the restoration by means of their respect for the torah. The interpretation attributed to James involves an application of Davidic vocabulary to Jesus, as is consistent with the claim of Jesus' family to Davidic ancestry. The transfer of Davidic promises to Jesus is accomplished within an acceptance of the terms of reference of the Scripture generally: to embrace David is to embrace Moses. There is no trace in James' interpretation of the Pauline gambit, setting one biblical principle (justification in the manner of Abraham) against another (obedience in the manner of Moses). Where Paul divided the Scripture against itself in order to maintain the integrity of a single fellowship of Jews and gentiles, James insisted upon the integrity of Scripture, even at the cost of separating Christians from one another. In both cases, the interpretation of Scripture was also—at the same moment as the sacred text was apprehended—a matter of social policy.

Within the context of Hellenistic Judaism as reflected in the Sibylline Oracles, then, a prohibition of blood to gentiles seems quite natural. If it is anachronistic to speak at this point of Noachian commandments, we may at least refer to the motif of Noah's instruction of all humanity as well established by the first century CE. Unfortunately, the Genesis Apocryphon from Qumran is fragmentary just as it speaks of Noah, but it is notable that Noah is told there that he is to rule over the earth and the seas and that "you shall not eat any blood" (1QapGen ar 7.1; 11.17). Both of those statements are more emphatic than what is said in the corresponding text of Genesis in Hebrew (Gen 9:2).

James' circle curated purity as part of devotion to the temple in Jerusalem. The ideal of devotion that James had in mind is represented in Acts 21. There, Paul and his companions arrive in Jerusalem and are confronted by a report from James and the elders that Paul's reputation in Jerusalem is that he is telling Jews in the diaspora to forsake Moses, and especially to stop circumcising their children (Acts 21:17-21). Paul is then told to take on the expense of four men who had taken a vow, entering the temple with them to offer sacrifice (Acts 21:22-26).

The nature of the vow seems quite clear. It will be fulfilled when the men shave their heads (so Acts 21:24). A Nazirite vow is evidently at issue.[34] As set out in Numbers 6, a Nazirite was to let his hair and beard grow for the time of his vow, abstain completely from grapes, and avoid approaching any dead body. At the close of the period of the vow, he was to shave his head and offer his hair in proximity to the altar (so Num 6:18). The end of this time of being holy, the Lord's property, is marked by enabling the Nazirite to drink wine again (6:20).

Just these practices of holiness are attributed by Hegesippus (as cited by Eusebius, *Ecclesiastical History* 2.23.3–9) to James. The additional notice, that he avoided oil and use of a traditional bath, is consistent with the especial concern for purity among Nazirites. They were to avoid any contact with death (Num 6:6-12); in fact the avoidance of all uncleanness—which is incompatible with sanctity—was essential. The avoidance of oil is also attributed by Josephus to the Essenes (*Jewish War* 2.123), and the reason seems plain: oil, as a fluid pressed from fruit, was considered to absorb impurity to such an extent that extreme care in its preparation was vital.[35] Absent complete assurance that oil was pure, abstinence was a wise policy. James' vegetarianism also comports with a concern to avoid contact with any kind of corpse uncleanness. Finally, although Hegesippus' assertion that James could actually enter the sanctuary seems exaggerated, his acceptance of a Nazirite regime, such as Acts 21 explicitly associates with him, would account for such a remembrance of him, in that Nazirites were to be presented in the vicinity of the sanctuary.

Acts presents James' thorough understanding of how gentiles remain gentiles, even as they keep those aspects of the torah demanded of non-Israelites. The purpose of those demands is that they might be part of the restoration of the house of David as predicted by the Prophets and take part in the Nazirite practice that James himself had organized in Jesus' name within the temple. The basis of this practice was the resurrection.

Purity's Foundation

James' focus was purity in the temple under the aegis of his risen brother, the Son of Man, but there is no trace of his requiring circumcision of gentiles. It needs to be kept in mind that Jesus himself had expelled traders from the temple, not as some indiscriminate protest about commercialism, and still less as an objection to the temple in itself, but as part of Zechariah's prophecy of a day when all the peoples of the earth would be able to offer sacrifice to the Lord without the intervention of commerce. James' Nazirite practice realized that prophecy in his brother's name.

The moment when James recognized his brother as the Son of Man who authorized an intense Nazirite practice is related, not in the New Testament, but in the Gospel of the Hebrews (cited by Jerome in *De viris illustribus* 2):

> The Gospel called according to the Hebrews, which was also recently translated by me into Greek speech as well as Latin, which Origen also frequently employs, after the savior's resurrection relates: When the Lord had given the linen to the priest's servant, he went to James and appeared to him. (Now James had vowed not to eat bread from that hour when he drank the Lord's cup until he should see him raised from those who sleep.) Again, after a bit: Bring—the Lord said—table and bread! And at once is added: He took bread and blessed and broke and gave to James the Just and said to him, My brother eat your bread, because the Son of Man has arisen from those who sleep.

Despite the fragmentary nature of what remains of the Gospel of the Hebrews,[36] Jerome—as translator of whatever remained of the document in his time—provides some welcome context.

In Jerome's Latin translation of Gospel of the Hebrews, Jesus presents a *sindonem* to the priest's servant, just the term used in Greek in Mark 14:51-52 (*sindona*), of the anonymous young man who fled naked after his linen garment was snatched from him.[37] The use of the Greek word rather than *linteamen* perhaps reflects Jerome's awareness of that connection. The term is also used in the Gospel of Peter 6:24 of Jesus' burial shroud, and linen is what a priest should wear next to his skin (Exod 28:42-43; Ezek 44:17). Such garments are associated with atoning powers in the Talmud (see b. Zebachim 88b). One talmudic story recounts that when Simeon the righteous entered the holy of holies on the Day of Atonement (a space no other human being could enter), he regularly saw an old man attired in white clothing, providing a good omen for the coming year; when he saw an old man dressed in black, he knew his death was near (b. Yoma 39b). Although the Gospel of the Hebrews speaks of a priest's servant, not the high priests, it seems to reflect a tradition of priestly followers of Jesus, to which Acts 6:7 briefly refers. Ultimately, the startling claim in the Epistle to the Hebrews 9:11-12, that Jesus had entered into the holy of holies, may owe its genesis to a visionary tradition among priests such as is represented in the Gospel of the Hebrews.

The Gospel of the Hebrews presents Jesus' appearance to James in the context of a vow. James' vow is symmetrical to the form of Jesus' just prior to his death, not to drink wine until he drinks it new in God's kingdom (see Mark 14:25; Matt 26:29; Luke 22:18).[38] James formally took up the Nazirite vow in the course of his practice in the temple (see Acts 21:18-26), but the Gospel of the Hebrews marks an extension of the vow, to include bread. An exceptional fast, related to mourning (cf. also Gos. Pet. 6:27), here becomes the setting for Jesus himself to appear after his death. He commands others (saying *adferte* [bring], a plural imperative) to bring a table and bread and invokes the basic procedure of Eucharist in order to assure James that the Son of Man has arisen. This pattern of emphasis upon the *bread*, as distinct from wine, is characteristic of the practice that emerged in Jerusalem (see Acts 2:42),[39] the apparent source of this allusively presented vignette.

Allusive though it is, the Gospel of the Hebrews account also preserves clear traces of the model that Jesus' appearance to James followed, a model drawn from Scripture. Reference to Jesus as "the Son of Man" draws from the book of Daniel, where "one like a son of man" takes his place before the throne of God (Dan 7:9-14). James' dedication to the risen Jesus as the Son of Man enthroned in heaven is independently shown by Hegesippus in his account of James' martyrdom. Set by allies of the high priest on a parapet of the temple and questioned concerning "the gate of Jesus,"[40] James replies, "Why do you ask me concerning Jesus, the Son of Man? He sits in heaven at the right of the great Power, and is about to come upon the clouds of heaven."[41] James was then thrown down from the parapet and killed with a club.

Hegesippus vividly describes James' ascetical practices, drawing from the language and imagery of the Nazirite vow (Eusebius, *Ecclesiastical History* 2.23.5–6):

> He was holy from his mother's womb,[42] and he drank no wine nor strong drink, nor did he eat flesh. No razor came upon his head; he did not anoint himself with oil[43] nor use the bath. He alone was permitted to enter into the Holy Place, because he wore not woolen but linen garments. And he was in the habit of entering alone into the Temple, and was frequently found upon his knees begging forgiveness for the people, so that his knees became hard like those of a camel, from his constantly bending them in his worship of God, and asking forgiveness for the people.

Similar practices are depicted in the book of Daniel, where fasting is the context of vision. Daniel speaks of his "mourning" for three weeks, a period in which he ate nothing extravagant and particularly avoided meat, wine, and oil (Dan 10:2-3).

Several human and angelic figures appear in the visions that follow, and sometimes the language used ("one in the likeness of the sons of men" [Dan 10:16]; "one as the appearance of a man" [10:18]) relates back to the Son of Man in chapter 7.[44] Repeatedly, these figures touch Daniel (10:10, 16, 18), with the result that, despite the weakness that has overcome him, he is strengthened to speak and receive the visions. At their close, after the classic reference to the resurrection at the opening of chapter 12, Daniel is dispatched with the promise that "many shall purify themselves, and make themselves white, and be refined" (Dan 12:10) unlike the wicked. Purity, that is, results from the combination of fasting and contact with the heavenly realm.

Those twin elements are present in the brief vignette Jerome quoted from the Gospel of the Hebrews. James' fasting culminates when the Son of Man, Jesus raised from the dead,[45] instructs him to eat bread again. The link with Daniel may also explain why James is described by Hegesippus as bearing the name *oblias*, which has caused understandable puzzlement, especially when Hegesippus' rendering of the term as "bulwark" is accepted. Yet Hegesippus assumes that this signification is Greek; James seems to be so named here because after his death the siege of Jerusalem was successful. But the term is easily related to the Aramaic term *'aval*, which means, "to mourn," and is used in Daniel 10:2. James was probably known as "mourner." A minor tractate of the Talmud lays down the rule that a mourner (*'aval*) "is under the prohibition to bathe, anoint [the body], put on sandals and cohabit"

(Semachoth 4.1). This largely corresponds to the requirements of a Nazirite vow and to Hegesippus' description of James' practice.

James' devotion to the temple and to his brother as the Danielic Son of Man after the resurrection made him the most prominent Christian leader in Jerusalem. His practice of the Nazirite vow was his distinguishing feature, and brought him widespread admiration in Jerusalem. Yet the focus of his devotion, his belief in his brother as the gate of heaven, the heavenly portal above the temple, made him controversial and finally led to his execution. Among Christians, he promulgated his understanding of the establishment of the house of David by means of his interpretation of Scripture, although he insisted that baptized, uncircumcised non-Jews had an ancillary role.

James' dedicated practice, the basis of his esteem in Jerusalem, in all probability survived his own death in 62 CE, but the Nazirite vow demanded the presence of the temple in order to be fulfilled. The destruction of the temple by the Romans meant that this distinctive and influential practice, in which the risen Jesus ordered the close of the period of fasting and announced the achievement of purity, could not survive. James' praxis was remembered in Acts only as the context of the final visit of Paul to Jerusalem rather than as the foundation of the purity that Jesus brought according to the teaching of James himself. Within the development of the New Testament, however, James' Nazirite practice remains central. In James' view of the resurrection, Jesus' angelic presence signaled the achievement of purity, a vital step in any process that involved, as the More Than Five Hundred mandated, the inclusion of the gentiles.

7

Seen by "All the Apostles"

Introduction

Some of the most familiar, powerful, and influential accounts of the resurrection at last come into play with Paul's reference to "all the apostles." Among that group, stories circulated in which Jesus rose from the dead in flesh and bone, eating fish in the presence of his followers (Luke 24:39-43). Another account has Jesus explaining the meaning of all the Scriptures in relation to his suffering and glory (Luke 24:25:27), while Mary Magdalene's visions feature in differing versions in all the Gospels.

Because Paul does not name the individuals in the group, which of them is the principal source of a given stream of tradition is a matter of inference. In the case of Mary Magdalene, her persistent association with a visionary tradition in the New Testament and early Christian literature is so striking that her major influence is evident. Other streams of tradition require closer scrutiny in order to be identified.

Within the Gospels and Acts, the apocalyptic presentation of the physical resurrection of Jesus as the Son of Man who is to judge the earth is both prominent and pervasive. Indeed, a fully material conception is today insisted upon as the only satisfactory view among many contemporary believers and theologians, whether they are avowed Fundamentalists or not. Yet within the New Testament, such an apocalyptic perspective remains unassociated with any named figure. The reference to the Son of Man and the imagery of Daniel, however, points to a figure associated with James, the brother of Jesus. Within the New Testament, Silas (also called Silvanus, the Latin version of his name) appears as such an apocalyptic teacher, with contacts and a range of influence that would account for the impact of this point of view.

The interpretation of Scripture also features at every level of the New Testament as a vital activity. An obvious precedent is offered by various approaches to the Torah and the Prophets among interpreters within Judaism, so that the methods of midrash and targum, as well as the exegetical approaches of writers such as Philo of Alexandria and Josephus, have been compared to early Christian literature.[1] Those comparisons are both productive and helpful in particular cases, but they do not explain a much broader and pervasive factor.

Most of those for whom the documents of the New Testament were intended knew them by listening, because they were illiterate. Only some of them had any deep experience of Judaism, and the vast majority were not in any sense expert in interpretation prior to seeking and receiving baptism in Jesus' name. Nonetheless, this movement of largely illiterate, nonexpert practitioners engaged in inquiry and controversy in regard to the Scriptures of Israel. Their interest was specifically christological, directed to the aim of finding Jesus, the risen Anointed, within those texts. Alongside apocalypse and vision, "all the apostles" endorsed interpretation as a medium in which Jesus was seen after his death.

Apocalypse, interpretation, and vision were all media in which early Christianity announced the resurrection. That process unfolded under the authority of "all the apostles."

Apocalypse in Motion

Uniquely among the Gospels, Matthew refers to an earthquake at the time of Jesus' crucifixion (Matt 27:51-53):

> And look: the curtain of the Temple was split from top to bottom in two, and the earth quaked, and the rocks were split, and the memorials were opened and many bodies of the holy ones who slept were raised; they came out from the memorials after his raising and entered into the holy city and were manifested to many.

This moment is linked to the resurrection, where the earthquake also features (Matt 28:2); taken together, the references convey an apocalyptic setting. The resurrection is portrayed as ground zero, the time from which the "holy ones," the saints, arise and begin to encounter those who are still alive. The boundary between the living and dead is fractured at the same moment the curtain in the temple splits;[2] an eschatological epoch sees its commencement in the specific case of Jesus.

By introducing the motif of an earthquake at the crucifixion, Matthew disrupts his own narrative sequence by referring to events in Jerusalem *after* Jesus' resurrection. In this regard, the apocalyptic significance of the depiction is manifest. Zechariah 14:3-7 presents an earthquake on the Mount of Olives as a key feature in a comprehensive eschatological triumph that will unite Israel and the nations in a temple that is open to all. The Targum Zechariah refers to that victory as when the kingdom of the LORD will be revealed upon all the dwellers of the earth.[3]

By his reference to this earthquake, Matthew structures his unique scene with a powerful and unmistakable dimension of vindication. Jesus' execution had been provoked by his action in the temple, where he and his followers had targeted the commerce there as an abuse. The prophetic program had been inspired by the same chapter of Zechariah in which the earthquake appears,[4] whose last words insist that on the LORD's day, there will no longer be a merchant in the temple (Zech 14:21). The collision between Jesus' prophetic perspective and Caiaphas' priestly authority had seemed to result in Jesus' defeat. The resurrection indicated otherwise.

Because Matthew is dealing with events that transcend time, the anachronism of conflating events concerning the crucifixion and the resurrection is not incidental[5] but a feature of the narrative, which makes chronology subservient to apocalypse. The Evangelist initiates the hearer of the Gospel into an aural palimpsest, in which crucifixion, resurrection, and parousia relate to one another in their final significance and in their power to shape the hearer's life in the present.

Jesus' death and resurrection become the trigger and also the assurance of eternal judgment. A work near in time to Matthew, but too late to feature as an actual source, provides a comparable model of the resurrection of the dead and the transition into a realm beyond death (2 Bar. 50:2-3):

> For the earth will surely give back the dead at that time; it receives them now in order to keep them, not changing anything in their form. But it has received them so it will give them back. And as I have delivered them to it so it will raise them. For then it will be necessary to show those who live that the dead are living again, and that those who went away have come back.

The bodily return of the "holy ones" to Jerusalem in Matthew 27:52-53 shares in the precise physicality of 2 Baruch.[6] In both 2 Baruch and Matthew's

Gospel, the tangible promise of the resurrection in 2 Maccabees—with the return of an enfleshed, restored body to vigorous life—clearly finds its voice in the period after the destruction of the Second Temple.

Where Matthew differs from both 2 Maccabees and 2 Baruch, of course, lies in its contention that the raising of Jesus occasioned and produced the raising of the holy ones.[7] His body is the pivot on which the ages turn, and apocalypse is set in motion; its initiation is a fait accompli, whose proof is Jesus' resurrection. That implies, however, that the physical custody of Jesus' body is assured: only then could doubt be removed that his appearance alive showed God had raised him from the dead in the initial act of raising all the just. By design rather than by coincidence, Matthew is the only Gospel that details a guard (Matt 27:62-66) that is set up to prevent the theft of Jesus' corpse.

The experience of the earthquake and the angel by the guards and their willingness to broadcast the lie (concocted by high priests and elders) that Jesus' body had been stolen (Matt 28:2-4, 11-15) are uniquely Matthean incidents that underscore the physical facticity of the resurrection. Because the earthquake has intervened, no inspection of the tomb of Jesus (as in Luke and John, the later gospels) is possible; the physical resurrection is declared by other means.[8]

The angel who sits on the remains of the tomb paralyzes the guards with fear before explaining what has happened to Mary Magdalene and the other Mary (Matt 27:5-7). Angelic interpretation, a feature of apocalyptic literature, provides one means of establishing the truth; the provision of the guard at the tomb, although intended by the high priests and the Pharisees[9] to foreclose any hint that Jesus was raised from the dead, proves to endorse the claim.

The assumption of the dialogue between the Pharisees and Pilate (Matt 27:62-63) is that Jesus' prediction that he would be raised from the dead is widely known, contradicting the theme in the Gospels of his secrecy concerning his true status (cf. Matt 17:9, for example). The exchange also does not highlight the pragmatic issue of the temple as the flashpoint of Jesus' controversy in Jerusalem with both Judaic and Roman authorities; instead, the resurrection itself is paramount. Anachronism is again manifest, since the controversy assumes that Jesus has been raised and that preaching in his name demands a response from the authorities. Likewise, Matthew's insertion portrays Pharisees as having charge of the police force associated with the temple, when in fact that was under the immediate control of the high priest; in Matthew's social imagination,[10] Pharisees are of high status (Matt 23:1-3) and have privileged access to Roman authorities (Matt 27:62).

One way to address this apparent lapse is to suppose that Pilate's statement in Matthew 27:65 should be inflected to mean, "Have a patrol," rather than, "You have a patrol." Although that is possible, by this stage in Matthew the high priests and elders have set the conditions necessary for the crucifixion by means of an armed force (see 26:4, 47, 50, 55). The issue in the appeal to Pilate is for permission to act outside the temple. But that finding only heightens the oddity of involving Pharisees at this stage, an oddity compounded by supposing that the events unfolded "after the Preparation," when the Sabbath would have begun (Matt 27:62). The appearance gains strength that Matthew relies on a tradition that intends to censure Jewish authorities, and the Pharisees in particular find themselves in his crosshairs.

The depiction of Jesus in Matthew 27:63, 64, as a "deceiver," and of his movement as "deceit," confirms this impression. The charge agrees with the wording of a later talmudic tradition (Sanhedrin 43a), according to which Jesus was executed (by stoning, and after judicious inquiry) for leading the people astray.[11] This tradition also considers Jesus a "deceiver" (*mesith*), as defined in Deuteronomy 13:1-11, who entices Israel to serve false gods. The punishment demanded is stoning, and that is the means of Jesus' death in the talmudic passage. Although this story is late, and loosely acquainted with the narrative of Jesus, the charge of deception, reflected in Matthew as well as in John 7:11 and Justin's *Dialogue with Trypho* (69.7; 108.2),[12] appears to have been an early objection to Jesus and his movement. The uniquely Matthean account of the guard at the tomb, later taken up and elaborated in the Gospel of Peter,[13] serves to insist that Jesus' body had been raised and that his message involved no deceit.

The tangibility of Jesus' risen body and the proof against any charge of deceit animate the contention in Matthew, and both themes are taken up by Luke in the Gospel and in Acts, albeit by different narrative means. Luke's Gospel provides the most direct evidence of Jesus' material presence after his death, by having him ask for food and eat a meal (Luke 24:36-42). Unlike other scenes of the resurrection, this vignette presents no commission to Jesus' followers on the basis of what they witness. Rather, the whole purpose of the appearance seems to be to insist that Jesus is not a "spirit"[14] but "flesh and bone" (vv. 37-39). His eating fish removes any doubt in that regard (vv. 41-43).

Under Luke's treatment, however, the passage extends into the commission that closes the Gospel (24:44-53) and provides the transition into the book of Acts. "You are witnesses of these things," Jesus tells "the Eleven and those with them" (v. 48; cf. v. 33). And he continues (vv. 49-53):

> "And look: I dispatch the promise of my father upon you, but you remain in the city until when you are clothed with power from on high." Yet he led them out to Bethany, and lifting up his hands, he blessed them. And it happened while he blessed them, he stood apart from them and was carried up into the heaven. They themselves worshipped him and returned to Jerusalem with great joy, and they were always in the sacred space blessing God.

This first ascension of Jesus is less well known than the scene that opens Acts, but it is crucial to Luke's entire presentation. Jesus' place in heaven is fully compatible with his physicality among his followers,[15] and the ascension is the mediating factor between his presence in heaven and on earth. His followers' presence in Jerusalem (the unique place of the resurrection in Luke's Gospel) assures the integrity of the message that God had raised Jesus from the grave *and* that he was taken up into heaven. The risen Jesus was *both* material *and* at home in heaven in this science of his resurrection.[16]

That same analysis of Jesus as risen from the dead permeates the story of his ascension in Acts (1:1-14). Here a commission resumes and expands what is said at the close of the Gospel, so that Jesus himself provides the narrative program of the book of Acts as a whole (1:4-11):

> He shared salt and commanded them not to depart from Jerusalem, but "to await the promise of the father, which you heard from me. Because John immersed in water, but you will be immersed in Spirit—Holy—after not many of these days." They then came together, questioned him, saying, "Lord, in this season will you restore the Kingdom to Israel?" But he said to them, "Not for you to know the seasons and times that the Father set by his own authority, but you will receive power when Holy Spirit comes upon you, and you will be my witnesses both in Jerusalem and all Judea, and in Samaria, and until the end of the earth." He said these things and, as they looked, he was taken upon and a cloud received him from their eyes. As they were staring into heaven and he proceeded, and look—two men stood by to them in white garments. And they said, "Galilean men, why do you stand gazing into heaven? This Jesus who was received up from you into heaven will come so, in the manner you observed him proceeding into heaven."

The broadening of the geographical range of activity as compared to what is envisioned in the Gospel, allusion to the new meaning of baptism (to be

detailed in Acts 2), and the caution in regard to eschatological anticipation all indicate that the scene is consciously crafted with the opening of
Acts in mind.

The apparent repetition of the scene with the close of the Gospel according to Luke has caused confusion, even prompting the suggestion that new
material came to Luke after the Gospel's composition that he incorporated
in Acts.[17] The beginning of Acts makes the transition as smooth as possible.
The "Eleven and those with them" of Luke 24:33 are now the delegates (or
apostles [*apostoloi*]; Acts 1:2), but the Eleven are actually named in Acts 1:13,
and those "with them" are identified in Acts 1:14. When, in Acts 1:2, Luke
refers to the day "he was received up," that recapitulates the statement that
he was "borne up into heaven" in Luke 24:51,[18] and it provides closure to
the forty days of his material presence with his closest followers, eating and
drinking with them while he spoke of God's kingdom (Acts 1:2). Those forty
days, however, do not correspond to the close of the Gospel, indicating that
Luke juggles differing traditions.[19]

The description of the ascension proper that follows is more detailed
than at the end of the Gospel.[20] Its message, crucial to Acts, is given by two
"men" (*andres*) who recollect the message of the two "men" at the tomb (Acts
1:10-11; Luke 24:4-7). But they say something never said before: that Jesus,
physically taken into heaven, is to return in like manner (Acts 1:11). Parousia,
a key term for Silas (1 Thess 4:15) and for apocalyptic material that bears his
imprint (see Matt 24:3, 27, 37, 39), finds its most elemental definition in Acts.

In effect, the passage as a whole is the bearer of two messages, one in
regard to apostolic authorization in Jesus' name and by God's Spirit, and the
other in regard to Jesus' parousia in the same flesh and bone with which he
rose from the dead (cf. Luke 24:39). The Eleven who receive this message are
exactly the Eleven whom Luke has mentioned from the beginning (albeit in a
different order; v. 13; cf. Luke 6:14-16), but they are now joined by unnamed
women, Jesus' mother, and his brothers.

This message for and of an apostolic community grounded in Jerusalem privileges the witnesses present as much as it insists upon Jesus' physical
presence. Indeed, the two conceptions are tightly woven together: only those
who know Jesus can speak of his physicality, and only that physical presence
corresponds to the parousia that is coming.

The first of Paul's letters, written with Silas and Timothy, includes a
comparable teaching, but one that stands in some dissonance with Paul's
own robust assertions in regard to his conception of a "spiritual body" in
1 Corinthians 15. Writing in harness with Silas—an apostolic delegate of

James (as well as a "prophet"; Acts 15:30-33) and an opponent of believing Pharisees who had wanted to require circumcision along with baptism—Paul and Timothy find themselves saying (1 Thess 4:15-18):

> This we say by a word of the Lord, that we who are alive, remaining until the *parousia* of the Lord will not precede those who have slept. Because the Lord himself by a command, with the sound of an archangel and with God's trumpet, will descend from heaven, and the dead in Anointed will arise first, then we who are alive, remaining, will be snatched up together with them in clouds to meet the Lord in the air, and so will we always be with the Lord. So reassure one another with these words.

Silas is the most likely source of this apocalyptic approach, which also exerted a powerful influence on the Gospels and Acts.[21] Once introduced into the book of Acts, however, the ascension/parousia seems to put a cap in the resurrection. Although Paul's conversion still lies in the future at this point, and for Luke he is indeed an apostle and encountered the reality of God's Anointed, the clear implication is that the Jerusalem community around the apostles was privileged with the knowledge of the direct, physical correspondence between the Jesus who died and the Jesus who was raised, ascended into heaven, and will return in the same way.

Opening the Scriptures

The scene of what occurred near Emmaus (Luke 24:13-35) stands out with a unique perspective, and so it has understandably been treated as both an unusual and an independent story, whatever its source. But Luke is careful to link the introduction to the scene immediately preceding: Peter's running to the memorial and looking in (Luke 24:12). Peter does what the women also do in Luke (24:3), establishing with several witnesses (and not only women)[22] that the body of Jesus was not present in the tomb. Luke's empty tomb, a major innovation among the Synoptic Gospels, makes that site pivotal to Jesus' resurrection. For that reason, the Emmaus scene closes with the return of Cleopas and his companion to Jerusalem (where Peter is again invoked as a witness in Luke 24:34), which Luke maintains as the center of a clearly delineated geographical focus.

Luke's integration of the Emmaus story within the wider presentation, however, reveals that it derives from an autonomous tradition.[23] Although the two disciples are described as traveling to and from nearby Emmaus on the same day (Luke 24:13, 33), the timing of the meal is marked in the body of the narrative as so near to sunset as to approach the next day (v. 29).

Immediately after the story, Luke has the disciples arise and return to Jerusalem "in the same hour" (v. 33), yet somehow still in time for supper there. That is scarcely plausible and suggests that Luke has ordered these stories liturgically, for a coordinated cycle of happenings "on the third day."

The autonomy of the tradition is also indicated by its tension with Luke's presentation of the same or related events. When Cleopas relates the passion of Jesus to the apparent stranger, he refers to Jesus as *Nazarênos* ("Nazirite"; Luke 24:19) rather than as Nazorean (*Nazôraios*). Elsewhere, Luke uses *Nazarênos* when sharing a tradition (4:34; cf. Mark 1:24).[24] Cleopas also imputes responsibility for the crucifixion solely to high priests and Jewish leaders, omitting reference to Pilate and the Romans, and says the disciples had hoped Jesus was about to redeem Israel (24:20-21), an aim Jesus does not state during the passion, although it coheres with Acts 1:6. Cleopas does, however, fully agree with the earlier formulation of the women not finding the body of Jesus (vv. 22-23; cf. v. 3), but he says "some" of the disciples, not only Peter, went to the tomb, confirmed what the women said, yet did not see Jesus (vv. 23-24; cf. v. 12). Cleopas says the women's vision is of angels (*anggeloi*) explicitly; when he and his companion return to Jerusalem, they are greeted with the news that "the Lord has been raised and was seen by Simon" (v. 34).[25] These are indications of a careful coordination of traditions.

The scene near Emmaus is more handsomely crafted than any other episode in the canonical Gospels concerning the resurrection, in order to convey a precise perspective:[26]

Journey of two disciples from Jerusalem (vv. 13-14)
    Jesus joins them unrecognized (vv. 15-17)
        Cleopas' précis of the passion (vv. 18-21)
        The women's story (vv. 22-24)
        Jesus' explanation from Scripture (vv. 25-27)
    Jesus recognized (vv. 28-32)
Journey to Jerusalem (vv. 33-35).

Following this scheme, we see that Jesus draws near (*enggisas*; v. 15) to the two disciples while they are engaged in deep discussion, but their eyes are prevented from recognizing him. Recognition (flagged by the use of the verb *epignônai*; v. 16) is a key interest of the narrative. Under the stranger's prompting, Cleopas rehearses the events of the passion, and then the stranger interprets the Scriptures to show—what the disciples, he insists, should have known—that it was necessary for the Anointed to suffer and enter into glory (vv. 25-27). There is still no recognition. Only when the stranger is pressed to remain with the disciples—and he reclines to eat, takes the bread, blesses and breaks it, and gives it to them—are their eyes opened: and at last they recognize him (vv. 28-31a-b). When he does what he did just prior to his death (Luke 22:19), and also during another evening meal, the Feeding of the Five Thousand (Luke 9:16), they know who Jesus is. Then he disappears (Luke 24:31c).

The meaning of that disappearance will occupy Luke later, but, when he says that Jesus became invisible (*aphantos*; v. 31c), the choice of the term is redolent. Josephus deploys the verbal equivalent, *aphanizomai*, to speak of the transfer of Moses and Elijah into heaven;[27] he speaks of them and Enoch as becoming *aphaneis*. For the moment, however, the disciples know only—in retrospect—that Jesus had been made known to them on the way to Emmaus during discussion and that they recognized him in the breaking of bread (v. 35). They do not even realize how much their heart[28] was burning as he spoke until after the fact, when they had recognized him (v. 32).

Two central activities are related within this narrative: the interpretation of Scripture and breaking bread. The former brings Jesus' living presence, and the latter brings recognition of who he is. Both are presented as crucial to the experience of the resurrection, but they do not quite occur together. One enriches the other, but each brings its own result, a sense of presence *or* a sense of identity; coordination comes only in hindsight. During the twentieth century, Werner Heisenberg developed the "uncertainty principle," that observers affect the target of their observations. As a result, in measuring an electron, one might calculate either its position in relation to the nucleus or its momentum, but not both at the same time.[29] So in the story of Emmaus, the risen Jesus is either recognized in breaking bread or felt in the opening of the Scriptures to the reality of his suffering and glory.

Because Cleopas himself underscores that the women had not found Jesus' body in the tomb (v. 23), the narrative associated with him raises the issue of how the resurrection can be known. To put the matter negatively, the same Synoptic Gospel that insists that the tomb is empty is also the one that indicates that this fact is not equivalent to knowing Jesus as raised from the dead. The resurrection is proved not by the disappearance of the body but by the appearance of the person.[30] Luke's presentation anticipates this observation and makes it the central focus of the narrative that follows immediately.

When Barnabas and Paul are presented together in Acts, the interpretation of Scripture is also a pivotal concern, and the speech at Pisidian Antioch (Acts 13:13-52) might be taken as an example of the use of Moses and all the Prophets (Luke 24:27) as well as the Psalms (Luke 24:44-47). Such traditions reflect the origin of the global assertion that the Anointed's suffering, death, and resurrection are attested in the Scriptures of Israel: that is what will enable repentance and forgiveness to be preached in his name (Luke 24:47; Acts 13:38) so that he will stand as the savior for Israel (Acts 13:23) and ultimately the gentiles (Acts 13:46; Luke 24:47). The story of the experience of two disciples who made their way to Emmaus after Jesus' death (Luke 24:13-35) articulates this global theology more clearly than any other single resurrection scene.[31]

The Eucharistic connection of the narrative of how Jesus appeared between Jerusalem and Emmaus extends to the disclosure of his identity during the meal. The gestures involved recollect both what Jesus did just prior to his death (Luke 22:19) and also during another evening meal, the Feeding of the Five Thousand (Luke 9:16). Although Barnabas is not named in the Gospels as a tradent of Jesus' teaching, he does fulfill that apostolic role according to Acts[32] and Paul.[33] His disagreement with Paul over arrangements of communal eating associates him with narratives concerning the feeding of multitudes—the five thousand (Mark 6:32-44; Matt 14:13-21; Luke 9:10b-17; John 6:1-13) and the four thousand (Mark 8:1-10; Matt 15:32-39). The two passages convey different messages, however, by their citation of differing numbers. The focus on Israel in Mark 6 is maintained by means of the number twelve. In Mark 8, the number seven conveys the extent of God's vigilance over the whole earth (see Zech 4:2, 10; and Acts 6:1-7) in its four compass points (Zech 6:1-5). The commentary on the miraculous feedings in Mark 8:17-21 indicates that the numbers cited in the two stories bear significance,[34] and that they show that Israel and the nations can be accommodated separately, just the arrangement that Paul styles as "hypocrisy" in Galatians 2:11-13.

Barnabas' disagreement with Paul in Antioch reflects his deep engagement with mealtime practice and interpretation. The unique story of what happened to Cleopas and another, unnamed member of the apostolic community (whom I infer to have been Barnabas) takes up this engagement and conveys the perspective that Jesus, known in the breaking of the bread, is effectively present in his disclosure of himself within Moses and the Prophets. Jesus' presence alone makes that hermeneutical insight possible,[35] providing a continuing contact with his resurrection by means of christological interpretation.

Transformative Vision

Mary Magdalene came to be called "the apostle to the apostles," because her vision at Jesus' tomb, along with variously identified associates in some accounts, provoked others to encounter Jesus.[36] The earliest version of this commission, given in Mark 16:7, provides access to its visionary context, since the imperative comes from an angelic figure, the "young man" (*nean-iskos*) whom Mary, Mary of James, and Salome see when they go to anoint Jesus' corpse (16:1, 5).

The account's prelude includes a description of the tomb, but this introduction varies widely from gospel to gospel. For that reason, the story of the tomb should be considered within a reading of how each Evangelist assimilated earlier materials into a narrative that conceptualizes the resurrection in a distinctive way (see chapter 8). In any case, the vision proper is where Mary Magdalene's source comes to expression most directly (Mark 16:5-8):

> They went towards the memorial and saw a young man sitting on the right appareled in a white robe, and they were bewildered. But he says to them, "Do not be bewildered. You seek Jesus the crucified Nazarene. He is raised; he is not here. See—the place where they laid him. But depart, tell his students and Rock that he goes before you to Galilee; you will see him there, just as he said to you." They went out and fled from the memorial, because trembling and frenzy had them. And they said nothing to any one; they were afraid, because—

The resonance of Jesus' name (*Nazarênos*) with Mary's (*Magdalênê*) comes out especially in the statement of the young man. The term *Nazarênos* is consistent in Mark from 1:24, where the unclean spirit addresses Jesus as a *Nazarênos*—and "the holy one of God"—rather than as "Nazorean" (*Nazôraios*), which predominates in other gospels. Mark reflects an Aramaic derivation of the term, from Nazirite, identifying Jesus as "the holy one of God" as compared to the world of uncleanness, whether in the form of unclean spirits or—in the case of Mark 16:6—of death itself.

This reference to Jesus' Aramaic designation invites consideration of the young man's statements in that language (Mark 16:6-7):[37]

> [6] *La' titmehan/! Ba'/yan 'atiyn yat Yeshu'/*
> *nazar/a' de'izdeqeyph/. Mita/qam;*
> *la' taman/ hu'.*
> *Chaza'ah/—yat koka'/ deshavi'u/hi beyh.*

> Don't be dazed! You are seeking Jesus:
> The Nazirite that was hanged. He is raised;
> He is not there.
> Look—the tomb where they laid him.

> [7] *'iyzeyl/a', 'eymar/a' letalmiydo/hiy*
> *veleKeyph/a' dena/pheyq qodam/kon*

leGaliylla'; taman/ tichzon/eyh,
'aph k'amar/ lekhon/.

Depart, say to his students
And to Rock that he goes before you
To Galilee; there you will see him,
He even said to you.

Jesus' designation as a Nazirite makes his contrast with the uncleanness of a cemetery emphatic—that he has no place there follows. Although Aramaic *zaqaph* (to hang) might contextually be rendered in terms of crucifixion, its basic meaning also associates it with the passage "cursed be he who is hanged on a tree" (Deut 21:23; as quoted by Paul in Gal 3:13) and with the prediction of the Johannine Jesus that he is to be lifted up as was the bronze serpent in the wilderness (John 3:14-15; 12:32; cf. Num 21:8-9). These motifs have a rich history within the New Testament and in early Christianity, and the Aramaic usage helps to explain their emergence.

From a prosaic point of view, the truncated finale of the passage makes the Gospel seem defective. How could anyone end a story by saying, "they were afraid, because—"? In Greek, the last words read, *ephobounto gar*. The term *gar* regularly occurs in writings of the period and throughout Mark's Gospel in what linguists call the postpositive position. That is, it is the second element in a clause, introducing an explanation, in the way "because" does in English. In every other occurrence in the Gospel, the expected explanation follows the use of *gar*, so its absence here deliberately produces a feeling of truncation, taking the place of *'arey* in Aramaic. The abrupt ending climaxes the primitive but effective art of Mark, signaling how hard and disruptive it was, even for those intimate with Jesus, to grapple with the vision that signaled he had overcome death.

An understanding of Aramaic syntax also helps in appreciating how the ending arose. The silence of the women at the tomb is the last word in the Gospel, and it is an approving word. The Markan community is thereby instructed to maintain reserve in the face of persecution.[38] But it is very clear what that reserve is about: the young man at the tomb (Mark 16:6, 7) and Jesus himself at an earlier stage (Mark 8:31; 9:9, 31; 10:33, 34) leave no doubt that the full disclosure of Jesus' identity lies in his resurrection.

Indeed, because the young man says what Jesus had said, the declaration intimates that the two are to be identified: the women realize the import of what they see, but not yet *whom* they see.[39] That is, the young man is not called an "angel" in Mark, despite his fulfilling an angelic function, because he stands in for Jesus, *unless he is Jesus himself.* As the Markan catechumen approaches the Paschal Mystery, when baptism will occur and full access to Eucharist will be extended for the first time, the door to the truth of Jesus' resurrection is opened in the Gospel, but actual entry to that truth awaits further instruction. Even this preliminary vision, without a conscious encounter with Jesus himself, involves a transformation of Mary, Mary of James, and Salome. "Fear and ecstasy" accompanied the command to convey the message that Jesus had been raised.

Although Matthew largely follows the narrative of Mark in this regard, the Evangelist makes Mary and her companion follow through on the command of the angel to them, and the term *anggelos* is now explicitly used (Matt 28:5-8). But Matthew also adds an encounter (Matt 28:9-10): Jesus meets the women (here Mary Magdalene and "the other Mary"; v. 1), whose feet they grasp as they worship him, and he tells them, "Depart, report to my brothers so that they go away into Galilee, and they shall see me there." The apparent redundancy of this passage as compared to the vision at the tomb proper raises the possibility that it derives from a different source.[40]

Mark 16:1-8, in its reference to the "young man," shows signs of ambivalence, in which the vision might be of the risen Jesus rather than an angel. Matthew 28:9-10 resolves any doubt, for the moment in any case, since Matthew will introduce a new kind of doubt in 28:17. The resolution comes with typically Matthean language; the women fall at Jesus' feet and "worship" him (v. 9), just the response that is appropriate (see v. 17, in the appearance to the Eleven).[41] Their grasping Jesus' feet, however, may well be an earlier feature of the story,[42] since it corresponds to usages elsewhere in the New Testament and the Hebrew Bible.

In this second story concerning Mary and the other Mary, Jesus tells them to report to his "brothers" (Matt 28:10), just as he does in John 20:17, and the term corresponds to Paul's brief reference to Jesus' being seen by "more than five hundred brothers at once" (1 Cor 15:6). If those usages are associated, they indicate a Galilean tradition in which hundreds of Jesus' associates, styled as "brothers" (cf. Mark 3:31-35; Matt 12:46-59; Luke 8:19-21), experienced him after his death. Mary's visions, angelic and of Jesus himself, feature as the prelude to both the disciples' encounter with Jesus and that of the "brothers." In both cases, the prelude is to further visions in Galilee, which is dedicated as the place of realizing the resurrection in both Mark and Matthew. Indeed, the abrupt transition to the second account in Matthew, and the lack of any geographical reference, opens the possibility that Mary Magdalene and the other Mary saw Jesus and recognized him in Galilee, rather than in Jerusalem.

Quite apart from the statements in Matthew and Mark, Luke obviously does not share a Galilean bias, and the "two males" at the tomb refer only to how Jesus spoke to his followers "when he was still in Galilee" (Luke 24:6), a cunning correction. Even then, the Eleven dismiss as nonsense (*lêros*) the account of Mary Magdalene and Joanna and Mary of James and the other women with them (Luke 24:8-11).

John is no less trenchant in a bias toward Jerusalem rather than Galilee, at least until chapter 21, and Mary Magdalene's visions are recounted in the greatest detail among the Gospels and in respect of Mary alone (John 20:11-13):

> But Mary stood at the tomb outside, weeping. So while she was weeping, she bent into the memorial and perceived two angels in white, sitting—one at the head and one at the feet—where the body of Jesus had lain. And they say to her, "Woman, why do you weep?" She says to them, "They have taken my Lord, and I do not know where they have placed him."

In an evident development of Luke's scene, and a shared depiction of an empty tomb, John disrupts a literal sense of the sequence of time. He refers to Mary standing outside the tomb, although—at the last mention of her—she had run *from* there to announce Jesus' absence from the tomb to Simon Peter and the other disciple (John 20:2).[43]

Mary "perceives" two angels (v. 12), just the verb used in Mark 16:4 (in regard to the stone). Instead of entering the memorial, as in Luke (24:3), Mary—who is on her own in John—is described as bending into it (v. 11), just as the beloved disciple did in verse 5; Simon Peter actually enters and perceives the linen and the kerchief (vv. 6-7). The description of the "white" garments in which Mary sees the angels clad (John 20:12) picks up the vocabulary of Mark (16:5; Matt 28:3). The report of the angelic explanation to Mary is also comparable to the synoptic presentation (Mark 16:6-7; Matt 28:5-7; Luke 24:5-8). Luke 24:5 even has the two "males" begin with a question, as in John, albeit a different question (John 20:13).

John's angels, however, *sit* where the head and feet of Jesus' body had been (John 20:12). Their posture may have inspired the posture the women anticipate *they* will take in the Gospel of Peter 12:53 as part of the process of mourning. That is what would be expected on the basis of biblical (e.g., Ezek 26:16) and rabbinic (e.g., Eval Rabbati 6:1) literature.[44] But are the angels here, as Mary in the Gospel of Peter anticipates, sitting in puzzled mourning, or is their position simply a result of being in the close quarters of the tomb? The motif of angelic mourning appears in midrashim concerning Abraham's offering of Isaac (Genesis Rabbah 65.10).[45] But the question the angels pose to Mary in verse 13 implies that their perspective is not (or is no longer) one of mourning.

Just as vocabulary in the description of Mary's actions ties it to the story about Simon and Peter and the beloved disciple, so the angelic address of Mary as "woman" (v. 13) anticipates the risen Jesus' question in the next scene (v. 15). It is a challenging usage,[46] introduced as such in John (2:4; 4:21), but then with obvious affection in 19:26.

The slight variation of Mary's response to the question in verse 13 ties it to her statement earlier in the chapter (v. 2), although now Mary uses singular pronominal and verbal forms. That prepares the way for her to be entirely alone when she meets Jesus in the next scene, and the plural usage earlier may signal that a traditional form of the story about Mary going to the tomb *with other women*, such as the Synoptics present, had been known to John. This impression is confirmed in the scene between Mary and Jesus that follows (vv. 14-18).[47] In John 20:15, as in Matthew 28:9-10, the risen Jesus repeats the angelic words earlier in both presentations. The reference to touch (v. 17) is reminiscent of the women's grasping Jesus' feet in Matthew 28:9. Of greater note, Jesus in both Matthew 28:10 and John 20:17 tells Mary (and her companion in the case of Matthew) to report to his "brothers," and the operative verb is (*ap*)*anggellō* (Matt 28:10; John 20:17-18; with differing placement and syntax). These are indications of a common tradition in Matthew and John, involving an appearance of Jesus to Mary after her initial vision.

Two features, however, radically differentiate John's presentation from Matthew's. Mary's confusion of Jesus with a gardener (John 20:15)[48] is consistent with the notice earlier, unique to John, that the tomb where Jesus was placed was in a garden near to where he was executed (19:41). A probably independent appropriation of the gardener motif is attested by Tertullian (*The Shows* 30.6), who reports the claim among disbelieving Jews that a gardener removed Jesus' body. A much more elaborate version of that claim appears in the later *Toledoth Jesu*.[49] Subsequent traditions of that kind show that the garden setting is not at all likely to be a Johannine invention. The use of the tradition in controversy also would help account for why, even if the setting of Jesus' tomb were remembered as being in a garden, that fact might not be mentioned.

The second innovative Johannine element, Jesus' reference to his ascending to the Father (John 20:17), is even more emphatically prepared for in the body of the Gospel.[50] In the interchange with Nathanael, Jesus is the generic Son of Man, an example of created humanity, on whom the angels of God ascend and descend. He makes a cognate vision possible for others (John 1:49-51). In the interchange with Nicodemus, the heavenly or angelic Son of Man is alone the one who ascends into heaven, because he came down from heaven (3:13). That figure is set in parallel to the generic Son of Man, who must be lifted up so that everyone who believes in him might have eternal life (3:13-14). As the Gospel unfolds, the generic and heavenly Son of Man are fused; Jesus' preexistence is made into an explicit theme. References to the Son of Man that follow in the Gospel take this fusion further, with Jesus portrayed as final judge (5:26-29), bread of life (6:27, 53, 62), lifted up (8:28), fully identified with the Son of Man (9:35-38), and glorified (12:23; 13:31). In several cases, "rabbi" appears prior to these assertions of Jesus' true identity (4:31; 6:25; 9:2; 11:8).[51]

Particular attention has been devoted to Jesus' avoidance of having Mary touch him.[52] In John's presentation, the purpose of Jesus' appearance to Mary Magdalene is that she should announce his ascension to his brothers. When he next appears, the hearer or reader is prepared for the possibility there will be differences in what he says and does—and perhaps even in who precisely he is and looks like. At the same time, in John, Mary Magdalene does not touch Jesus even *prior* to the resurrection. The physical separation of Jesus from Mary runs through the entire Gospel—expressing an ambivalence toward Mary and feminine sexuality that is fiercely assertive. In the crucial scene of Jesus' anointing prior to his death, John (12:1-8) explicitly names Mary of Bethany, the sister of Martha and Lazarus, as the anointer who is an anonymous woman in the Synoptic Gospels. Having Jesus anointed by a woman who had a male protector (Lazarus), rather than Mary Magdalene, contributes to the pattern of the Magdalene's marginalization. John does more than suppress the anointer's identity (as happens in the Synoptics); he switches her identity. In the same way, only Joseph of Arimathea and Nicodemus anoint Jesus' corpse (19:38-42). Mary takes no part whatever in preparing his body for burial, any more than her anointing portends his death.

Mary Magdalene, rather than Simon Peter, is the first person in John's Gospel to say, "I have seen the Lord" (John 20:18). To this extent, John contradicts Paul's list. Yet touching is denied Mary; direct contact will come in the Fourth Gospel only when the risen Jesus breathes Holy Spirit into his followers (20:22). Seeing him is not an invitation to touch him; not even Thomas does that (20:27-28). Rather, any touch is at Jesus' initiative.[53] The specifically visionary medium of Mary's account raises the issue of how substantial her knowledge was, because her announcement is of the possibility of greater contact with Jesus. That element of doubt corresponds to her confusion of Jesus with a gardener (v. 15).

A later document, the Gospel of Mary 10:6-20, investigates the nature of her vision by means of a later dialogue between Jesus and Mary:

I saw the Lord in a vision and I said to him, "Lord, I saw you today in a vision." He answered and said to me, "You are privileged, because you did not waver at the sight of me. For where the mind is, there is the treasure." I said to him, "Lord, now does he who sees the vision see it through the soul or through the spirit?" The Savior answered and said, "He sees neither through the soul nor through the spirit, but the mind which is between the two—that is what sees the vision and is—"

Then the document breaks off for several pages.

Whatever Mary goes on to say in the missing part of the document, Peter and Andrew together rebuke Mary after her speech. Their anger—summed up in a rhetorical question—stems both from what she says and from what their paternalism considers her inferior gender (Gos. Mary 17:9–19:1): "Has he revealed these things to a woman and not to us?" Mary's articulate insight and her gender upsets Peter and his cohort. A woman had had a visionary breakthrough that permitted her to see Jesus' purpose in reaching out to gentiles before Peter himself did. The Gospel of Mary also understands that, in portraying the resurrection in trenchantly visionary terms (as the perception of the "mind," not of physical eyes or ears or hands), Mary directly contradicted a growing fashion in Christianity that conceived of Jesus in the flesh as victorious over the grave.

This Gospel reflects not only Mary's theory of vision as she had articulated it from the first century but also the controversies of later periods, using the characters of Peter and Andrew to portray the reaction against Mary within the Catholic Church during the second and third centuries of the Common Era. As theologians became increasingly materialistic in their conception of how Jesus rose from the dead and how all believers were to be resurrected, sources such as the Gospel of Mary fell into disrepute. The bishop of Lyons, Irenaeus—having inherited the millenarian theology of his teachers in Asia Minor—preached a physical resurrection of the flesh (*Against Heresies* 2.29; 4.18; 5.7–16, 36). Despite what Paul had clearly said in 1 Corinthians 15, Irenaeus dismissed anyone who did not go along with this millenarian literalism as a heretic. The Catholic Church of this period largely defined itself by its opposition to gnostic teachers, and therefore by an emphatic assertion of the value of the flesh, even if that meant contradicting Saint Paul. Mary's vision fell into disfavor.

The Gospel of Mary stood by Mary Magdalene's vision. Seeing Jesus here is unashamedly a perception of the "mind" (*nous* in both Greek and Coptic). Paul, whose view of the resurrection is compatible with Mary's, also articulated a theology of "mind" that agrees with this (1 Cor 2:9; 14:19).[54]

"Mind," for Paul as well as for the Gospel of Mary, was the instrument of lucid vision.

Paul's list, then, reflects not only different followers of Jesus (named and unnamed) but also differing cosmologies and views of the resurrection so distinctive that at moments contradiction among them becomes apparent. Questions typically raised about Jesus' appearance after his death (such as, Why do some of his acquaintances not recognize him? And how does he appear and disappear and yet eat and invite his students to touch him?) go beyond matters of detail. They even transcend the historian's desire to know whether the resurrection happened, because they raise the issue whether the resurrection can be thought of as a happening in the physical world at all.

Particularly among "all the apostles," the variation of views is manifest. The opening of the graves of the holy ones in Silas' conception is quite different from Barnabas' opening of the Scriptures, and neither aligns well with Mary Magdalene's claim—Paul to the contrary—that she was the first to "see the Lord," such that vision was the only permissible medium of contact with him. Paul himself attempted to assimilate his list of earlier apostles within his own cosmology of a spiritual body in the resurrection, but others would evidently have seen the matter differently. Indeed, the time after Paul's death saw a vigorous effort at a different assimilation of the apostolic testimony and efforts toward a resurrection science that have continued into our time. In an attempt to resolve those problems, Acts and the Gospels attempted by narrative means to coordinate differences into a master account. The idiom of Acts was prophecy; that of the Gospels was the story of the tomb. Both reflect efforts at reasoning with the resurrection.

III
Reasoning with the Resurrection

8

After Paul, beyond the Tomb

Introduction

The people listed by Paul by whom Jesus was seen after his death shared the claim that God had raised him from the dead: Peter, the Twelve, the More Than Five Hundred, James, All the Apostles (in particular, Silas, Barnabas, and Mary Magdalene),[1] and Paul himself affirmed their encounters. The very existence of the list (1 Cor 15:3-8) shows that by 56 CE—despite differences, inconsistencies, and outright contradictions among the sciences of the witnesses—it was possible to assert the singularity of the catalyst for these differing views: the resurrection itself.

Paul leans heavily on the language of tradition (already established in 1 Cor 11:2, 23) in the opening of his statement (15:3) of what the catalyst was and who was involved in the reaction it provoked. The list itself, together with the claim of a common catalyst, goes back to his meeting in Jerusalem with Peter (the chief exponent of the Galilean resurrection) and James, the brother of Jesus (the chief exponent for the Jerusalem school of the resurrection), in 35 CE.

Yet for all Paul's eagerness for unity in 1 Corinthians, a letter that sees him deploy the risen body of the Anointed as an identifying principle of the church generally (12:12-31),[2] when it comes to explaining how Jesus was raised from the dead, he insists on his own science, the most detailed in the New Testament. He had earlier joined with Silas in a more apocalyptic perspective (1 Thess 4:13-17), but in his own voice Paul became categorical in his assertion of the "spiritual body" of the Anointed in his resurrection and its implications for the resurrection of all (1 Cor 15:35-50). Faced with the reality that his traditional list reflected different views—some of them mutually exclusive—of how Jesus was raised from the dead, Paul set out his own science, grounded in his own experience as the basis for evaluating other accounts.[3]

Within the Gospels, the strands of tradition sometimes appear so closely woven together that the narrative represents a hybrid. John assigns Petrine forgiveness to Jesus' encounter with the Twelve (John 20:23; see chapter 5). Matthew gives the Twelve the worldwide mission conferred to the More Than Five Hundred in Galilee (Matt 28:19a; see chapter 5). In Acts, James' distinctive practice of Nazirite purity in connection with the resurrection is swallowed up by the account of Paul's last visit to Jerusalem (Acts 21:18-26; see chapter 6). "All the Apostles" (Silas, Barnabas, and Mary Magdalene) find their perspectives embedded within the larger narrative of the Synoptic Gospels and John (see chapter 7) so that they appear within a new context and for the most part anonymously.

Such interweaving of sources, up to and occasionally including hybridization, is common among the Gospels quite aside from the resurrection; passages such as the baptism, the transfiguration, and the crucifixion offer ready comparison. In that comparison, however, it is obvious that distinctive sources are more prevalent in the case of Jesus' resurrection, because the degree of variation among the Gospels is very high. Paul's list provides insight into why at that point each Gospel becomes unique. In any case, no impetus to develop a new science emerges when events such as the baptism, the transfiguration, and the crucifixion are concerned. They unfold within identifiably first-century cosmologies, and they conflict with even modern worldviews only partially. But a direct contradiction of an axiom of reality, such as the axiom that death is final, is not at issue.[4]

The process of amalgamating sources—a standard feature in the development of oral tradition into written manuscripts—is well represented within the evolution of the texts of the resurrection. But amalgamation alone could not have produced coherent accounts, because the sciences involved were too disparate. Alongside the usual evolution of tradition and its conflation of sources, there is another process at work in the Gospels. Each of them develops a take on the resurrection so as to coordinate traditions available but also to prefer the most intelligible explanation (according to the Evangelist) of how Jesus rose from the dead. This process was part of the overall develop-ment of understandings of the resurrection in the New Testament.

The resurrection featured for writers of the New Testament, not only the Evangelists but also authors such as Paul, as a key element of preach-ing and teaching. Coherence in regard to God's raising of Jesus from the dead, by means of either an immediate statement or the clear prospect of an explanation that would provide coherence, emerged as crucial over and above the circumstantial adjustments that traditions in the process of formation go through.

Two major innovations addressed this challenge: (1) Jesus' resurrection was rationalized as a prophetic announcement, so that continuity with the prophets of Israel *and* with the emergence of ongoing Christian prophecy provided an authoritative structure of meaning. During the same period, (2) a narrative of the circumstances in which Jesus' tomb was found offered a pivot for understanding the faith of his disciples. Both idioms of reasoning through the resurrection resulted not in any new science but in a coordinated preference among the sciences available at the time and in the place that each text was produced.

Prophetic Resurrection after Paul

Paul does not devote himself to a description of his own experience, leaving only allusions to an encounter with Jesus that might be described as either seeing the Lord or having the Son revealed within (1 Cor 9:1-2; Gal 1:15-16). He also refers circumstantially to "returning to Damascus" after a sojourn in Arabia; only then, three years later, did he go to Jerusalem and meet *Kêpha'* and James (Gal 1:17-19).

These incidental references are transformed within three different accounts in the book of Acts, resulting in similar but also mutually con-tradictory accounts of Jesus' appearance to Paul (Acts 9:1-22; Acts 22:3-21; Acts 26:8-20). In substance, each of these accounts provides its own view of the content of Paul's experience and of the means by which it unfolded. In effect, they correct Paul's vision in the direction of their own conception of prophecy. Prophetic presentation takes over Paul's own account and turns his experience into three related but different stories. They share a family resem-blance with Paul's own language. He refers to the prophetic moment that God's Son was revealed in him as "when it pleased the one who separated me from my mother's belly" (Gal 1:15; see chapter 4), an allusion to Isaiah (49:1) and Jeremiah (1:5).

Luke presents the stories as offering, in aggregate, a prophetic moment as decisive as Peter's vision at Joppa that caused him to visit the house of Cornelius and therefore offer baptism in Jesus' name to Godfearers (Acts 10:1-48; 11:1-18; 15:6-11; see chapter 6). Together, Peter and Paul in Luke's narrative represent the decisive movement toward non-Jewish populations;[5] in each case their moment of commissioning for this purpose is recounted three times. The variation in the case of the accounts concerning Paul is greater (although the Petrine accounts also vary), but Luke's aggregative presentation in the case of both apostles is evident.

As in the case of the presentation of Peter's vision, variation is to some extent natural, because the first iteration is direct narrative (Acts 9:1-22 [concerning Paul] and 10:1-48 [concerning Peter]), the second is the principal's own discourse (Acts 21:40–22:21 [Paul before the people on the temple steps] and 11:1-18 [Peter before the apostles and brothers in Jerusalem]), and the third appears in a forensic setting (Acts 26:1-23 [Paul's appeal to Herod Agrippa II] and 15:6-11 [Peter's account of himself before the meeting of the apostles and elders in Jerusalem]). Luke's mastery of this material is evident, but so are the inconsistencies involved in the presentation of Paul's commission to be an apostle.

The discrepancies among the three accounts of Paul's encounter with Jesus in Acts are all the more striking because they also overlap in their vocabulary. They share key narrative features that set them apart from what Paul himself says in Galatians and 1 Corinthians:

❖ Saul receives letters from the high priest(s) to bring followers of Jesus from Damascus to Jerusalem.
❖ A light and voice appear, identifying themselves as Jesus, whom Saul persecutes.

Both Acts 9 and Acts 22 present additional elements that may be assumed in the more summary version of events in Acts 26:

❖ Saul is led blinded into the city.
❖ Ananias meets him there.
❖ Saul is healed, baptized, and takes up his apostolate.

Given such consistency in structure and the coordination of vocabulary, differences from one account to the next can hardly be oversights. In Acts 9, Paul's companions on the way hear the voice but see no one (v. 7), while in Acts 22 they "perceived the light, but they did not hear the voice" (v. 9).[6] Acts 26 (vv. 13-14) is not as explicit in its description but perhaps accords more with Acts 22 than with Acts 9. Discrepancies of this kind raise the possibility

of marks of earlier traditions that Luke has incorporated, each with idiosyn-
crasies that have not been edited away.

These discrepancies, however, are less consequential than differences in
regard to how Paul's (or Saul's) apostolate is mediated to him, and what its
content is. In Acts 9, Ananias—simply described as a "student" (v. 10)—
has a vision contemporaneous with Paul's call, in a manner reminiscent of
the coordinated visions of Peter and Cornelius in Acts 10:1-33. In Acts 9,
however, Ananias' visionary insight is greater than that of the Godfearer
Cornelius in Acts 10. In fact, Ananias—despite his initial reluctance to heal
a persecutor (vv. 13-14)—learns *before Paul refers to his own purpose* that
the former persecutor is "a vessel of choice for me to bear my name before
nations, and even kings of sons of Israel!" (v. 15). Ananias' contact and that of
other, unnamed students (v. 19) triggers Paul to announce Jesus as both Son
of God (v. 20) and the Anointed (v. 22).

Acts 9 does not have Ananias formally give Paul his commission to
preach to the nations, but the inference remains that Paul on his own would
not have understood his purpose. The underlying conception might be that
Paul came to know his purpose when he was baptized (vv. 18-20, a moment
he himself does not mention in Galatians), so that Ananias would play an
instrumental role both for Paul in bringing him to baptism and for the hearer
in explaining Paul's purpose.

In Acts 22, Ananias' message to Paul is that he has seen the "just" or
"righteous" one (v. 14) precisely the way Jesus is identified in the speeches
of Peter (Acts 3:14) and of Stephen (Acts 7:52). The language accords with
Luke's Christology (cf. Luke 23:47), which is reminiscent of the Wisdom of
Solomon's (2:18).[7] Stephen's example is specifically cited by Paul (Acts 22:20),
and in a unique context; his departure from Jerusalem is motivated by an
additional vision of Jesus while "in ecstasy," which includes his dispatch to the
nations (vv. 17-21). Although Paul in his own letters speaks as a man who has
had several "visions and revelations of the Lord" (2 Cor 12:1), his personal
account of his commission in Galatians 1:16 does not appear to allow for a
lapse of time and a repeated vision before his realization that he was sent to
the gentiles,[8] as Acts 22:16-21 insists was the case.

Finally, Acts 26 has Paul dispense with any reference to Ananias during
the course of narrating his vision near Damascus and has the self-identified
risen Jesus quote a metaphor about kicking against the barbs that derives
from Euripides (v. 14).[9] More consequentially, an enriched paraphrase of Isaiah 42 also features, to articulate the purpose of leading the nations to God
by means of repentance (vv. 16-18).

So the three accounts of Paul's conversion involve three interrelated but different versions of how Paul came to his apostolic purpose of preaching to the gentiles. In Acts 9, Ananias is the first person mentioned to learn of this from the risen Jesus (Acts 9:15); in Acts 22, Ananias—no longer simply a "student" of Jesus but "devout according to the Law" and well regarded by the Judaic population—also plays a crucial role (Acts 22:12-16), but Paul himself has received instruction from the risen Jesus to address the gentiles during a second vision in the temple (vv. 17-21); Acts 26, finally, makes Paul the sole recipient of "the heavenly vision" and its imperative (vv. 15-20). Although Luke has beautifully coordinated the three accounts, their differing views of how the insight of Jesus' resurrection came to be delivered undermines the claim that a single community tradition explains the presentation of Acts.[10] Rather, in each case, a distinctive prophetic circle comes to voice.

The variations among the episodes are less drastic than the discrepancy with Paul's own statement, since Galatians 1:16-17 seems to exclude contact with Ananias or anyone else. After all, here Paul says, "I did not confer at once with flesh and blood, nor did I go up to Jerusalem to those who were apostles before me, but I departed to Arabia, and again returned to Damascus." The reference to Damascus offers a bridge to the episodes in Acts, but no reference or allusion to Ananias can be found in Paul's own succinct account.

The perspective he insists upon in Galatians might suggest why that is the case. Paul's explanation for what occurred near Damascus is that God decided to "uncover" (*apocaluptô*) his Son within Paul (Gal 1:15). Similarly, he says that he received his message through an "uncovering (*apokalupsis*) of Anointed Jesus" (vv. 11-12). Paul uses the same noun, *apokalupsis*, to explain why he went from Antioch to Jerusalem fifteen years later to lay out his message before the other apostles (2:1-2). The embassy in regard to circumcision is reported as ordered from Antioch in Acts 15:1-2, but the leadership in that city has already been described as prophetic, acting under the command of the Holy Spirit (Acts 13:1-3). Paul can refer to contact with prophetic circles as a matter of apocalypse,[11] rather than as consultation with "flesh and blood." He glossed over Ananias for the same reason he glossed over his own baptism: for Paul, both were incidental instruments of the substantial reality of the revelation of the Anointed within him.

The people comprising the prophets and teachers in Antioch are identified along with Paul in Acts 13:1-3 as Barnabas, Symeon called Niger, Lucius of Cyrene, and Manaen, a companion of Herod Antipas; prayer, fasting, and communal devotion to the Lord occasion the speech of the Spirit in the scene. Although Luke is sparing with detail, sporadic or incidental references indicate that Ananias was another such prophetic figure in Damascus, while others—some of them named (Agabus, Judas, Silas)—are described as from Jerusalem and depicted as active as far away as Antioch (Acts 11:27-28; 15:27, 32; 21:10-11). Ananias' explanation to Paul might have been the source of the apostle's conviction that Jesus was both Son of God and the Anointed (Acts 9:20, 22), terms Paul himself uses in the corresponding section of Galatians (1:12, 16).

The complete absence of reference to Arabia in any of the episodes in Acts is a factor that demands correction from Galatians 1:17, and Paul's usage of Arabia elsewhere in the letter (Gal 4:24-25) suggests that his experience there caused him to see the law in a manner relegated to Christ.[12] Luke sees the contrast in far less stark terms, and "Arabia" as a place for the contrast between the torah and the risen Jesus is either not in his tradition or not on his intellectual horizon.

The Christology of the "just one" in Acts 22:14 suggests the prophetic circle of Hellenists—Greek-speaking Jews in Jerusalem—of whom Stephen was the most famous example among the disciples (Acts 6:1-10; 7:52). The addendum in Acts 22:17-21, concerning Paul's vision of Jesus in the temple,[13] assumes Paul's eventual contact with Hellenists in Jerusalem, the mortal hostility of some of them, and the decision of "the brothers" to send Paul away (Acts 9:26-30). Luke somehow sees the descriptions in Acts 9:26-30 and 22:17-21 as compatible, which they are *if and only if* the decision to depart from Jerusalem (the link between the two passages) is regarded as of a prophetic order.

Luke implies such an understanding in Acts 26, when he has Paul's commission spelled out (vv. 14-18) without any reference to Ananias, whose crucial role has already been detailed. In the prophetic world of Acts, content takes precedence over human instrumentality, as it did in Paul's own account of his experience. In the case of Acts' version of Paul's commission (Acts 26:17-18, 20), the goal agrees with the prophetic charge in Acts 13:1-3, which involves programmatic, geographical movement into the nations. Luke himself, in the narrative strategy developed in Acts, takes on the mantle of the prophets and teachers of his native Antioch,[14] whose program he adapted in literary terms.

The content of all three accounts in the book of Acts is prophetic, and the way Paul's experience is recounted mirrors the vision of Daniel, a classic model for the belief that seers could be given personal messages by angels that they were to convey to the faithful. In chapter 10 of Daniel, the angel (perhaps Gabriel; cf. 9:21) provides the seer with the secret of the end of days.

Daniel's vision of the angel is much more detailed than any account of Paul's vision, but the emphasis on light is a common element, as Gabriel, with a face like lightning and eyes flashing fire, is described as clothed in linen and girdled with gold (Dan 10:5-6). As compared to Acts' narrative about what happened on the road to Damascus, the very next sentence in Daniel is truly striking (Dan 10:7):

> And I, Daniel, alone saw the vision, and the men that were with me did not see the vision. But a great quaking fell upon them, so that they fled to hide themselves.

That corresponds to what Acts narrates about Paul's companions (Acts 9:7), so frightened they are "speechless, hearing a voice, but seeing no one."

Given that pivotal Scripture, it is telling that Acts 22:9 agrees Paul's companions were frightened but has them *see the light*, without *hearing the voice*. Obviously, Acts is more comfortable about the subjectivity of Paul's revelation than are some literally minded commentators in the modern period.[15] The point of both Acts and Daniel is that the companions do not fully share the experience, although they know an apocalypse is going on. Luke's third iteration of Paul's apocalypse (Acts 26:13-18) addresses a Jewish king as well as a ruler designated directly by Rome. This description comes closest to Daniel 10, because Paul refers to what he personally saw and heard, while his fellow travelers simply collapse in a heap on the ground.

Jerusalem seems to have been the source of the second version of the prophetic tradition in Acts 22, just as Damascus likely donated the material in Acts 9. In a focus even more tightly on Paul, Acts 26:18 cites Isaiah 42:7, 16, but enhances the apostle's standing as compared to the prophet in the biblical text, so that he will move those who hear him from the authority of Satan to that of God and so have a share among those sanctified by faith. Here, it is the risen Jesus himself that "was seen" by Paul (v. 16); a figure such as Ananias is less consequential. In these stories in aggregate, the last perhaps from Antioch, the disclosure of the risen Jesus occurs in a prophetic context.

That context enjoyed a long life. Although the biblical Apocalypse is often treated as a text of a completely different genre from those that narrate Jesus' resurrection, the author tells of how Jesus, specifically as risen from the dead (Rev 1:17-18), came to him. On the island of Patmos, during worship on Sunday, the Lord's Day (1:1-9), Jesus commissions John to write seven letters to each of seven churches (1:10–3:22) in Asia Minor. This commission is built into the outset of the book, which says that it is "an apocalypse of Anointed Jesus" (Rev 1:1).

In writing to the seven churches (Ephesus, Smyrna, Pergamon, Thyatira, Sardis, Philadelphia, and Laodicea), John sometimes alludes to the difficulties they face. In Ephesus, false apostles (2:2); in Smyrna, defamation from the "synagogue of Satan" (2:9); in Pergamon, martyrdom (2:13) and false teaching (2:14-15) in the city where "Satan dwells" on his throne; in Thyatira, a seductress styled as Jezebel who encourages fornication and eating meat sacrificed to idols (2:20); and varying degrees of faintheartedness in the last three—Sardis, Philadelphia, and Laodicea (3:1-22). The situation of each community is, by definition, unprecedented, since their religion is new. The risen Jesus specifies problems that the historical Jesus never confronted. False teaching and lack of enthusiasm are the most frequent problems cited; the tension between experience on earth and the promises of heaven is produced less by a particular edict of government than by the seer's realization of how far his world is from the new Jerusalem.

Apocalyptic prophecy was typically attributed to a figure in the distant past. For example, the putative author of the biblical book of Daniel lived centuries before the Seleucid crisis; he therefore appeared to predict events accurately until the time that the apocalypse was written during the second century BCE. The failure of their predictions after the period of their composition permits apocalypses to be dated. Pseudonymity—in this case, attribution to Daniel, a Babylonian figure made to "predict" the Seleucid crisis—is a characteristic of apocalyptic writing. Daniel's apocalypse involved surreal, sequential images, whose meaning was explained by angelic intervention from the heavenly court through the pseudonymous author. The impact of the whole was designed to provide authoritative hope and the resolve to assure the temple's restoration, when judgment is given to "one like a son of man" (Dan 7:13), the heavenly representative of Israel. In the case of the Apocalypse, however, the author is identified as a figure of the present (Rev 1:9), not the past, so that the issue of what he sees, rather than who he is, becomes paramount.

The Revelation of John is committed to the world of heavenly vision, to what the seer sees and hears beyond this world, as well as to interaction with the heavenly court of angels. These fundamental components of apocalypse are depicted in searing detail, reflecting a deep commitment to these elements and a determined drive to interpret the meaning of what is seen and heard. In fact, heavenly seeing, heavenly hearing, and engagement with angels—judged in terms of the proportion of the text they cover and their intensity—are pressed to a new level in the Revelation as compared to Daniel and other apocalypses. At the same time, John of Patmos takes up scriptural antecedents: the seraphic hymn of Isaiah (6:1-5 in Rev 4:6b-11), the throne visions of Ezekiel (1:4-28) and Zechariah (3:1-9, both reflected in Rev 4:1-6a), as well as the identification of God's agent of judgment as "Son of Man." Key components of John's vision of the risen Jesus confirm its participation in the genre of apocalypse: he is the Danielic "son of man" who comes on the clouds (Rev 1:7, 13; Dan 7:13) and receives a kingdom and glory that all shall serve (Rev 1:5-6; Dan 7:14).[16] Even the appearance of this Son of Man (Rev 1:13-15) is reminiscent of what Daniel says of both God (Dan 7:9) and of an angelic figure (Dan 10:5-6). These elements are woven together in order to concentrate on Jesus, but they are also redolent of the divine throne, with its seven spirits (Rev 1:4), an apparent allusion to Zechariah 3:9. By means of an apocalyptic style of prophecy, the Revelation deploys the dynamic, shared language of vision within the Scriptures of Israel.[17] But it does so not merely on the basis of verbal interplay but within the genre of an actual cosmic vision.[18]

The reference in 1:18 to the keys of Hades, drawn from Isaiah 22:22 (cf. also Rev 3:7), features language already taken up in Matthew 16:18-19, and by the time of John of Patmos much of the scriptural imagery used in his Revelation had already been used by Jesus' followers.[19] This may explain the rapid progression of visionary images in the Apocalypse. After the letters to the seven churches, the visionary scene shifts. Instead of the seer opening his eyes to Christ's presence on earth, he looks into heaven itself, invited to enter an open gate or door to see the throne of God in heaven, where Christ appears as a slain Lamb and as a Lion (4:1–5:14). The seer no longer sees heavenly realities on earth but looks into the secrets of heaven itself, where angelic worship echoing the temple liturgy in Jerusalem surrounds the divine throne. The Wedding of the Lamb (19:6-10) and the portrayal of Christ as the conquering Word of God who defeats all enemies (19:11-21) show that the Apocalypse deliberately avoids fixity in its pursuit of the reality of the Son of God but engages in a visionary polysemy that gives the Apocalypse its distinctive character.

The Apocalypse explicitly designates itself as "words of prophecy" (Rev 1:3); John of Patmos concludes his book (22:7-21) with a solemn warning not to tamper with it in any way. The text conveys power in its cadences as well as in its visions. At one level, the warning not to change John's wording (22:18-19) is surprising, since the Revelation's Greek is basic—on occasion to the point of being formally ungrammatical. These mistakes are so obvious that they sometimes appear deliberate. In addition to employing a form of the Koine dialect that took his message out of the literary mainstream, the author called special attention to some of what he said by means of disruptions in the expected grammar. Either directly or as artifice, these disruptions represent an underlying Semitic grammar that interrupts the normal flow of Greek.

The integrity of those visions requires faithful transmission and grappling with vision *as* vision rather than as code or calendar or plan of battle. Neither adding to nor subtracting from John's words (Rev 22:18-19) means taking his rugged expression of what he calls "signs" (12:1, 3; 15:1) for what they are, insights into heaven granted to those on earth because God has "signaled" them (1:1).

In the prophetic tradition from which the Apocalypse draws, a sign is a perception that opens up the prospect of the divine realm to those who dwell in this world. For that reason, no sign, no vision, can be reduced to the conditions of the politics or circumstances of any passing moment. Rather, they await the witness of those who see the signs in their own terms, as invitations to join in the reality of God's power in heaven. This perspective opened up a remarkable literature, in which Jesus is depicted as alive and continuing to teach the community dedicated to his resurrection.

The Gospel of Thomas presents itself as the words of the "living" Jesus, conferred to Didymus Judas Thomas.[20] The sense in which Jesus is "living" and teaching in such a way that he can promise—"The one who finds the interpretation of these sayings will not taste death" (preface and saying 1)—is brought out through the Gospel of Thomas as a whole. Saying 22, however, is the most specific analysis within the Gospel of Thomas of what this deathless state entails:

> When you make the two one, and when you make the inner like the outer and the outer like the inner, and the upper like the lower, and when you make male and female into a single one, so that the male will not be male nor the female be female, when you make an eye in the place of an eye, a hand in place of a hand, a foot in place of a foot, an image in place of an image, then you will enter the Kingdom.

One aspect of the saying, making "male and female into a single one," is singled out for explanation at the close of the Gospel of Thomas. There, Simon Peter declares that Mary should go away from the disciples altogether (saying 114): "Let Mary depart from us." His position becomes trenchant as he goes on to say: "Females are not worthy of the life," referring to resurrected, spiritual life. Peter's declaration would mean that Mary—and women in general—cannot be involved in interpreting Jesus' words. They would not even be included among the disciples who remembered and treasured Jesus' teaching. Peter's judgment in the Gospel of Thomas implies that men alone could recall, understand, and benefit from Jesus' wisdom, and that resurrection was for men only.

That antagonism may reflect tension between the increasingly patriarchal hierarchy of those who called themselves Catholic and the attempt of many Christians to maintain Mary's leading role among disciples as a teacher of vision. Over time, the latter group came to be called "gnostic," but there has been a tendency to forget that the distinction between them and "Catholic" identity was far from firm in early Christianity.[21] Because Peter had been a foundational apostle in great cities such as Jerusalem, Antioch, and Rome, he was a natural symbol of male leadership in Catholic Christianity. The contrast with Mary Magdalene was inevitable, and Peter's contradiction of Mary emerges as a trope in some gnostic sources.

But it would be superficial to claim that Simon Peter's intervention, "Let Mary depart from us," and the trenchant antifeminism it articulates, reflects programmatic disagreement between the Gospel of Thomas' community and the emerging hierarchy of Catholic Christianity. Peter appears in the Nag Hammadi library more often than Mary does, and in an unequivocally positive light as a hero of the gnostic quest. He is much more than a straw man to represent Catholic authoritarianism.

In the Gospel of Thomas, Jesus rebukes Peter's rejection of Mary with the book's last words: "Every female who makes herself male will enter the kingdom of heaven" (saying 114). The Coptic text of the Gospel of Thomas leaves no doubt about the meaning of these words, because "female" and "male" are the particular words for sexual difference, as in English. Saying 22 makes sexual transformation one aspect of becoming one with the heavenly counterpart that people are searching for in their lives. The final result is androgyny, because "the male will not be male nor the female be female." The whole process occurs within a total reconciliation with one's heavenly image,[22] the divine template from which humanity was created. The Gospel of Thomas presents the "living Jesus" as a persistent reality; integration with him fulfils the promise of transcending death.

The Gospel of Philip, a third-century Coptic text, also speaks of salvation as a matter of uniting with one's heavenly image, in a way that serves as a commentary on the Gospel of Thomas 22. The Gospel of Philip specifies by means of symbolic language how and where marriage with a divine image can occur (II.3.67.29–34):[23]

> The Lord did everything in a mystery, a baptism and a chrism and a Eucharist and a redemption and a bridal chamber. The Lord said, "I came to make

the things below like the things above, and the things outside like those inside, I came to unite them in that place."

The "bridal chamber," the apex in the sequence of mystery, is the "place" where above and below and outside and inside are reconciled, where a person merges with one's heavenly counterpart.

The Gospel of Philip never gives a prosaic description of the "bridal chamber," but its emphasis on the value of anointing suggests that unction was involved. According to the Gospel of Philip (II.3.74.13–23), "Anointing is superior to baptism, for it is from the word 'anointing' that we have been called 'Christians,' certainly not because of the word 'baptism.'" Taking off from the basic meaning of the term Christ (*khristos* in Greek, "anointed"), this teaching discovers the essence of Christianity in the ointment offered by Jesus and his followers.[24] The esoteric meaning of being anointed, a prominent sacrament throughout the ancient period of Christianity, proves central to the emerging portrayal of Mary Magdalene and her later legacy.

Just before Mary Magdalene first appears in this Gospel, the Gospel of Philip comments on the inner, spiritual sense conveyed by the kiss (II.3.59.2–5):

> For it is by a kiss that the perfect conceive and give birth. For this reason we also kiss one another. We receive conception from the grace that is in each other.

The Gospel of John also details the practice as part of the ritual of earliest Christianity, when the risen Jesus (John 20:19) greets his disciples with the traditional greeting in Aramaic, *Shelema'*—"Peace." A kiss on the mouth often went with this greeting, and John shows that is the case here, because Jesus next "breathes on" his disciples, infusing them with Holy Spirit and the power to forgive sins (John 20:21-23). The breath of Spirit went with the exhalation of one practitioner into another in an ancient practice that stretched from the Gospel of John through the Gospel of Philip and included Hippolytus, the third-century Roman liturgist.[25] The Gospel of Philip explains the kiss in purely spiritual terms, relating the practice to understanding the nature of true intercourse (Gos. Phil. II.3.78.25–31): "So spirit mingles with spirit, and thought consorts with thought, and light shares with light."

Even as supplemented with the commentary in the Gospel of Philip (which in any case comes from a century later than the Gospel of Thomas), the precise practice involved in the conception of the Gospel of Thomas remains elusive. Yet it does appear to be a ritual and visionary process. There are hints of a connection to the appearance to James in the Gospel of the

Hebrews. Clement of Alexandria attributes to the Gospel of the Hebrews a statement that also appears in the Gospel of Thomas 1: that in the quest for the interpretation of the living Jesus' words, one should continue seeking until one finds, is dismayed, then is astonished, and finally will reign over all. Although it might be that Clement assigns the reference by error, his identification seems emphatic.[26] In addition, the Gospel of Thomas itself (in saying 12) directs Jesus' disciples for guidance, no matter where they come from, to "James the Just, for whose sake heaven and earth came into existence." James is identified as a source of wisdom after the resurrection, understood in a fashion that confers leadership on him and maintains a link with Jesus.

Yet the streams of tradition that flow into and from the Gospel of Thomas appear multiple. Although the Gospel of Philip provides a ritual context for saying 22, and a connection with James may seem plausible, the Acts of Peter attributes to Peter himself, as he is crucified upside down, a version of the saying. He quotes "the Lord" as teaching that "knowledge of the Kingdom" comes only from the inversion of which the saying speaks, because it stands for reconciliation with the primal man (Acts Pet. 38).[27] Although the Acts of Peter need not be taken to contradict the setting implied in the Gospel of Philip, it clearly shapes interpretation in terms of repentance, which the cross occasions, rather than anointing.

Although the precise practices of visionary transformation are difficult to specify, confidence in that process is palpable within the New Testament and well beyond. Texts styled as gnostic participate in this confidence, but it is not possible to limit prophetic engagement with the resurrection to sectarian sectors within Christianity. Christian prophecy is a powerful adaptation of conceptions of vision from Second Temple Judaism, in which the one who "sees" becomes part of what is seen, transferred to the heavenly realm (as in the Apocalypse) or united with a heavenly counterpart (as in the Gospel of Thomas and the Gospel of Philip).

The fundamental question raised by the process is not the reality of the resurrection, taken for granted to a degree that indicates how powerfully it permeated the environment of early Christianity with all its variety. As a catalyst, it both triggered—and then altered—a series of resurrection sciences. But variegation in how Jesus was seen as raised from the dead provoked the issue of identifying Jesus as the actual source of transformative vision.[28] The more visionary his presence, the greater the potential for doubt concerning who exactly was present. Mary Magdalene, identified persistently within the prophetic, visionary idiom of the resurrection, also appears as the anchor of another idiom: the narrative tradition of the tomb of Jesus, which attempted to remove such doubt.

Emptying Jesus' Tomb

Mary Magdalene, in a variety of tellings of the narrative, is placed at Jesus' tomb, as the location from which encounters with him after his death are promised. The critical connection is between Jesus as buried and Jesus as risen: that alone permits identification of the one who is risen with the person who was known by his followers, because he was known to have died. That issue becomes all the more fraught when accounts of encounters with him after death involve a failure to recognize him,[29] doubt,[30] or in Paul's case a lack of personal familiarity with the living Jesus in the first place.[31]

As the scene develops in the trajectory through the Gospels, the link between the gravesite and the eventual encounters with Jesus is articulated differently. The claim of the tomb being empty, which has obsessed modern interpretation to the point that it is projected into texts that mention no such thing, represents only one such articulation.[32] Along the trajectory of development, the grave becomes empty rather than starting that way. Even more important, interest is by no means restricted to the issue of not finding a corpse. Other emphases intrude, in some cases seizing greater prominence than descriptions of the tomb.

In Mark, who represents the beginning of the trajectory, three women— Mary Magdalene and Mary of James and Salome—have a vision at the *opening* of the tomb. What they see turns them around, directing them to instruct Jesus' disciples and Peter, so that they might "see" Jesus in Galilee (Mark 16:1-8). The three women are the first to know that Jesus had been raised from the dead. As named, they are the same three that appear in Mark's account of Jesus' death, with usage of the term "Sabbath" a linguistic echo of the timing of the burial,[33] and they are listed in the same order as in 15:40.

The only difference is that "Mary, mother of James the less and Joses," in the earlier passage becomes "Mary of James" at the tomb, a change easily explicable as abbreviation. It is much less straightforward to appreciate why, in the intervening scene of the interment (Mark 15:47), Salome is omitted and the second Mary is called "Mary of Joses." The variation may reflect variant traditions of who all the women were, but in each case the verb *theôreô* (meaning to "perceive" or "observe"; cf. Mark 16:4) is used. With that degree of coordination, the variation of the named witnesses becomes more striking and at the same time difficult to account for, although Mary Magdalene's identification throughout Mark is stable.

In the present state of the text, Mark underlines Mary Magdalene's importance. The threefold use of her "perceiving" (at the death, 15:40; at the interment, 15:47; and at the visit to the tomb, 16:4) may be compared to

Paul's creedal assertion in 1 Corinthians 15:3-4 that Christ died, was buried, and rose again.[34] Only Mary Magdalene and Mary of (James and) Joses correlate to that threefold claim of witness in Mark. At the same time, the variation of the naming of witnesses and the overlap with Paul's apostolic tradition tell against the analysis that Mark should be seen as the inventor of the story of the tomb.[35]

Mary Magdalene appears first in this account, and her surname "the Magdalene" resonates with Jesus': "the Nazarene." Mary is on her way with Mary of James and Salome to anoint Jesus' corpse, and that confirms the inference that the Magdalene had been the nameless anointer who prepared Jesus before his death for burial (Mark 14:3-9). That action and Jesus' response is crucial to an understanding of her experience that God had raised Jesus from the dead. Her first anointing encouraged Jesus to accept death, while her second attempt at anointing occasioned her assurance of his triumph over death.

The characteristically choppy style of Mark is evident in chapter 16, mitigated in one textual stream (represented by the later manuscripts Koridethi and Beza).[36] The stream adds a participle (*poreutheisai*, "proceeding") prior to the verb "purchased" in verse 1, providing Mark with at least a modicum of the hypertaxis preferred in Greek literary style. With or without that addition, the timing of Mark suggests liturgical usage. Sabbath has passed at sundown, but the rising of the sun marks the women's approach to the tomb. This timing reflects primitive practices of worship. In the earliest non-Christian account of worship within the church, Pliny the Younger reported to the emperor Trajan that, under torture, believers admitted that they "gathered regularly before light on a set day in order to join in saying a hymn to Christ as to a god" (*Letter to Trajan* 10.96).[37]

The belated concern of the women (Mark 16:3) over the removal of the stone that two of them had seen rolled into place (Mark 15:46-47) pivots into the following scene. But then their initial action itself is also belated, in that they wish to complete the preparation of the body, a task that Joseph of Arimathea had not fulfilled in Mark's conception. Their timing is off as compared to the action they intend, but it will prove exactly commensurate with what is to be disclosed.

The action of the women as described in Mark 16:5 is not articulated so as to emphasize, or even to establish, that the tomb is empty. The stone has been removed, and the women "went" (reading *elthousai* with Vaticanus, among the two earliest continuous manuscripts) toward (*eis*) the site when they are interrupted by their seeing a young man. Later manuscripts read that they "went into" the site (*eiselthousai* with *eis*). That wording without much question at all implies entry into the tomb or cave, which makes Mark comparable to Luke 24:3, where a different set of women explicitly enters the tomb and do not find Jesus' body. Such harmonizations of Mark with later Gospels are common in the manuscript tradition; their purpose is to make the earliest Gospel agree with the fuller texts of Gospels that came to be more widely used. Efforts of this kind are rightly taken by textual critics—as a matter of course—to indicate a later "correction" of texts toward a canonical standard. This same process also resulted in Mark's being provided with an artificial ending (vv. 9-20), which is a summarized pastiche of references chiefly drawn from Luke.[38] In any case, no matter what manuscript is consulted, there is no statement in Mark as there is in Luke of the women's proceeding into the cave past the entrance and to the ledge where a corpse would be placed in a burial cave.

Once the account in Mark is taken on its own terms, terms donated by the source derived from Mary Magdalene discussed in the last chapter, the ending of the Gospel emphasizes Jesus' purity, his incompatibility with the place of death, and the understandable astonishment of the women. The tomb in every version—whether or not it is described as empty—produces astonishment,[39] but for differing reasons. By itself, it provides no proof of the resurrection in any version of the account. In the case of Mark, the trajectory of surprise is that the women go to anoint Jesus' corpse but then are turned away.

In Matthew, the pattern of a mandate for vision elsewhere, in Galilee rather than Jerusalem, is emphasized by an earthquake and the active intervention of an angel, elements that transform the scene (Matt 28:1-8). Matthew has Mary Magdalene go to the tomb with "the other Mary" (Matt 28:1) and uses the plural of "Sabbath" to signal the opening of the entire week, but evidently during the night. Where Mark represents one kind of liturgical timing for the events, Matthew aligns with the vigil of Easter, which was kept from the evening when Sabbath begins, and marks the resurrection as the light that dawns in darkness. This accords with sources such as the *Peri Paskha* of Melito of Sardis,[40] where the sacrifice of lambs during the night of Passover offers a type of Christ's death.

It is unclear whether the "other" Mary is supposed to be the same person as Mark's "Mary of James" (Mark 16:1), and Matthew loses track of Salome—unless, following a harmonizing tradition of interpretation, she is taken as "the mother of the sons of Zebedee" in Matthew 27:56[41]—although Mark names her as one of the women at the tomb. These are indications that this key story was reshaped prior to the writing of the Gospels, and that reshaping came at the cost of destabilizing the memory of particular women.

At least, however, Matthew's language of Mary Magdalene and "the other Mary" is consistent (unlike Mark's) between the scene of the interment (Matt 27:61) and their visit to the tomb after the Sabbath. Although the verb "perceive" is absent in the earlier case (as compared to Mark 15:47), Matthew preserves the usage in 28:1. That is a residue of preparation for a visionary narrative comparable to Mark's, which has largely been overtaken by the apocalyptic intervention (from the tradition of Silas, as described in the last chapter) of an earthquake and an angel.

Matthew makes the young man at the tomb described in Mark into the explicitly heavenly representative of the previously introduced, physically verifiable earthquake (Matt 28:2 and 27:51-53). The scene is no longer purely visionary, as in Mark, but details a supernatural intervention into the physical world with tangible consequences. Matthew's explanation that the guards (another unique element among the Synoptics) became "as dead" (Matt 28:4) permits the women to become the center of attention. In contrast, the Gospel of Peter 9:35–10:40 makes the guards (now Roman soldiers) into principal witnesses before the women arrive on the scene. Yet even so, the women are utterly passive in Matthew and without the specific purpose in arriving at the tomb that they have in Mark. They are less crucial to the scene than in Mark, because in Matthew the young man of the earlier Gospel explicitly becomes an angel with the appearance of lightning and in a white garment, and divine intervention is as unmistakable as the earthquake. The paralysis of the guards attests the angel's presence, and the women do not keep silent, as in Mark; great joy overcomes their fear, and they report their experience to Jesus' disciples.

Mary Magdalene survives Matthew's preference for apocalyptic materials derived from Silas and his signature earthquake, but she appears in a reduced role. Matthew ignores her purpose in coming to the tomb. She and the "other" Mary come not to anoint Jesus but only to "perceive" (28:1) his grave; the threefold usage in Mark—to signal the women's witness of the death, burial, and vision—is not maintained. That change breaks a link with the woman with the alabaster jar, although Matthew preserves this narrative (26:6-13), while Luke omits it completely. The delicate poetics of Mark are progressively overruled and discarded as the synoptic tradition unfolded: Mary is marginalized, and her deep connection with anointing is submerged.

Matthew overshadows the connection between Mary's ritual anointing and Jesus' resurrection with its unique earthquake, the second reference to the earthquake in the Gospel. The first is anachronistically embedded within the crucifixion (27:51-53): "And look: the curtain of the Temple was split from top to bottom in two, and the earth quaked, and the rocks were split, and the memorials were opened and many bodies of the holy ones who slept were raised; they came out from the memorials after his raising and entered into the holy city and were manifested to many." Matthew is ambivalent about his own chronology, and so the earthquake is allusively invoked in this first reference. Presumably, it coincides with the moment of Jesus' resurrection, because Matthew's conception is that this moment alone marks an apocalyptic breakthrough that shows how believers will be raised. The new element represents a literally seismic shift to a physical and apocalyptic rather than visionary belief in Jesus' resurrection.

At the same time, the earthquake features an angel (cf. Matt 1:20, 24; 2:13, 19) as a divine response to the sealing of the tomb by the guard (Matt 27:62-66). The destructive force unleashed together with the angel's rolling of the stone and interpretation of the events (Matt 28:2-7) obviates any reference to the women wishing to anoint Jesus. Ordinary arrangements of burial are gone, and the role of explanation has been appropriated to the point that Matthew does not retain the role of the women from Markan tradition. The focus is on the messenger as the Lord's, and his function implicitly includes opening the memorials of the holy ones at the same time.

The Matthean earthquake literally changes the geography of Jerusalem, rendering the physical status of many tombs in the area indeterminate. What Matthew's approach achieves, at the cost of reducing the role of the women and making any categorical statement about Jesus' place of burial impossible, is a distinctive emphasis on the apocalyptic transformation of the righteous dead, with Jesus' resurrection as the vanguard of that change. Matthew's procedure is to bring the initially visionary narrative of Mary Magdalene into line with the apocalyptic reasoning that he prefers. This result is achieved by deploying an angel, an explicitly angelic interpretation, an earthquake, resisters against revelation subject to punishment (the guards), as well as favored witnesses (the women), all elements that also feature in the uniquely Matthean expansion of the "Little Apocalypse" (Matt 25). In effect, Jesus is raised here—and only here—in a manner fully commensurate with the Matthean parable of how the Son of Man comes in glory (Matt 25:31-46) in his parousia. Apocalypse emerges as the substance of vision.

With Matthew's apocalyptic conception, disruption is more vital than continuity. That is exemplified by the imagery of the angel sitting on what is left of the tomb and explaining the significance of events to the women (Matt

28:3-7). The tomb is neither inspected nor found empty. The angel directs the women to look at something (v. 6) that had once been a burial cave, but is no longer. The explicit absence of Jesus' body features not in the angel's announcement but in the *false* story concocted by the high priests and elders (Matt 28:11-15), that Jesus' students had stolen his corpse. For Matthew, the absence of the body does not prove the resurrection; only Jesus' apocalyptic presence—together with the saints that rose with him (Matt 27:52-53)—can do that, and even then there is room for doubt (Matt 28:17). The physicality of the resurrection proceeds from its status as the definitive and first moment of the age that is coming, not because it extends the terms and conditions of the present age. The Matthean angel uniquely explains that Jesus "is not here, *because* he has been raised" (v. 6). The resurrection determines physical reality rather than being its product.

While Matthew insists on the physical disruption of Jerusalem's cemeteries, Luke specifies the *integrity* of the site of Jesus' burial. The change of emphases—hand in hand with evident differences over facts on the ground—signals a new way of reasoning the resurrection. Among the Synoptic Gospels, Luke alone has the women search for, and fail to find, Jesus' body (Luke 24:1-11, 23), a result that is then confirmed by Peter (v. 12), who does see linen wrappings. Luke at first does not name Mary and her companions, although Mary Magdalene is belatedly mentioned in Luke 24:10 with Joanna and Mary of James and other unnamed women. This approach may be taken to finesse the variation of names within traditions prior to Luke.

The women search the tomb and find it empty. The Lukan treatment of the scene produces a certifiably empty tomb, because the women go in and inspect it (Luke 24:3). It is notable that Luke also has the angelic "males" (*andres*) say, "He is not here, but has been raised" (24:6 in Greek editions), signaling a logical progression that becomes a hallmark of Luke–Acts. Instead of the resurrection requiring the apocalyptic transfer of Jesus' body as well as the bodies of the saints (Matthew's conception), Luke makes the emptiness of the tomb a requirement of the resurrection. This would suggest that Luke's additional notice, that the women did not find the body, intends to specify that the announcement does more than insist on the identity of the person raised, whose grave can be seen in one state (Mark 16:6) or another (Matt 28:6). Luke also maintains that the body could not be found (Luke 24:3) and then was announced as raised (Luke 24:6), such that it was *moveable* within space,[42] without local constraint.

The purpose of the women, an indeterminate number, since unnamed others are referred to in 24:10, coincides with Mark's presentation, although the notice is much reduced as well as delayed, and their real function becomes one of pragmatic witness: the stone has been rolled off, and they enter the tomb, certifying that Jesus' corpse is not there (24:3). Although this passage is referred to generically in all the Gospels as the narrative of "the empty tomb,"[43] it is first in Luke (and then in John) that the tomb's emptiness, rather than its place as the location of a supernatural event (Mark's vision or Matthew's earthquake), becomes the governing concern.

Likewise, Luke will have the risen Jesus insist on his own physical reality: only in this Gospel does Jesus explicitly say (24:39): "See my hands and my feet, that I am myself. Feel me and see, because a spirit does not have flesh and bone just as you perceive I have." Jesus even eats some fish to make his point (vv. 41-42)—which is more specifically Luke's point: the resurrection is substantially and significantly material, in some ways more physical than in any of the other gospels, even as Jesus' body defies strictures of location.

Since the women's experience after verse 4 appears as nothing other than an angelic vision (as Luke 24:23 confirms), rather than a physical encounter, this makes for an aporia within Luke's own presentation, since the empty tomb would seem to anticipate the women will meet with Jesus' risen and physical body. The narrative concerning Mary Magdalene and her companions stands in contrast to Luke's apparently physical perspective. The women in Luke do not take part in Jesus' interment, not even implicitly. They only watch and wait through the Sabbath with the ointment they have bought (Luke 23:55-56); they see the body (Luke 23:55) in the very place they will not find it (Luke 24:3) later. But the significance of their ointment—and Mary's connection to the anointing ritual—is obscured in Luke, because the entire story about Mary's anointing of Jesus prior to his death, the pivot of the narrative concerning her in Mark, has been removed.

Mary and her companions do not succeed in convincing the other disciples that their vision was authentic; the men reject their testimony as "nonsense" (*lêros*; Luke 24:11), a matter of "idle tales" from women. Apart from tangible, physical substance, Luke dismisses women's vision and testimony with a single word. They provide the correct meaning of the events, because it is given to them by the angels, but not the confirmation of what had happened.

For Luke's Gospel, only Jesus personally, raised from the dead in flesh and bone (Luke 24:39), can explain his resurrected presence among his disciples. The book of Acts (1:3) sets aside a period of forty days during which the risen Jesus teaches his followers in and around Jerusalem, not Galilee.

The ambivalent "body" (Luke 24:3)—tangible and yet uncontainable—is the sole evidence of the resurrection.

Luke's conception of the palpable proof of the resurrection, however, is conditioned by time. During forty days, between Passover and Pentecost, Jesus presented himself alive to his apostles by means of proofs (Acts 1:1-5); they are "witnesses handpicked in advance by God, who ate and drank with him" (Acts 10:39-41). Only those apostolic witnesses can attest the physical appearance of Jesus. And they are also witnesses of his disappearance: from a meal near Emmaus (Luke 24:31), from the midst of the Twelve and those with him (Luke 24:33-51), and definitely until his parousia at the ascension (Acts 1:6-11). By ordering his account as he does, Luke makes Silas' ascension scene into the capstone and limit of the resurrection traditions of Mary Magdalene (Luke 24:1-12), Barnabas (Luke 24:13-32, 44-46), Peter (Luke 24:12, 34), the Twelve (Luke 24:33, 47-49), and Silas himself (Luke 24:36-43, 50-53). The result of that ordering turns the tradition of the More Than Five Hundred into scenes involving thousands in Jerusalem at Pentecost, when the Holy Spirit, rather than physical presence, becomes the means by which Jesus is disclosed from heaven (Acts 2:33 within vv. 1-36).

One casualty of Luke's periodization is Paul's apostolic status, which is relegated together with that of Barnabas and the "prophets" also mentioned within Acts. But that is a small price to pay for the resourceful achievement of Luke–Acts (and no price at all, if one of its purposes is to tame Pauline influence). Luke promised in his prologue to write "in order" (*kathexês*; Luke 1:3)—a key element in fulfilling the pledge involved making the resurrection an event that could be chronicled with an end point. In that way, only the apostles could be its witnesses; they and only they can attest to its reality. Reasoned through in this fashion, the resurrection became a historical fact that was no longer palpable in the way it had been. Thereafter, in the environment of the ascension and Pentecost, Jesus could be known, but not on earth, and longing for the parousia replaced the certainty of Jesus' presence claimed by the apostles.

Luke's achievement is embodied in many understandings of the Apostles' Creed, with its stark, rhythmic assertion that, on the third day, Jesus "rose from the dead, ascended into heaven, sat on the right of God the Father Almighty."[44] That may be understood along the lines of Luke's chronology, and in any case the liturgical calendar of Easter, Ascension, and Pentecost makes discrete sequence—with each event taken separately—a likely interpretative approach. But the creed may be read as easily against the background of 1 Corinthians 15 as against that of Luke–Acts. Those who pledged themselves to God's Anointed by means of baptism, the creed's earliest application, did so after a preparation that might have resorted to Mark and Matthew as much as, or more than, to Luke–Acts. The visionary reasoning of Mark and the apocalyptic reasoning of Matthew found literary successors in early Christianity alongside the historical reasoning of Luke. The Gospel of Thomas continues a visionary perspective on the resurrection, for example; Papias, an apocalyptic perspective; and Hegesippus, a historical perspective.[45]

The modern period, of course, has seen a predominantly historical lens applied to understanding the resurrection. That has implied a preference for Luke's periodization. But in the midst of that discussion, a vital factor has not been taken into account sufficiently: Luke's view of history makes the resurrection a historical fact only for those who believe the apostles. Whether it can be taken as fact otherwise and how it should be understood as a whole are issues that remain disputed and that can be addressed only within a consideration of how history features in apprehending the resurrection.

9

Resurrection, History, and Realization

Noli Me Tangere

The development of the Synoptic Gospels unfolded in a way that permitted Luke–Acts to set out its periodized presentation of traditions of how Jesus was raised from the dead. His resurrection then occupied a discrete place within a larger cycle that closed with his ascension and exaltation. John's Gospel takes a different direction; incorporating distinctive traditions, John portrays resurrection, ascension, and exaltation as unconditioned by time. Each occurs in relation to the others, but without chronological constraint. Consequently, the act of believing for John represents an awareness that Jesus is alive in all those ways at once. John's treatment of the resurrection lays bare a way of reasoning that interacts with earlier approaches.

John extends all previous narratives of the tomb. The manner of extension conveys a perspective on the resurrection that coordinates the scenes in the final two chapters of the Gospel, and it provides insight into the character of the traditions prior to John. Where Mark reasons the resurrection along the lines of vision, Matthew along the lines of apocalypse, and Luke along the lines of revelation history, John is absorbed by the issue of belief in Jesus (20:30-31) as raised from the dead.

Mary Magdalene does not enter Jesus' tomb in John but reacts only to the removal of the stone (John 20:1-2); the extent of her contact with the tomb, as Mark also describes (Mark 16:3-6), does not include actual entry. John makes emphatic a trait in Mark that might be overlooked (and has been overlooked): Mary Magdalene never goes into the tomb. But in John she comes to precisely the wrong conclusion on the basis of what she sees. She supposes that Jesus' body has been removed: "They have taken the Lord from the tomb, and we do not know where they have laid him" (John 20:2). Since Mary is described as on her own, usage of the first-person plural here seems an artifact of an earlier tradition, where several women visited the tomb. Mary Magdalene's use of the impersonal "they" to refer to the removal of the corpse covers the cases of virtually anyone taking the body away. Later traditions of the *Toledoth Jesu*,[1] where a gardener is responsible, might even find their echo in her general statement. In any case, seeing the tomb does not amount to believing in the resurrection.

Two male students, Peter and his companion, run to the tomb and observe the remaining grave clothes (John 20:3-8). Just as Mary's non-entry of the tomb (vv. 1-2) echoes Mark (16:4-5), so Peter's entry and sight of the grave clothes (*othonia*; v. 6) echoes Luke (24:12). But John uniquely has the "other" disciple, "whom Jesus loved," join in the sight with Peter; only he believes on the basis of what he sees. He stands for believers who know Jesus as raised from the dead and therefore have the advantage over even Peter, who is not yet described as coming to faith.

At this point, John explains Peter's limitation, as well as Mary's (and the incomprehension of students yet to be encountered): no one had understood the Scripture that Jesus had to be raised from the dead (John 20:9). John follows the Synoptics in insisting on the christological reading of Scripture without specifying a passage. Earlier, John's Jesus had used the example of the bronze serpent that Moses raised in the wilderness to explain how the Son of Man would be lifted up (3:14-15; cf. 12:32-33; and Num 21:4-9), and he had spoken of the temple as his body (2:18-22). For John, Scripture was replete with types because prophets saw Jesus' "glory" (John 12:41) before the eternal word became flesh (1:14).

The resurrection is the pivot for John's Gospel that enables disciples to move from their natural limitation of understanding to a faithful appreciation of Jesus as the Anointed, the Son of God (20:30-31). Anticipated from the outset of the Gospel, the nature of his "glory" only emerges fully at its close. Once that is known, however, even Jesus' death is a moment of his glorification (John 13:31; 17:1-5).[2] Belief is the means of access to knowledge of Jesus' glory, a leitmotif of the diverse traditions in John that reaches its climax— but for the denouement that caps the whole in chapter 21—in 20:27-31.

Focused at first on the grave clothes with the story of the now-emptied tomb, John's emphasis falls on the issue of belief (20:8-9). One possible interpretation of the description of the linens is that Jesus' body has passed through the clothing that had suited it for death,[3] much as later it would pass into the locked room where his students had gathered (20:19). But John's additional detail (in comparison to Luke) that the cloth for Jesus' head lay wrapped in a place apart (v. 7) tells against this possibility; it rather suggests Jesus' deliberate agency in departing from the tomb. In this way, John underscores Jesus' volition in both his absence from the place he was expected to be in and his presence in those places that he chose to visit. Jesus' resolve is the central factor. Similarly, the offer to Thomas physically to touch Jesus awakens his recognition of "My Lord and my God" (John 20:27-28),[4] but physical contact is not involved in the recognition itself, only the willingness of Jesus to extend himself to whatever lengths necessary to instantiate faith.

Rather than privileging physical contact, Jesus tells Mary—in part of the extended tomb scene in John—not to touch him (John 20:17; *mê mou haptou* in Greek, *noli me tangere*[5] in Latin). The apparent oddity, that this limitation is because he has "not yet" ascended to the Father, is *only* an apparent oddity. For John, ascension is not the capstone of encounters with Jesus, as it is in Luke–Acts, but a principle that enables him to engage ever more intimately with those who know him. In fact, John—in a brilliantly calibrated presentation—reverses the polarity of touching. After Jesus has ascended to his Father, it is *he* that touches his students. Jesus breathes into them so that they receive the Holy Spirit (v. 22; cf. 7:37-39), just the encounter for which Mary has prepared them. The interaction with Thomas follows, in order to make the transition to the penultimate ending of the Gospel, with its expression of God's pleasure in those who do not see (and implicitly, do not touch) and yet believe (v. 29; cf. v. 31).

The continuation of the Gospel into chapter 21, a seeming addendum, rounds out the Johannine portrait of how faith relates to the resurrection. Jesus speaks of the student whom he loved, "If I will him to remain until I come, what is that to you?" (vv. 22, 23). His statement is twice cited verbatim, and the same disciple is named as the principal witness of the Gospel (v. 24). Jesus sets out the statement of his will to Peter, so that he and the beloved disciple, just the two students who first entered the tomb and saw the grave clothing in John (20:2-9), and uniquely in John, are also the last named to engage with Jesus.

Being the last named, however, does not make Peter and the beloved student the final witnesses of Jesus' resurrection. John goes on to claim that if everything Jesus did were written, the world would not suffice to contain all the scrolls that would result (21:25). That is, the Gospel closes deliberately, and in a fashion coordinated with the opening of the resurrection narrative in chapter 20 by means of reference to Peter and the beloved disciple, in order to leave the issue of further appearances of Jesus open. By denying that the promise implies the beloved student would not die (v. 23), John implicitly endorses the view that the resurrection is a continuing reality, beyond the lifespan of anyone but Jesus himself.

The final two chapters of John not only shape traditions into a coherent whole; they also imitate structurally a characteristic feature of those traditions. That is, John's reasoning of the resurrection emphasizes a trait already deep within the individual narratives of the Gospels generally. In each case, the resurrection unfolds by describing the absence of Jesus, his being seen and recognized, and providing instruction prior to his departure.[6] But the absence at the opening of each tradition is not the same as the situation at its close. Every story ends with an absence that is now only conditional. By disrupting the static absence that follows death, Jesus produces a dynamic absence that is shaped by his presence and might be interrupted again. (As John 21: 22, 23 has Jesus say, "If I will him to remain until I come, what is that to you?") So when he says, "*Noli me tangere*" (John 20:17), it is to prepare his followers for the even more intimate approach of infused Spirit that will make absence dynamic.

John lays bare a characteristic feature of resurrection accounts throughout the Gospels and related literature. Jesus articulates imperatives when he is "seen" that endure long after his appearance, becoming more powerful and more plain during his absence. He shapes the actions of those who follow him in a way that makes him present while he is absent. "*You* follow me," Peter is told in John (21:22); he is to implement the forgiveness conveyed by Jesus, to the point of death (vv. 15-19). The Twelve are promised Jesus' presence "until the end of the age" (Matt 28:19-20) as they engage in making *talmidin*; the More Than Five Hundred are filled with Holy Spirit (Acts 2:4) for the purpose of the baptism of others for receiving the same Spirit (v. 38). James practices a *halakhah* of fasting for purity determined by the risen Jesus (Jerome, *De viris illustribus* 2), while Silas anticipates the parousia as a matter of programmatic practice (Acts 1:11). The Anointed is continuingly revealed in the Scriptures for Barnabas (Luke 24:27), and Mary Magdalene incites others to vision (Mark 16:7) as persistently as Paul conceives of that vision as transformative (2 Cor 3:18).

Throughout, there is a family resemblance among the various sciences of resurrection in the New Testament and associated literature. The differing ways of reasoning through the resurrection also accord in regard to the same vital element: they all insist that the content of seeing Jesus involved an imperative that he, and he alone, revealed to his followers. That pattern also persists in the varying attempts to synthesize these sciences within the prophetic and narrative styles of presentation exhibited by each of the Gospels, Acts, and their literary progeny.

None of these revelatory imperatives even approaches being describable as a return to the status quo ante. That previous state, never to be returned to, is alluded to in various ways. Peter encounters Jesus while attempting to return to his fishing (John 21:3), an activity that will no longer describe his purpose, except as a metaphor. The Twelve meet alone in a locked room (John 20:19) so as to engage in a pattern of behavior that will ultimately observe no barriers. The More Than Five Hundred are gathered "in one place" (Acts 2:1) and receive a Spirit poured out by Jesus upon "all flesh" (v. 17) everywhere. Jesus commandeers meals in the tradition of James (Jerome, *De viris illustribus* 2) that involve an ever-more focused purity in the wake of fasting, but as a result fasting can never again seem to epitomize mourning. Silas' *anticipation* of the parousia (Acts 1:11) specifically rules out "looking into heaven," as if the risen Jesus would appear by calendrical calculation (v. 7). Barnabas' christological interpretation of Scripture (Luke 24:27) implies new christological hermeneutics that animate the Gospels. A visit to the tomb, variously characterized, stands at the outset of the tradition of Mary Magdalene and her associates (Mark 16:1-2), but in such a way that they never again confuse the realm of the dead with the realm of the living. The imperatives that result from Jesus' being seen relate to the description of his absence, but in such a way as to interrupt that absence definitively—although not continuously.

Non Habeas Corpus

Of all the depictions of Jesus' absence that preface his being seen after death, the tomb has without doubt attracted the most attention in recent years. Despite the fact that the tomb is only one preface among several, and the fact that it only became "empty" with the depictions of Luke and John, "the empty tomb" has become a metonym for the resurrection itself in a vigorous strand of scholarship. Several factors have favored that identification, to the point that it is claimed that to assert Jesus was raised *must* mean the tomb was empty, because that was its "inspiration."[7] Those factors include a tendency to harmonize Gospel texts, a preference for the Gospels over Paul in assessing Jesus, and the familiarity of accounts concerning the tomb from liturgies of Easter Day.

Such factors lie in the background of readers. But partisanship of the primacy of the "empty tomb" is by no means limited to those who treat the Gospels as an undifferentiated whole, bypass Paul, and limit their attention to the readings of the first Sunday of Easter. Taken together, they would not have produced the fixation on the tomb's emptiness in a great deal of current discussion. The impetus to use "the empty tomb" as a logical proof of the resurrection derives from two axioms of Fundamentalism, which arose at the dawn of the twentieth century in the United States, and has increasingly influenced discussion of the Bible—and the resurrection in particular—over the past several decades.

First, the insistence that all Scriptures are inerrantly true is basic to "the Fundamentals," a set of principles that came to prominence in 1910.[8] On this basis, Paul is not ignored but read in such a way that he agrees with the Gospels. This informing principal is not at all the same as a literal reading of Scripture, with which Fundamentalism is frequently confused; it is more accurately described as dedicated to a concordant understanding of the Bible. This often results in using one passage to interpret another, whether or not they can be shown to be critically related to one another. Forceful harmonization is more characteristic of Fundamentalist readings than is literalism.

Second, Fundamentalists insist that Jesus' resurrection must be in "the same body" in which he died in order to be considered true. Although the Fundamentals were established at the beginning of the twentieth century, emphasis on this axiom has grown since that time.[9] The empty tomb, taken as an amalgam of all the Gospels and projected into Paul's account in 1 Corinthians 15, delivers a reading of Scripture that honors both principles of Fundamentalism in a stroke.[10] Approached in this way, "the empty tomb" has to have been believed for any statement about the resurrection to have been made. That putative logic is then deployed to make the tomb in all the narratives equally "empty," despite the crucial variations from passage to passage.

The problems of essentializing the resurrection to the point of identification with the account of the "empty" tomb are not only exegetical and logical. Once the datum to be explained was absence taken by itself, rather than absence as the prelude to Jesus' presence, revisionist explanations flourished. Examples included having Jesus' corpse removed from the tomb by Joseph of Arimathea before the women's visit[11] or simply having the women muddled about which tomb to attend to.[12] When the empty tomb is taken as a provable fact in order to mount an apologetic argument for the resurrection,[13] a restrictive focus on that element alone can easily be turned to argue against the resurrection. That is all the more likely to occur if it is maintained (contrary to the evidence) that all the accounts present the tradition of the tomb and its emptiness.

Claims that Jesus had survived the crucifixion and walked out of the tomb were deployed to justify elaborate legends of his visits to Kashmir, Glastonbury, and Japan (sometimes to spawn progeny);[14] they thrived during the nineteenth and twentieth centuries. But they have been surpassed more recently by baroque schemes, designed to deny that Jesus' corpse had ever been put in the tomb that Mary Magdalene and her companions visited. The dead body was either dumped and left to dogs[15] or moved about from tomb to tomb.[16] Each of these scenarios has been subjected to analysis and found wanting, and considering them helps to sharpen appreciation of both the texts involved and the archaeology of the period. That consideration, however, also reveals the common foible of such schemes. They short-circuit analysis, bypassing an exegesis of what texts say in a rush to make claims of history. Their textual truncation includes considering only the "empty tomb," without regard to the substance of the claims of Jesus' disciples, that they encountered him after his death.

The apologetic argument that "the empty tomb"[17] lies at the core of the resurrection has spawned an inadvertent progeny of theories crafted to deny Jesus was raised from the dead at all. Since the Gospels themselves portray the removal of Jesus' body as a rational (John 20:2) or malicious (Matt 28:11-15) conclusion to draw from his uninterpreted absence, that is scarcely surprising.

Just as Jesus' survival of crucifixion, however improbable, cannot be dismissed formally as a possibility, theft and confusion over the gravesite are also not impossible.[18] Indeed, the challenge of an argument grounded in the alleged emptiness of the tomb is that it must exclude other arguments and account for the range of experiences of the resurrection as indicated by diverse texts. That helps explain the increasing tendency of partisans of one view or another to assert that their explanation of the physical emptiness of the tomb is the "fact" that provides the best point of departure. That is, they conflate their own hypothesis for why the tomb was "empty" with the alleged unanimity of the Gospels in respect of that emptiness.

An obvious response to the problem is to emphasize encounters with Jesus rather than the tomb. But that strategy has resulted in such a focus on "visions" of Jesus after his death[19] that in the modern period the issue of subjectivity naturally arises.[20] Efforts have been made, both anecdotal[21] and disciplinary,[22] to portray visions as related to or at least consistent with objective reality, but they have not yet yielded an agreed result.

Some support for the view that the resurrection should chiefly be seen as a prophetic *optasia* ("vision") may be claimed from New Testament usage itself, especially in Luke–Acts. The term is used of Zechariah's vision of an angel (Luke 1:22), the women at the tomb (Luke 24:23), and Paul's experience (Acts 26:19), while the related verb is used of Jesus in Acts 1:3. The synonym *horama* refers to the transfiguration (Matt 17:9), Moses' encounter at the burning bush (Acts 7:31), the experience of Ananias (Acts 9:10), Peter's vision in Joppa (Acts 10:3, 17, 19; 11:5 [cf. 12:9]), Paul's seeing a man of Macedonia (Acts 16:9, a usage with the verb *ōphthē*), and Paul's reassurance by "the Lord" in Corinth (Acts 18:9). The related term *horasis* appears for descriptions of heaven (Rev 9:17) and for prophetic insight (Acts 2:17). The breadth of the category of "vision" only becomes more striking when the sense of passages is not limited to the use of these particular words but is allowed to unfold from their narratives in context.

Yet caution is required in deploying the category of vision, basic though it seems. Within modern sensibilities, visions are easily conflated with hallucinations, so as to prejudice any assessment of the reality of the resurrection.[23] That has recommended the category to those who wish to argue that some form of self-delusion lies at the heart of the matter.[24] "Vision" alone within the usage of the New Testament does not resolve the issue of the subjectivity or objectivity of what was seen (and Acts 12:9 reflects an awareness of that). Further, the very fact that vision is a broad category within the New Testament means that passages not originally associated with vision might have been co-opted into the category. Presumably, a wide range of experience is subsumed in Paul's list in 1 Corinthians 15:5-8, for example, and "vision" might not have been the preferred description of all those involved, although it clearly grew to become a major paradigm for appreciating the resurrection. The last book of the New Testament makes this crystal clear.

The problem remains to avoid the pitfall of either privileging religious experience (as if it were so primal as to escape criticism) or dismissing it as a matter of cultural projection (amounting to no more than hallucination). At the moment, despite a great deal of interest in "vision," and assertions of its primacy,[25] no categorical finding can be recommended for applying it to the resurrection as an adequate explanation.

Historically speaking, the problem of the resurrection is that all approaches to it are by means of texts that speak of its impact but not of the event in itself. No account[26] refers to the quickening of a dead body, to the moment of transfer of that body to another kind of existence, or to a replacement of one mode of being with another. Precisely that lack produces the indeterminacy in categorizing the resurrection.[27] But because nothing like a witness of the event appears, the more basic issues emerges: Should the resurrection be considered historical in the first place?

Historical Christophany

The understanding of what history is has passed through a revolution that has affected the humanities as a whole. That change is basic to the study of the New Testament, no matter what the topic at hand. But this changed view of history has also been adapted specifically to cope with the resurrection, raising the issue of whether historiography should ever be customized for a particular inquiry.

The historian's responsibility to seek out sources as near as possible to the events to be analyzed is basic, as is the need to interrogate those sources and correct for their biases.[28] But many events—including deaths and murders, marriages and sexual affairs, births, illnesses, recoveries—are real, yet not archived or even witnessed to the extent of current knowledge. So in addition to their critical task of sifting evidence, historians also enter into the experiences and thoughts that motivated human agents in the past. Listening to what they say moved them to act enables the historian to assess the underlying causes of the often surprising, disruptive events of which history is made.[29]

That process involves canvassing the breadth of the evidence to be evaluated. By identifying disagreement within and among sources, the historian might find that they inadvertently offer points of view that vary from their intended statements. Unfolding patterns of tradition can also inform historians of the perceived meaning of events.[30] When meaning is taken as the key to history, then the evolution of meaning becomes the focal concern. That is an especial challenge in the case of the resurrection, where the pluralism of early Christian tradition from the New Testament onward[31] must be factored in.

Just that pluralism, however, has been portrayed as a strength of the resurrection in an influential stream of discussion since the Second World War. If historical intentions and events are disruptive by nature, confusion might be taken as a mark of reality; in that case the raising of Jesus from the dead in its uniqueness appears to *exemplify* the historical.[32] On this analysis, history arises precisely when events are *not* fully explained; an attempt at total explanation results in the dissolution of history into allegedly constant factors of human behavior. History is the record of reactions to unique events in a plurality of forms, not of successful efforts to explain events away, on whatever grounds.

Approaches derived from this point of view pursue the claim that the resurrection is an event of history, despite the lack of witnesses to the phenomenon itself. But that of course implies that the phenomenon can be reliably inferred without being witnessed directly.[33] What is witnessed, in one way or another in all the texts—however they are presented—is the awareness that Jesus is alive after his public execution. The execution is public, as are consequences of the resurrection, but the resurrection itself is not. The conviction that those consequences resulted from God raising Jesus from the dead is not in itself a historical event but an interpretation that involves experiencing him alive after death.

The resurrection—understood as the assertion that God raised Jesus from the dead—may be understood as a historical event only if that interpretation is combined with accepting the claim that Jesus transcends death and can be experienced alive. That is precisely what occurs within theological discourse practiced inside the bounds of the church,[34] but that assumes a specialized perspective on history.

Resurrection implies that human nature itself has been transformed; among those who agree to that new frame of reference, a collective, but still not fully public, agreement to speak of the history of "the Christ-event" can be and has been deployed.[35] Sometimes, this sense of the ongoing transformation flagged by the resurrection is interpreted in terms of an eschatological event.[36] But if an "event" is alleged to arrive at the end of history, generated from outside history itself, the methods of history by definition cannot be deployed to understand it.[37] Although "eschatological event" is much less likely to be applied to visions of the risen Jesus than was once the case, the concept survives among those who champion the primacy of the "empty tomb." But that, as is by now obvious, has proven to be a weaker support for the objectivity of the resurrection than some recent contributors have argued.

The resurrection as an eschatological event—as the final happening that sublimates all previous truths—is not a finding of history, although it is an exegetical meaning (especially within the tradition of Silas), or at least the implication, of texts associated with the resurrection. But this insight was never for "all the people," as Acts has Peter say in the house of Cornelius (Acts 10:39-41), but for those who had been chosen to eat and drink with

Jesus after he arose. Even so, Matthew retains its note of doubt on the part of some of those in the presence of the risen Jesus (Matt 28:17).[38]

A text from the second century CE, the Treatise on the Resurrection investigates the dichotomy between historical event and eternal truth by declaring that "one ought to maintain the world is an illusion, rather than resurrection."[39] In this case, a lack of fit between ordinary perception and the reality of vision is held to mark the greater truth of the latter. Resurrection is taken—in this effective, moving, but ahistorical assertion—to be a truth prior to the conditions of mortality. John's Gospel has Jesus make the same kind of claim more directly in the statement, "Before Abraham was, I am" (John 8:58). Using the language of historical sequence, the primacy of history is denied.

Even from the point of view of those who have argued for categorizing the resurrection as an "eschatological event," where a happening in history is held to point to transcendence, statements of sheer transcendence such as in the Treatise on the Resurrection and John's Gospel may seem extreme. But the resurrection in fact regularly appears on a transcendent basis among the sources of the New Testament and related literature.

Those portrayals develop so as to insist on the continuity between Jesus before and after death, so that his transcendence is momentarily focused within immanence, and then he departs. That is why the departure, his dynamic absence, is crucial: immanence can express transcendence, but what is transcendent must in the end take leave of conditional existence in order to remain true to itself. The lack of any ostentation in appearances of the risen Jesus (unlike the transfiguration) underscores that he is present in that way only temporarily. His ordinary aspect, so commonplace that he can be mistakable for some other ordinary person, emerges so briefly that signs are required to show his significance. The focal articulation of transcendence, in fact, does not usually lie in the particular description of Jesus after his death. That is a trait more of the figures associated with the risen Jesus than with Jesus himself: Mark's young man (Mark 16:5), Matthew's angel (Matt 28:2-3), Luke's two dazzling males (Luke 24:4), John's two angels (John 20:11-12), and the Gospel of Peter's three males and a cross (Gos. Pet. 10:38-42). In the last case, the male supported by the other two is presumably Jesus (although only the cross speaks on his behalf), but the emphasis on transcendence is achieved more by those who support than the one who requires help.

Despite being seen postmortem, Jesus in his appearance seems more immanent than transcendent. Transcendence comes to unmistakable emphasis, however, in the imperatives that he then delivers. The activities directed by the risen Jesus either vivify his teaching during life or demand new departures.[40] In either case, they are transcendent in relation to the particular conditions of Jesus' followers and in relation to their own interests. The first three entries in Paul's list—*Kêpha'*, the Twelve, and the More Than Five Hundred—involve imperatives whose supernatural power is conveyed by their direct association with God's Spirit.

The imperatives of the resurrection are embedded within their particular sciences. Paul—providing the fullest cosmological account—sees his own being, like those of his readers, as being transformed from the physical "tent" of mortal life to the spiritual body that shares in the Spirit of the Anointed (2 Cor 5:1-5). He leaves no doubt of his confidence in the complete triumph of Spirit over matter and flesh by means of the resurrection, just as he portrays the encounter with the risen Jesus as interior and prophetic (Gal 1:15-16). The extent to which Paul's cosmological model might have been shared by others on his list of principal sources of resurrection teaching cannot be known, but in many cases contrast is easier to perceive than agreement.

Peter's overwhelming emphasis upon the imperative of forgiveness is too complete (John 21:1-19; 20:23; Matt 16:17-19), and the traditions associated with him too fragmentary, for a cosmology comparable to Paul's to emerge. This helps to explain why the much later Second Letter of Peter supplements Peter's own characteristic emphasis upon repentance and forgiveness (expressed in 2 Pet 3:9). Second Peter 1:12-21 builds out a cosmology, combining Pauline language of being in the "tent" of the body (v. 13), the Johannine prediction of Peter's death (v. 14), allusion to either the transfiguration or Matthew's resurrection scene on the mountain (vv. 16-18), and a Barnaban construction of how Scripture functions christologically (vv. 19-21). The whole is balanced with the promise of becoming "participants in divine nature" (v. 4) and entering into the kingdom (v. 11). Traditional language is framed to fashion and convey a fresh reasoning of human participation in the divine.

Yet nearer its point of origin, the Petrine tradition shows a different character. The strong connection between forgiveness and restoration to health—a signature insistence within the Petrine tradition (see Mark 2:1-12; Matt 9:1-8; Luke 5:17-26)—implies that when the risen Jesus forgives Peter and gives him authority to forgive, the result is to effect a profound and pragmatic transition. To this extent, comparison is more natural with 2 Maccabees' presentation of what it means to be raised from the dead than with the model of Jubilees, Paul's natural counterpart. Palpably different cosmological perspectives are involved. As in the case of Matthew 16:17-19, the issue in

John 21:1-15 is only incidentally Peter's status. The gravamen of the imperative is that *intentional* forgiveness is to be offered. Jesus' imperative to forgive
breaks the rule of sin's inevitable consequences, whether from generation to
generation (Exod 34:6-7; Deut 5:9-10) or within the life of an individual (2
Kgs 14:5-6; Ezek 18:1-4). The transcendent impact is not to shift from the
flesh to the Spirit, as in Paul's science, but to effect a change within the constitution of the person who is forgiven.

The Twelve's signature concern, to extend Jesus' halakhic teaching by
making *talmidin* (Matt 28:16-20), presupposes programmatic action "until
the end of the age" but in such a way that Jesus is "with" them at every
point in time (v. 20). Transcendence, as in the case of Peter's imperative, is
more episodic than it is the ontological rupture that Paul posits. Similarly,
when the bodily presence of Jesus is described in John 20:19-20, little or no
theoretical interest in the nature of Jesus' body seems to prevail. Rather, the
concern is to present Jesus as the source of the Spirit on the strength of which
forgiveness is not only possible but also an apostolic mandate (vv. 21-23),
and to identify this imperative as coming from the very Jesus who had been
tortured. His hands and his side show why forgiveness is necessary, while the
Spirit he breathes on his disciples transforms them into agents of forgiveness.
John has prepared for understanding of this transformation, because the
Spirit has already been identified as what leads Jesus' followers into all truth
(16:12-15), including and beyond his own teaching (14:26).

The More Than Five Hundred, in their association with God's Spirit as
poured out by Jesus (Acts 2:1-41), pursue an inclusion of gentiles in baptism
that strains and ultimately obviates the full application of the torah. Jesus'
own program had involved proclaiming God's kingdom on the authority of his
possession of God's Spirit (see Matt 12:28). Now, as a consequence of the resurrection, Jesus had poured out that same Spirit upon those who would follow
him. Baptism in the Spirit (see Acts 1:4-5) and baptism into the name of Jesus
were one and the same for that reason. That was why believing that Jesus was
God's Son and calling upon his name were the occasions on which the Spirit
was to be received. In the new environment of God's Spirit that the resurrection signaled, baptism was indeed, as Matthew 28:19 indicates, an activity and
an experience that involved the Father (the source of one's identity), the Son
(the agent of one's identity), and the Holy Spirit (the medium of one's identity).
Jesus' resurrection, his exaltation, and his directing the Spirit are known to the
More Than Five Hundred as a result of what they see and hear. Each is asserted
on a distinctive basis, respectively:[41] the awareness of those who concluded

Jesus was alive after he died, the acceptance of Jesus within the heavenly court, and then his direction of the Spirit toward believers on that basis.

The risen, exalted Jesus prompts the apostolic imperative to engage, and finally to baptize, representatives of the nations of the earth. Even with its stylized account, Acts 2 cannot quite say, as Matthew 28:19 does, that Jesus' imperative is to baptize all nations, since in Acts Peter's acceptance of that stance is a matter of sequenced vision, not a single, initial revelation. The pattern of moving directly from the resurrection to the announcement to the nations is Paul's in Galatians 1:16.[42] To this extent, the Pauline pattern seems to have influenced sources associated with Peter over time. This is the explanation for why Acts anticipates the extension of God's Spirit to the gentiles in the Pentecost scene in chapter 2 but cannot deliver on that promise until chapter 10: the source grounded in the Twelve had received the Petrine mandate of forgiveness and the imperative to extend forgiveness within Israel on the basis of receiving the Spirit with immersion. But the more radical extension to the gentiles occurred under the impetus of other forces. The numbers involved in accepting this new immersion (hundreds or thousands, depending on whether Paul in 1 Cor 15:6 or Luke in Acts 2:41 is followed) prompted an expansion, but Paul's influence also proved powerful. Especially as worked out in Acts,[43] however, the link between Jesus' transcendent status and the redrawing of the lines that define Israel and the nations is emphatic. This is not only a science, but in particular a social science, of the resurrection.

Where social transcendence is demanded by a transcendent source in the case of the More Than Five Hundred, James directly addressed the issue of purity. The account of his preaching in the temple given by Hegesippus (quoted in Eusebius' *Ecclesiastical History* 2.23.12–14) represents Jesus as the Son of Man who is to come from heaven to judge the world. Those who agree cry out, "Hosanna to the Son of David!" Hegesippus shows that James' view of his brother came to be that he was related to David (as was the family generally) and was also a heavenly figure who was coming to judge the world. When Acts 15:13-21 and Hegesippus are taken together, they indicate that James contended Jesus was restoring the house of David because he was the agent of final judgment (the "Son of Man" of Dan 7:13) and was being accepted as such by gentiles with his Davidic pedigree. The distinction between the groups, unlike in Paul's teaching, is categorically maintained. Focus on purity in eating is also a feature of the single account of the resurrection associated with James, from Jerome's *De viris illustribus* 2. The setting is James' fast, which he had vowed to keep from the time he drank "from the Lord's cup" until he had seen him risen from those who sleep (see also Gos. Pet. 7:27). Fasting—particularly in the Nazirite tradition—is a well-established feature of James' circle (see Acts 21:17-26).

Jesus' intervention as the Son of Man risen from those who sleep is tied directly to the practice of fasting since the time of one Eucharist until the next: abstention from the Lord's "cup" occasions the offer of bread from the Son of Man. Association with the temple was implicit in the case of the Nazirite vow, although the temple need not feature in most eucharistic practice. In James' case, however, the offer of bread from the Son of Man comes after the Lord had given the linen to the servant of the priest. According to Hegesippus, James himself wore only linen and enjoyed special access to the temple (Hegesippus, in Eusebius, *Ecclesiastical History* 2.23.6), and a priest attempted to rescue James from execution (*Ecclesiastical History* 2.23.17). Linen features as a priestly (Lev 6:3), a high-priestly (Lev 16:4), and also an angelic (Dan 10:5) marker, but the meaning here is that resurrection links the Son of Man in heaven and the temple-related practice of Eucharist on earth. The destruction of the temple helps account for the relative absence of James' teaching in the New Testament proper, but his science of purity in relation to Jesus' resurrection had its effect in the conviction (Heb 9:11-12) that the true locus of Jesus was in the heavenly sanctuary.

The insistence of Acts 1:9-11 that Jesus will come in judgment in the same manner that he departed has embarrassed even commentators who insist that the resurrection should be conceived of in physical terms.[44] Silas' source indeed shows a deep connection to apocalyptic, but there is no indication within its presentation that it takes the resurrection, and the associated ascension and parousia, to be a matter of imagery. In fact, the rebuttal of any attenuated view of the resurrection is directly stated in Luke 24:36-43. As presented, the purpose of the passage is to contradict the surmise that Jesus is a "spirit" (vv. 37, 39): any such view is ruled out by his "flesh and bone" (v. 39), wounds on his hands and feet (v. 40), and his request for and consumption of fish (v. 41-43). The choice of language in Luke 24:39, "flesh and bone," echoes Ezekiel 37:1-14, a passage that by the first century was read in association with eschatological resurrection.[45]

Indeed, in this case the narrative swallows up an explicit imperative, uniquely among the stories in the Synoptic Gospels. The instruction conveyed by the encounter is implicit in what Jesus tells his disciples when he appears among them: not to be led astray by frightened thoughts into any but a corporeal understanding of the resurrection (Luke 24:38-39). By intent as well as impact, the Silan source winds up the most influential within the

New Testament (see Acts 1:1-14; Matt 27:51-53; 27:62-66; 28:1-2, 11-15; Luke 24:36-43, as well as Gos. Pet. 8:28-33; 9:34-37; 10:38–11:49). Its science is direct, and its focal insistence on the parousia[46] remains a robust contribution.

The earthquake endures as a firm aspect of the apocalypse that Zechariah anticipates (Zech 14:4) and that Matthew and the Gospel of Peter take up. Likewise, any source that sees Jesus as the Danielic Son of Man, as the Silan tradition does, would need to engage Daniel's promise of a resurrection of "many that sleep in the dust of the earth" (Dan 12:1-3), a promise realized in Matthew 27:52-53. These elements (also reflected in Gos. Pet. 5:15–6:21) are not simply decorative embellishments but feature into a conviction of judgment exercised at the time of the resurrection. At each stage in the development of the tradition, the element of physical description is related to the nature of the judgment that Jesus as Son of Man is to exercise.

Luke 24:36-43 (from the Silan source) seems to correct the description of Jesus' disappearance in Luke 24:31.[47] The Emmaus story, Luke 24:13-35, which we have associated with Barnabas, is focally concerned with the globally christological use of Scripture and with the Eucharist.[48] Key to the Barnaban meaning of Luke 24:26 is that Scripture mandates that it is the *Anointed* who is to suffer. Of the many meanings that may be attributed to the term, specific distance is put between Jesus (before or after the resurrection) and the restoration of the kingdom to Israel (see Acts 1:6). In the Lukan presentation, Jesus was already anointed by God's Spirit in Galilee (Luke 4:18; citing Isa 61:1), and his resurrection permits him to pour out that same Spirit on his followers (Acts 2:32-33). Just as references to the Scripture are broadened to investigate how the necessity of the Anointed's suffering was to be understood, so the definition of what makes Jesus the Anointed becomes more precise.

As occurring after the crucifixion, the Emmaus narrative provides a fresh meaning to the Eucharist: it is a meal that Jesus may join even after his death. For this reason, the textual moments of the recognition of Jesus, and then his departure, are pivotal. Both of them represent developments of the themes of seeing the Lord and then acknowledging his departure in other narratives. In the case of Emmaus, however, the recognition is delayed, and the departure is oddly truncated.

Although Cleopas and his companion do not recognize Jesus (Luke 24:16), his exasperation is provoked not by this lack of insight but by their failure to understand the Prophets—and, it turns out, the Torah and the rest of Scripture, as well (Luke 24:25-27). Their desire for the apparent stranger to remain with them might derive from their benefit from his instruction, but their offer is also framed along the lines of a care for others that accords with Jesus' teaching (vv. 28-29; cf. 10:25-37). That is the setting in which he breaks bread, is at last recognized—and disappears (vv. 30-31). The Lukan usage may mean that Jesus was taken away, as Philip was in Acts 8:39-40, but there the Spirit snatches up Philip (*harpazô*), the eunuch sees him no longer, and he appears in Azotus. "Disappearing from them" is less categorical than, although similar to, the later statement that Jesus "stood apart from them, and was carried up into the heaven" (Luke 24:51). It might of course be that the Barnaban source and Luke vary in their expression, but another possibility is that when Jesus was no longer apparent to Cleopas and his companion, what remained was the unknown stranger.[49]

The imperative embedded in Mary Magdalene's vision[50] insists on a change of place, because Jesus is identified as the Nazirite (Mark 16:6), extending a Markan (and ultimately Magdalene) characterization of Jesus. The purity of the one who has been raised is incompatible with the place of death, and he must be sought elsewhere, as Galilee becomes a place of privilege for the reason that it hosted Jesus' presence initially and defined the characteristic (and peculiar) purity that he championed there.

The imperative does not disclose itself immediately but is staged through the women's preparation (Mark 16:1-2; Matt 28:1a; Luke 24:1), their approach to the tomb and their entry in Luke's case (Mark 16:3-5a; Matt 28:1b; Luke 24:2-3), and the announcement they receive (Mark 16:5b-7; Matt 28:5-7; Luke 24:4-7). It is also followed by a clear indication of their attitude (Mark 16:8; Matt 28:8; Luke 24:8-9). These are indications of liturgical development, emerging from a ritual of death.[51] Death is just the reality, however, that is interrupted and then reversed by the proclamation of Jesus' incompatibility with the place of death. Vision becomes an engine for seeking the one who is alive apart from the region of death, a dedicated practice of discovering the life that has not, in the end, been destroyed.

Each of the sources assumes a science of the resurrection; the extent of their assumption means that they usually include only fragmentary statements of their cosmologies. Yet the impact of each remains palpable, in the sources and in the practices of those influenced by the sources. These are human actions, describable deeds that claim a transcendent origin for the imperatives they fulfill, richly attested by participants and observers, and imbued with intentional meanings.[52] Once in the field of people acting as agents, historical inquiry becomes possible—and necessary if their actions are to be understood.

So apprehended, the resurrection—although not in itself a historical event—becomes historical when Jesus' agency exerts itself among his followers. It then emerges within their human actions, programmatic responses to the living Jesus, to which historians would appropriately respond by understanding as best they can the meaning of those programs of action. History is regularly a matter of inference. The historian enters into the evidence and gathers as much as possible, but in the end each investigator must use his or her own mind in order to recover the mind behind the events to hand.[53] In the case of the resurrection, historians may deploy both evidence and inference, and on that basis recover the minds of those who shaped the sources, and in shaping them reflected their sense of the agency of Christ. Their sense belongs to demonstrably human agents, but to speak of the agency of Christ itself, the very content of the resurrection, is an inference drawn *from* historical inference.

Within the movement of Jesus itself, believers conceived that Jesus, alive after his death, appeared in visions, conveyed purity, assured the promise of the coming age, provoked an extension of the message beyond historic Israel by means of baptism, authorized programmatic forgiveness, insisted that his teaching should be used to call new disciples and seek out new meanings in Scripture by means of Spirit, and provided his followers means to stand on the right side of the final judgment. What he had spoken of in association with God's activity—the kingdom of God revealing itself—became his own activity,[54] and on a larger scale than before the crucifixion. That identification with divine dimensions of action opened christological questions in ways that invited not only the usage of laden terms to understand Jesus (Son of Man, Son of God, Messiah, Just One) but an active investigation over centuries to understand him in relation to God. Jesus became an agent of greater change than when he was alive, and in that sense the resurrection influenced history with all the impact of an event, while holding itself back from entering history.

When those who acted on Jesus' behalf referred to him as the living, transcendent source of their actions, their claims exited the realm of history. Their actions are fully historical, while their accounts of their motivations deliberately depart from a claim of sequenced happenings in order, in a variety of ways, to privilege unexpected and astonishing disruption. Their explanation that Jesus had been raised from the dead by God might be accepted, or alternative explanations might be sought, but it is as incontrovertible in its influence as it is capricious in its attestation, in history and yet not of history.

Corporeal Sciences

The breadth of the narratives concerned is scarcely captured by the routine remark that early Christianity cannot be explained apart from faith in the resurrection. Its impact goes beyond being an object of belief; it is a subject that has moved history, summarized by the Johannine Jesus during a resurrection appearance: "As the Father delegated me, I also send you" (John 20:21). The emergence of imperatives within each source—fresh commands, some of them involving radical departure—marks the moment at which Jesus is not only "seen" but becomes the subject who determines how the disciples themselves are to be seen. From the point of view of their historical actions, which are a matter of public record, he is the motivating factor.

The particular challenge in evaluating the resurrection involves assessing disciples' claims to have encountered Jesus and their understanding of how Jesus was alive after his death. The range of the actions of which Jesus is named as the impetus, as well as the array of witnesses, tells against attempts to reduce all the accounts to a single simple cause. The problem persists, no matter the direction of the reduction. Attempting to explain all the texts on the basis of an alleged guilt complex on Peter's part[55] works as poorly as trying to project "the empty tomb" onto every stage of every tradition. The fallacy is not the deployment of the argument to appropriate texts but the attempt to derive the whole array of accounts from a singular cause.

A major reason for the drive to find the single causative trigger of the resurrection is that, although ancient sciences could frame views of transcendence, modern science is widely held to exclude any such possibility. The use of electricity, it is commonly said, is incompatible with belief in anything like the resurrection.[56]

Although the mechanical model of physical existence has often been far less exclusive of the transcendent than is often supposed,[57] the idea of science as a self-contained, indisputable system profoundly influenced theology during the twentieth century. The result, however, was not—except in a few cases—denial of the resurrection. Instead, the resurrection came to be portrayed as the occasion for a response of faith in its purest form, apart from and if necessary despite scientific or historical proof.[58] Departure from the empirical world came to be portrayed as a mark of greater, indeed primordial, faith. The bifurcation between faith and reason over the issue of Jesus' resurrection became predominant in discussion after the Second World War; partisanship of the "empty tomb" developed more from this approach than any other, offering a deliberate emphasis on physical impossibility as an occasion for faith.

Yet the claim that physical science excludes any claim of Jesus' resurrection has found robust challenges. Perennial discussion in regard to the Shroud of Turin provoked the thought that radiation, produced by the resurrection, was responsible for the image on the cloth.[59] The shroud itself proved incapable of sustaining any reasonable claim of a connection with Jesus, yet the thought remained that the resurrection might involve a process in which Jesus' material corpse in some way made a transfer to another mode of existence.[60]

The twentieth century saw an increasing confidence in a science of matter and the mechanical relations among material entities, so that many theologians despaired of making claims that contradicted that science. But at the same time that confidence grew, matter itself became susceptible to a radically different approach, at first at the level of electrons, but then more generally. The electron that once was supposed to be a subatomic unit that orbited around a nucleus no longer appeared as such. Rather, the electron might sometimes be measurable as a value of energy and sometimes as a particle, but not as both at the same time. Expressed at the level of the atom, that may seem an abstract observation, but it proves to pose a fundamental challenge to a mechanical model of physical nature.

A physicist named Erwin Schrödinger developed an equation that showed that particles could best be described as waves of energy. But if that is the case, could a particle really be in more than one place at the same time, like a wave of light? Schrödinger denied that idea and worked out a thought experiment, known as "Schrödinger's Cat,"[61] to express his objection. Quantum physics would have it that an electron's actual location in space and time only holds for the moment of observation; uncertainty shrouds where it is at another time or for another observer. To illustrate why that issue is troublesome, Schrödinger imagined a cat put at risk of poisoning inside a sealed box. The release of the poison was conditional on a Geiger counter detecting radiation at a marginal level that was also sealed in the box. Such a value might or might not be picked up, since the precise position of all subatomic particles involved (in the source of radiation and the Geiger counter) could not be determined in advance. Quantum uncertainty suggested that the cat would only be dead or alive when an observer opened the box. Schrödinger demurred, insisting that the cat was either dead or alive, independently of what someone might see after the fact of this strange experiment.

Schrödinger's illustration backfired after he set it out. Some physicists took his thought experiment, as well as his fundamental equation that represents quanta in terms of waves, to show that every quantum really might occupy several positions at once. Only an observation can say what occurs in any given case. This means that the occurrence is true for that observation, and only that observation.[62] That implies that *each* position of particles such as electrons corresponds to different universes; at all times, then, people also might inhabit many worlds. Popularly called the "multiverse," this interpretation has proven extremely popular[63] and profoundly controversial. It was just the corollary that Schrödinger (and his friend Albert Einstein) disputed. Specifically, the multiverse has been applied as a modern science of resurrection. In this application,[64] the moment of death marks a transfer from one universe into another, with personality remaining intact.

Although the multiverse has proven very popular, it has also attracted trenchant criticism. And after all, Schrödinger himself had devised his thought experiment to undermine such speculation. In his mind, whatever happens at the quantum level, by the time classic observation of the real world is involved, cats are either alive or dead. But even a strict reduction of applying quantum theory to physics at a subatomic level has resulted in yet another possible resurrection science in our time.

If it is the case that all objects are subject to "superposition," such that they might be in one place or in other places, and if the multiverse is an unconvincing conclusion to draw from that, then there must be a better model. In one robust—but also controversial—theory, the superposition resolves itself as a result of the gravitational attraction between the possible locations. They snap into place in what is conceived of as a resolution of time and space by "orchestrated objective reduction."[65] That resolution is the origin of consciousness, in that the brain is capable of assimilating these moments when multiple potentials are resolved into single realities.

The divide among quantum models of physics and their relationship to views of resurrection may seem baffling, until current controversies are seen in relation to their ancient counterparts. Origen pioneered a version of the multiverse,[66] while Augustine was convinced of the eternity of consciousness and its connection to physical reality.[67] Neither of them, of course, was a quantum physicist, yet their conclusions were no less rooted in the science of their times than today's discussion is. Moreover, current controversies in relation to basic physics can no longer be said to be any less striking than their ancient counterparts. The idea of a single Enlightenment natural philosophy has long since been exploded among scientists, and theologians should catch up to that realization.

The resurrection has catalyzed possible views of how the dead might live, because it predicates that the possible has become real. How that happened has been a question that has been answered differently, and disagreements among those named on Paul's list have contributed to a controversial progeny, down to current disputes that can be framed in terms of quantum physics. But in the midst of that persistent (and perhaps inevitable) disagreement, the character of how the resurrection discloses itself should not be ignored. No matter what the source cited by Paul and reflected in the New Testament, the resurrection produces imperatives, which constitute its enduring trace in history. Although the differing tradents disagreed in their explanations of how Jesus had been raised from the dead, they all took up their imperatives, some of them involving radically new activities compared to earlier models of what it meant to follow Jesus.

Risen from the dead in the experience of his disciples, Jesus inscribed fresh patterns of action in the bodies of his followers, and he did so because they perceived him as corporeal consciousness.[68] The inscription of his imperatives on their bodies was possible because they could recognize Jesus, accept new directions from him as a human agent, and discover these activities within their own capacities. Their sciences sometimes put them at odds with one another and contributed starkly different portrayals of the resurrection. Differences among Mary Magdalene, Peter, and the Twelve might have offered matters for compromise, but Silas and Paul do not seem to have reached an accord, and the More Than Five Hundred, James, and Barnabas contributed their own distinctive paradigms. Yet they all live together, not only on Paul's list (a list that he was given by Peter and James), but also within the pages of the New Testament. As the sciences differed, so did the imperatives, and yet those imperatives were embraced by the differing groups as coming from the same risen Lord, who made new conscious choices and was seen with a recognizable body.

The resurrection in this sense, as the apprehension of embodied consciousness that impels the follower to new action in Jesus' name, emerges as the common trait among the various imperatives articulated in the sources identified. Owing to that commonality, the principals at the time could accept their differences in regard to how Jesus appeared, what he said, and the ways their practices should be implemented in response to that appearance. Their direct experience of Jesus as risen from the dead is not historical, and the sources in their various ways keep the moment of resurrection hidden for that very reason. But his followers' responses to their experiences were and remain powerfully historical.

The catalytic impact of the risen Jesus upon their expectations resulted in the variety of conceptions that have been traced, but in each case the identity of the embodied catalyst as Jesus features as the central factor. The pluralism of ancient sciences of resurrection that Jesus' resurrection influenced and vivified makes current controversies concerning physics, the status of embodiment, and how consciousness relates to meaning appear relatively straightforward by comparison.

The particular paths scientific discussion might take obviously cannot be predicted. And because the resurrection is a datum of history in its effects but not in the moment of its happening, no insistence on its status as a publicly verifiable event is likely ever to be convincing. But the embodied consciousness that the sources in aggregate refer to remains a viable element within consideration of how human beings relate to transcendent meaning within their mortal existence.

The post-Enlightenment ferment of scientific discussion is a fertile ground for new evaluations of what the resurrection means. Those assessments can be conducted both within communities of faith that honor Jesus' resurrection as a reality and among investigators for whom the claim of Jesus' being raised is influential but unverifiable. For many believers, the philosophical dimension of inquiry might seem dispensable, but claims of transcendence in any form always and necessarily open at least the possibility of philosophical investigation. For many who take up a stance outside the tradition of Christianity, embodied consciousness might appear an unattractive proposition if applied to Jesus, but then they need to confront their own inclination to presume that Christian concepts are not sufficiently sophisticated for them.[69] In either case, whether from the point of view of believers or nonbelievers, the embodied consciousness that the earliest sources represent, and that continues to offer itself in the living tradition of those sources, stands as an option for investigating how human awareness participates in transcendent meaning so as to share the life of God. The resurrection is present in history in its results, exerts an influence on cosmology then and now, yet stands astride both history and cosmology because, in defying objectification, it offers itself as embodied consciousness.

Conclusion

Surprises, Decisions, and Adjustments

Any act of learning, especially when extended over a course of investigation, will involve decisions and surprises. Inquirers engage their curiosity, lighting upon a phenomenon or question that attracts attention. The resurrection has been treated both as phenomenon and as question; diverse findings have been forwarded, sometimes with a degree of confidence that their mutual contradictions belie. So, readers of current studies encounter the assured finding that the resurrection was a historical event and the equal certainty that it was a scientific impossibility.[1] An initial surprise likely to confront any inquiry into the resurrection lies in the degree—and often the passion—of trenchant disagreement.

Controversy is only exacerbated by questions along the lines of, "What really happened?" As explained in the introduction, pursuit of inquiry in those terms has resulted in apologetic defenses of Protestant, Catholic, and various revisionist interpretations of the evidence. The telltale sign that the effort is as much dogmatic as exegetical is that many investigators have attempted to reduce the texts in *all* their variety to an amalgam, "the empty tomb," which is an artifact of selective reading. That amalgam has been enlisted in claims both to prove and to refute claims that Jesus rose from the dead.

Surprise at the present state of discussion might come as disappointment, but it is nonetheless a surprise for all that, and it invites a fresh decision.

Adjusting the question from "What happened?" to "*How* did the disciples believe in the resurrection?" changes the ground of discussion. The revised question encourages inquiry to trace the texts through their development over time, allowing characteristic beliefs to emerge in their individuality. Exegetical consideration of most topics usually proceeds in this way, with an eye on chronology. In contrast, recourse to harmonizing interpretations, and readings that use later texts to understand earlier texts, characterizes many studies of the resurrection; those characteristics suggest that, in those cases, exegesis is being used in the service of a predetermined finding. Exegetical awareness also sensitizes readers to issues of context. Explicit statements by Jesus' followers manifest differing understandings of how the transcendence of death should be understood, and they locate themselves differently within their cultures and among the cultures that surrounded them.

Any claim of transcending death raises the question of the view of the world, the cosmology or the science, that would both make that claim extraordinary and yet provide it with credibility. Although a great deal of territory is covered in chapter 1, "Resurrection and Immortality before Jesus," the Sumerian, Egyptian, Greek, and Syrian examples together evince a pattern. Their heroes function at the boundary of the human and the divine, but they never control that border. Gilgamesh is denied his quest for immortality; Osiris rules only the underworld, while his progeny represents the cycle of eternity in Egypt; Dionysos offers regeneration for worshippers who never escape their own mortality; Tammuz does not govern the seasons, because their pattern determines his fate year in and year out.

The rich development of these traditions, all substantially preliminary to the emergence of the Hebrew Bible, offers insight into the cosmological universes in which the transcendence of death was investigated as a human possibility. That very discussion, however, does not support the claim that a general expectation of afterlife pervaded cultures prior to Israel. Death is only exceptionally and partially transcended, while the gods jealously guard their immortality. That finding then plays into a pair of surprises when it concerns the traditions of Israel.[2]

Early Israel is often portrayed as relatively unconcerned with the entire question of afterlife. This generalization turned out to be both sustainable and misleading. The great exception to the rule that people's place is in life rather than the realm of the dead is set out by means of the prophets Samuel and (especially) Elijah. The absence of a theoretical account of how their transcendence of death might be explained cosmologically warrants the generalization of the relative lack of concern for the issue. Yet the theory that is largely missing, as compared with what was available elsewhere within the ancient Near East, did not prevent First Temple Judaism from coming to a result comparable to that of surrounding cultures: an extremely parsimonious view of the possibility of transcending death.

That changed, however, with the advent of Second Temple Judaism, which brings the second surprise from the traditions of Israel. Eschatological expectation of the restoration of Israel carried within itself the potential, *and then the actuality*, of promising individual transcendence. This movement came in the idiom of vision, such as in the books of Ezekiel and Enoch. But far afield from Judaism, in the emergence of Platonism, the truism of human mortality came to be challenged philosophically with a conception of personality as enduring death; Judaism proved to be amenable to some forms of philosophy in a way it had not been to the cosmologies of its neighbors. Philosophical and visionary assertions of transcending death could then find themselves blended—for example, in the commentary of Philo of Alexandria.

The Maccabean revolution galvanized and weaponized the hope of transcending death, because martyrs could hope that the physical bodies they sacrificed in confrontation with their opponents and tormenters would be restored, limb by limb, in the resurrection of the dead. A palpable, material transcendence of death became one feature within a larger movement, in which Second Temple Judaism pushed past the reserve of the earlier period and made resurrection a central feature. Even Maccabean writings, however, deploy various models to express how vindicated bodies are to be raised. They share in the spectrum of hope expressed by Judaic literature of the period, which depicts resurrection in terms of God raising up spirits, stars, angels, and souls, as well as flesh.[3] Resurrection sciences varied, so that existence could be described in ways so different as to become incompatible. Cosmologically, Second Temple Judaism shows the influence of earlier conceptions within the ancient Near East and Hellenism, although without the same degree of cosmological detail.

The hybrid products of mixed sciences of resurrection were available by the first century, and their influence within early Christianity is palpable.[4] Where it concerns Jesus' resurrection, however, the sources of the New Testament—even as they illustrate variety in conceptions of how his body was raised—mark another seismic reconfiguration of earlier possibilities. By following Paul's dataset of those by whom Jesus was seen after he had died, the innovative force of his resurrection comes into view.

Paul himself provides the earliest account in the New Testament, and from the perspective of a science of resurrection the most complete account.

His anthropology of three states of bodily existence—material, psychic, and spiritual—derives from his own encounter with Jesus as spiritual body. This last Adam marks the eschatological aim of humanity as such, and, in 1 Corinthians, Paul makes a contrast between the spiritual body that is to come and stars, spirits, angels, flesh, and soul—just the options explored elsewhere in Second Temple Judaism.

Paul's science is robust, which suggests that with a fuller representation of views from other tradents in the New Testament, greater detail in the cosmologies in which the resurrection made sense to them would also be available. As the evidence stands, strong variation in the depiction of how Jesus appeared after his death offers an index of varying conceptions of what the resurrection involves. The distinctive strands of witness make sense within the variety of Second Temple Judaism, but that concern is pushed into a secondary position, as compared to an innovative feature of the New Testament that demands a fresh adjustment of approach.

The foregrounding of a new element, emphatic and all-consuming, characterizes texts of the resurrection. Among the apostles that Paul's list provides, which coordinates with sources represented in the New Testament, the emphasis of each witness falls on the imperative that Jesus gives after his death.

In every case, the mandate represents a shift from Jesus' teaching prior to the crucifixion, and sometimes a departure. *Kêpha'* receives a commission for forgiveness that applies to his own status first of all: his denial of Jesus prior to the crucifixion made his restitution necessary. But the identity he recovers is enhanced. Jesus appears in John 21 as hosting a meal, a palpable but mysterious presence; he gives Spirit to *Kêpha'* (John 20:22-23) so that the forgiveness that restores him is conveyed to others. The circle of activity is not limited to a community in which repentance and forgiveness are necessary; the imperative is for an outward, programmatic extension. Similarly, the Twelve's commission turns on their continuing Jesus' activity as rabbi by making *talmidin* for his *mishnah*; his words, guarded and extended so as to mediate Jesus' presence, are to outlast the world (Matt 28:19-20).[5] The radical extension that involved the commission to both *Kêpha'* and the Twelve is matched by a description of Jesus' appearance as immediate and yet mysterious, so that uncertainty is built into the encounter (Matt 28:17) to the point that some of his followers nearly asked, "Who are you?" (John 21:12).

The depiction of the scene of Pentecost in Acts shifts what is considered palpable in the resurrection, because the endowment of Spirit takes over from Jesus' personal presence as the active element. Yet any uncertainty is resolved concerning the resurrection or the identity of the one who was raised. Jesus as exalted to the throne of God is identified as the source of a gift intended for humanity as a whole (Acts 2:17, 32-33), ultimately including gentiles. Baptism, now a distinctive ritual of immersion endorsed by the group Paul calls "More Than Five Hundred," joins the emerging practice of Eucharist, so that the resurrection is marked sacramentally by means of rituals that are precedented within Second Temple Judaism but radically revised.[6] The issue of purity raised by the programmatic inclusion of gentiles finds particular address in the tradition associated with James, the brother of Jesus. He associated Daniel's Son of Man with Jesus' living presence, understood as determining the moment when the dedicated practice of purity had achieved its intended result. James' usage of "Son of Man" (in Jerome's *De viris illustribus* 2) also implies Jesus' exaltation, in a manner comparable to that of the More Than Five Hundred, although the angelic emphasis is stronger than in the Pentecostal scene.

The overtly physical depiction of Jesus having "flesh and bone" (Luke 24:39) obviously contrasts with Paul's conception but also with that of *Kêpha'* and the Twelve, where an element of mystery or doubt is introduced. Similarly, the announcement of Jesus' exaltation at Pentecost and his identification to James as the angelic Son of Man described in Daniel offer fleeting allusions to different cosmologies and, with them, varying sciences of resurrection. These distinctive worldviews take an ancillary position to the imperatives developed, and there is a relationship between what is commanded and the view of how Jesus had been raised from the dead. In the case of the apocalyptic depiction of Jesus' return in flesh and bone, the clear command to await the parousia (Acts 1:10-11),[7] an ethically engaged action, occupies the center of attention.

The account of what occurred near to Emmaus evidently offers another, differing science of resurrection, in which Jesus disappears just as he is recognized in the breaking of bread (Luke 24:31). But that evanescent presence is contrasted with the interpretative heart of the narrative: opening the Scriptures by means of the risen Jesus' hermeneutic, in which he discloses himself in the texts, constitutes his persistent, palpable presence (Luke 24:32). That contact is influential and yet eludes specification. The situation is similar in sources involving Mary Magdalene, where vision persistently promises an encounter with Jesus, but the identity of the one who is seen is elusive, and touch is excluded.

Two major efforts are made within the New Testament to reason through these various traditions with their distinctive imperatives.[8] In one of them, an encounter with the risen Jesus casts those who see him in a prophetic role (see, for example, Acts 9:7 with Dan 10:7). When Jesus as the Son of Man— the beginning and the end (Rev 1:12-20)—commissioned John of Patmos, the result was prophecy—from first (1:3) to last (22:18-19). Another means of coordination is represented by the differing depictions in each gospel of the first visit to the tomb after Jesus' death. In their variation in naming those involved and their disagreement over what exactly transpired, the Gospels set out a framework for recommending whose accounts of the resurrection should be preferred.

In their characteristic ways, the prophetic line of reasoning and the narrative line do justice to the streams of tradition that they make sense of, because they allow the imperatives given by the risen Jesus to pervade even the absence that always follows his being seen. These imperatives are the most durable, historical signs of the resurrection. History accommodates the encounter with the risen Jesus in the actions of his followers. But history has not captured the resurrection, and, in the present state of knowledge and information, history cannot do so. The absence of any source that depicts God raising Jesus may reflect an awareness virtually from the moment the resurrection was believed that it did not belong to the ordinary run of human events. Speculating on the state of the tomb, the disciples' state of mind, or the psychology of vision are all interesting exercises but speculative for all that.

Within a pattern of differing but sometimes overlapping imperatives, contradictory cosmologies refer to a raised body that can be conceived along a spectrum from the physical to the spiritual (with astral and angelic in between). Modes of reasoning with these traditions pursue sometimes prophetic and sometimes narrative rationalizations. Yet an inner consensus among the traditions and the strategies to reconcile those traditions within the New Testament emerges as the final surprise.

The body that is raised might appear in a variety of media, but, in every case, Jesus' embodied consciousness is what directs those who see him. Throughout these traditions, derivable from sources as near as conceivable to the resurrection, what is recognizable is a body, giving an innovative command that can only come from a conscious human being. The confluence of body, imperative, and sentience makes the resurrection and produces the ancient claim, "I have seen the Lord" (John 20:18).

Consequences

Decisions come from strategies to learn within a given domain, but they also result from surprise over what is learned. The cosmological diversity that preceded the Hebrew Bible and continued long thereafter was predictable, once the question of "how" was put to conceptions of afterlife. However unexpected it might seem, the seismic adjustment that Second Temple Judaism made to its conditions, producing an explosive commitment to hope for human resurrection, has been well documented. But the range of cosmologies within Judaic expectations, and their intersections with both visionary and philosophical developments in the Hellenism that became Judaism's context, remains startling.

Within the New Testament, selective fluency with these cosmologies is apparent, with the result that readers are today put in the position of having to adjust to different views of science in order to understand any given assertion. And no cosmology within the sources has exerted any claim to viability within the modern world. Paul makes his personal view unmistakably plain, but it has not proven normative within Christianity or elsewhere; some of the sources he refers to in his invaluable list proved more influential than what he said himself, and he does not even refer to Jesus' tomb. The power of innovation ripples through all his sources, even when their cosmologies are fragmentary, and their commitment to the imperatives of the risen Jesus is fierce.

Discussions of whether the resurrection is historical have, from the point of view of these traditions, missed the trajectory of action that they embody. History from the point of view of the apostolic dataset of the resurrection is produced by what is done in response to risen Jesus, rather than by his historical action. He is present as a conscious body that prompts actions by other conscious bodies, but he only becomes historically palpable in their response to him.

The imperatives of the sources are so strong that, except in the case of Paul, the sciences of resurrection are largely inferential. Nonetheless, later Christian writers show that the conceptions of Judaism, and the earlier sciences of the ancient Near East, could provide crucial insight for those who engaged with the issue of how to conceive of and grapple with Jesus' living presence.

The sciences of the past, interesting though they are, do not and no doubt should not compete with the science that unfolds contemporaneously. Some ways in which modern efforts to cope with the relationship between mind and perception, cognition and physics, body and consciousness are alluded to in the last chapter.[9] Because these are current endeavors, they are far from definitive or even reliable findings. But two factors persist strongly as features of investigation today: consciousness is a feature that relates to the universe as well as to the mind, and consciousness emerges in relation to a body. As the attempt to understand who people are in their universe continues, the resurrection's model of embodied consciousness will remain as a marker of human transcendence.

The degree of commitment the resurrection elicits will, of course, vary from person to person, and it always has. That fact should long ago have cautioned interpreters who have attempted to make it into a simple fact *or* a groundless fantasy. But by pursuing the "how" of belief, and adjusting to the surprises that the texts have brought to an attentive reading, interpretation can and should do something new. By speaking of embodied consciousness as the common term in how Jesus' first followers saw him after his death, critical interpretation can offer accounts of texts that are exegetically sensitive, historically cautious, applicable within theological discussion, and sensible even to those for whom the resurrection is a foreign idea.

Belief that God raised Jesus from the dead did not arise because it was a matter of convention; conventional nostrums for understanding the resurrection—as simple historical fact, delusion, grave robbery, and the like—are most unlikely to succeed. How it happened and happens that Jesus was and is apprehended to be a living and commanding reality requires unconventional means to understand. Once those means are identified and deployed, the result can help explain the nature of Christian conviction and its prospects for believers and unbelievers alike.

Notes

1 Such views are detailed in this book. Examples of Protestant, Catholic, and revisionist arguments respectively include the positions of Rudolf Bultmann, Jean-Luc Marion, and Gerd Lüdemann. They are considered together in chapter 9, and discussions are cited below. For general treatments, see Michael R. Licona, *The Resurrection of Jesus: A New Historiographical Approach* (Downers Grove, Ill.: InterVarsity, 2010); James Crossley, "Manufacturing the Resurrection: Locating Some Contemporary Scholarly Arguments," *Neotestamantica* 45, no. 1 (2011): 49–75; Simon J. Joseph, "Redescribing the Resurrection: Beyond the Methodological Impasse?" *Biblical Theology Bulletin* 45, no. 3 (2015): 155–73.

2 John Macquarrie, *The Scope of Demythologizing: Bultmann and His Critics* (New York: Harper & Row, 1966); Joanne Miyang Cho, "Karl Jaspers' Critique of Rudolf Bultmann and His Turn toward Asia," *Existenz* 5, no. 1 (2010): 11–15. Gerd Theissen has for this reason (and in the spirit of his revisionism) called the resurrection "the corpse in the basement of the Protestant Church"; see the article by Manfred Klein entitled "Christus ist die Leiche im Keller der Kirche," *Lokalexpress*, September 11, 1996.

3 For all the emphasis on the collective identity of the church within the proceedings of the Second Vatican Council, *Lumen Gentium* 25 insists that "this infallibility with which the Divine Redeemer willed His Church to be endowed in defining doctrine of faith and morals, extends as far as the deposit of Revelation extends, which must be religiously guarded and faithfully expounded." See "Dogmatic Constitution on the Church *Lumen Gentium* Solemnly Promulgated by His Holiness Pope Paul VI

on November 21, 1964," available at http://www.vatican.va/archive/hist_councils/ii_vatican_council/documents/vat-ii_const_19641121_lumen-gentium_en.html. Philosophically, Jean-Luc Marion has argued that love with this kind of obedience leads to a higher form of knowing: *Prolegomena to Charity: Perspectives in Continental Philosophy*, trans. Stephen E. Lewis (New York: Fordham University Press, 2002). See also Brian V. Johnstone, "The Resurrection in Phenomenology: Jean-Luc Marion on the 'Saturated Phenomenon Par Excellence,'" *Pacifica* 28, no. 1 (2015): 23–39.

4   See John C. O'Neil, review of *The Resurrection of Jesus*, by Gerd Lüdemann, *Theology* 99 (1996): 154–56.

5   Leonard Eisenberg, "A New Natural Interpretation of the Empty Tomb," *International Journal for the Philosophy of Religion* 80, no. 1 (2016): 133–43.

6   The Harvard Library's HOLLIS catalog lists more than eighty-four thousand entries for the phrase (https://hollis.harvard.edu).

7   Joseph ("Redescribing the Resurrection") gives some examples; others are detailed during the course of this discussion. See also Anders S. Tune, "Quantum Theory and the Resurrection of Jesus," *Dialog* 43, no. 3 (2004): 166–76.

1 – RESURRECTION AND IMMORTALITY BEFORE JESUS

1   For both ancient and modern influence, see John Maier, ed., *Gilgamesh: A Reader* (Wauconda, Ill.: Bolchazy-Carducci, 1997); and Theodore Ziolkowski, *Gilgamesh among Us: Modern Encounters with the Ancient Epic* (Ithaca: Cornell University Press, 2012). Ziolkowski refers to the sense of "immediacy" that discovery of the epic in the late nineteenth century produced: "Unencumbered by the cultural or religious associations that shape and constrain our relationship to the Greek and Roman classics or to the Bible, it encountered an increasingly secularized public that was eager to find surrogates for its lost religious faith" (191). More recently, see David Damrosch, *The Buried Book: The Loss and Rediscovery of the Great "Epic of Gilgamesh"* (New York: Holt, 2007).

2   Since 1872, when George Smith gave a lecture entitled "The Chaldean Account of the Deluge" (later published in the *Transactions of the Society of Biblical Archaeology* 2 [1873]: 213–34), comparison with the Noah story has been pursued. See Irving Finel, *The Ark before Noah: Decoding the Story of the Flood* (New York: Anchor, 2014).

3   See the translations of Alexander Heidel, *The Gilgamesh Epic and Old Testament Parallels: A Translation and Interpretation of the Gilgamesh Epic and Related Babylonian and Assyrian Documents* (Chicago: University of Chicago Press, 1963); Maureen Gallery Kovacs, *The Epic of Gilgamesh: Translated, with an Introduction* (Stanford: Stanford University Press, 1989); and John Gardner, John Maier, and Richard A. Henshaw, *Gilgamesh: Translated from the Sîn-legi-unninnî Version* (New York: Vintage, 1985). References are to the Akkadian tablets, in this case: I ii 1; IX ii 16 (cf. line 14 and X B I 7) in Heidel's presentation; and I 46 IX 58 in Kovacs's. Gardner and Maier generally follow Heidel in their system of citation. For the history of composition and reception history of the *Epic*, see Jeffrey H. Tigay, *The Evolution of the Gilgamesh Epic* (Philadelphia: University of Pennsylvania Press, 1982); Daniel

E. Fleming and Sara J. Milstein, *The Buried Foundation of the Gilgamesh Epic: The Akkadian Huwawa Narrative*, Cuneiform Monographs (Leiden: Brill, 2010); and Alhena Gadotti, *"Gilgamesh, Enkidu, and the Netherworld" and the Sumerian Gilgamesh Cycle*, Untersuchungen zur Assyriologie und Vorderasiastischen Archäologie 10 (Berlin: de Gruyter, 2014).

4 Tigay, *Evolution of the Gilgamesh Epic*, 25n10.

5 See, for example, Robert M. Price, *Deconstructing Jesus* (Amherst, N.Y.: Prometheus, 2000), 86–94. Price is a self-aware scholar, with a rich knowledge of the New Testament bibliography that he deploys to offer a new version of the by-now exhausted argument that Jesus is a mythic construction.

6 Plutarch wrote a compendium of the stories told about Isis and Osiris within his *Moralia*; see "Isis and Osiris" 20, in *Plutarch: Moralia*, vol. 5, ed. Frank Cole Babbitt, LCL 306 (London: Heinemann, 1936). Plutarch's perspective is represented in *Drei religionsphilosophische Schriften: Über den Aberglauben, Über die späte Strafe der Gottheit, Über Isis und Osiris*, ed. Herwig Görgemanns et al., Sammlung Tusculum, Plutarch übersetzt und heraugegeben (Düsseldorf: Artemis & Winkler, 2003).

7 David O'Connor, *Abydos: Egypt's First Pharaohs and the Cult of Osiris*, New Aspects of Antiquity (London: Thames and Hudson, 2009). See p. 16 on Ramesses II. The crucial importance of the New Kingdom in the development of the myth is detailed by Mark Smith, *Following Osiris: Perspectives on the Osirian Afterlife from Our Millennia* (Oxford: Oxford University Press, 2017), 166–270.

8 The relationship of a broad swath of Egyptian evidence to the exodus is argued in James K. Hoffmeier, *Israel in Egypt: The Evidence for the Authenticity of the Exodus Tradition* (New York: Oxford University Press, 1996). He opposes the recent contention that the exodus is implausible. That view, however, does not deny that it is "one of a number of alternative immigration stories." See Philip R. Davies, *In Search of "Ancient Israel": A Study in Biblical Origins*, 2nd ed., Cornerstones (London: T&T Clark, 2015), 105. In that mention is made of a city named Ramesses in Exod 1:11; 12:37; Num 33:3, it would seem that some in Israel, whether or not their families fled from Egypt, had knowledge of this pharaoh.

9 The Egyptologist Claude Traunecker has remarked that, within Egyptian cosmology, Osiris "was a means of expressing all cyclical phenomena, whether of vegetation, the Nile inundation, or even life and death." See Traunecker, *The Gods of Egypt*, trans. David Lorton (Ithaca: Cornell University Press, 2001), 12.

10 O'Connor, *Abydos*, 43–61.

11 See John H. Taylor, *Death and Afterlife in Ancient Egypt* (London: British Museum Company; Chicago: University of Chicago Press, 2001), 48, 79.

12 Toby A. H. Wilkinson, *Early Dynastic Egypt* (London: Routledge, 1999), 220–22.

13 Taylor, *Death and Afterlife*, 32–39.

14 The texts representing this development within the Osiris cycle, and its amalgamation with the myth of Ra, come from the New Kingdom, when the development of the ritual in Abydos took place. They are known as the *Books of the Underworld*: the

Amduat, the *Book of Gates*, and the *Book of Caverns*. They are well described in Taylor, *Death and Afterlife*, 198–99.

15 The phrase "Democratisation of the Afterlife" has been applied by Egyptologists to this potentially broad extension. But Harold M. Hays has brilliantly challenged this view, in "The Death of the Democratisation of the Afterlife," in *Old Kingdom, New Perspectives: Egyptian Art and Archaeology 2750–2150*, ed. Nigel Strudwick and Helen Strudwick (Oxford: Oxbow, 2011), 115–30. This challenge has been deepened by M. Smith, *Following Osiris*, 166–270. Cf. also p. 123. More accurately, we might speak of the oligarchization of afterlife, with the limits of participation expanding and contracting over time and from place to place.

16 For a description of the ritual, see Robyn Gillam, *Performance and Drama in Ancient Egypt* (London: Duckworth, 2005), 69–73.

17 Nicely explained in M. Smith, *Following Osiris*, 47, 235.

18 Taylor (*Death and Afterlife*, 146) refers to their presentation of "the tomb as cosmogram." In particular, he calls attention to how the arrangement of rooms and wall paintings "replicated the environment of the underworld though which the sun journeyed by night."

19 That designation has been given a durable place in recent secondary literature by Joseph Campbell in *Flight of the Wild Gander: Explorations in the Mythological Dimension* (Novato, Calif.: New World Library, 2002), 106. He refers to Osiris, Tammuz, and Dionysos and links them to Jesus (p. 62). See also his *Oriental Mythology: The Masks of God* (New York: Viking Penguin, 1962); *Occidental Mythology: The Masks of God* (New York: Viking Penguin, 1964). He takes his concept from James George Frazer, who names the same gods, saying they are "of essentially one nature" and examples of "supposed death and resurrection"; Frazer, *The Golden Bough: A Study in Magic and Religion*, part 4, *Adonis Attis Osiris* (New York: St. Martin's, 1990), 1:6.

20 See Emilio Suárez de la Torre, "Apollo and Dionysos: Intersections," in *Redefining Dionysos*, ed. Alberto Bernabé, Miguel Herrero de Jáuregui, Ana Isabel Jiménez San Cristóbal, and Raquel Martín Hernández (Berlin: de Gruyter, 2013), 58–81; M. Smith, *Following Osiris*, 410.

21 See John J. Winkler and Froma I. Zeitlin, eds., *Nothing to Do with Dionysos? Athenian Drama in Its Social Context* (Princeton: Princeton University Press, 1990).

22 Marco Antonio Santamaría, "The Term *Bakkhos* and Dionyos *Bakkhios*," in Bernabé et al., *Redefining Dionysos*, 38–57.

23 M. L. West, *The Orphic Poems* (Oxford: Clarendon, 1998), 74, 139–75.

24 As a result, two recent schools of thought have contended over the issue of whether *The Bakkhantes* enacts the ritual of Dionysos or mounts something by way of parody or criticism. See Richard Seaford, *Euripides: Bacchae, with an Introduction, Translation and Commentary* (Warminster, UK: Aris & Phillips, 1996); and the response by Rainer Friedrich, "Dionysos among the Dons: The New Ritualism in Richard Seaford's Commentary on the 'Bacchae,'" *Arion: A Journal of Humanities and the Classics* 7, no. 3 (2000): 115–52; as well as Jean Bollack, *Dionysos et la tragédie: Le dieu homme dans "Les Bacchantes" d'Euripide* (Paris: Bayard, 2005); and the response

of Bernard Mezzadri in *L'Homme* 187/188 (2008): 541–45. Fortunately, that issue does need to be settled for the point of view of the play to be appreciated. Wendy Doniger O'Flaherty has successfully shown that it is not necessary for scholars of religion to assume that a work is ritual in order to assess its religious perspective. See O'Flaherty, *Other Peoples' Myths: The Cave of Echoes* (Chicago: University of Chicago Press, 1988), 103–11. A balanced appraisal is offered by Reginald Gibbons and Charles Segal, "Bacchae [Bakkhai]," in *The Complete Euripides IV: Bacchae and Other Plays*, ed. Peter Burian and Alan Sjapiro (Oxford: Oxford University Press, 2009), 199–362.

25   See the commonly available Greek edition in Arthur S. Way, *Euripides with an English Translation*, vol. 3, LCL 11 (London: Heinemann, 1924).

26   This has been called "the spell that every competent playwright casts on his audience," and it helps account for the deep link between Dionysian worship and drama as such. The phrase is included in the incisive treatment of Gilbert Norwood, "The *Bacchae* and Its Riddle," in *Essays on Euripidean Drama* (Berkeley: University of California Press, 1954), 52–73, 62. Perhaps the spell was cast as far as Acts 16:22-28.

27   See Daniel Mendelsohn, *Gender and the City in Euripides' Political Plays* (Oxford: Oxford University Press, 2002), 228–30.

28   *The Life of Crassus* 33, nicely treated by Page du Bois, *Out of Athens: The New Ancient Greeks* (Cambridge, Mass.: Harvard University Press, 2010), 27–39.

29   See the discussion in Gardner, Maier, and Henshaw, *Gilgamesh*, 154, and the speculation on Isa 17:10.

30   An allusion to Tammuz appears already in the *Epic of Gilgamesh* tablet 6, lines 46–47. The principal texts are described in Tzvi Abush, "Ishtar's Proposal and Gilgamesh's Refusal: An Interpretation of 'The Epic of Gilgamesh,' Tablet 6, Lines 1–79," *History of Religions* 26, no. 2 (1986), 143–87; Tammi J. Schneider, *An Introduction to Ancient Mesopotamian Religion* (Grand Rapids: Eerdmans, 2011), 46–49. The Akkadian text is taken as the point of departure in the translation by Stephanie Dalley, "The Descent of Ishtar to the Underworld," in *Myths from Mesopotamia: Creation, the Flood, Gilgamesh, and Others* (Oxford: Oxford University Press, 1989), 154–62. The longer, Sumerian version is available in an accessible form in Diane Wolkstein and Samuel Noah Kramer's *Inanna, Queen of Heaven and Earth: Her Stories and Hymns from Sumer* ([New York: Harper & Row, 1983], 51–89) and must be used to complement the Akkadian version. Electronic resources are also available: *Cuneiform Digital Library Initiative, Electronic Text Corpus of Sumerian Literature*, and *Melammu*.

31   Wolkstein and Kramer particularly bring this out in "The Courtship of Inanna and Dumuzi," in *Inanna*, 29–49.

32   During the twentieth century, James George Frazer used Tammuz as a chief example for how dying and rising gods were inextricably linked to agricultural cycles. We have already seen reason to question whether such expansive categories—which are designed to fit the likes of Gilgamesh/Utnapishtim, Osiris, and Dionysos, as well as Tammuz into one designation—obscure the specific cosmologies that each god

functions within. Recently, Louise M. Pryke has challenged Frazer and his followers, showing that the aim of the enterprise was to amalgamate disparate (and sometimes fragmentary) myths into a single reductionist pattern. See Pryke, *Ishtar, Gods and Heroes of the Ancient World* (London: Routledge, 2017), 188–90. The purpose of the exercise, as long ago shown by Edwin M. Yamauchi, was to conflate many elements into a model that resembled the claims of Christianity, so that that the whole could be reduced to a form of nature worship. See Yamauchi, "Tammuz and the Bible," *JBL* 84, no. 3 (1965): 283–90.

2 – ISRAEL'S REVOLUTION OF HOPE

1   Alan F. Segal observed, "In contrast to the plethora of different ideas about life after death, in the great rivers cultures surrounding Israel, early Bible traditions seem uninterested in the notion of an afterlife." See Segal, *Life after Death: A History of the Afterlife in the Religions of the West* (New York: Doubleday, 2004), 121. As in the case of several of his findings, I will show the value of this remark but also indicate its limitations. In this instance, I hold that there is more agreement than disagreement between the Hebrew Bible and other sources from the Near East where it concerns the finality of death. The issue is nicely dealt with in Lidija Novakovic, *Resurrection: A Guide for the Perplexed* (London: T&T Clark, 2016), 7–47.

2   Once the story of Noah was established in biblical tradition, it appears that alternative readings offered purchase to motifs reminiscent of Utnapishtim. See John C. Reeves, "Utnapishtim in the Book of Giants?" *JBL* 112, no. 1 (1993): 110–15.

3   See Patrick E. McGovern, "The Noah Hypothesis," in *Ancient Wine: The Origins of Viniculture* (Princeton: Princeton University Press, 2007), 16–39.

4   For discussion of that story within the setting of human sacrifice, see Bruce Chilton, *Abraham's Curse: Child Sacrifice in the Legacies of the West* (New York: Doubleday, 2008), 18–43.

5   See Hennie J. Marsman, *Women in Ugarit and Israel: Their Social and Religious Position in the Context of the Ancient Near East*, OTS 49 (Leiden: Brill, 2003), 605–9; Jer 7:18; 44:15-27.

6   See Megan Bishop Moore and Brad E. Kelle, *Biblical History and Israel's Past: The Changing Study of the Bible and History* (Grand Rapids: Eerdmans, 2011). The issue of the exodus, which came up in the last chapter (see n8), features within this discussion, as well, in a sometimes strident controversy pitting "minimalists" (who assert that the biblical sources developed from very little by way of historical events) against "maximalists" (who see the documents as historical and written near in time to the events they reflect).

7   Of course, other stunning changes are also involved. For example, the assertions that sacrifice may occur only in Jerusalem and that every god except Yahweh is nonexistent are foreign to the earliest stages of biblical development. My point of view is reflected in Bruce Chilton, ed., *The Cambridge Companion to the Bible*, 2nd ed., with contributions from Howard Clark Kee, Eric M. Meyers, John Rogerson, Amy-Jill

Levine, and Anthony J. Saldarini (Cambridge: Cambridge University Press, 2008), 189–201.

8	This is well brought out in the distinction between disreputable and honorable death in the Hebrew Bible traced by Kevin J. Madigan and Jon D. Levenson's "Who Goes to Sheol—and Who Does Not?" in *Resurrection: The Power of God for Christians and Jews* (New Haven: Yale University Press, 2008), 69–80. They suggest that Sheol "is best conceived as a kind of continuation of the end of the deceased's life" (76). But it is not hell, even for those who might deserve punishment, and heaven is not its opposite. Rather, insofar as there is an antipode to Sheol, it is the temple in Jerusalem.

9	See Jan Assmann, *Moses the Egyptian: The Memory of Egypt in Western Monotheism* (Cambridge, Mass.: Harvard University Press, 1997).

10	Homer, *Odyssey* 11.489–491. The setting is sacrifice to which the souls of the dead are attracted and engage Odysseus; see *Homer: The Odyssey Books 1–12 with an English Translation*, ed. A. T. Murray, rev. George E. Dimock, LCL 104 (Cambridge, Mass.: Harvard University Press, 1995).

11	Segal (*Life after Death*, 120–38) has helpfully documented how widely represented this view is within the Hebrew Bible, and he contrasts it with Canaanite rituals that valorized the dead. Although the precise contours of Canaanite cosmology and ritual have not yet been described fully, it is plausible to see them as the immediate conduit of many of the conceptions of the ancient Near East—some of which are outlined in the last chapter—to which Israel responded, whether positively or negatively. As Madigan and Levenson ("Heaven on Earth," in *Resurrection*, 81–106) point out, this also implies that the temple itself provides access to paradise. Concentrated attention to this theme is developed in Terje Stordalen's *Echoes of Eden: Genesis 2–3 and Symbolism of the Eden Garden in Biblical Hebrew Literature*, CBET 25 (Leuven: Peeters, 2000), 306–14.

12	Uncertainty as to the meaning vexed patristic and rabbinic interpretation and supported the view among Christian interpreters that the episode was a demonic delusion. See K. A. D. Smelik, "The Witch of Endor: 1 Samuel 28 in Rabbinic and Christian Exegesis till 800 A.D.," *VC* 33, no. 2 (1979): 160–70, 168, 174, 176. As he shows, however, the other possibilities mentioned are more natural. Christians saw necromancy as such as demonic and also wished to rebuff the accusation that the resurrection could be explained as a conjuring.

13	*Enggastrimuthos* in Greek implies a form of ventriloquism (literally, "stomach-speech"). That usage was cited to support the charge of deceptive necromancy (see the previous note).

14	See 1 Sam 13:8-15. In this case, as well, the issue is obedience to the LORD, but the incident involves Saul's failure to wait for Samuel to offer sacrifice, and his usurpation of that role. Given Samuel's delay in arriving, however, Saul's fault is portrayed as less egregious.

15	The narrative opens less magnificently than Josh 3:1–4:24, but then it closes in an even more spectacular fashion. On this and similar connections, see Joel S. Burnett,

"'Going Down' to Bethel: Elijah and Elisha in the Theological Geography of the Deuteronomistic History," *JBL* 129, no. 2 (2010): 281–97, here 287.

16 So Burnett, "Going Down," 297. He also develops a plausible analysis that the youths represent a royal opposition to Elisha and the prophetic movement.

17 The additions correspond to chapters 40–55 (known as the Second Isaiah) and chapters 56–66 (the Third Isaiah). Chapters 24–27 are also to be associated with these additions; cf. Chilton, *Cambridge Companion to the Bible*, 189–201.

18 For discussion, see Martha Himmelfarb, *Tours of Hell: An Apocalyptic Form in Jewish and Christian Literature* (Philadelphia: University of Pennsylvania Press, 1983), 116–19; Richard Bauckham, *The Fate of the Dead: Studies on the Jewish and Christian Apocalypses*, NovTSup 93 (Leiden: Brill, 2001), 134–35.

19 So Claudia Setzer, *Resurrection of the Body in Early Judaism and Early Christianity: Doctrine, Community, and Self-Definition* (Boston: Brill Academic, 2004), 8.

20 Theodore A. Bergren, "Plato's 'Myth of Er' and Ezekiel's 'Throne Vision': A Common Paradigm?" *Numen* 64, nos. 2–3 (2017): 153–82. See also H. S. Thayer, "The Myth of Er," *History of Philosophy Quarterly* 5, no. 4 (1988): 369–84.

21 Plato, *Republic* 10.614–621; see Plato, *The Republic with an English Translation*, ed. Paul Shorey, LCL Plato 6 Republic 2 (London: Heinemann, 1970). As in the case of the *Odyssey*, many other renderings are also available, but the Loeb collection presents a generally sound Greek or Latin text opposite its translation and provides a good resource.

22 See, for example, Paul M. Fullmer, *Resurrection in Mark's Literary-Historical Perspective* (London: T&T Clark/Continuum, 2007).

23 See George W. E. Nickelsburg, *1 Enoch 1: A Commentary on the Book of 1 Enoch, Chapters 1–36; 81–108*, ed. Klaus Baltzer, Hermeneia (Minneapolis: Fortress, 2001), 7–28; Michael A. Knibb, *Essays on the Book of Enoch and Other Early Jewish Texts and Traditions*, SVTP 22 (Leiden: Brill, 2009); Gabriele Boccaccini and John J. Collins, eds., *The Early Enoch Literature*, Supplements to Journal for the Study of Judaism 12 (Leiden: Brill, 2007).

24 See Elliot R. Wolfson, *Through a Speculum That Shines: Vision and Imagination in Medieval Jewish Mysticism* (Princeton: Princeton University Press, 1994). Although the Middle Ages saw the flowering of kabbalistic literature, its roots are biblical. See James R. Davila, *Descenders to the Chariot: The People behind the Hekhalot Literature*, Supplements to the Journal for the Study of Judaism 70 (Leiden: Brill 2001); Frederick E. Greenspahn, ed., *Jewish Mysticism and Kabbalah: New Insights and Scholarship*, Jewish Studies in the 21st Century (New York: New York University Press, 2011); Moshe Idel, *Ascensions on High in Jewish Mysticism: Pillars, Lines, Ladders, Pasts Incorporated*, CEU Studies in the Humanities 2 (Budapest: Central European University Press, 2005).

25 Indeed, not only modern readers—the Wisdom of Solomon is included in the oldest canon of the New Testament, alongside the Gospels and the Letters of Paul. See Mark W. Elliott, "Wisdom of Solomon, Canon and Authority," *Studia Patristica* 63 (2013): 3–16.

26 This allegorical reading exerted a palpable influence on Augustine, when he came to write *The City of God*; see Johannes van Oort, *Jerusalem and Babylon: A Study into Augustine's City of God and the Sources of His Doctrine of the Two Cities*, Supplements to Vigiliae Christianae 14 (Leiden: Brill, 1991), 235–53. Van Oort wisely observes that Augustine adapts the conception in a way that makes his view distinctive from Philo's.

27 For Philo's relationship to Plato, see C. D. Elledge, *Resurrection of the Dead in Early Judaism 200 BCE–CE 200* (Oxford: Oxford University Press, 2017), 113–17. Philo's texts are available in *Philo Volume II*, ed. F. H. Colson and G. H. Whitaker, LCL 227 (Cambridge, Mass.: Harvard University Press, 1991); and *Philo Volume VI*, ed. F. H. Colson, LCL 289 (Cambridge, Mass.: Harvard University Press, 1994).

28 See Josephus, *Jewish Antiquities* 4.326; 9.28; available in *Jewish Antiquities, Books I–IV*, ed. H. St. J. Thackery, LCL Josephus 4 (London: Heinemann, 1930); and *Jewish Antiquities, Books IX–XI*, ed. Ralph Marcus, LCL Josephus 6 (London: Heinemann, 1937); Bruce Chilton, "The Transfiguration: Dominical Assurance and Apostolic Vision," *NTS* 27 (1980): 115–24.

3 – BODIES RAISED IN ISRAEL'S VINDICATION

1 See Albert I. Baumgarten, ed., *Sacrifice in Religious Experience*, Numen Book Series 93 (Leiden: Brill, 2003); Jeffrey Carter, ed., *Understanding Religious Sacrifice: A Reader*, Controversies in Religion (New York: Continuum, 2003); Bruce Chilton, *Abraham's Curse: Child Sacrifice in the Legacies of the West* (New York: Doubleday, 2008); Ann W. Astell and Sandor Goodhart, eds., *Sacrifice, Scripture and Substitution: Readings in Judaism and Christianity* (Notre Dame, Ind.: Notre Dame University Press, 2011).

2 Specified by Ezek 44:15 as the high priestly family; see Menaham Haran, "Ezekiel, P, and the Priestly School," *VT* 58, no. 2 (2008): 211–17. In this regard, see the discussion in regard to the Sadducees below.

3 And which are not always present in any case. The Revelation to John, for example, does not appear to be pseudepigraphal in the same sense that Daniel is. Cf. Robert L. Webb, "'Apocalyptic': Observations on a Slippery Term," *JNES* 49, no. 2 (1990): 115–26; Michael Anthony Novak, "*The Odes of Solomon* as Apocalyptic Literature," *VC* 66 (2012): 527–50; Bruce Chilton, *Visions of the Apocalypse: Receptions of John's Revelation in Western Imagination* (Waco, Tex.: Baylor University Press, 2013), 131–33.

4 See Alan F. Segal, *Life after Death: A History of the Afterlife in the Religions of the West* (New York: Doubleday, 2004), 289: "As opposed to prophecy, when repentance can avert any of God's threats, in the vision the predicted end will come, regardless of human behavior."

5 "Younger" only within the tradition of millennia that Zoroastrianism represents and—according to a now-prevalent hypothesis—antedating Enoch and Daniel. Good discussions are available in Bryan Rennie, "Zoroastrianism: The Iranian Roots of Christianity?" *CSSR Bulletin* 36, no. 1 (2007): 3–7; Shaul Shaked, "Eschatology i:

In Zoroastrianism and Zoroastrian Influence," *Encyclopedia Iranica* 7, no. 6 (1996): 565–69. I agree with their findings of a relatively early and robust insistence upon eschatological rewards and punishments but demur at the claim of the universalism of the scheme. The latter element emerged during the Sassanian period in my view, after both Judaism and Christianity had made their distinctive contributions. But if Shaked's analysis is accepted, then the broadening of hope in the resurrection can be attributed first not to Israelite sources but to Zoroastrian theology. The late attestation of the manuscripts compared to the point of composition, combined with clear evidence for the layered production of texts over time, makes source criticism of the Bible and related sources seem an accurate science by comparison. A basic consideration in the assessment of when a feature emerges within a literature, however, is its *Sitz im Leben* within the cultural life of the community of production. The Sassanian period of Zoroastrianism posed the challenge of accounting for an empire and its global aspirations, as contrasted with an earlier focus on an ethical elite.

6 See *The Dead Sea Scrolls: Hebrew, Aramaic, and Greek Texts with English Translations*, vol. 2, *Damascus Document, War Scroll, and Related Documents*, ed. James H. Charlesworth (Tübingen: Mohr, 1995); Florentino García Martínez and Julio Trebolle Barrera, *The People of the Dead Sea Scrolls*, trans. Wilfred G. E. Watson (Leiden: Brill, 1995); James C. VanderKam, *The Meaning of the Dead Sea Scrolls: Their Significance for Understanding the Bible, Judaism, Jesus, and Christianity* (San Francisco: HarperSanFrancisco, 2002).

7 See *The Dead Sea Scrolls: Hebrew, Aramaic, and Greek Texts with English Translations*, vol. 1, *Rule of the Community and Related Documents*, ed. James H. Charlesworth (Tübingen: Mohr, 1994).

8 See Lidija Novakovic, *Raised from the Dead according to the Scripture: The Role of Israel's Scripture in Early Christian Interpretation of Jesus' Resurrection*, T&T Clark Jewish and Christian Texts Series 12 (London: T&T Clark, 2012), 87–88. See also George W. E. Nickelsburg, *Resurrection, Immortality, and Eternal Life in Intertestamental Judaism and Early Christianity: Expanded Edition*, HTS 56 (Cambridge, Mass.: Harvard University, 2006), 47–49, 219–23; addressing Oscar Cullmann, *Immortalité de l'ame ou réssurection des mort? Le témoignage du Nouveau Testament* (Paris: Delachaux & Niestle, 1956). Cullman's attempt to make resurrection and immortality mutually exclusive categories remains influential, but it has not stood up to criticism. Nickelsburg is to be credited with showing that it is not critically viable and is probably motivated by apologetic considerations. Nickelsburg's attempt to date Jubilees prior to Daniel, on the other hand (pp. 65–66), has not prevailed, and he has revised his chronology since the original publication of his book in 1967.

9 For discussion, see James C. VanderKam, *The Book of Jubilees: A Critical Edition*, CSCO 510, Scriptores Aethiopici 87 (Peters: Louvain, 1989), xn5. His reserve has since been largely overcome, although the fragmentary nature of the evidence remains a factor; cf. Florentino García Martínez and Eibert J. C. Tigchelaar, eds., *The Dead Sea Scrolls, Study Edition* (Leiden: Brill, 1999), 361–63.

10 So an early and influential study: R. H. Charles, *The Apocrypha and Pseudepigrapha of the Old Testament in English* (Oxford: Clarendon, 1913), 1:59. The suggestion in regard to the Sadducees is his.

11 Their name reflects loyalty to the position—and no doubt the genealogy—of Zadok, also a key dimension within the Dead Sea Scrolls. See Alison Schofield and James C. VanderKam, "Were the Hasmoneans Zadokites?" *JBL* 124, no. 1 (2005): 73–87. The authors, in a brilliant analysis, answer that question in the affirmative, in the face of received opinion (which they document). Although the matter is perhaps not conclusively settled, their suggestion is plausible, and in any case it is clear that the Maccabees needed to reckon with Sadducean claims. One reason for that is that, although they may have been Zadokites, they had evidently not belonged to the elite families that made claims to the high priesthood in the period prior to the revolt against the Seleucids.

12 See Josephus, *Jewish War* 2.165; Mark 12:18; Matt 22:23; Luke 20:27; Acts 23:8; m. Sanhedrin 10.1.

13 See Paul's accusation in 1 Cor 15:12: "Some among you say there is not resurrection from the dead." Yet in the same letter, he complains about those who say that they "already" reign (1 Cor 4:8). This is the point of departure for the article of Anthony C. Thiselton: "Realized Eschatology at Corinth," *NTS* 24 (1978): 510–26. Writing in response to criticism of his views, Thiselton then revised his position to accommodate problems posed in Corinth by "concerns about self-promotion, the psychological insecurity generated by status inconsistency, competitive pragmatism, and the radical pluralism which we have identified with David Harvey's 'postmodern mood' of the social construction of a 'virtual reality.'" See Thiselton, *The First Epistle to the Corinthians: A Commentary on the Greek Text*, NIGTC (Carlisle, UK: Paternoster; Grand Rapids: Eerdmans, 2000), 40. Historically, "realized eschatology" appears increasingly plausible the more the alternatives are couched in terms of options that did not feature on Paul's horizon.

14 So Nickelsburg (*Resurrection*, 133–34, 162), a skilled interpreter who has opened up this seam within 1 Macc in his magisterial work.

15 Cf. N. Clayton Croy, *3 Maccabees*, Septuagint Commentary Series (Leiden: Brill, 2006).

16 See Robert Doran, *2 Maccabees: A Critical Commentary*, Hermeneia (Minneapolis: Fortress, 2012).

17 See, for example, Norman L. Geisler, "In Defense of the Resurrection: A Reply to Criticisms," *JETS* 34, no. 2 (1991): 243–61.

18 See John J. Collins, "Sibylline Oracles," in *The Old Testament Pseudepigrapha*, ed. James H. Charlesworth (Garden City, N.Y.: Doubleday, 1985), 1:317–472, here 389 (see marginal note).

19 So Segal, *Life after Death*, 381, 607; citing Josephus, *Jewish War* 2.163 and m. Sanhedrin 10.1.

20 See Genesis Rabbah 28.3, Leviticus Rabbah 4, and Ecclesiastes Rabbah 12.5.1; and the brief but illuminating discussion in Robert Shapiro, "The Mystical Bone of

Resurrection," *Radiology* 163, no. 3 (1987): 718. The Midrashim are easily available in *The Midrash Rabbah*, ed. H. Freedman and Maurice Simon (London: Soncino, 1977); within the collection, H. Freedman translated Genesis, J. Israelstam translated chapters 1–19 of Leviticus, and A. Cohen translated Ecclesiastes.

21 Hugh Anderson, "4 Maccabees," in Charlesworth, *Old Testament Pseudepigrapha*, 2:531–64, here 538.

22 Cf. 10:12; 15:28; 16:20.

23 C. D. Elledge puts the matter well: "Resurrection certainly restores the dead to some type of embodied existence, yet the more precise details of that existence remained open to a variety of explorations." Elledge, *Resurrection of the Dead in Early Judaism 200 BCE–CE 200* (Oxford: Oxford University Press, 2017), 6.

24 So Oscar Cullmann, successfully refuted by Nickelsburg, *Resurrection*, 219–23. Cullmann's position has been resuscitated in the work of N. T. Wright: *The Resurrection of the Son of God*, Christian Origins and the Question of God 3 (London: SPCK; Minneapolis: Fortress, 2003). His book's argument turns on according a monopoly status to the view of resurrection taken in 2 Macc.

25 Nickelsburg, *Resurrection*, 3–5. The works he refers to are dealt with elsewhere in the present discussion, and so they are not treated here. He usefully reviews the secondary literature that appeared in the period between his initial publication and the new book. The disagreement he addresses turns on his own disinclination to assume that resurrection in Judaism was "bodily" and to allow for "immortality of the soul." Given the controversy over the issue, that is a natural typology for modern discussion, but the primary texts do not seem patient of a neat division along those lines. Nickelsburg himself observes in his conclusion that "there is a movement toward resurrection of the body as the standard means and mode for making possible a post-mortem judgment." But having made that judgment, he immediately has to acknowledge that 4 Macc accords with the Essene "belief in assumption or immortality" (216–17).

26 Because this is a "long time" rather than eternity, John J. Collins questions whether eternal life is at stake. See Collins, "The Afterlife in Apocalyptic Literature," in *Judaism in Late Antiquity*, ed. Jacob Neusner, Alan J. Avery-Peck, and Bruce Chilton (Boston: Brill, 2001), 3:119–39, 122. But since, as Collins agrees, the fragrant tree is the tree of life, whose capacity is limitless (see Gen 3:22), a restrictive reading seems unnatural.

27 O. S. Wintermute, "Jubilees," in Charlesworth, *Old Testament Pseudepigrapha*, 2:35–142, here 102 (see marginal note and footnote p). As he points out, "spirits" might be taken poetically to refer to the more collective view of an earlier period. But this is only a possible interpretation when the term is abstracted from the wider scenario in which it features.

28 Collins ("Afterlife," in Neusner, Avery-Peck, and Chilton, *Judaism in Late Antiquity*, 3:129) remarks, "It is not the Greek idea of the soul, but neither is it a physical body." But Collins attributes this idea to Daniel, as well, where the language and conception are different, and he does not include Jubilees in his analysis.

29 So John Collins, *The Apocalyptic Imagination: An Introduction to the Jewish Matrix of Christianity* (New York: Crossroad, 1998), 113.

30 So Mark T. Finney, *Resurrection, Hell and Afterlife: Body and Soul in Antiquity, Judaism and Early Christianity* (New York: Routledge, 2016), 67.

31 For this reason, when Pseudo-Phocylides 103–104 says that the remains of the departed will come to light again and "afterward they will become gods," that is a probable reference to angelic status. See P. W. van der Horst, "Pseudo-Phocylides," in Charlesworth, *Old Testament Pseudepigrapha*, 2:565–73, 582.

32 The expression is borrowed from Isa 28:14-19, an indication that, as Nickelsburg argues, Wisdom used Isaiah as a template; see Nickelsburg, *Resurrection*, 83–87.

33 See, for example, Thorleif Boman, *Hebrew Thought Compared with Greek*, trans. J. L. Moreau (Philadelphia: Westminster, 1960); and the response from James Barr, *The Semantics of Biblical Language* (London: Oxford University Press, 1961), 46–88.

34 Cf. Wis 3:6.

4 – PAUL ON HOW JESUS "WAS SEEN"

1 To encounter sciences that compete with Paul's in terms of comprehensive cosmological detail, one must await the discussions of Origen of Alexandria during the third century (in *First Principles*) and Augustine of Hippo at the opening of the fifth century (in *The City of God*). Even in those cases, the updated sciences are developed in a conscious dialogue with Paul; see Bruce Chilton and Jacob Neusner, *Comparing Spiritualities: Formative Christianity and Judaism on Finding Life and Meeting Death* (Harrisburg, Pa.: Trinity Press International, 2000), 68–91; and Chilton, "One Afterlife of Nickelsburg's Resurrection, Immortality, and Eternal Life," in *George W. E. Nickelsburg in Perspective: An Ongoing Dialogue of Learning*, ed. Jacob Neusner and Alan J. Avery-Peck, Supplement to the Journal for the Study of Judaism (Leiden: Brill, 2003), 2:315–34.

2 For an orientation within Paul's life and theology, see Anthony C. Thiselton, *The First Epistle to the Corinthians: A Commentary on the Greek Text*, NIGTC (Carlisle, UK: Paternoster; Grand Rapids: Eerdmans, 2000), 29–46; and Bruce Chilton, *Rabbi Paul: An Intellectual Biography* (New York: Doubleday, 2004), 147–221.

3 See Lidija Novakovic, *Resurrection: A Guide for the Perplexed* (London: T&T Clark, 2016), 59–64.

4 On Stoic influences within Christianity, see Sabine MacCormack, "Cicero in Late Antiquity," in *The Cambridge Companion to Cicero*, ed. Catherine Steele (Cambridge: Cambridge University Press, 2013), 251–305, citing Augustine's *Against the Academics* 1.7; Marcia L. Colish, *The Stoic Tradition from Antiquity to the Early Middle Ages*, vol. 2, *Stoicism in Christian Latin Thought through the Sixth Century* (Leiden: Brill, 1990); Dougal Blyth, "Cicero and Philosophy as Text," *CJ* 106, no. 1 (2010): 71–98. Evidently, 4 Maccabees develops a view of resurrection that is compatible with the later Christian conception, also showing the influence of Stoicism.

5 See, for example, Ted Cabal, "Defending the Resurrection of Jesus: Yesterday, Today and Forever," *Southern Baptist Journal of Theology* 18, no. 4 (2014): 115–37.

6 So, for example, N. T. Wright, *What Saint Paul Really Said: Was Paul of Tarsus the Real Founder of Christianity?* (Grand Rapids: Eerdmans, 1997), 50. Out of his own assumption that Paul speaks of a physical resurrection, just what Paul overtly denies, Wright also imposes the "empty tomb" on Paul. His argument maintains that because Paul referred to Jesus being buried (1 Cor 15:4) and then being raised, he implied the tomb was empty. See Wright, *The Resurrection of the Son of God*, Christian Origins and the Question of God 3 (Minneapolis: Fortress, 2003), 321, where the line of thought is casuistic:

The fact that the empty tomb itself, so prominent in the gospel accounts, does not appear to be specifically mentioned in this passage, is not significant; the mention here of "buried, then raised" no more needs to be amplified in that way than one would need to amplify the statement "I walked down the street" with the qualification "on my feet."

But if the exegetical thread of the text is followed, rather than the reductive logic of the interpreter, the bare statement of Jesus' burial is connected immediately to the claim that he was raised on the third day. Paul says these events happened "according to the Scriptures." If that phrase applies to both the burial (not only the death) and the resurrection, then Paul would be the earliest source available for a connection between the passion and the song of the suffering servant in Isaiah 52:13–53:12, where it is said that the servant will be buried with a rich man (Isaiah 53:9). Taken in that way, Paul's bare assertion might also be taken to allude to the reference to Joseph of Arimathea in the Gospels, although it is obvious that no specific tradition apart from the fact of burial is stated.

7 Quite unlike the modern view of cellular differentiation, this view relies on Aristotle's conception of differing orders of flesh. See David Sedley, *Creationism and Its Critics in Antiquity*, Sather Classical Lectures 66 (Berkeley: University of California Press, 2007), 167–204.

8 On modern views of the body, see Daniel Lord Smail and Andrew Shryock, "Body," in *Deep History: The Architecture of Past and Present* (Berkeley: University of California Press, 2011), 55–77; and John Robb, "Material Culture, Landscapes of Action, and Emergent Causation: A New Model for the Origins of the European Neolithic," *Current Anthropology* 54, no. 6 (2013): 657–83.

9 See Rom 15:27; 1 Cor 3:3; 9:11; 2 Cor 1:12; 10:4. The sense of the related term *sarkinos* seems to me more negative in Rom 7:14 and 1 Cor 3:1, but 2 Cor 3:3 shows a high valuation of "fleshly hearts." The usage shows that "flesh," in its wide associations, stands at the origin of both adjectives. In the last case, the influence of Ezek 11:19 is palpable. Robert G. Bratcher, "The Meaning of *Sarx* ('Flesh') in Paul's Letters," *BT* 29, no. 2 (1978): 212–18.

10 Except as noted, these comparisons are drawn from the electronic resource "Bible Study Tools" (https://www.biblestudytools.com/).

11 See *The New Testament: A New Translation* (London: Hodder and Stoughton, 1915). The Weymouth Bible offered the rendering "animal body," which can be understood

but scarcely clarifies Paul's meaning. The Wycliffe rendering, "beastly body," is also impenetrable, but possibly the most enjoyable of any translation I have encountered.

12 The wording is that of the Septuagint, while the Masoretic Text reads, "Who has directed the LORD's Spirit?" Targum Jonathan extends the sense, "Who has established the Holy Spirit in the mouth of all the prophets?" Paul thinks so flexibly about mind, Spirit, and the capacity of human cognition to fathom the divine that he might have had all these renderings in the background of his thought. For citation of the most accurate editions and commentary, see Bruce Chilton, *The Isaiah Targum: Introduction, Translation, Apparatus, and Notes*, ArBib 11 (Wilmington, Del.: Glazier, 1987).

13 The linkage of themes through the letter supports the carefully developed argument in Thiselton, *First Epistle*, that 1 Corinthians is not simply episodic in the topics that it addresses.

14 As James Ware argues, this militates against the argument that flesh and soul and spirit are completely different substances in Paul's understanding. See Ware, "Paul's Understanding of the Resurrection in 1 Corinthians 15:36-54," *JBL* 133, no. 4 (2014): 809–35, here 832–33. Ware is critical of attempts to claim that resurrection involves a new substance of being, preferring the finding that the spiritual body is "the risen body given life by the Spirit."

15 In view of Paul's insistence, James Ware goes beyond the evidence of Paul in asserting that "the body of flesh and bones" is raised in Paul's understanding; Ware, "Paul's Understanding," 835. Rather, to Paul's mind, the victory of both Christ and the believer (vv. 54-55)—which he expresses as the true meaning of Isaiah's prophecy of resurrection (Isa 25:8)—involves a change in the body that had once been only flesh, then soul, and, at its best, spirit. Just as the end of the entire process is that God becomes "all in all" (1 Cor 15:28), so those raised from the dead "bear the image of the man of heaven" (1 Cor 15:49). As Stefan Alkier concludes, "The Crucified One who was raised is therefore no revivified dead man who comes back to his former life. He is rather the beginning of the eschatological raising of the dead." See Alkier, *The Reality of the Resurrection: The New Testament Witness*, trans. Leroy A. Huizenga (Waco, Tex.: Baylor University Press, 2013), 25.

16 Conventionally translated "first fruit," this term refers sacrificially in the Septuagint (Lev 23:10) to the initial portion of any kind of offering, animal or plant. In this case, the resurrection marks a shift as crucial as the death of Adam. Adam's death means ours, just as Jesus' resurrection means ours (1 Cor 15:22). Paul can also use the term of the gift of the Spirit (Rom 8:23) that longs for "the redemption of our bodies." See Christian Grappe, *L'au-delà dans la Bible: Le temporal et le spatial*, Le Monde de la Bible 68 (Fribourg: Labor et Fides, 2014), 197–98.

17 "Gospel" is the traditional rendering. The term refers initially to news of victory in pitched battle, corresponding to *besorta'* in Aramaic. In the book of Isaiah, in its Aramaic version (the Targum), for example, the verbal form *basar* is used to speak of the final tidings of God's triumph (Isa 52:7) and also of the message of the prophet who speaks that promise (Isa 53:1). These two passages are of especial interest, because

they form a precedent for Jesus' preaching. In these quotations, where the Targum introduces new wording as compared to the Hebrew text of Isaiah, italics are used, so that the particular meaning of Isaiah for Aramaic speakers will be clear:

How beautiful upon the mountains *of the land of Israel* are the feet of him who announces *victory*, who publishes peace, who announces good *victory*, who publishes redemption, who says to *the congregation of* Zion, *The* King*dom of* your God *is revealed*. (Isa 52:7)

Who has believed *this*, our *message of victory?* And to whom has *the strength of* the *mighty* arm of the LORD been *so* revealed? (53:1)

Not only do we find here the Aramaic wording (*besora* and *basar*) that stands behind "gospel" (*euanggelion*) and "preach the gospel" (*euanggelizomai*) in the New Testament, but also the exact equivalent of Jesus' signature concern, the kingdom of God.

18 And probably did not know Jesus personally, despite a recent vigorous argument to the contrary. See Stanley E. Porter, *When Paul Met Jesus: How an Idea Got Lost in History* (New York: Cambridge University Press, 2016). The crucial passage is 2 Cor 5:16, where Paul refers to having known the Anointed "according to flesh" (*kata sarka*). In the same breath, Paul asserts that he now knows no one *kata sarka*; his concern is not to claim a personal, authoritative relationship but to explain the means by which persons are rightly known.

19 As Gerd Lüdemann has pointed out, the disclosure of God's Son within Paul is compatible with a visual element (cf. Rev 1:1-2); cf. Lüdemann, *The Resurrection of Jesus: History, Experience, Theology*, trans. John Bowden (Minneapolis: Fortress, 1994), 51–52. The relationship between Paul's apocalypse and his time in Arabia is developed in Chilton, *Rabbi Paul*, 67–71.

20 Adolf von Harnack, followed more recently by Ernst Bammel, posited that two lists are actually combined here, one headed by *Kêpha'* (v. 5) and the other by James (v. 7). See Adolf von Harnack, *Die Verklärungsgeschichte Jesu, der Bericht des Paulus (I. Kor. 15, 3ff) und die beiden Christusvisionen des Petrus*, Sitzungsberichte der Königlich Preussischen Akademie der Wissenschaften zu Berlin (Berlin: Walter de Gruyter, 1922); and Bammel, "Herkunft und Funktion der Traditionselemente in 1 Kor 15,1-11," *Theologische Zeitung* 11 (1955): 401–19.

21 In Gordon Fee's explanation, Paul picks up a negative reference to himself current in the community at Corinth, which would account for the use of the definite article. This self-designation, with its implication of an untimely event, plays out the emphasis on sequence through the passage. By way of translation, Fee suggests "any kind of premature birth (abortion, stillbirth, or miscarriage)." The point, as Fee shows, is that Paul was "born" as a believing apostle out of time—while persecuting the church of God (v. 9). See Gordon D. Fee, *The First Epistle to the Corinthians*, NICNT (Grand Rapids: Eerdmans, 1987), 733.

22 So Lüdemann, *Resurrection of Jesus*, 38–39. Harnack's analysis is predicated, as Gerd Lüdemann has shown (p. 85), on the thesis of an active suppression of the claims to authority of Peter and James at a later stage in the tradition (primarily by Matthew and Luke).

23 Joachim Jeremias' assertion that we are dealing with an Aramaic tradition appears an attractive explanation, although that would not exclude the influence of both *Kêpha'* and James. See Jeremias, "Artikilloses *Khristos*: Zur Ursprache von 1 Cor 15,3b-5)," *ZNW* 57 (1966): 211–15.

24 See Bernd Janowski and Peter Stuhlmacher, eds., *The Suffering Servant: Isaiah 53 in Jewish and Christian Sources*, trans. Daniel P. Bailey (Grand Rapids: Eerdmans, 2004).

25 On the Targumic interpretation and its connection to the New Testament, see Paul Flesher and Bruce Chilton, *The Targums: A Critical Introduction* (Waco, Tex.: Baylor University Press, 2011), 183–98.

26 As argued convincingly by Anthony J. Guerra, *Romans and the Apologetic Tradition: The Purpose, Genre and Audience of Paul's Letter*, SNTSMS 81 (Cambridge: Cambridge University Press, 1994), 72–74. Although the dating of 4 Maccabees puts a connection in doubt, the linguistic invocation of martyrdom seems evident. See Douglas A. Campbell, *The Rhetoric of Righteousness in Romans 3.21-26*, JSNTSup 65 (Sheffield: Sheffield Academic Press, 1992), 219–28.

27 Whatever the relationship between 1 Corinthians and the Gospels, C. K. Barrett seems right to recognize that "the Pauline list and the gospel narratives of resurrection appearances cannot be harmonized into a neat chronological sequence." See Barrett, *The First Epistle to the Corinthians*, BNTC (Peabody, Mass.: Hendrickson, 1993), 342.

28 Jeremias believed the passive can be explained by *'ytchamy* in Aramaic; Jeremias, "Artikilloses," 211–15. Studies of Aramaic dialects since his time make it plain that we should rather think in terms of the verb *chaza'*, but apart from this correction his point stands. See Stephen A. Kaufman, ed., *The Comprehensive Aramaic Lexicon Project*, http://cal1.cn.huc.edu, accessed Pentecost 2018. Like Jeremias himself, Hans Conzelmann concludes that the balance of probability favors the finding of an Aramaic source. See Conzelmann, *1 Corinthians: A Commentary on the First Epistle to the Corinthians*, trans. James W. Leitch, ed. George W. MacRae, references by James W. Dunkly, Hermeneia (Philadelphia: Fortress, 1975), 252–54.

29 Conzelmann was quite open about the concern, even as he acknowledged the grammatical special pleading: "The idea is that the exalted Lord appears on each occasion"; Conzelmann, *1 Corinthians*, 256. The same line of reasoning is followed by Lüdemann, *Resurrection of Jesus*, 48. He goes to the extreme of saying that the passive is "ruled out" because the preposition "by" (*hupo* in Greek) does not appear. Conzelmann's reference to Euripides and other sources shows that is not the case, and in any event an Aramaic original should not be expected to produce elegant Greek in translation.

30 Gordon Fee appropriately insists that seeing in Paul's mind is linked to his view, discussed in vv. 20-58, of the resurrection as bodily; Fee, *First Epistle*, 728.

31 Jer 1:5; Isa 49:1-6; Krister Stendahl, *Paul among Jews and Gentiles and Other Essays* (Philadelphia: Fortress, 1976), 7–23.

32 Dieter Mitternacht, "Foolish Galatians? A Recipient-Oriented Assessment of Paul's Letter," in *The Galatians Debate: Contemporary Issues in Rhetorical and Historical Interpretation*, ed. Mark D. Nanos (Peabody, Mass.: Hendrickson, 2002), 408–33, 415. In that the
experience involves transcendence, Gerd Lüdemann remarks that Paul's statement does
not preclude a visionary element or a sense in which the preposition *en* might be rendered
as "to" as well as "in me"; Lüdemann, *Resurrection of Jesus*, 51–52. But in this connection
and others, Lüdemann has his own sort of apologetic motivation. Concerned to leave the
practice and belief of Christianity behind him, he sometimes makes Paul's theology seem
cruder than it was; see his book, *The Great Deception: And What Jesus Really Said and Did*
(London: SCM Press, 1998), 1–9.

33 Part of its significance for him was that the risen Jesus represented the fusion of his
Tarsan heritage and his Judaic faith. Texts such as Cicero's "The Dream of Scipio"
(Cicero, *Republic* 6.24) and 1 Enoch came together in a moment of realization. See
Chilton, *Rabbi Paul*, 51–53. As angels had once guided Scipio and Enoch, a supernatural guide, a "Son" representing the divine Father, brought Paul to the heaven
within himself. Alan F. Segal has masterfully contexted Paul's mysticism within the
Merkabah practice of early Judaism. See Segal, *Life after Death: A History of Afterlife
in the Religions of the West* (New York: Doubleday, 2004), 407–10. I disagree with
him, however, in portraying 2 Cor 12:1-10, where Paul describes being snatched up
in the Merkabah, as the same moment as when the Son was revealed within him. In
2 Cor 12:2-3, Paul does not know whether he is "in body or out of body," while in
Gal 1:16, the Son is within him (and the Son is bodily for Paul). In 2 Cor 12, Paul
refers to a later mystical experience in 42 CE, when was sent out from Antioch and
began to tell gentiles that they became Israelites if they believed in the Anointed.
See Chilton, *Rabbi Paul*, 113–15. While Wright seems unable to conceive of any
resurrection without flesh, Segal appears reluctant to admit of its bodily dimension.
In their differing ways, they miss the focus of Paul's conception. A more balanced
treatment is offered by Carey C. Newman, who has argued that Paul's reference to
Jesus as "the Lord of Glory" in 1 Cor 2:8 identifies him with the human figure on
the divine throne as depicted in Ezek 1:28. See Newman, *Paul's Glory-Christology:
Tradition and Rhetoric*, NovTSup 69 (Leiden: Brill, 1992), 244 (also citing 1 En.
63:2). Bodily reality in this conception is consistent with divine glory.

34 See Mark 11:15-17; Zech 14:21; and Bruce Chilton, *Rabbi Jesus: An Intimate Biography* (New York: Doubleday, 2000), 213–68.

35 See Brigitte Kahl, *Galatians Re-imagined: Reading with the Eyes of the Vanquished*,
Paul in Critical Contexts (Minneapolis: Fortress, 2010), 276–78.

36 See A. J. M. Wedderburn, *Baptism and Resurrection: Studies in Pauline Theology
against Its Graeco-Roman Background*, WUNT 44 (Tübingen: Mohr Siebeck, 1987),
6–37; Alkier, *Reality of the Resurrection*, 25.

37 As Segal (*Life after Death*, 439) observes, this "was not based on the empty tomb nor
was it a belief in a proposition. It is the experience of transformation from mortality
to immortality in the real presence of the Spirit of the risen Lord, which in turn,

guaranteed his intercession in heaven and the coming transformation of those who believed in him."

38 See Ethelbert Stauffer, *New Testament Theology*, trans. John Marsh (New York: Macmillan, 1955), 299n544; Barrett, *First Epistle*, 362–64; Grappe, *L'au-delà dans la Bible*, 238–39.

39 A temporal extension elsewhere pictured spatially in the descent of Christ into the realm of the dead (1 Pet 3:18–4:6). Grappe, *L'au-delà dans la Bible*, 212–18, 238.

5 – Seen "by *Kêpha'*," Then "by the Twelve"

1 In referring to the "Evangelist," I refer to the editorial agency that frames the document as a whole, without any claim to know the persons or persons involved independently of the Gospels.

2 Not that it had to have continued. The manuscript evidence is quite clear that 16:8 closed the Gospel with a deliberately abrupt ending. Composed with baptism in view, Mark deliberately leaves some instruction to oral teaching, both at the elementary level (the Lord's Prayer, for example) and at the advanced level (the resurrection above all). Even N. T. Wright, who denies the Gospel intentionally ended when it does and who speculates lavishly on what the original conclusion might have been, acknowledges that the evidence of the textual remains offers us no insight beyond Mark 16:8. See Wright, *The Resurrection of the Son of God*, Christian Origins and the Question of God 3 (London: SPCK; Minneapolis: Fortress, 2003), 617–24.

3 Although Matthew enhances Peter's position in key passages, such as the famous promise of the keys of heaven (Matt 16:18-19, discussed below), his view of the resurrection is largely determined by another apostolic source, discussed in chapter 7.

4 Earlier in the narrative, the eyes of the students are described as "kept from recognizing him" (Luke 24:16), so that seeing and knowing are correlated in Luke's presentation. Still, two different kinds of cognition are indicated, even if they are related, and that is a matter that we will also consider in chapter 7.

5 And it is a sound, something said, explicitly cited by Luke in 24:33-34. Wright (*Resurrection of the Son of God*, 592) objects that "tracing the relationship between hypothetical sources is like looking for a black cat in a dark room." But in this case, Luke tells us about the cat, and its sound may be heard in traditions that refer to Peter by name. There is a tendency among scholars who wish to argue that the Gospels are historical to invoke visual terms of reference, when in fact the line of tradition was explicitly oral and aural (in addition to Paul's list, see Luke 1:1-4). Another example of this tendency is the title of Richard Bauckham's *Jesus and the Eyewitnesses: The Gospels as Eyewitness Testimony* (Grand Rapids: Eerdmans, 2017), which actually turns on the consideration of *ear*witness testimony. In Wright's case, his impatience with sources is that they do not mention his empty tomb. After his remark about looking for a black cat in a dark room, he goes on to say, "or, indeed, for a body in a tomb when the stone is still rolled against the door."

6　Paul Foster makes the connection to a variant of Mark 3:18, reading "Levi," instead of "James," "of Alphaeus," which Origen knew. See Foster, *The Gospel of Peter: Introduction, Critical Edition, and Commentary*, TENTS (Leiden: Brill, 2010), 510–11. This would make Levi one of the Twelve. But Mark 2:13-14 in any case puts Levi in Capernaum as well as by the "Sea"; his role in the Gospel of Peter may be more as a local Galilean student than one of the Twelve. Although Foster stresses the possible independence of the narrative from John's, for some reason he then attempts to harmonize references to the persons involved. Harmonization occurred as the traditions developed rather than at their points of origin.

7　Peter Van Minnen suggests the story was truncated already at the time of copying, owing to the limited space in the manuscript; Van Minnen, "The Akhmîm *Gospel of Peter*," in *Das Evangelium nach Petrus: Text, Kontexte, Intertexte*, ed. Thomas J. Kraus and Tobias Nicklas, TUGAL 158 (Berlin: de Gruyter, 2007), 53–60, here 58. Perhaps for that reason, the location in Galilee remains implicit in the Gospel of Peter; overt reference would have spoiled the concentration on the feast, since narrating the journey back would entail a lapse of time. The double motivation for returning home, the end of the feast in v. 58 and the mourning of the Twelve in v. 59, suggests that the temporal placement of the story is secondary, a splice comparable to John's recourse to the use of an addendum.

8　N. T. Wright (*Resurrection of the Son of God*, 691) conflates the scene with Luke 24:41-43, admitting that "the text does not say explicitly that Jesus ate," and going on to conclude, "but it is surely implied." The result is a failure to develop the eucharistic connections. Those are well brought out by Alan F. Segal in *Life after Death: A History of Afterlife in the Religions of the West* (New York: Doubleday, 2004), 457–58, although his thematic focus prevents him from developing the exegetical resonance of John 21 in this regard.

9　This leads me to reverse a brilliant suggestion by Caroline Bammel. She argued that "Peter, while at Jerusalem, experienced a vision in which he was encountered by the risen Jesus at the Sea of Galilee." Were John 21 truly an addendum, this approach would be plausible. But in fact its way is prepared within the Gospel so carefully that its location is emphatic. The tentative connection is really Jerusalem, so perhaps the late introduction of Peter into accounts of the visit to the tomb (Luke 24:12; John 20:3-10) reflects such a visionary background as Bammel suggests. See C. P. Bammel, "The First Resurrection Appearance," in *John and the Synoptics*, ed. Adelbert Denaux, BETL 101 (Leuven: Peeters, 1992), 620–31, here 625.

10　See Raymond E. Brown, *The Gospel according to John (xiii–xxi)*, AB 29A (Garden City, N.Y.: Doubleday, 1970), 1074–76.

11　I owe this observation to Jason Byassee, *Praise Seeking Understanding: Reading the Psalms with Augustine* (Grand Rapids: Eerdmans, 2007), 130.

12　For the present discussion, engagement with the issue of the student whom Jesus loved (vv. 20-25) is unnecessary. In my opinion, however, the approach of tracing links with the body of the Gospel is key to the meaning of the material, as in the case of Peter. With Deirdre Good, I am inclined to see the figure as representing the readership of the Gospel; see Bruce Chilton and Deirdre J. Good, *Studying the New Testament: A Fortress Introduction* (Minneapolis: Fortress, 2011), 113.

13 See John 18:17, 25, 26-27, in particular; and Roger Aus, *Simon Peter's Denial and Jesus' Commissioning Him as His Successor in John 21:15-19: Studies in Their Judaic Background*, Studies in Judaism (Lanham, Md.: University Press of America, 2013), 260, 262, 264.

14 This phrasing derives from that of Raymond Brown, *Gospel according to John*, 1110–12. Brown also concludes, as I agree, that the forgiveness of Peter actually preceded the scene involving the Twelve in the tradition prior to John's Gospel, as Paul's list would indicate. Wright (*Resurrection of the Son of God*, 676) repeats Brown's language about the restitution of Peter but does not take up Brown's suggestion that the scene, given the students' hesitancy to recognize Jesus, is implicitly prior to earlier scenes. Yet Wright dismisses that suggestion (675n35) as "purely imaginary" when it is taken up by Peter Carnley (*The Structure of Resurrection Belief* [Oxford: Oxford University Press, 1987], 17). That is odd, since Wright himself remarks (p. 629) that the mention of Peter in Mark 16:7 implies his rehabilitation.

15 This is now a current view of the Acts of Peter. See Christine M. Thomas, *The Acts of Peter, Gospel Literature, and the Ancient Novel: Rewriting the Past* (New York: Oxford University Press, 2003), 3–13, 87–105. Tertullian also makes a connection to Peter's crucifixion, although without reference to the position of the victim in this brief notice of a list of martyrdoms. See *Scorpiace* 15 in Giovanna Azzali Bernardelli, *Tertulliano, Scorpiace*, Biblioteca Patristica (Florence: Nardini, 1991).

16 See Robert Stoops, "The *Acts of Peter* in Intertextual Context," in *The Apocryphal Acts of the Apostles in Intertextual Perspectives*, ed. Robert F. Stoops Jr., Semeia 80 (Atlanta: Scholars Press, 1997), 57–86, here 77–79; Wilhelm Schneemelcher, "The Acts of Peter," in *New Testament Apocrypha*, ed. Edgar Hennecke and Wilhelm Schneemelcher, trans. R. McL. Wilson (Philadelphia: Westminster, 1964), 2:259–322, here 275.

17 In the words of Roger Aus, Peter is commissioned "to be the spiritual leader of everyone in the Christian community, from the newly converted or baptized lambs, to younger members, to the older matures ones." See Aus, *Simon Peter's Denial*, 225–27, 262.

18 Generally, my preferred standard. Deviations from Vaticanus on the basis of earlier witnesses seems reasonable to me, but I avoid conjectural emendations or the corrections of later witnesses, except in the case of evident errors. Cf. Kurt Aland, Barbara Aland, Johannes Karavidopoulos, Carlo M. Martini, and Bruce M. Metzger, eds., *Novum Testamentum Graece* (Stuttgart: Deutsche Bibelgesellschaft, 2012).

19 Commentators such as Rudolf Bultmann have been able to deny the pivotal importance of forgiveness within the scene, on the grounds that the actual language of repentance and absolution is missing. See Bultmann, *Das Evangelium des Johannes*, KEK (Göttingen: Vandenhoeck & Ruprecht, 2011), 551. But Raymond Brown's view (*Gospel according to John*, 1112) that a comprehensive "rehabilitation" implying forgiveness is at issue has prevailed. See T. Söding, "Erscheinung, Vergebung und

Sendung: Joh 21 als Zeugnis entwickelten Osterglaubens," in *Resurrection in the New Testament: Festschrift J. Lambrecht*, ed. Reimund Bieringer, Veronica Koperski, and B. Lataire, BETL 165 (Leuven: Leuven University Press, 2002), 207–32.

20 So Rudolf Bultmann, *A History of the Synoptic Tradition*, trans. John Marsh (New York: Harper & Row, 1968), 259.

21 See W. D. Davies and Dale Allison, *A Critical and Exegetical Commentary on the Gospel according to Saint Matthew: Commentary on Matthew VIII–XVIII*, ICC (Edinburgh: T&T Clark, 1991), 2:615. It is even conceivable for them that John's Gospel reflects an awareness of the scene at Caesarea Philippi in Matthew (2:608).

22 See Thomas Finley, "'Upon This Rock': Matthew 16.18 and the Aramaic Evidence," *AS* 4, no. 2 (2006): 133–51.

23 Joseph Fitzmyer suggested *'ntah hu' Kepha' veal kepha' denah 'bneh*; Fitzmyer, "Aramaic *Kepha'* and Peter's Name in the New Testament," in *To Advance the Gospel: New Testament Studies* (New York: Crossroad: 1981), 112–24, here 118.

24 So that in this case, Brown's conclusion that "Matthew's localization of the saying has no authoritative claim" seems unwarranted. See Brown, *Gospel according to John*, 1039–45, 1040. Similarly, his attempt to claim that John 21 does not depict "a specific exercise of power in the Christian community" (1044) appears strained to me. Cases in which I depart from Brown's exegesis are not numerous, and for this reason they seem worth noting. In this case, my differences with him derive from my lesser willingness to argue for the transposition of blocks of tradition and from his greater concern to caution against use of New Testament passages in order to support the power of the Catholic magisterium.

25 See Bruce Chilton, "Shebna, Eliakim, and the Promise to Peter," in *The Social World of Formative Christianity and Judaism: Essays in Tribute to Howard Clarke Key*, ed. Jacob Neusner, Peder Borgen, Ernest S. Frerichs, and Richard Horsley (Philadelphia: Fortress, 1989), 311–26, here 325–26.

26 Dale Allison, *Resurrecting Jesus: The Earliest Christian Tradition and Its Interpreters* (New York: T&T Clark, 2005), 254–59. Joseph A. Fitzmyer went so far as to refer to Luke 5:8 as a "suture-verse," on the grounds that "one would expect a comment of awe or gratitude toward the wonder-worker rather than a confession of unworthiness." See Fitzmyer, *The Gospel according to Luke I–IX: Introduction, Translation, and Notes*, AB 28 (Garden City, N.Y.: Doubleday, 1981), 1:561.

27 Cf. Walter T. Wilson, *Healing in the Gospel of Matthew: Reflections on Method and Ministry* (Minneapolis: Fortress, 2014). Wilson wisely writes on p. 312, n. 28: "Healing in fact belongs to a set of communal practices that enact the authority to forgive conferred on the church by the Son of Man." He rightly relates this practice to eschatology (cf. 151–59), so that "the forgiven are now drawn into a social and eschatological drama" (159). That points to the specific connection to the resurrection developed here.

28 See, for instance, Ps 103:3; and Barbara A. Elliott, "Forgiveness Therapy: A Clinical Intervention for Chronic Disease," *Journal of Religion and Health* 50, no. 2 (2011): 240–47. Elliott finds on p. 244 that "forgiveness reportedly results in beneficial

physiologic changes, including lower heart rate, increased rate of cardiovascular recovery, reduced resting blood pressure, less EMG tension and reduced skin conductance," and that it can "impact the structure and function of the brain."

29   The term is used of Jesus in the Gospels more than any other single designation (Matt 26:25, 49; Mark 9:5; 10:51; 11:21; 14:45; John 1:38, 49; 3:2; 4:31; 6:25; 9:2; 11:8). Obviously, the term did not yet carry the institutional associations it did with the rise of Rabbinic Judaism in the second century. It simply referred to a teacher. See Bruce Chilton, "Master/Rabbi," in *Encyclopedia of the Historical Jesus*, ed. Craig A. Evans (New York: Routledge, 2008), 395–99.

30   See Jim Popkin, "I Covered the Rajneesh Cult: Here Is What 'Wild Wild Country' Leaves Out," *Huffington Post*, March 28, 2018, https://www.huffingtonpost.com/entry/cult-wild-wild-country-netflix_us_5ab2b37de4b054d118df49c1.

31   "A man must speak in the words of his master" is a basic principle of Rabbinic Judaism, discussed by John Bowker in *The Targums and Rabbinic Literature* (Cambridge: Cambridge University Press, 1969), 49. A chilling admonition had it that "whoever forgets a word of his Mishnah, scripture accounts it as if he had lost his soul" (Pirqe Aboth 3.9). See Michael F. Bird, *The Gospel of the Lord: How the Early Church Wrote the Story of Jesus* (Grand Rapids: Eerdmans, 2014), 74–113.

32   The use of *distazô* in 28:17 and in 14:31 raises the question whether the story of the invitation to Peter to walk on the water might be another fragment of a Petrine resurrection narrative, comparable to Matt 16:17-19. Wright (*Resurrection of the Son of God*, 644) takes the reference to show "the risen Jesus both was and was not 'the same' as he had been before." Stefan Alkier shares this point of view and concludes that the resurrection "is not accessible through the power of the factual," so that "it becomes plausible only through trust in the immeasurable might of the royal rule of God and the concomitant conviction that this has been brought to effective expression in the words and deeds of Jesus." See Alkier, *The Reality of the Resurrection: The New Testament Witness*, trans. Leroy A. Huizenga (Waco, Tex.: Baylor University Press, 2013), 113 (cf. also 161, 163). Kenneth Grayston has suggested that the usage following the reference to worship means that the students doubted the effect of throwing themselves at Jesus' feet; Grayston, "The Translation of Matthew 28.17," *JSNT* 21 (1984): 105–9. In any case, he shows that an attempt to restrict the number of the Eleven who doubted is not supported by the grammar. A response by K. L. McKay, it seems to me, does not answer Grayston's challenge, since the usage *hoi* is resumptive of the subject given in v. 16 (*hoi hendeka*). See McKay, "The Use of *hoi de* in Matthew 28.17: A Response to K. Grayston," *JSNT* 24 (1985): 71–72. Grayston concludes, "Will our biblical translators please now rid us of an ancient reverential misunderstanding of Matthew's intention?" Discussion of the meaning of *proskunô* is developed in Matthew L. Bowen, "'They Came and Held Him by the Feet and Worshipped Him': Proskynesis before Jesus in Its Biblical and Ancient Near Eastern Context," *Studies in the Bible and Antiquity* 5 (2013): 63–89.

33   Otto Michel provided the insight that while John (20:29) makes faith the response to doubt, in Matthew (28:19-20) the commission to make disciples of all peoples

performs that role. The connection between these passages is detailed below, confirming Michel's suggestion. See Michel, "The Conclusion of Matthew's Gospel: A Contribution to the History of the Easter Message," trans. Robert Morgan, in *The Interpretation of Matthew*, ed. Graham Stanton, IRT 3 (London: SPCK, 1983), 30–41.

34 So Jane Schaberg, *The Father, the Son, and the Holy Spirit: The Triadic Phrase in Matt 28:19b*, SBLDS 61 (Chico, Calif.: Scholars Press, 1982), 111–41; and Reginald H. Fuller, *The Formation of the Resurrection Narratives* (New York: Macmillan, 1971), 82–88; followed by Wright, *Resurrection of the Son of God*, 643.

35 See Dale C. Allison, *The New Moses: A Matthean Typology* (Minneapolis: Fortress, 1993), 262–66.

36 So Otto Michel, "Conclusion of Matthew's Gospel," in Stanton, *Interpretation of Matthew*, 33–40; cf. Fuller, *Formation*, 90–93. Redaction criticism once made such suggestions more widespread than they are now.

37 Cf. Bruce Chilton, "'Not to Taste Death': A Jewish, Christian, and Gnostic Usage," in *Studia Biblica 1978: Papers on the Gospels; Sixth International Congress on Biblical Studies*, JSNTSup 2 (Sheffield: JSOT Press, 1980), 2:29–36.

38 Cf. 18:20; and Robert H. Gundry, *Matthew: A Commentary on His Handbook for a Mixed Church under Persecution* (Grand Rapids: Eerdmans, 1994), 597.

39 See David B. Howell, *Matthew's Inclusive Story: A Study in the Narrative Rhetoric of the First Gospel*, JSNTSup 42 (Sheffield: Sheffield Academic Press, 1990), 225–29, 258–59. Segal (*Life after Death*, 463–67) presses his case too far, in my judgment, in arguing that the transfiguration is a retrojected account of the resurrection. Cf. Bruce Chilton, "The Transfiguration: Dominical Assurance and Apostolic Vision," *NTS* 27 (1980): 115–24. As Wright (*Resurrection of the Son of God*, 604) points out, in the transfiguration, unlike the resurrection, "the disciples have no problem recognizing Jesus."

40 The issue of prophecy in the New Testament has become confused. In a desire to refute the claim that Christian prophets invented sayings of Jesus that were then imputed to him within the Gospels, some interpreters have minimized the entire phenomenon of prophecy as a part of Jesus' movement. See David Hill, *New Testament Prophecy* (Atlanta: John Knox, 1979). More balanced accounts are available in David E. Aune, *Prophecy in Early Christianity and the Ancient Mediterranean World* (Grand Rapids: Eerdmans, 1991); and Thomas W. Gillespie, *The First Theologians: A Study in Early Christian Prophecy* (Grand Rapids: Eerdmans, 1994).

41 See the Epistle of Barnabas 15.9, with its reference to "the eighth day in which Jesus also rose from and dead and appeared and ascended into heaven." Cf. Bart D. Ehrman, ed., *The Apostolic Fathers*, vol. 2: *Epistle of Barnabas, Papias and Quadratus, Epistle to Diognetus, the Shepherd of Hermas*, LCL 25 (Cambridge, Mass.: Harvard University Press, 2003); Wright, *Resurrection of the Son of God*, 671.

42 So Brown, *Gospel according to John*, 1046. Many of Brown's insights have informed my reading of this passage, although I disagree with his assessment that "there is not much likelihood that John xx 24-29 preserves elements of an early narrative" (1032).

He did not deal with the correspondences between John and Matthew that in my judgment evidence the tradition of the Twelve. Segal (*Life after Death*, 457) slips into the assumption that Thomas touched Jesus. The issue is nicely covered in Glenn W. Most, *Doubting Thomas* (Cambridge, Mass.: Harvard University Press, 2005), 250–56.

43 See Exod 4:16; 7:1; cf. Philo, *Moses* 1.158; and John Lierman, *The New Moses: Christian Perceptions of Moses and Israel in the Setting of Jewish Religion*, WUNT 173 (Tübingen: Mohr Siebeck, 2004), 230–32.

44 See James M. Robinson, ed., *The Coptic Gnostic Library: A Complete Edition of the Nag Hammadi Codices* (Leiden: Brill, 2000).

6 – Seen "by More Than Five Hundred," Then "by James"

1 So Ernst Haenchen, *The Acts of the Apostles: A Commentary*, trans. Bernard Noble, Gerald Shinn, Hugh Anderson, and R. McL. Wilson (Philadelphia: Westminster, 1971), 173–75. Within his discussion, it seems to me that he does not allow enough for Luke's overall conception, which Etienne Trocmé discovered in his comparison to the story of the Tower of Babel (Gen 11:1-9). See Trocmé, *Le livre des Actes et l'histoire* (Paris: Presses Universitaires de France, 1957), 202–6. This perspective has been taken up to powerful effect by Dean Philip Bechard, *Paul outside the Walls: A Study of Luke's Socio-geographical Universalism in Acts 14:8-20*, AnBib 143 (Rome: Pontificio Istituto Biblico, 2000), 211–24. Bechard also skillfully shows the influence of traditional elements within Lukan composition. For an older but still incisive treatment, see C. Freeman Sleeper, "Pentecost and Resurrection," *JBL* 84, no. 4 (1965): 389–99.

2 This is the term used, and the number given, in Acts 1:15 (with variant readings easily explicable), representing a correspondence with Paul's statement in 1 Cor 15:6. In that an unstated lapse of time lies between the end of that scene and the opening of the Pentecost account, "more than five hundred" might not be a bad estimate of the number of "brothers" gathered. That number is implausible for a house in Jerusalem, but so are the numbers that follow; both the city and the enclosed space come of deracinating the scene from Galilee.

3 Bechard's delightful remark is appropriate: the textual evidence "renders suspect any attempt to solve this problem through the convenience of textual emendation, the sanctified genius of Augustine and Jerome notwithstanding"; Bechard, *Paul outside the Walls*, 214n116. Yet the point is that Augustine (as well as other ancillary witnesses) is aware of the problem; see the citation of witnesses in Barbara Aland, Kurt Aland, Johannes Karavidopoulos, Carlo M. Martini, and Bruce M. Metzger, eds., *Novum Testamenetum Graece* (Stuttgart: Deutsche Bibelgesellschaft, 2012).

4 The verb is *anistēmi* rather than *egeirō*. Rather than treat them as synonyms, I rely on the base meanings in both cases when translating. As Alan F. Segal observes, in this passage "the identification of resurrection with enthronement is evident"; Segal, *Life after Death: A History of the Afterlife in the Religions of the West* (New

York: Doubleday, 2004), 462. Variations between *anistêmi* and *egeirô* reflect differing emphases. Segal goes on to argue that it was the crucifixion itself, "originally the inscription on the cross," that prompted enthronement as an interpretation. One of the weaknesses of recourse to ideas of enthronement to explain the resurrection is that they too often wind up trying to explain it away. But as the narrative of Pentecost shows, resurrection and enthronement are mutually predicating. Cf. Timo Escola, *Messiah and the Throne: Jewish Merkabah Mysticism and Early Christian Exaltation Discourse*, WUNT 142 (Tübingen: Mohr Siebeck, 2001), 352.

5   Following Papyrus 46 in reading simply "his Spirit" rather than "the Spirit of his Son." This is a case in which the more difficult and earlier formulation may be more accurate than what the manuscripts of the fourth century attest. In either case, however, Paul shows an awareness of the dual motifs of the release of the Spirit and baptism.

6   In this connection, see N. T. Wright, *The Resurrection of the Son of God*, Christian Origins and the Question of God 3 (London: SPCK; Minneapolis: Fortress, 2003), 325.

7   Hence the Hebrew term "Weeks" (*Shavuot*) as used for the feast, as in Deut 16:10. Further associations of Pentecost in the time prior to Acts are discussed in Bruce Chilton, *Redeeming Time: The Wisdom of Ancient Jewish and Christian Festal Calendars* (Peabody, Mass.: Hendrickson, 2002), 49–51.

8   In the Septuagint, Luke's Bible at this point, Joel 3:1-5. C. K. Barrett (*The Acts of the Apostles*, ICC [Edinburgh: T&T Clark, 1994], 1:129–57) shows how deep an influence the quotation is. Stefan Alkier captures this in saying that the quotation shows that "the eschatological and the cosmological dimensions" of the Spirit's arrival "are coming to fruition." See Alkier, *The Reality of the Resurrection: The New Testament Witness*, trans. Leroy A. Huizenga (Waco, Tex.: Baylor University Press, 2013), 135.

9   When Paul says that the Anointed did not send him to baptize (1 Cor 1:14-17), although he occasionally did so, that may signal his awareness that he did not act with the same commission that came to "more than five hundred brothers."

10   The number derives from the seventy grandsons of Noah in Gen 10. In the Septuagint, the count comes to seventy-two. For this reason, the variation at Luke 10:1 shows an awareness of the significance of the number.

11   A point well observed by Haenchen, *Acts of the Apostles*, 175. He rationalizes the observation, however, by remarking that Luke "can hardly have the mission's first 3,000 converts, the nucleus of the community secured from among them, streaming off to the four corners of the world within a week of conversion!"

12   See David Lertis Matson, *Household Conversion Narratives in Acts: Pattern and Interpretation*, JSNTSup 123 (Sheffield: Sheffield Academic Press, 1996), 129–34.

13   See Matson, *Household Conversion Narratives*, 90–92. The strength of the motif helps explain the implausible reference to the "house" in Acts 2:2.

14   So Linda M. Maloney, *"All That God Had Done with Them": The Narration of the Works of God in the Early Christian Community as Described in the Acts of the Apostles*, AUSTR 91 (New York: Lang, 1991), 76.

15 See Lars Hartman, *"Into the Name of the Lord Jesus": Baptism in the Early Church,* SNTW (Edinburgh: T&T Clark, 1997), 133–36.

16 For a discussion, see Bruce Chilton and Jacob Neusner, *Judaism in the New Testament: Practices and Beliefs* (London: Routledge, 1995), 99–104, 108–11.

17 Hartman, *"Into the Name,"* 140; citing Acts 8:37; 22:16.

18 N. T. Wright attempts to evade this conclusion, by making the citation of Ps 16:8-11 in Acts 2:25-28 into the "key text to interpret the extraordinary events of Easter"; Wright, *Resurrection of the Son of God,* 455. Because "David" in the Psalm says that God will not permit his "holy one to see corruption," that means "Jesus' physical body did not decay." This attempt to shift the focus of interest ignores the vital importance of Spirit in the narrative of Pentecost, where David appears as a step on the way in the explanation. "Corruption" in Ps 16:10b stands for "pit" in the Hebrew text and is used in parallelism for Sheol in v. 10a. So the point is that the figure spoken of is not to be left in the realm of the dead. In the speech, Peter argues that David in fact died, so that in the psalm the Anointed is prophesied, who was "neither left to Hades nor did his flesh see corruption" (Acts 2:31). That is a paraphrase of Ps 16:10, not an account of "the empty tomb," to which Wright tries to relate it. In fact, he goes on to argue it is "futile" to mention the absence of reference to the empty tomb within Peter's speech in the house of Cornelius. As in the case of Paul in 1 Cor 15, "it is clearly assumed." Once the assumption is let loose on one text, the only futility would be in trying to stop it invading others.

19 See W. Hall Harris, *The Descent of Christ: Ephesians 4:7-11 and Traditional Hebrew Imagery* (Leiden: Brill, 1996), xv–xvii. Harris continues to uphold Pauline authorship (p. 184), a view I have opposed, although I find his exegesis compelling. See Bruce Chilton, *Rabbi Paul: An Intellectual Biography* (New York: Doubleday, 2004), 255.

20 Cf. also Acts 2:39.

21 The role of Peter and John in the passage (vv. 14-25) maintains contact with the central role of Holy Spirit within baptism as well as with the Lukan conception of Jerusalem as the focal center of Jesus' movement.

22 So C. K. Barrett, *The Acts of the Apostles,* ICC (Edinburgh: T&T Clark, 1994), 1:108. See also Hartman (*"Into the Name,"* 131–33), who observes the coherence with Luke 24:44-49. That is a telling remark, because it shows, together with the preaching attributed to Peter in the house of Cornelius, that the narrative of Jesus' passion was connected with the catechesis that led to baptism from a primitive stage.

23 Kirsopp Lake, "The Apostolic Council of Jerusalem," in *The Beginnings of Christianity,* ed. F. J. Foakes Jackson and Kirsopp Lake (Grand Rapids: Baker, 1979), 5:195–212, here 208–9, with a citation of the Greek text. For an English rendering and fine introductions and explanations, see John J. Collins, "Sibylline Oracles: A New Translation and Introduction," in *The Old Testament Pseudepigrapha,* vol. 1, ed. James H. Charlesworth (Garden City, N.Y.: Doubleday, 1983). Collins dates this work within the first century but after the eruption of Vesuvius in 79 CE (1:381–82). With due caution, he assigns book 4 a Syrian provenience.

24 Cf. the usage of the cognate noun in Luke 1:23, and Paul's usage in Rom 13:6 and 15:16. *Leitourgeô* in Acts 13:2 corresponds to *proskuneô* in Matt 28:17.

25 See Moshe Bildstein's *Purity, Community, and Ritual in Early Christian Literature,* Oxford Studies in Abrahamic Religions (Oxford: Oxford University Press, 2017), which details a voluminous secondary literature. My interest in purity as a necessary category within the study of Jesus is developed in Bruce Chilton, *The Temple of Jesus: His Sacrificial Program within a Cultural History of Sacrifice* (University Park: Pennsylvania State University Press, 1992).

26 See, for example, Susan Haber, *"They Shall Purify Themselves": Essays on Purity in Early Judaism,* ed. Adele Reinhartz, EJL 24 (Atlanta: Society of Biblical Literature, 2008); Thomas Kazen, *Jesus and Purity Halakhah: Was Jesus Indifferent to Impurity?* Coniectanea Biblica New Testament Series 38 (Stockholm: Almqvist & Wiksell, 2002).

27 For recent secondary literature on James, together with an explanation of its significance, see Bruce Chilton, "James, the Brother of Jesus," *Oxford Bibliographies,* last modified July 26, 2017, http://www.oxfordbibliographies.com/view/document/obo -9780195393361/obo-9780195393361-0242.xml.

28 See Martin Hengel, "Jakobus der Herrenbruder—der erste 'Papst'?" in *Glaube und Eschatologie: Festschrift für Werner Georg Kümmel zum 80. Geburtstag,* ed. E. Grässer and O. Merk (Tübingen: Mohr, 1985), 71–104, 81.

29 See James H. Charlesworth, *The Pesharim and Qumran History: Chaos or Consensus?* (Grand Rapids: Eerdmans, 2006).

30 See Markus Bockmuehl, "The Noachide Commandments and New Testament Ethics," in *Jewish Law in Gentile Churches: Halakhah and the Beginning of Christian Public Ethics* (Edinburgh: T&T Clark, 2000), 145–73.

31 See Ethelbert Stauffer, *Jesus and His Story,* trans. R. Winston and C. Winston (New York: Knopf, 1960), 14–15.

32 See Vincent J. Rosivach, *The System of Public Sacrifice in Fourth-Century Athens,* American Classical Studies 34 (Atlanta: Scholars Press, 1994).

33 Eusebius on several occasions refers to James as having been the first bishop of Jerusalem, and once he cites a source of the second century to do so (*Ecclesiastical History* 2.1.1–4; 2.23.1; 7.19; referring in the first passage to Clement's *Hypotyposes*). The term *episkopos* means "overseer," as does *mebaqqar,* an office with responsibility to do many of the same things that an *episkopos* was to do: to teach the torah (even to priests) as well as the particular traditions of the Essenes, to administer discipline, and to see to the distribution of wealth (see CD 13.7–8; 14.8–9, 13–14; and 1 Tim 3:1-7). Cf. Bruce Chilton, "Jesus, Levitical Purity, and the Development of Primitive Christianity," in *The Book of Leviticus: Composition and Reception,* ed. Rolf Rendtorff and Robert A. Kugler, VTSup (Leiden: Brill, 2003), 358–82, here 375–77.

34 See Roger Tomes, "Why Did Paul Get His Hair Cut? (Acts 18.18; 21.23-24)," in *Luke's Literary Achievement: Collected Essays,* ed. C. M. Tuckett, JSNTSup 116 (Sheffield: Sheffield Academic Press, 1995), 188–97. Tomes rightly points out that there

is considerable deviation from the prescriptions of Num 6 here, but Mishnah (see below) amply attests such flexibility within the practice of the vow.

35   See Josephus, *Jewish War* 2.590–594; m. Menahoth 8.3-5; and the whole of Makhshirin. The point of departure for the concern is Lev 11:34.

36   At the close of a comprehensive and adventurous discussion, Pier Franco Beatrice concludes, "The Aramaic *Gospel of the Hebrews* is a work that we know only through Greek and Latin translations and paraphrases, in a fragmentary and imprecise manner, that is true, but it is nevertheless a written text, the existence of which is well documented." See Beatrice, "The 'Gospel according to the Hebrews' in the Apostolic Fathers," *NovT* 48, no. 2 (2006): 147–95.

37   Craig Evans represents the view that the priest's servant is the servant of the high priest wounded at Jesus' arrest, named as Malchus in John 18:10 (cf. Matt 26:51; Mark 14:47; Luke 22:50). See Evans, *From Jesus to Church: The First Christian Generation* (Louisville: Westminster John Knox, 2014), 60.

38   It has been argued that, at this point, Jesus invokes a Nazirite vow. See P. Lebeau, *Le vin nouveau du Royaume: Etude exégétique et patristique sur la Parole eschatologique de Jésus à la Cène* (Paris: Desclée, 1966); M. Wojciechowski, "Le naziréat et la Passion (Mc 14,25a; 15:23)," *Biblica* 65 (1984): 94–96. But the form of Jesus' statement has not been rightly understood, owing to its Semitic syntax. He is not promising never to drink wine, but to drink wine only in association with his celebration of the kingdom. See Bruce Chilton, *A Feast of Meanings: Eucharistic Theologies from Jesus through Johannine Circles*, NovTSup 72 (Leiden: Brill, 1994), 169–71. While Jesus indeed taught principles of holiness, it was his brother who turned that teaching into a formal practice associated with the temple.

39   Cf. Chilton, *Feast of Meanings*, 75–92.

40   See John 10:7, with its connection to the Feast of Dedication (v. 22), and Ps 24:7-10; Bruce Chilton, *Redeeming Time: The Wisdom of Ancient Jewish and Christian Festal Calendars* (Peabody, Mass.: Hendrickson, 2002), 86.

41   The high priestly source of the action is not clear from Hegesippus but is explicitly cited by Josephus, *Jewish Antiquities* 20.197–203, and named as Ananus. Hegesippus' account appears in Eusebius, *Ecclesiastical History* 2.23. The claim of James' prominence is confirmed by Clement, who portrays James as the first elected bishop in Jerusalem (also cited by Eusebius, *Ecclesiastical History* 2.1.1–6), and by the pseudo-Clementine *Recognitions*, which makes James into an almost papal figure, who provides the correct paradigm of preaching to gentiles. Paul is so much the butt of this presentation that *Recognitions* (1.43–71) even relates that, prior to his conversion to Christianity, Saul physically assaulted James in the temple. Martin Hengel refers to this presentation as an apostolic novel (*Apostelroman*), deeply influenced by the perspective of the Ebionites, and probably to be dated within the third and fourth centuries. See Hengel, "Jakobus," in Grässer and Merk, *Glaube und Eschatologie*, 81.

42   Cf. Judg 13:2-7; 1 Sam 1:21-28.

43 Avoidance of oil is also attributed by Josephus to the Essenes (*Jewish War* 2.123). James' connection with the Essenes is not immediately germane to this discussion. Still, I think that as the bishop or overseer (*mebaqqer*, in the Dead Sea Scrolls) of his community, he exercised a function that entered the Greek language as *episkopos*. Both terms mean "overseer," and the *mebaqqer* was charged to do many of the same things that an *episkopos* was to do, as discussed in n. 33. The particular roles of the *mebaqqar* appear commensurate with that of the *episkopos*, although the latter term in Greek carried less status. The association with James as *mebaqqar* gave *episkopos* a new meaning. See Bruce Chilton, "James and the (Christian) Pharisees," in *When Judaism and Christianity Began: Essays in Memory of Anthony J. Saldarini*, vol. 1, *Christianity in the Beginning*, ed. Alan J. Avery-Peck, Daniel Harrington, and Jacob Neusner, Supplements to the Journal for the Study of Judaism 85 (Leiden: Brill, 2004), 19–47. The influence of James' circle is reflected in the New Testament and later literature (including the Gospel of Thomas, the Secret Book of James, the Protevangelium of James, the First and Second Apocalypse of James, the Gospel of Peter, the Apocalypse of Peter, the Kerygma Petrou, the Kerygmata Petrou, the Acts of Peter, the Letter of Peter to Philip, and the Acts of Peter.

44 The shift back to Hebrew from Aramaic by this point, however, means that identity of language is not in question. See also the man in 12:6.

45 The clear focus of the narrative. Although Alan Segal does not refer to the passage, he comes to this conclusion: "I suspect the visions of Peter and even James and the others were similar: They convinced Jesus' followers that he not only survived in a new spiritual state but that that state was as the manlike figure in heaven, 'the Son of Man.'" See Segal, *Life after Death*, 448. For Segal such a conviction derives from "an RASC experience of the risen Jesus" (463), his abbreviation of "Religiously Altered States of Consciousness." He points out, "If we know that the brain produces religious experiences, we may still affirm that God made our brains so as better to communicate with us" (725). Since Segal published, a quantum theory of consciousness has provoked both support and attack. See Stuart Hameroff and Roger Penrose, "Consciousness in the Universe: A Review of the 'Orch OR' Theory," *Physics of Life Reviews* 11, no. 1 (2014): 39–78. Even allowing for an argument for the reality of visions, I cannot agree with Segal's generalization of his finding to all cases, or with his psychological explanation. Still, he captures the sense of James' vision. Its rich detail and clearly visionary emphasis rule out Wright's suggestion that the story was spun out of the bare reference to James in 1 Cor 15:7; Wright, *Resurrection of the Son of God*, 325, 560. It is obviously not the kind of account that Wright prefers, even as Segal embraces it.

7 – Seen by "All the Apostles"

1 For discussion and reference to some of the vast secondary literature on this comparison, see G. K. Beale and D. A. Carson, eds., *Commentary on the New Testament Use of the Old Testament* (Grand Rapids: Baker Academic, 2007).

2 As Stefan Alkier remarks, this "must be conceptualized as an intertextually motivated eschatological sign act." See Alkier, *The Reality of the Resurrection: The New Testament Witness*, trans. Leroy A. Huizenga (Waco, Tex.: Baylor University Press, 2013), 109.

3 Targum Zechariah 14:9; cf. Kevin Cathcart and Robert P. Gordon, eds. and trans., *The Targum of the Minor Prophets*, ArBib 14 (Wilmington, Del.: Glazier, 1989).

4 See Cecil Roth, "The Cleansing of the Temple and Zechariah XIV.21," *NovT* 4 (1960): 174–81; Victor Eppstein, "The Historicity of the Gospel Account of the Cleansing of the Temple," *ZNW* 55 (1964): 42–58; Bruce Chilton, *The Temple of Jesus: His Sacrificial Program within a Cultural History of Sacrifice* (University Park: Pennsylvania State University Press, 1992), 91–136; Simon Joseph, *Jesus and the Temple: The Crucifixion in its Jewish Context*, SNTSMS 165 (Cambridge: Cambridge University Press, 2016).

5 N. T. Wright provides a good catalog of the loose ends left by the text; Wright, *The Resurrection of the Son of God*, Christian Origins and the Question of God 3 (London: SPCK, 2003), 631–36. He comes to the conclusion that Matthew relates an earlier tradition with his preferred theology: "that with the combined events of Jesus' death and resurrection the new age, for which Israel has been longing, has begun" (635). That is a useful description of the apocalyptic purpose of both the tradition and its presentation, which makes it all the more surprising to find this statement on the next page: "Some stories are so odd that they may just have happened" (636). Since, on Wright's view, people believe in resurrection only as a result of finding tombs empty, that would imply a great increase in vacant mortuary real estate in the vicinity of Jerusalem and necessitate some motivation on the part of the families of the holy ones to visit the sites they then found empty. Matthew feels no compulsion to construct such a scenario, contenting himself with reference to the tombs opening, the bodies being raised, and their manifestation to many in the city (Matt 27:51-52). Their being manifested is the first reference Matthew makes to any witnesses' awareness of events.

6 Armand Puig i Tàrrech suggests that Matthew here represents a "primitive apocalyptic fragment" based on Ezek 37. See Armand Puig i Tàrrech, "Els sants que ressusciten (Mt 27,51b-53)," in *Estudis de Nou Testament*, Col·lectània Sant Pacià 108 (Barcelona: Facultat de Teologia de Catalunya, 2014), 131–69, quoting 161; cf. 135, 148–49, 167–68. See also Christian Grappe, *L'au-delà dans la Bible: Le temporal et le spatial*, Le Monde de la Bible 68 (Fribourg: Labor et Fides, 2014), 211–12.

7 In both cases, it is more accurate to refer to a "raising" (*ergesis*), as in Matt 27:53, than an *anastasis*, "resurrection." The latter term, linked with the verb *anistemi* rather than with *egeirô*, might refer more to Jesus' status in regard to God than to his physical presence, as—for example—in the tradition of the More Than Five Hundred.

8 Wright (*Resurrection of the Son of God*, 638) rightly sees the vignette as "an apologia for the bodily resurrection of Jesus" (by which he means "physical resurrection") but does not observe that the Matthean earthquake had created the conditions that make the explanation necessary. Rather, he insists that in this story "the empty tomb was an absolute and unquestioned datum." In this case, it is so "unquestioned" that

Matthew does not mention it, while portraying the tomb as damaged by an earth-quake. For Wright, without the empty tomb "there is no chance that even the most devout of Jesus' former followers would have said he had been raised" (626), so that it meets the standard of a historical event (709). This perspective helps to explain why he projects "the empty tomb" onto texts where it is not referred to.

9   So Matt 27:62; they become high priests and elders in 28:11-12. I take the variation to indicate that Matthew in the entire complex of the custody of the tomb represents an earlier tradition. The Evangelist has adjusted the language to develop his critique of Pharisaic Judaism in particular.

10 This factor, together with Matthew's evident acquaintance with Essenes, suggests Damascus as the provenience of the Gospel. The first Gospel shows a keen inter-est in how Jesus' life and work fulfills prophecies in the Scriptures of Israel, in the final judgment that is to accompany the end of the world, in the teaching of ange-lology, and in the emerging custom of celibacy among believers (Matt 19:1-12). All of these features suggest a Syrian provenience, and particularly from Damascus (although Antioch has also been suggested); Elisha had healed the Syrian general who came from Damascus (2 Kgs 5:1-14). There were disciples of Jesus present from shortly after the resurrection, and other Jewish communities thrived. Among them, the Essenes also featured prominently, and some distinguishing characteristics of Matthew's Gospel, especially its presentation of Jesus as the authoritative teacher of the law, echo features of the Dead Sea Scrolls, where the figure called the Teacher of Righteousness is also portrayed in Mosaic terms. On the survival of the Essenes after the destruction of the temple, see Joshua Ezra Burns, "Essene Sectarianism and Social Differentiation in Judaea after 70 C.E.," *HTR* 99, no. 3 (2006): 247–74. Edwin K. Broadbent makes a compelling case for Matthew as a composition in dialogue with Judaism(s), but he opts for Antioch rather than Damascus as the city of provenience. See Broadbent, *The Gospel of Matthew on the Landscape of Antiquity*, WUNT 378 (Tübingen: Mohr Siebeck, 2017). But Daniel J. Harrington soberly explains that Damascus and Edessa are equally good candidates; Harrington, *The Gospel of Matthew*, SP 1 (Collegeville, Minn.: Liturgical, 1991), 8–10. Damascus has the advantage of a connection with the Essenes.

11 See Michael Meerson and Peter Schäfer (with Yaacov Deutsch, David Grossberg, Avigail Manekin, and Adina Yoffie), *Toledot Yeshu: The Life Story of Jesus, Two Volumes and Database* (Tübingen: Mohr Siebeck, 2014), 1:101–3.

12 See Philippe Bobichon, *Justin Martyr: Dialogue avec Tryphon, édition critique*, Para-dosis 47/1–2 (Fribourg: Academic, 2003).

13 See 8:28-33; 9:34-37; 10:38-11:49. Against the argument of John Dominic Cros-san's *The Cross That Spoke: The Origins of the Passion Narrative* (San Francisco: Harper & Row, 1988), the Gospel of Peter appears derivative. Cf. Timothy P. Henderson, *The Gospel of Peter and Early Christian Apologetics: Rewriting the Story of Jesus' Death, Burial, and Resurrection*, WUNT 2/301 (Tübingen: Mohr Siebeck, 2011).

14 Alan Segal remarks that "Luke explicitly denies" the language Paul uses in 1 Cor 15:44. See Segal, *Life after Death: A History of the Afterlife in the Religions of the West*

(New York: Doubleday, 2004), 459. But he acknowledges that Paul there speaks of a "spiritual body," so the difference should not be exaggerated. Luke's innovation is in insisting upon the flesh and bone of the risen Jesus. Wright (*Resurrection of the Son of God*, 657–59) interprets the passage in that way, although for him, of course, the resurrection must be physical whenever it is mentioned. Yet he points out that when Paul refers to flesh, it "always designates that which is corruptible, and often that which is rebellious" (658), while the risen flesh of Jesus is part of "the new creation" in Luke's conception. Later, Augustine would make the distinction between flesh as it now is and flesh that is raised, saying, "The spiritual flesh will be subject to spirit, but it will still be flesh, not spirit; just as the carnal spirit was subject to the flesh, but was still spirit, not flesh" (*The City of God* 22.21); see Brian E. Daly, *The Hope of the Early Church: A Handbook of Patristic Eschatology* (Cambridge: Cambridge University Press, 1991), 131–50. In contrast, Origen had asserted that when Paul called the body "spiritual," "it seems absurd and contrary to his meaning to say it is still entangled in the passions of flesh and blood" (*First Principles* 2.10.3); see Bruce Chilton and Jacob Neusner, *Classical Christianity and Rabbinic Judaism: Comparing Theologies* (Grand Rapids: Baker Academic, 2004), 231–37. Yet whatever their differences, Origen and Augustine allow more for one another's positions than do Segal and Wright.

15 Ascension accommodates within itself two models of the resurrection: as exaltation and as encounter with the living Jesus. Wright (*Resurrection of the Son of God*, 654–55) analyzes the ascension as the solution to the problem of how Jesus can be both "physical" and "transphysical." I can agree it addresses such an uncertainty, but formulation in those terms begs the question: Then why insist the resurrection is physical and can be nothing else?

16 As Alkier (*Reality of the Resurrection*, 131) summarizes, "Here again the resurrected body, which Luke represents in materially correct ways, no longer obeys the bounds of space and time."

17 So Joseph A. Fitzmyer, *The Gospel according to Luke X–XXIV: Introduction, Translation, and Notes*, AB 28A (Garden City, N.Y.: Doubleday, 1985), 2:1588.

18 So rightly Haenchen, *Acts of the Apostles*, 139.

19 Alkier (*Reality of the Resurrection*, 134) refers to an "irreconcilable contradiction" between the Gospel and Acts. He goes on to point out that Luke produces a problem for himself when it concerns later appearances of Jesus (Acts 7:56; 9:3), where "the exalted one becomes visible only when the heavens are opened."

20 Fitzmyer (*Gospel according to Luke*, 2:1587) describes it as "decked out with apocalyptic stage props: rapture with motion upward through the heavens, a cloud as the elevator, and angel interpreters," while Ernst Haenchen (*Acts of the Apostles*, 151) characterizes the same scene as "austere."

21 He was also involved in the composition of 1 Peter (1 Pet 5:12), and the similarity between the teaching in 1 Thessalonians and the "little apocalypse" in the Synoptic Gospels has been carefully detailed. See David Wenham, *The Rediscovery of Jesus' Eschatological Discourse*, Gospel Perspectives 4 (Sheffield: JSOT Press, 1984). Wright

(*Resurrection of the Son of God*, 215) cautions against the "astonishing literalness in popular fundamentalism and critical scholarship alike" in interpreting this passage. He attempts to read the passage in terms of 1 Cor 15, but, by the time he wrote to the Corinthians, Paul had broken with Silas during a dispute in Antioch concerning food sacrificed to idols and table fellowship among gentile and Jewish believers. See Bruce Chilton, *Rabbi Paul: An Intellectual Biography* (New York: Doubleday, 2004), 162–70. That may be why Paul does not cite the "word of the Lord" of 1 Thess 4:15 in 1 Cor 15.

22 Cf. Mishnah Rosh Hashanah 1:8, in Philip Blackman, *Mishnayoth: Pointed Hebrew Text, English Translation, Introductions, Notes, Supplement, Appendix, Indexes, Addenda, Corrigenda* (Gateshead, UK: Judaica, 1990). Segal (*Life after Death*, 459–61) sees confirmation of the story of the tomb as a major purpose of the Emmaus pericope. In this regard, he and Wright (*Resurrection of the Son of God*, 657) are in agreement, despite their championing of mutually exclusive views of what the resurrection is.

23 See David Catchpole, *Resurrection People: Studies in the Resurrection Narratives of the Gospels* (London: Darton, Longman & Todd, 2000), 88–102.

24 Mark is not only consistent in the spelling of *Nazarênos*; every time it appears, a linkage with other usages appears. When the blind Bartimaeus appeals to Jesus in Mark 10:47, his appeal echoes the demonic statement in 1:24; when the young man calls Jesus the *Nazarênos* in Mark 16:6, he uses the identification of Jesus that Peter denied in 14:67. Mark's usage echoes the treatment "Nazirite" in the Septuagint of Num 6:1-21; Judg 16:17. The term *Nazôraios* might well be linked with the village Nazareth (although the transliteration would be not straightforward, since it should be *natzoraios*; cf. Stephen Goranson, "Nazarenes," in *Anchor Bible Dictionary*, ed. David Noel Freedman et al. [New York: Doubleday, 1992], 4:1049–50, here 1049). Since the village Nazareth does not appear in the Hebrew Scripture, it is difficult to see what geographical text Matthew might have in mind, so that Isa 11:1 is frequently proposed as the scriptural locus, the "branch" (*netzer*) from Jesse. That form of the name is perhaps preserved as a name for Jesus' movement in Acts 24:5, and its link to Nazareth is reflected in the Syriac *Natzraya* (in this case more easily related to Nazareth). The Hebrew for *Notsrim* is the equivalent form.

25 See Fitzmyer, *Gospel according to Luke*, 2:1545, 1569.

26 The helpful schematic developed by Joel B. Green is here adapted. See Green, *The Gospel of Luke*, NICNT (Grand Rapids: Eerdmans, 1997), 842–51.

27 See Josephus, *Jewish Antiquities* 4.326; 9.28; in *Josephus*, ed. H. St. J. Thackeray, Ralph Marcus, Allen Wikgren, and Louis H. Feldman, LCL 203, 210, 242, 292, 326, 365, 433, 456, 487, 489, and 490 (Cambridge, Mass.: Harvard University Press, 1926–1965). Alkier (*Reality of the Resurrection*, 131) describes Jesus' body as now "similar to the angels, just as was stated in the debate between Jesus and the Sadducees about the resurrection of the dead."

28 The singular is Luke's usage in Greek, unlike the majority of translations into English. The King James Version, however, captures the original.

29 See Jan Hilgevoord and Jos Uffink, "The Uncertainty Principle," in *The Stanford Encyclopedia of Philosophy*, ed. Edward N. Zaita (Stanford: Metaphysics Research Lab, 2016), revised July 12, 2016, https://plato.stanford.edu/archives/win2016/entries/qt-uncertainty/.

30 See Elias Bickermann, "Das leere Grab," in *Zur neutestamentlichen überlieferung von der Auferstehung Jesu*, Wege der Forschung 522 (Darmstadt: Wissenschaftliche Buchgesellschaft, 1988), 272–84, here 277.

31 Richard B. Hays aptly deploys this pericope as foundational to typology within the church. As he points out, typology is not a particular technique of interpretation but "before all else a trope, an act of imagination," and he sees Paul as contending that the Anointed discloses "a previously uncomprehended narrative unity in Scripture." See Hays, *Echoes of Scripture in the Letters of Paul* (New Haven: Yale University Press, 1989), 100, 157. When Hays turns to the Gospels, he describes this process as "reading backwards" or "figural reading," and he subtitles his concluding chapter "Did Not Our Hearts Burn within Us?" (Luke 24:32). See Hays, *Echoes of Scripture in the Gospels* (Waco, Tex.: Baylor University Press, 2016), 347, 358.

32 See 4:35-37; 9:26-28; 11:21-30; 12:24-25; 13:1-3, 6-8; 13:42-50; 14:1-4, 11-15, 19-24; 15:1-3, 11-13, 21-26, 34-40; and Bernd Kollmann, *Joseph Barnabas: Leben und Wirkungsgeschichte*, SBS 175 (Stuttgart: Verlag Kathlisches Bibelwerk, 1998); Kollmann, *Joseph Barnabas: His Life and Legacy*, trans. Miranda Henry (Collegeville, Minn.: Liturgical, 2004).

33 See 1 Cor 9:5-7; Gal 2:1-3, 8-10, 12-14; Col 4:9-11.

34 Cf. *A Comparative Handbook to the Gospel of Mark: Comparisons with Pseudepigrapha, the Qumran Scrolls, and Rabbinic Literature*, ed. Bruce Chilton (general ed.), with Darrell Bock (associate ed.), Daniel M. Gurtner (ed. for the Pseudepigrapha, Josephus, and Philo), Jacob Neusner (ed. for Rabbinic Literature), and Lawrence H. Schiffman (ed. for the Literature of Qumran) with Daniel Oden, New Testament Gospels in Their Judaic Contexts 1 (Leiden: Brill, 2010), 251–64.

35 So also Alkier, *Reality of the Resurrection*, 130.

36 The phrase is well explained in David Mycoff, *The Life of Saint Mary Magdalene and of Her Sister Saint Martha: A Medieval Biography Translated and Annotated*, Cistercian Studies Series 108 (Kalamazoo: Cistercian, 1989), lines 240–51, 876–903, 1959–61; cf. Bruce Chilton, *Mary Magdalene: A Biography* (New York: Doubleday, 2005), 111–18.

37 This transliteration is designed to help the reader gain a sense of the sound of the original Aramaic. For that reason, the system is simplified, and the symbol "/" is used to indicate where stress falls so as to establish a meter. For a full explanation, see Chilton, Bock, Gurtner, Neusner, and Schiffman (with Oden), *Comparative Handbook to the Gospel of Mark*, 48–60.

38 The association of the Gospel with Rome is, of course, inferential, but in my judgment it is also sound (cf., for example, Mark 15:21; and Rom 16:13). A good treatment of the question is available in Brian Incigneri, *The Gospel to the Romans: The Setting and Rhetoric of Mark's Gospel*, BibInt 65 (Leiden: Brill, 2003).

39 Alkier (*Reality of the Resurrection*, 85) takes the women to be "negative examples" of a failure to perceive, but in my view they instantiate the opening into insight that is the theme of the Gospel's close. When Mark accuses people of hardheartedness, he is quite direct (cf., for example, the string of condemnations in chapter 12).

40 Comparison with John 20:14-18 is fairly common. See Daniel A. Smith, *Revisiting the Empty Tomb: The Early History of Easter* (Minneapolis: Fortress, 2010), 126–31. Robert Gundry has attempted to specify the source of the tradition; Gundry, *Matthew: A Commentary on His Handbook for a Mixed Church under Persecution* (Grand Rapids: Eerdmans, 1994), 591. He argues that the material derives from a lost ending of Mark, which motivated the women to overcome their fear and tell Jesus' followers that he was risen.

41 John C. Fenton, *The Gospel of St Matthew* (Baltimore: Penguin, 1963), 450. In this regard, any negative characterization, such as Alkier suggests in Mark (cf. *Reality of the Resurrection*, 85), is ruled out.

42 So Konrad Weiss, "*pous*," in *Theological Dictionary of the New Testament*, ed. Gerhard Friedrich, trans. Geoffrey W. Bromiley (Grand Rapids: Eerdmans, 1968), 624–31, here 628–31. The usage does not directly imply a recognition of Jesus as God but is motivated by Matthew's conviction that he deserves worship as the Anointed (see Matt 2:10) and, in particular, by the baptismal formula that closes the final resurrection appearance and the Gospel as a whole (Matt 28:18-20).

43 Brown sees in this awkwardness an editorial seam, indicating the "joining of once independent episodes." See Raymond E. Brown, *The Gospel according to John (xiii–xxi)*, AB 29A (Garden City, N.Y.: Doubleday, 1970), 988. The real seam might be in v. 2 itself, since—if the story of Simon Peter and the other disciple (vv. 3-10) is ignored—the incident regarding Mary Magdalene is comparable to the Synoptic Gospels with their plurality of women, although distinctive in its presentation. Indeed, by saying Mary "runs" (*trekhei*), John provides a resonance with the more crucial usage of the same verb in v. 4. Her running in v. 2 and her bending to see what is in the memorial (v. 11) connect her to the description of the beloved disciple in vv. 4, 5. Indeed, both of those verbs are associated with Peter in Luke 24:12, but only *after* the vision of Mary Magdalene and her companions. John delays Mary's vision until after the race to the tomb between Peter and the beloved disciple.

44 See Isidore Epstein, ed., *The Babylonian Talmud, Translated into English with Notes, Glossary, and Indices* (London: Soncino, 1961).

45 See Moshe J. Bernstein, "Angels at the Aqedah: A Study in the Development of a Midrashic Motif," in *Reading and Re-reading Scripture at Qumran*, vol. 1, *Genesis and Its Interpretation*, STDJ 107 (Leiden: Brill, 2013), 323–52.

46 Raymond Brown's contention that this is a "normal, polite way of addressing women" stumbles when Matt 15:28; Luke 13:12, with their plainly discourteous context, are taken into account. See Brown, *The Gospel according to John (i–xii)*, AB (Garden City, N.Y.: Doubleday, 1966), 99.

47 I make this observation in full agreement with Brown, *Gospel according to John*, 989.

48 Alkier (*Reality of the Resurrection*, 161) points out that Jesus' body has become "something other than what it was prior to the resurrection."

49 See Peter Schäfer, Michael Meerson, and Yaacov Deutsch, eds., *Toledot Yeshu ("The Life Story of Jesus") Revisited: A Princeton Conference* (Tübingen: Mohr Siebeck, 2007); Meerson and Schäfer, *Toledot Yeshu*, 1:101–3.

50 Brown (*Gospel according to John*, 994) observes that "Jesus has frequently spoken about going to his father (*hypagein* in vii 33, xvi 5, 10; *poreuesthai* in xiv 12, 28; xvi 28)."

51 The natural inference is that John intends a theology of Jesus' preexistence as the Son of Man and uses "rabbi" as an introductory counterpoint. See Bruce Chilton, "The Gospel according to John's Rabbi Jesus," *Bulletin for Biblical Research* 25, no. 1 (2015): 39–54.

52 Brown attempts to argue that the sense of the prohibition is that Mary should not "cling" to Jesus, because John's purpose lies in "contrasting the passing nature of Jesus' presence in his post-resurrectional appearances and the permanent nature of his presence in the Spirit." See Brown, *Gospel according to John*, 1015. But this depends on an unduly restrictive rendering of *haptô*, albeit one that has convinced the translators of the English Standard Version.

53 The distinction is cognate with Paul's distinction between knowing God and being known by him (Gal 4:9).

54 The Nag Hammadi Library, the principal source of ancient gnostic writings, actually begins with the Prayer of the Apostle Paul, which addresses Christ by saying, "You are my mind: bring me forth! You are my treasure: open for me!" (I.1.6–7). This agrees with the Gospel of Mary. There are also echoes of Mary's conception in the Wisdom of Jesus Christ (III.4.98.9–22); Dialogue of the Savior (III.126.16–23; III.134.20–135.5); Thunder: Perfect Mind (VI.2.18.9–10); Paraphrase of Shem (VII.1.5–15); Second Discourse of Great Seth (VII.2.64.9); and Teachings of Silvanus (VII.4.103.1–10)—all available in *The Coptic Gnostic Library: A Complete Edition of the Nag Hammadi Codices*, ed. James M. Robinson (Leiden: Brill, 2000). I have developed the connection between Mary and gnostic sources in Bruce Chilton, *Mary Magdalene: A Biography* (New York: Doubleday, 2005), 119–37.

8 – AFTER PAUL, BEYOND THE TOMB

1 These teachers are listed among "all the apostles" in view of their connection to identifiable streams of tradition in the Gospels, as developed in the last chapter. Others, such as Apollos (1 Cor 1:12; 3:5, 22), Andronicus, and Junia (Rom 16:7) might also have been on Paul's mind.

2 This statement, coming as it does after Paul has argued for unity on the basis of a common possession of God's Spirit (1 Cor 12:1-11), suggests the influence of the More Than Five Hundred (as detailed in chapter 6). But it also ties in to his earlier mandate in regard to "discerning the body" within the Eucharist (11:27-32), which reflects the influence of Barnabas (see chapter 7).

3 In this regard, one might explain his strong emphasis on the "body," and not on Spirit alone, in his anthropology of resurrection (Jesus' and others') on the basis of Silas' influence. Hybridization emerges among strands of tradition within the Gospels, and there is no reason to exclude that possibility in the evaluation of Paul. In any case, a survey of conceptions of resurrection within Second Temple Judaism (as in chapter 3) rules out generalizations of the type: "As a Jew, but also as a native Greek speaker, Paul cannot imagine a self outside the body, an existence without a body"; so François Bovon, "The Soul's Comeback: Immortality and Resurrection in Early Christianity," *HTR* 103, no. 4 (2010): 387–406, here 401. It has been some time since the discipline has taken Judaism somehow to exclude philosophies of its various periods; a return to that habit would be unfortunate.

4 For this reason, the cases of Jairus' daughter (Mark 5:22-24, 35-43; Matt 9:18-19, 23-26; Luke 8:41-42, 49-56) and Lazarus (John 11:1-44) also differ from the resurrection, in that those resuscitated are not said to live forever. These healings point forward to the resurrection in the treatment of the Synoptics and of John, but they differ in kind from the case of Jesus.

5 So Ernst Haenchen, *The Acts of the Apostles: A Commentary*, trans. Bernard Noble, Gerald Shinn, Hugh Anderson, and R. McL. Wilson (Philadelphia: Westminster, 1971), 328.

6 Emphasis on "light" has been taken to be a primitive feature of the experience of the resurrection. See James M. Robinson, "Jesus—From Easter to Valentinus (or to the Apostles Creed)," *JBL* 101 (1982): 5–37, here 7. Acts 22:14, however, has Ananias tell Paul that he has seen Jesus, although the light is supposed to have been perceived by all present. Gerd Lüdemann suggests that 2 Cor 4:6 supports the primacy of light. See Lüdemann, *The Resurrection of Jesus: History, Experience, Theology*, trans. John Bowden (Minneapolis: Fortress, 1994), 53. Taken in the same sense, 2 Cor 3:18 intimates the richness of Paul's own visionary vocabulary.

7 See John Kilgallen, *The Stephen Speech: A Literary and Redactional Study of Acts 7,2-53*, AnBib 67 (Rome: Biblical Institute Press, 1976), 98–100; and chapter 3. In the case of Peter, the "righteous" one is also the "holy" one.

8 This aspect of Acts 22 is particularly surprising, since there is a tendency toward elision, rather than expansion, within the speech. Acts 22:3, for example, has been taken to mean that Paul grew up in Jerusalem. See Haenchen, *Acts of the Apostles*, 625. But I understand the statement to be a result of a compression that conflates periods of Paul's life. Similarly, Acts 22:18 refers to a vision of a "him" whose antecedent might be taken to be Ananias, except for how the "Lord" then features (v. 19).

9 The quotation comes from his *Bacchanals* (794–95), discussed in chapter 1. By the time of Acts, it has already been mediated by means of Second Temple Judaism. See Vadim Wittkowsky, "'Pagane' Zitate im Neuen Testament," *NovT* 51, no. 2 (2009): 107–26, here 119–24. As Wittkowsky observes, having Paul/Jesus cite Euripides in an audience with Festus is apposite, but the fact of the innovation remains.

10 So Haenchen, *Acts of the Apostles*, 328, for example.

11 See Tony Costa, "Paul's Calling as Prophetic Divine Commissioning," in *Christian Origins and Hellenistic Judaism: Social and Literary Contexts for the New Testament*, vol. 2 of *Early Christianity in Its Hellenistic Context*, ed. Stanley E. Porter and Andrew W. Pitts, TENTS 10 (Leiden: Brill, 2013), 203–35, here 210–18.

12 See Bruce Chilton, *Rabbi Paul: An Intellectual Biography* (New York: Doubleday, 2004), 65–71. Similarly, the assignment to Paul of powers from the high priest(s) to bind and force Jesus' followers to travel to Jerusalem to be punished (9:2, 21; 22:4-5) is widely regarded as inaccurate. But when Ananias himself is quoted in Acts 9:14, he refers to an authority to "bind" but not to the power to take prisoners to Jerusalem (cf. the wording of 26:12). Luke's Paul refers to violent activity in Jerusalem in Acts 22:19-20, including complicity in Stephen's death. The traditions incorporated by Luke may have referred to Paul's reputation as a persecutor in Judea (as in Gal 1:22-24). His embassy to Damascus no doubt was aimed to undermine followers of Jesus there, but the high priest could scarcely confer powers of detention and forced transfer to Jerusalem.

13 C. R. A. Morray-Jones has argued that this is a Merkabah vision, and associates the commission with 2 Cor 12:1-4. See Morray-Jones, "Paradise Revisited (2 Cor 12:1-12): The Jewish Mystical Background of Paul's Apostolate; Part 2; Paul's Heavenly Ascent and Its Significance," *HTR* 86, no. 3 (1993): 265–92, here 284–92. I have agreed with the setting of such visions (of which Paul himself alludes to a number in 2 Cor 12:1), but for chronological reasons I have associated the ascent to Paradise in 2 Corinthians with his prophetic commission in Acts 13:1-3; Chilton, *Rabbi Paul*, 114–16. The connection of Paul to the practice of Merkabah mysticism has been broadly accepted. See also John Bowker, "'Merkabah' Visions and the Visions of Paul," *JSS* 16 (1971): 157–73; Seyoon Kim, *The Origin of Paul's Gospel*, WUNT 2.3 (Tübingen: Mohr, 1981); Morray-Jones, "Paradise Revisited (2 Cor 12:1-12): The Jewish Mystical Background of Paul's Apostolate; Part 1; The Jewish Sources," *HTR* 86, no. 2 (1993): 177–217; Carey C. Newman, *Paul's Glory-Christology: Tradition and Rhetoric*, NovTSup 69 (Leiden: Brill, 1992). Even strong partisans of the view that the tomb was empty have become convinced by this line of investigation that a mystical element was present in Paul's experience. When N. T. Wright acknowledges that Paul had been influenced by the Merkabah in such a way, he inadvertently allows that the resurrection does not necessitate reference to the "empty tomb." See Wright, *The Resurrection of the Son of God*, Christian Origins and the Question of God 3 (London: SPCK, 2003), 394, 397.

14 See Luke Timothy Johnson, *Prophetic Jesus, Prophetic Church: The Challenge of Luke–Acts to Contemporary Christians* (Grand Rapids: Eerdmans, 2011).

15 Attempts to finesse the contradiction are recounted in Charles W. Hedrick, "Paul's Conversion/Call: A Comparative Analysis of the Three Reports in Acts," *JBL* 100, no. 3 (1981): 415–32, here 428–32.

16 See Thomas Hieke, "The Reception of Daniel 7 in the Revelation of John," in *Revelation and the Politics of Apocalyptic Interpretation*, ed. Richard B. Hays and Stefan Alkier (Waco, Tex.: Baylor University Press, 2012), 47–67, 65–67.

17 So Steve Moyise, *The Old Testament in the Book of Revelation*, JSNTSup 115 (Sheffield: Sheffield Academic Press, 1995), 138.

18 See Bruce Malina, *On the Genre and Message of Revelation: Star Visions and Sky Journeys* (Peabody, Mass.: Hendrickson, 1995), 68.

19 See Philip Edgcumbe Hughes, *The Book of Revelation: A Commentary* (Leicester: Inter-Varsity, 1990), 25–31; as well as the discussion in chapter 5.

20 See James M. Robinson, ed., *The Nag Hammadi Library in English* (San Francisco: Harper & Row, 1978); and Robinson, ed., *The Coptic Gnostic Library: A Complete Edition of the Nag Hammadi Codices* (Leiden: Brill, 2000). This is the most widely used translation of the ancient library of gnostic books discovered in Egypt in 1945, and it also includes the Gospel of Mary. Its reliance on all the canonical Gospels shows that the Gospel of Thomas must have been composed after the first century. See Bruce Chilton, "The Gospel according to Thomas as a Source of Jesus' Teaching," *Gospel Perspectives* 5 (1985): 155–75. For a good version of the Coptic text, and a translation with notes and a nice bibliography, see Marvin Meyer, *The Gospel of Thomas: The Hidden Sayings of Jesus* (San Francisco: HarperSanFrancisco, 1992). Further references are available in his *Secret Gospels: Essays on Thomas and the Secret Gospel of Mark* (Harrisburg, Pa.: Trinity, 2003); and in Stephen J. Patterson, *The Gospel of Thomas and Jesus*, Foundations and Facets Reference Series (Sonoma, Calif.: Polebridge, 1993).

21 See Karen King, *What Is Gnosticism?* (Cambridge, Mass.: Harvard University Press, 2003).

22 See Marvin Meyer, "Making Mary Male: The Categories 'Male' and 'Female' in the Gospel of Thomas," *NTS* 31 (1985): 554–70; Meyer, *The Gospel of Thomas: The Hidden Sayings of Jesus* (San Francisco: HarperSanFrancisco, 1992), 109; Meyer, *Secret Gospels: Essays on Thomas and the Secret Gospel of Mark* (Harrisburg, Pa.: Trinity, 2003), 76–106.

23 Citations follow the unfolding of volumes, books, pages, and lines within the Nag Hammadi Library, as presented by Robinson. The Gospel of Thomas is unusual in having been assigned numbers to its sayings by modern editors.

24 See Hans-Martin Schenke, *Das Philippus-Evangelium (Nag-Hammadi-Codex II, 3)*, TU 143 (Berlin: Akademie, 1997), 270; Elaine Pagels, "Ritual in the *Gospel of Philip*," in *The Nag Hammadi Library after Fifty Years: Proceedings of the 1995 Society of Biblical Literature Commemoration*, ed. John D. Turner and Anne McGuire, Nag Hammadi and Manichaean Studies 44 (Leiden: Brill, 1997), 280–91; Bruce Chilton, *Mary Magdalene: A Biography* (New York: Doubleday, 2005), 54–70, 113–17, 139–43.

25 See Paul Bradshaw and Carol Babawi, *The Canons of Hippolytus* (Bramcote, UK: Grove, 1987), canon 18.

26 See A. F. J. Klijn, *Jewish-Christian Gospel Tradition*, Supplements to Vigiliae Christianae 17 (Leiden: Brill, 1992), 4–6; citing Clement, *Miscellanies* 2.9.45. Clement appears to be well informed in regard to gnostic tradition, as when he attributes to

Valentinus the view that Jesus ate and drank, but did not eliminate, presumably after his resurrection (Clement, *Miscellanies* 3.59.3).

27 The Acts of Peter stand in a position to the Gospels not unlike that of the Gospel of Thomas and the Gospel of Peter. See Robert F. Stoops Jr., "The *Acts of Peter* in Intertextual Context," in *The Apocryphal Acts of the Apostles in Intertextual Perspectives*, ed. Robert F. Stoops Jr., Semeia 80 (Atlanta: Scholars Press, 1997), 57–86.

28 An early example of this type of problem is addressed by Paul's assertion that "no one speaking by God's Spirit says, Jesus is *anathema*, and no one is able to say, Jesus is Lord, except by Holy Spirit" (1 Cor 12:3). See Clint Tibbs, *Religious Experience of the Pneuma: Communication with the Spirit World in 1 Corinthians 12 and 14*, WUNT 2/230 (Tübingen: Mohr Siebeck, 2007), 147–80. As Tibbs shows, speech by means of the Spirit is a feature of prophecy before and after Paul.

29 The failure to recognize Jesus is a theme that is more widely represented and durable than is often accounted for, including a variety of tradents. See (apart from the possibility that Mark 16:5 refers to Jesus; cf. chapter 7) Luke 24:15-16, 18, 31; John 20:14-18, 20. This feature is more prominent than either the emphasis that Jesus ate (Luke 24:41-43) or the reference to his sudden appearance in the midst of his disciples (Luke 24:36-37; John 20:19).

30 Most crucially voiced in Matt 28:17 and most famously in John 20:26-29.

31 For this reason, as we have seen, in Luke's accounts, Jesus needs to identify himself to Paul; see Acts 9:5; 22:8; 26:15. The continuity of the Jesus who was buried with the Jesus who was risen is also central to Paul's apostolic asseveration in 1 Cor 15:3-4. As we have seen, Paul is likely to have included Mary Magdalene among "all the apostles" (v. 7); in our present state of knowledge, she appears to be the source of the tradition concerning Jesus' burial.

32 To this point, Wright has been mentioned specifically in this connection throughout our discussion, because he makes the strongest case for the physicality of the resurrection. For a treatment of the question, see Lidija Novakovic, *Resurrection: A Guide for the Perplexed* (London: T&T Clark, 2016), 77–102.

33 See Mark 15:42-47. The plural usage in respect of the week in 16:2, common in the New Testament, contrasts with *hebdomas* in Hellenistic usage. Henry George Liddell and Robert Scott, eds., *A Greek-English Lexicon* (New York: Oxford University Press, 1996), 466.

34 Christopher Bryan has attempted to ignore the pattern and to dismiss the usage of *theôreô* to imply "perception," but then he takes *theôreô* in v. 4 to refer to "a faint beginning of hope," an overinterpretation determined more by eagerness to confirm the hypothesis of "the empty tomb" than by the verb at issue. See Bryan, *The Resurrection of the Messiah* (New York: Oxford University Press, 2011), 283n50.

35 Among scholarly proponents of this view, see Dennis R. MacDonald, *The Homeric Epics and the Gospel of Mark* (New Haven: Yale University Press, 2000). If the account can be put off until as late as Markan redaction, it feeds the argument that the resurrection was essentially visionary and only acquired physical features for apologetic reasons. In this case, I suspect that the desire for that outcome has influenced some

interpreters' exegetical decisions. In this regard, see the review of MacDonald's book by Robert J. Rabel, in *Bryn Mawr Classical Review* 9, no. 16 (2000), http://bmcr .brynmawr.edu/2000/.

36 The former witness also changes "purchased" to "prepared." See Kurt Aland, Barbara Aland, Johannes Karavidopoulos, Carlo M. Martini, and Bruce M. Metzger, *Novum Testamentum Graece* (Stuttgart: Deutsche Bibelgesellschaft, 2012).

37 See Betty Radice, ed. and trans., *Pliny: Letters, Volume II, Books 8–10, Panegyricus*, LCL 59 (Cambridge, Mass.: Harvard University Press, 1969).

38 So, for example, the reference to Mary (Mark 16:9) reflects Luke 8:2 rather than the body of Mark's Gospel. Mark 16:10-11 recapitulates Luke 24:9-11; the short epitome in Mark 16:12-13 severely truncates the Lukan story of the disciples who traveled to Emmaus (Luke 24:13-35). For these and other indications that the "Longer Ending" is late and synthetic, see Martin Hengel, *Studies in the Gospel of Mark*, trans. John Bowden (London: SCM Press, 1985), 168; Paul Collins, "Polymorphic Christology: Its Origins and Development in Early Christianity," *JTS* 58, no. 1 (2007): 66–99.

39 See Stefan Alkier, *The Reality of the Resurrection: The New Testament Witness*, trans. Leroy A. Huizenger (Waco, Tex.: Baylor University Press, 2013), 85, 160–61.

40 See *Peri Paskha* 5, 7, 32–33, 60, 67, 69, 71; and the edition of Stuart J. Hall, ed. and trans., *Melito of Sardis, Peri Pascha and Fragments*, OECT (Oxford: Clarendon, 1979).

41 In recent years, an identification forcefully argued by Richard Bauckham, "The Relatives of Jesus," *Themelios* 21, no. 2 (1996): 18–21. Whatever the merits of that case, I would caution that there is a persistent tendency to argue about gnats that indicate a difference between the Markan and Matthean accounts, when an earthquake bigger than a camel is the real issue.

42 Richard C. Miller has shown that Luke's treatment in particular offers a correlation between the case of Jesus and the translation of Romulus in classical sources. See Miller, *Resurrection and Reception in Early Christianity* (New York: Routledge, 2015), 173–77.

43 See, for example, Kurt Aland, *Synopsis Quattuor Evangeliorum* (Stuttgart: Deutsche Bibelgesellschaft, 2005), 495. Once this heading is used for every pericope involving the tomb, the impact on exegetes is predictable.

44 See Markus Vinzent, *Der Ursprung des Apostolikums im Urteil der kritischen Forschung*, Forschungen zur Kirchen- und Dogmengeschichte 89 (Göttingen: Vandenoeck & Ruprcht, 2006). Gerhard Ebeling has skillfully shown how the resurrection is the lynchpin of everything that is said in the second part of the creed. Ebeling, *The Nature of Faith*, trans. Ronald Gregor Smith (Philadelphia: Fortress, 1961), 60–63.

45 I restrict my examples to the second century, for the sake of convenience. For Papias' apocalypticism, see Bruce Chilton, *Visions of the Apocalypse: Receptions of John's Revelation in Western Imagination* (Waco, Tex.: Baylor University Press, 2013), 13–26.

9 – Resurrection, History, and Realization

1   See Peter Schäfer, Michael Meerson, and Yaacov Deutsch, eds., *Toledot Yeshu ("The Life Story of Jesus") Revisited: A Princeton Conference* (Tübingen: Mohr Siebeck, 2007); Michael Meerson and Peter Schäfer (with Yaacov Deutsch, David Grossberg, Avigail Manekin, and Adina Yoffie), *Toledot Yeshu: The Life Story of Jesus*, 2 vols. and database (Tübingen: Mohr Siebeck, 2014), 1:101–3.

2   These are only examples of a pervasive theme of glory through John's Gospel. See John Ashton, "The Johannine Christ," in *The Gospel of John and Christian Origins* (Minneapolis: Fortress, 2014), 181–200.

3   Following a suggestion by John A. T. Robinson (cf. n. 59 below), N. T. Wright states that the description of the grave-clothes "carefully described in verse 7, suggests that they had not been unwrapped, but that the body had somehow passed through them, much as, later on, it would appear and disappear through locked doors." See Wright, *The Resurrection of the Son of God*, Christian Origins and the Question of God 3 (London: SPCK, 2003), 689.

4   As Richard C. Miller has observed, Jesus' "somatic palpability" in the resurrection serves the interests of worship rather than realism as such. See Miller, *Resurrection and Reception in Early Christianity* (New York: Routledge, 2015), 166–67 and 192n61.

5   In an otherwise lucid study, Jean-Luc Nancy misconstrues the Latin of the Vulgate as restricted to the desire to touch. In fact, *noli* is used as a straightforward prohibition. See Nancy, *Noli me tangere: On the Raising of the Body*, trans. Sarah Clift, Pascale-Anne Brault, and Michael Naas (New York: Fordham University Press, 2008), 37. With this caveat, Nancy's conclusion can be recommended: Jesus "is withdrawing into this dimension from which alone comes *glory*, that is, brilliance of more than presence, the radiance of what is in excess of the given, the available, the disposed" (17). Still, one could have wished that Nancy had engaged in a more disciplined exegetical preparation for his work. See the review by Jay Twomey in *Bible and Critical Theory* 6, no. 2 (2010): 52.1–52.3.

6   Following the analysis of Reginald H. Fuller, *The Formation of the Resurrection Narratives* (New York: Macmillan, 1971), 161. Fuller here extends the characterization of C. H. Dodd in "The Appearances of the Risen Christ: An Essay in Form-Criticism of the Gospels," in *More New Testament Studies* (Manchester: Manchester University Press, 1968), 102–33, here 118. Both are taken up in the helpful description of the development of traditions offered by Darryl W. Palmer, "The Resurrection of Jesus and the Mission of the Church," in *Reconciliation and Hope: New Testament Essays on Atonement and Eschatology*, ed. Robert Banks (Grand Rapids: Eerdmans, 1974), 205–23. Fuller's analysis is especially interesting, however, in that he calls attention to the continuing importance of absence within the texts both before and after appearance. He takes that to indicate the resurrection was not understood "as the resuscitation of Jesus' earthly body, but as the transformation of his whole being into the new mode of eschatological existence" (170; cf. 22). His recourse to both form criticism and eschatology is no longer fashionable, but his work is of enduring value.

7   Jane Schaberg, for example, speaks of the "emptiness" of the tomb as the "inspiration" of belief in the resurrection. See Schaberg, *The Resurrection of Mary Magdalene: Legends, Apocrypha, and the Christian Testament* (New York: Continuum, 2002), 282–91, 289. She also is aware of the indeterminacy of the "empty tomb," taken alone: "But I do not think this commits me to the belief that the resurrection must be thought of as the resuscitation of a corpse; rather, it is compatible with a lost or stolen corpse, and compatible with exaltation/ascent, and compatible with the mystery of the unknown fate of the corpse, and compatible with the destruction of the corpse" (284).

8   See the helpful discussion of Malise Ruthven, *Fundamentalism: The Search for Meaning* (Oxford: Oxford University Press, 2004), 10–11. He refers to Milton Stewart and Lyman Stewart in their publication of *The Fundamentals: A Testimony of Truth*.

9   See, for example, Norman L. Geisler, "The Apologetic Significance of the Bodily Resurrection of Jesus," *Bulletin of the Evangelical Philosophical Society* 10 (1987): 15–37.

10 This is how the argument of William Lane Craig is developed. See Craig, "The Historicity of the Empty Tomb of Jesus," *NTS* 31 (1985): 39–67, 40, 40–42, 56, 61–62n16; citing Karl Bornhäuser, *Das Wirken des Christus durch Taten und Worte*, BFCT (Gütersloh: Bertelsman, 1921), 26, 33. Ten years prior to Craig's article, Raymond E. Brown contested the equation of Paul with the Gospels. See Brown, *The Virginal Conception and Bodily Resurrection of Jesus* (London: Chapman, 1973), 83–84. But the trajectory of discussion turned away from Brown's approach. Craig's insistence that "saying that Jesus died—was buried—was raised—appeared, one automatically implies that the empty grave has been left behind" ("Historicity," 40) became the basis of N. T. Wright's assertion of Paul's agreement with the story. Wright is careful, however, to avoid identification with the "same body" argument of Fundamentalism, since he stresses the difference of the body that is raised from the body that was buried. Wright also, like Craig, appeals to Paul's background as a Pharisee, pitting the apostle "with his fellow Jews against the massed ranks of pagans; with his fellow Pharisees against other Jews"; Wright, *Resurrection of the Son of God*, 190–202, 271–76, quoting 272.

11 Jeffrey Jay Lowder, "Historical Evidence and the Empty Tomb Story: A Reply to William Lane Craig," *Journal of Higher Criticism* 8, no. 2 (2001): 251–93, here 264.

12 Kirsopp Lake, *The Historical Evidence for the Resurrection of Jesus Christ* (New York: Putnam, 1907), 250–53. Roger Aus has recently taken up this position, observing, "Since *all* of his followers had abandoned" Jesus, the women "did not know where Jesus had been buried." See Aus, *The Death, Burial, and Resurrection of Jesus, and the Death, Burial, and Translation of Moses in Judaic Tradition*, Studies in Judaism (Lanham, Md.: University Press of America, 2008), 321.

13 Wright even asserts that "the empty tomb was an absolute and unquestioned datum." See Wright (*Resurrection of the Son of God*, 614, 638) in the latter case referring to Matthean additions in regard to the guard at the tomb. In an astute analysis, Marianne Sawicki pointed out that the custody of Jesus' body was interrupted shortly

after his death, so that absolutes are not in play. See Sawicki, *Seeing the Lord: Resurrection and Early Christian Practices* (Minneapolis: Fortress, 1994), 257–75.

14 The largest recent impact among these theories has been exerted by the version of Hugh J. Schonfield, *The Passover Plot: New Light on the History of Jesus* (New York: Geis Associates, 1965), although the conspiracy to fake a resurrection was thwarted, on Schonfield's revision of the hypothesis, by the soldier's lance in John 19:34. See also Simon J. Joseph, "Jesus in India? Transgressing Social and Religious Boundaries," *JAAR* 80, no. 1 (2012): 161–99. Glastonbury's many alleged connections are well explained in Roberta Gilchrist, *Glastonbury Abbey: Archaeological Excavations 1904–1979* (Reading: University of Reading, Trustees of Glastonbury Abbey, 2015). The Japanese connection is discussed in Fritz Lidz, "The Little-Known Legend of Jesus in Japan," *Smithsonian Magazine*, January 2013, https://www.smithsonianmag.com/history/the-little-known-legend-of-jesus-in-japan-165354242/.

15 John Dominic Crossan has propagated this picture recently, which derives from the century-old work of Alfred Loisy. See Crossan, "The Dogs Beneath the Cross," in *Jesus: A Revolutionary Biography* (San Francisco: HarperSanFrancisco, 1994), 123–58; Loisy, *Les évangiles synoptiques* (Ceffonds: A. Loisy, 1907–1908), 700–712; and Loisy, *"The Birth of the Christian Religion" (La naissance du christianisme) and "The Origins of the New Testament" (Les origines du Nouveau Testament)*, trans. L. P. Jacks (New Hyde Park, N.Y.: University Books, 1962), 89–91. The claim is refuted by archaeological evidence: the remains of a man who had been crucified in an ossuary. See Craig Evans, *Jesus and the Ossuaries: What Jewish Burial Practices Reveal about the Beginning of Christianity* (Waco, Tex.: Baylor University Press, 2003), 91–122. Loisy's scholarship could not have taken the ossuary into account, and he typified foibles of his time in ignoring Judaic evidence for the burial of crucified people.

16 See Simcha Jacobovici and Charles R. Pellegrino, *The Jesus Family Tomb: The Discovery, the Investigation, and the Evidence That Could Change History* (New York: HarperCollins, 2008); and James D. Tabor and Simcha Jacobovici, *The Jesus Discovery: The Archaeological Find That Reveals the Birth of Christianity* (New York: Simon and Schuster, 2012). The multiple suppositions involved have been laid bare in such publications as Eric Meyers, "The Jesus Tomb Controversy: An Overview," *NEA* 69, nos. 3/4 (2006): 116–18; Amos Kloner and Shimon Gibson, "The Talpiot Tomb Reconsidered: The Archaeological Facts," in *The Tomb of Jesus and His Family? Exploring Ancient Jewish Tombs Near Jerusalem's Walls*, ed. James H. Charlesworth, Princeton Symposium on Judaism and Christian Origins (Grand Rapids: Eerdmans, 2013), 29–52.

17 Alan F. Segal calls it a "modern, rationalized apologetic synthesis." See Segal, "The Resurrection: Faith or History," in *The Resurrection of Jesus: John Dominic Crossan and N. T. Wright in Dialogue*, ed. Robert B. Stewart (Minneapolis: Fortress, 2006), 121–38, quoting 135. In N. T. Wright's argument, the stories about the tomb are generalized to produce "emptiness" throughout (rather than stages that eventually make emptiness their part of their assertion), the generalization is equated with history, and then "the bodily resurrection of Jesus proves a necessary condition" for the

alleged emptiness; Wright, *Resurrection of the Son of God*, 17. This procedure appears to contradict Wright's stated principle of method (under the banner of "critical realism"), which denies the enterprise of "tradition-historical study" as building "castles in the air," to the extent that he finds "the lengthy tradition-historical analysis of Lüdemann almost entirely worthless." See Wright, *Resurrection of the Son of God*, 19, 319. Yet Gerd Lüdemann in fact concludes that Paul thought of the tomb as empty without explicitly drawing that conclusion or referring to the tradition in the Gospels. See Lüdemann, *The Resurrection of Jesus: History, Experience, Theology*, trans. John Bowden (Minneapolis: Fortress, 1994), 46–47. To that extent, his difference from Wright is not as great as one might think from reading Wright's characterization without reference to Lüdemann's own work. That is because the issue of the tradition of the tomb being empty was elevated by the time Wright contributed to a position it did not occupy at the time that Lüdemann wrote. It is also notable that Wright does not portray the empty tomb as a sufficient condition for belief in the resurrection, only as a necessary condition. See Wright, "Resurrection Faith," *Christian Century*, December 18–31, 2002, 28–31.

18 For this reason, it is fatuous of Christopher Bryan to invoke Sherlock Holmes' principle that "when you have eliminated the impossible, whatever remains, *however improbable*, must be the truth." See Bryan, *The Resurrection of the Messiah* (New York: Oxford University Press, 2011), 39, 171. Without citing Arthur Conan Doyle's "The Sign of Four," where Holmes invokes his principle, Wright reverts to the same argument. Stewart, *Resurrection of Jesus*, 22.

19 So, for example, Alan F. Segal, *Life after Death: A History of the Afterlife in the Religions of the West* (New York: Doubleday, 2004), 441, 393–94: "spiritual visions" are conflated with Jesus' "transformed, angelic state." In his own way, Segal engages in the reductionism that he criticizes Wright for. He short-circuits the narrative of the tomb, while Wright short-circuits the pervasive understanding that Jesus "was seen" (*ôphthê*) after his death. Segal has been criticized for claiming that the earliest rabbis were not concerned with identifying afterlife with the "fleshly body" (607–8); cf. Jon Douglas Levenson, *Resurrection and the Restoration of Israel: The Ultimate Victory of the God of Life* (New Haven: Yale University Press, 2006), 232. Yet rabbinic literature attributes to the second-century teacher Joshua ben Hananiah the view that God will generate people from an indestructible bone in the spinal column (Genesis Rabbah 28:3); see Dale C. Allison, *Resurrecting Jesus: The Earliest Christian Tradition and Its Interpreters* (New York: T&T Clark, 2005), 219–22.

20 Indeed, Gerd Lüdemann argues for the centrality of "visions and auditions" and then finds that "if you say that Jesus rose from the dead biologically, you would have to presuppose that a decaying corpse—which is already cold and without blood in its brain—could be made alive again. I think that is nonsense." See Lüdemann, *Resurrection of Jesus*, 69; and Lüdemann, *Jesus' Resurrection, Fact of Figment? A Debate between William Lane Craig & Gerd Lüdemann*, ed. Paul Copan and Ronald K. Tacelli (Downers Grove, Ill.: InterVarsity, 2000), 45. See also Bart Ehrman,

How Jesus Became God: The Exaltation of a Jewish Preacher from Galilee (New York: HarperOne, 2014), 174.

21 See Allison, *Resurrecting Jesus*, 269–99.

22 See Colleen Shantz, "Opening the Black Box: New Prospects for Analyzing Religious Experience," in *Experientia*, vol. 2: *Linking Text and Experience*, ed. Colleen Shantz and Rodney A. Werline (Atlanta: Society of Biblical Literature, 2012), 1–15; Shantz, *The Neurobiology of the Apostle's Life and Thought* (New York: Cambridge University Press, 2009), 27, 57. In association with her work, see István Czachesz, "Filled with New Wine? Religious Experience and Social Dynamics in the Corinthian Church," in Shantz and Werline, *Experientia*, 2:71–90; and the volume Czachesz edited with Tamas Sndor Biro, *Changing Minds: Religion and Cognition through the Ages*, Groningen Studies in Cultural Change 42 (Leuven: Peeters, 2012).

23 In his study, Gary R. Habermas uses the emergence of the category to argue that in contrast, by a wide margin, scholars prove to be "moderate conservatives," in the sense that they hold that "Jesus was actually raised from the dead in some manner, either bodily (and thus extended in space and time), or as some sort of spiritual body (though often undefined)." See Habermas, "Resurrection Research from 1975 to the Present: What Are Critical Scholars Saying?" *Journal for the Study of the Historical Jesus* 3, no. 2 (2005): 135–53, quoting 136, 139–40.

24 Lüdemann (*Resurrection of Jesus*, 180) is convinced, on the grounds of his deployment of the same category, that "we can longer understand the resurrection of Jesus in a literal way."

25 Such as Lüdemann's (*Resurrection of Jesus*, 173–79, 249n679) view that it is "a primary experience that bears the religious truth completely within itself." We have encountered the interpretive problems involved in the last chapter. Until recently, however, this was a widely accepted position. C. F. D. Moule suggested that, by placing his own experience in association with that of the witness to the resurrection before him, Paul shows that "the Evangelists, who wrote later, are objectifying, localizing, and limiting what was really in the nature of a vision, with all the elusiveness and ubiquity of vision." See Moule, introduction to *The Significance of the Message of the Resurrection for Faith in Jesus Christ*, ed. C. F. D. Moule, trans. Dorothea M. Barton and R. A. Wilson, SBT 8 (Naperville, Ill.: Allenson, 1968), 1–11, quoting 5.

26 Gos. Pet. 10:38-42 presents a unique scene, largely embellished from Matthew:

Then those soldiers, having seen, awakened the centurion and the elders, because they also were present, guarding. And while they explained what they had seen, again they see three males come out from the tomb—and two supporting the one, and a cross following them, and the head of the two reaching into heaven, but that of the one being led by hand by them transcending the heavens. And they heard a voice from the heavens saying, Have you proclaimed to those who sleep? And a response was heard from the cross that: Yes.

By the application of logic that escapes me, scholars such as Bryan call this a description of the resurrection itself. See Bryan, *Resurrection of the Messiah*, 117. Obviously, the emergence from the tomb of these entities is not the moment of the resurrection in itself. Yet to Bryan, this seals his view of a "transphysical" event. There can be little doubt of the "trans," in any case. The Gospel of Peter may be read as a palimpsest of the Johannine story of Lazarus as well as the Matthean tradition of the guard, by having witnesses when three figures and the cross exit the tomb, but the cosmic figure they see is only recognizable in light of what the divine voice says, and how the cross features. If it were the case that the ancient texts were as concerned to focus attention on the physical body of Jesus as some modern interpreters do, it is difficult to avoid the impression that the texts would have been composed differently. See John Dominic Crossan and Sarah Sexton Crossan, *Resurrecting Easter: How the West Lost and the East Kept the Original Easter Vision* (New York: HarperOne, 2018), 2–3, 184.

27 See Segal, *Life after Death*, 448, within the discussion on 446–63. He argues that the eventual emptiness of the tomb is designed to "face and then finesse the issue that no one saw Jesus rise."

28 See Marc Bloch, *The Historian's Craft*, trans. Peter Putnam (Manchester: Manchester University Press, 1992 [from the 1953 ed., a translation of the French original of 1949]).

29 This was the breakthrough understanding of R. G. Collingwood, *The Idea of History* (Oxford: Clarendon, 1946), 208.

30 Collingwood, *Idea of History*, 213, 214.

31 See Outi Lehtipuu, *Debates over the Resurrection of the Dead: Constructing Early Christian Identity*, OECS (Oxford: Oxford University Press, 2015).

32 As Richard R. Niebuhr argues in a classic study, "In the resurrection of Christ the spontaneity, particularity and independence of historical events rise to the surface in a single eruption." See Niebuhr, *Resurrection and Historical Reason: A Study of Theological Method* (New York: Scribner's, 1957), 177; cf. 147. Jean-Luc Marion has recently taken up Niebuhr's understanding, to characterize events as "unrepeatable, unable to be assigned a unique cause, and unable to be foreseen." So Robyn Horner, *Jean-Luc Marion: A Theo-logical Introduction* (Farnham, UK: Ashgate, 2005), 124; cf. 37–40; citing a position Marion argues in Jean-Luc Marion, *De Surcroît: Études sur les phénomènes saturés* (Paris: Presses universitaires de France, 2001), 43. The latter work is available in English as *In Excess: Studies of Saturated Phenomena*, trans. Robyn Horner and Vincent Berraud (New York: Fordham University Press, 2002). In the description of Shane Mackinlay, "Phenomena are neither caused by some other reality nor constituted by a subject." Mackinlay, *Interpreting Excess: Jean-Luc Marion, Saturated Phenomena, and Hermeneutics* (New York: Fordham University Press, 2010), 81.

33 The category of "event" might be applied in the sense of a "language event" (part of the tradition within which Niebuhr and Marion emerge), but that takes the resurrection out of the usual explanation of happenings that history involves. "Saturated phenomena," in Marion's language, involving awareness of what cannot be fully explained, are hardly historical events, philosophically interesting though they are. A seam of philosophical inquiry largely defined by Martin Heidegger qualifies "event" (*Ereignis*) as a personal cognitive moment, as an awareness of "our own

intrinsic self-absence that draws us into openness." See the discussion in Thomas Sheehan, "*Kehre* and *Ereignis*: A Prolegomenon to *Introduction to Metaphysics*," in *A Companion to Heidegger's Introduction to Metaphysics*, ed. Richard Polt and Gregory Fried (New Haven: Yale University Press, 2001), 3–16, 12. Marion has preferred a greater emphasis on the phenomenon than on the observer, and has been criticized for that, but a cognitive construction of "event" remains a philosophical option. See James K. A. Smith, "Liberating Religion from Theology: Marion and Heidegger on the Possibility of a Phenomenology of Religion," *International Journal for Philosophy of Religion* 46, no. 1 (1999): 17–33. Anthony J. Kelly has pioneered a thorough analysis of the resurrection and ascension along lines he pursued from Jean-Luc Marion's work. Kelly on that basis returns to language of "the total phenomenon of the Christ Event," in which "Christ has left the death-bound world behind, and, in his humanity, carried that world into the deathless realm of God and eternal life." See Kelly, *Upward: Faith, Church, and the Ascension of Christ* (Collegeville, Minn.: Liturgical [Michael Glazier], 2014), 48. Kelly deliberately simplifies at this point in his discussion, but he illustrates the conflation of philosophy, theology, and faith when issues of cognition are involved. For that reason, even when seen as cognitive, rather than "eschatological," caution will be necessary in understanding the resurrection as an event, to avoid confusion with historical events as usually understood.

34 For Niebuhr, the resurrection can be known "only through the memory of the church"; Niebuhr, *Resurrection and Historical Reason*, 94–95. He here shows the influence of John Knox, *The Man Christ Jesus* (Chicago: Willett, Clark, 1941), 24–27. "Church" in the usage of Knox and Niebuhr is a transhistorical reality, such that "the church is not only the ground of the twentieth-century Christian's knowledge of Jesus, but it is the condition of his contemporaries' knowledge of him." See Niebuhr, *Resurrection and Historical Reason*, 94–95.

35 See, for example, Dennis Edwards, "Divine Action in the Christ Event," in *How God Acts: Creation, Redemption, and Special Divine Action* (Minneapolis: Fortress, 2010), 15–34.

36 See Franz Mussner, *Die Auferstehung Jesu*, Biblische Handbibliothek 7 (Munich: Kösel, 1969), which aligns with the approach of Reginald Fuller, *Formation*.

37 So Gerd Lüdemann, *Resurrection of Jesus*, 211; as well as his later works: *The Resurrection of Christ: A Historical Inquiry* (Amherst, N.Y.: Prometheus, 2004); and (with Tom Hall), *The Acts of the Apostles: What Really Happened in the Earliest Days of the Church* (Amherst, N.Y.: Prometheus, 2005).

38 Stephen Davis' statement that "the risen Jesus was a physical body that was objectively present to the witnesses in time and space" needs to be conditioned by the New Testament's awareness that some of those who might have been witnesses were not, and that even those who were could remain uncertain. See Davis, "Seeing the Risen Jesus," in *The Resurrection: An Interdisciplinary Symposium on the Resurrection of Jesus*, ed. Stephen T. Davis, Daniel Kendall, and Gerald O'Collins (Oxford: Oxford University Press, 1997), 126–47, quoting 146. Although the presentation of Gos. Pet. 9:35–11:49 might at first sight appear to break this rule, even in that text what

260 NOTES TO PAGES 189–194

is seen at the tomb, although graphically described, does not generate faith. There is a dichotomy between what can be observed and the reality of the resurrection.

39 Also known as the Epistle to Rheginos; see I.4.48.6–49.8, in James M. Robinson, *The Nag Hammadi Library in English* (San Francisco: Harper & Row, 1978).

40 Richard Miller's comparison of the risen Jesus with the translated Romulus is weak, because the charge of Romulus to those who come after him (hardly his "Great Commission," as Miller calls it) simply involves carrying on the work of empire that had already begun, without the distinctive new imperatives involved in the resurrection; cf. Livy, *History* 1.16.1–8. See Miller, *Resurrection and Reception*, 68–69.

41 For that reason, it is not accurate to assert that "the resurrection, the exaltation, and the gift of the spirit were one undifferentiated experience." See S. MacLean Gilmour, "The Christophany to More Than Five Hundred Brethren," *JBL* 80, no. 3 (1961): 248–52, quoting 151; and Lüdemann, *Acts of the Apostles*, 49–50.

42 But Paul's expression here does not exclude Jesus' exaltation. Exaltation as well as resurrection feature in Col 1:13-23; and Gal 4:4-7 assumes a tight connection between Jesus as Son, the identity of believers, and the Spirit.

43 "Luke–Acts collects extant sources and creates its own literary memory theater for early Christianity, where past stories are newly used, transformed, and embedded in the narrative." See Laura Nasrallah, "The Acts of the Apostles, Greek Cities, and Hadrian's *Panhellenion*," *JBL* 127, no. 3 (2008): 533–66, quoting 553.

44 Christopher Bryan, for example, remarks that although the description of Jesus "might be heard as claiming for him a literally physical, upward movement," in fact in this case "Luke is using the language and imagery of apocalyptic." See Bryan, *Resurrection of the Messiah*, 119.

45 See Karin Schöpflin, "The Revivification of the Dry Bones: Ezekiel 37:1-14," in *The Human Body in Death and Resurrection*, ed. Tobias Nicklas, Friedrich V. Reiterer, and Joseph Verheyden, Deuterocanonical and Cognate Literature, Yearbook 2009 (Berlin: Walter de Gruyter, 2009), 67–85. By that time, as well, a process was underway in which—as Maureen Bloom has explained—the description of God himself also became more physical and anthropomorphic in response to mounting confrontation with Roman power. See Bloom, *Jewish Mysticism and Magic: An Anthropological Perspective*, Routledge Jewish Studies Series (Abingdon: Routledge, 2007), 158–59.

46 Emphasis on the substantial reality of God also resulted in the tradition within the Merkabah of the physical description of God himself. Moshe Idel quotes the challenge of *Midrash Mishlei* 10, where the question is posed to a scholar, "Since you studied Talmud, did you gaze at the Chariot, did you gaze at my greatness?" The interrogation goes on to refer to the *hashmal*, the radiance of Ezek 1:4, 27, and even to God's physical attributes and dimensions. See Idel, *Absorbing Perfections: Kabbalah and Interpretation* (New Haven: Yale University Press, 2002), 171–72. *Midrash Mishlei*, of course, is far too late (perhaps from the eighth century CE) to be used as a source for interpreting the New Testament. A concerted effort has been made to link meditation on God's dimensions (the *Shi'ur Qoman*) to the angel Metatron, and to connect Metatron and Enoch. See Andrei A. Orlov, *The Enoch-Metatron Tradition*,

Texts and Studies in Ancient Judaism 107 (Tübingen: Mohr-Siebeck, 2005), 86–147. Although evocative, these materials are also attested from after the period of the New Testament.

47 Bryan compares this to the vanishing of Apollo in the *Aeneid* 9.656–658 (Bryan, *Resurrection of the Messiah*, 114). This dimension of analysis has been greatly extended by Richard C. Miller, who shows that from the time of Justin's first *Apology*, patristic authors compared the resurrection to stories of translations of "sons of Zeus." Miller, *Resurrection and Reception*, 1–19.

48 So Joseph A. Fitzmyer, *The Gospel according to Luke (X–XXIV): Introduction, Translation, and Notes*, AB 28A (Garden City, N.Y.: Doubleday, 1985), 2:1558–59; and Raymond A. Blacketer, "Word and Sacrament on the Road to Emmaus," *CTJ* 38 (2003): 321–29, here 323–26.

49 Abraham Abulafia, the thirteenth-century kabbalist, spoke of how spirit might overflow a soul, so that a practitioner "is called angel of God, and his name will be called as the name of his master, which is Shaddai" (*Hayyei ha-Olam ha-Ba* fol. 12a); see Elliott R. Wolfson, *Language, Eros, Being: Kabbalistic Hermeneutics and Poetic Imagination* (New York: Fordham University Press, 2007), 240–41. It would obviously be unwarranted to make Abulafia the context of Luke's source but equally unwise to exclude the possibility of such a reading from the original, pre-Lukan setting.

50 Mark 16:1-8; Matt 28:1-8; Luke 24:1-11; Matt 28:9-10; John 20:1-2, 11-18; Gos. Pet. 12:50–13:57; Gos. Mary 10:6-20.

51 Marianne Sawicki, *Seeing the Lord*, 243–75; and Angela Standhartinger, "'What Women Were Accustomed to Do for the Dead Beloved by Them' ('Gospel of Peter' 12.50): Traces of Laments and Mourning Rituals in Early Easter, Passion, and Lord's Supper Traditions," *JBL* 129, no. 3 (2010): 559–74. Gos. Pet. 12:50–13:57, although a derivative text, reflects the liturgical background.

52 In his analysis of "event" as it applies to a historian, Collingwood observed that it involves investigating "not mere events (where by a mere event I mean one which has only an outside and no inside) but actions." Collingwood, *Idea of History*, 213–14. In this sense, I will go on to observe that the resurrection is action, but not event, because it is all "inside," in Collingwood's sense of the term.

53 See Collingwood, *Idea of History*, 209; and Giuseppina D'Oro, *Collingwood and the Metaphysics of Experience* (London: Routledge, 2002), 103–24.

54 That is why Origen referred to Jesus as *autobasileia*, "kingdom itself"; see *Commentary on Matthew* 14.7; and Benedict T. Viviano, *The Kingdom of God in History* (Eugene, Ore.: Wipf and Stock, 1988), 40.

55 So Gerd Lüdemann's effort to explain Peter's vision as "the initial spark" of the entire resurrection complex, where it is best interpreted "psychologically as failed mourning and the overcoming of a severe guilt complex," does not answer to the case; see Lüdemann with Alf Ôzen, *What Really Happened to Jesus? A Historical Approach to the Resurrection*, trans. John Bowden (Louisville: Westminster John Knox, 1995), 129–30.

56 The number of such statements is incalculable, but Rudolf Bultmann is frequently cited: "We cannot use electric lights and radios and, in the event of illness, avail ourselves of modern medical and clinical means and at the same time believe in the spirit and wonder world of the New Testament." See Bultmann, *The New Testament and Mythology and Other Basic Writings*, trans. Schubert M. Ogden (Philadelphia: Fortress, 1984), 4.

57 Isaac Newton himself inferred that the force of gravity, as he had demonstrated it, operates by means of a "most subtle Spirit" among large and small bodies, "electric bodies," and differing forms of light. Even "animal bodies" move by "vibrations of this Spirit"—an anticipation of the views of Roger Penrose discussed below. See Nancy K. Frankenbury, "Isaac Newton (1643–1727)," in *The Faith of Scientists: In Their Own Words* (Princeton: Princeton University Press, 2008), 102–21, 117 (quoting from the "General Scholium"). As she shows, Newton specifically refuted the closed mechanical universe that his work has been used to posit. Cf. also Rob Iliffe, *Priest of Nature: The Religious Worlds of Isaac Newton* (New York: Oxford University Press, 2017), 94–95, where the vacuum of space complements the nature of God as bodiless.

58 Gerhard Ebeling, Bultmann's ablest student in this regard, portrayed belief in the resurrection not as "a new object of faith, but the coming into being, the being awakened and coming alive of faith itself." See Ebeling, *The Nature of Faith*, trans. Ronald Gregor Smith (Philadelphia: Fortress, 1961), 62. In my reading, Niebuhr, Fuller, and Marion, whose views are discussed above, are also part of this movement, which locates the resurrection within the field of cognition.

59 John A. T. Robinson suggested that we should take the Shroud of Turin as evidence that the image was produced, not by a medieval artist, but by a form of "dematerialization" involved in the resurrection. That was his way of "envisaging the relationship between flesh and spirit, matter and energy, of being 'changed' or 'clothed upon' with a body of 'glory.'" See "The Shroud and the New Testament," in *La Sindone e la scienza*, ed. P. Coero-Borga, Atti del II Congresso Internazionale di Sindonologia (Turin: Paoline, 1979), 265–88, quoting 270. But claims of the authenticity of the shroud have been overturned. See Walter C. McCrone, *Judgement Day for the Turin Shroud* (Chicago: Microscope, 1997); and Giulio Fanti and Roberto Maggiolo, "The Double Superficiality of the Frontal Image of the Turin Shroud," *Journal of Optics A: Pure and Applied Optics* 6 (2004): 491–503.

60 Moule suggested that Jesus' physical body was "*transformed* into a different mode of existence." See Moule, introduction to *Significance of the Message*, 1–11, quoting 10. He also envisages the resurrection as consistent with resurrection generally, suggesting that "the total matter of this space-time existence is destined by the Creator not to be 'scrapped' but to be used up into some other existence," along the analogy of fuel being used up in energy.

61 Mani Bhaumik, "Is Schrödinger's Cat Alive?" *Quanta* 6, no. 1 (2017): 70–80.

62 "As soon as the observation is performed, the composite state is split into a superposition for which each element describes a different object-system state and an

observer with (different) knowledge of it." See Hugh Everett, "The Theory of the Universal Wavefunction" (Ph.D. diss., Princeton University, 1955), in *The Many-Worlds Interpretation of Quantum Mechanics*, ed. Bryce DeWitt and R. Neil Graham, Princeton Series in Physics (Princeton: Princeton University Press, 1973), 98. Everett is clear, however, that the stance of the observer is collective, so he is not positing individualistic subjectivity. He also uses Schrödinger's own wave equation to brilliant effect, against Schrödinger's criticism of a many-worlds interpretation.

63 Cf. Michio Kaku, *Higher Worlds: A Journey through Creation, Higher Dimensions, and the Future of the Cosmos* (New York: Doubleday, 2004); and Michael Crichton, *Timeline* (New York: Knopf, 1999).

64 Most notably by John Hick in *Death and Eternal Life* (New York: Harper & Row, 1976). Hick's "replica theory" has been taken up and modified by Eric Steinhart, "The Revision Theory of Resurrection," *RelS* 44, no. 1 (2008): 63–81.

65 See Stuart Hameroff and Roger Penrose, "Consciousness in the Universe: A Review of the 'Orch OR' Theory," *Physics of Life Reviews* 11, no. 1 (2014): 39–78. Deepak Chopra has championed this theory; see his article with Stuart Hameroff, "The 'Quantum Soul': A Scientific Hypothesis," in *Exploring Frontiers of the Mind-Brain Relationship*, ed. Alexander Moreira-Almeida and Franklin Santana Santos, Mindfulness in Behavioral Health (New York: Springer, 2012), 79–93.

66 Origen insists, again following Paul's analysis, that the body that is raised in resurrection is continuous with the physical body in principle, but different from it in substance (*First Principles* 2.10.3). See Lehtipuu, *Debates over the Resurrection*.

67 Augustine is well aware, as was Origen before him, that Paul speaks of a "spiritual body," and he acknowledges, "I suspect that all utterance published concerning it is rash." And yet he can be quite categorical that flesh must be involved somehow: "The spiritual flesh will be subject to spirit, but it will still be flesh, not spirit; just as the carnal spirit was subject to the flesh, but was still spirit, not flesh" (*The City of God* 22.21).

68 Graham Ward has suggested that, in the light of the resurrection, corporality as ordinarily perceived, in matter, needs to be "read" allegorically, in that bodies are designed to be eternal. See Ward, "Transcorporality: The Ontological Scandal," *Bulletin of the John Rylands Library* 80, no. 3 (1998): 235–52, here 244. For an attempt to work that insight out in terms of biology, see Holmes Rollston III, "Divine Presence—Causal, Cybernetic, Caring, Cruciform: From Information to Incarnation," in *Incarnation: On the Scope and Depth of Christology*, ed. Niels Henrik Gregersen (Minneapolis: Fortress, 2015), 255–87.

69 Hameroff and Penrose, "Consciousness in the Universe," 41, for example, illustrate consciousness with reference to "Buddhist writings," making that their privileged field of comparison.

Conclusion

1 Relevant literature is cited within the previous chapters. Notes and references within the epilogue refer to the chapters where bibliography is most easily located. In this case, see the introduction and chapter 9, "Resurrection, History, and Realization."

2 Traced in chapter 2, "Israel's Revolution of Hope."

3 Detailed in chapter 3, "Bodies Raised in Israel's Vindication."

4 A late starter, the conception of the soul as resurrected, a view consonant with the growing Stoicism of patristic thinkers, becomes dominant by the time of Saint Augustine. All the other types of resurrection body are instanced within the New Testament, and precedent for the later development is offered by Rev 6:9-11 (cf. 1 En 22:3-14). In aggregate, the chapters in part 2, "Catalyst of Transformation," deal with this development. The interesting focus on "soul" as the medium of resurrection after the period of the New Testament is discussed in chapter 4, "Paul on How Jesus 'Was Seen.'"

5 See chapter 5, "Seen 'by *Kêpha*,' Then 'by the Twelve.'"

6 Chapter 6, "Seen 'by More Than Five Hundred,' Then 'by James.'"

7 Chapter 7, "Seen by 'All the Apostles.'"

8 Chapter 8, "After Paul, beyond the Tomb."

9 Chapter 9, "Resurrection, History, and Realization."

Bibliography

Abush, Tzvi. "Ishtar's Proposal and Gilgamesh's Refusal: An Interpretation of 'The Epic of Gilgamesh,' Tablet 6, Lines 1–79." *History of Religions* 26, no. 2 (1986): 143–87.

Aland, Barbara, Kurt Aland, Johannes Karavidopoulos, Carlo M. Martini, and Bruce M. Metzger, eds. *Novum Testamentum Graece*. Stuttgart: Deutsche Bibelgesellschaft, 2012.

Aland, Kurt. *Synopsis Quattuor Evangeliorum*. Stuttgart: Deutsche Bibelgesellschaft, 2005.

Alkier, Stefan. *The Reality of the Resurrection: The New Testament Witness*. Translated by Leroy A. Huizenga. Waco, Tex.: Baylor University Press, 2013.

Allison, Dale C. *The New Moses: A Matthean Typology*. Minneapolis: Fortress, 1993.

———. *Resurrecting Jesus: The Earliest Christian Tradition and Its Interpreters*. New York: T&T Clark, 2005.

Ashton, John. "The Johannine Christ." In *The Gospel of John and Christian Origins*, 181–200. Minneapolis: Fortress, 2014.

Assmann, Jan. *Moses the Egyptian: The Memory of Egypt in Western Monotheism*. Cambridge, Mass.: Harvard University Press, 1997.

Astell, Ann W., and Sandor Goodhart, eds. *Sacrifice, Scripture and Substitution: Readings in Judaism and Christianity*. Notre Dame, Ind.: Notre Dame University Press, 2011.

Aune, David E. *Prophecy in Early Christianity and the Ancient Mediterranean World*. Grand Rapids: Eerdmans, 1991.

Aus, Roger. *The Death, Burial, and Resurrection of Jesus, and the Death, Burial, and Translation of Moses in Judaic Tradition.* Studies in Judaism. Lanham, Md.: University Press of America, 2008.

———. *Simon Peter's Denial and Jesus' Commissioning Him as His Successor in John 21:15-19: Studies in Their Judaic Background.* Studies in Judaism. Lanham, Md.: University Press of America, 2013.

Bammel, C. P. "The First Resurrection Appearance." In *John and the Synoptics*, edited by Adelbert Denaux, 620–31. BETL 101. Leuven: Peeters, 1992.

Bammel, Ernst. "Herkunft und Funktion der Traditionselemente in 1 Kor 15,1-11." *Theologische Zeitung* 11 (1955): 401–19.

Barr, James. *The Semantics of Biblical Language.* London: Oxford University Press, 1961.

Barrett, C. K. *The Acts of the Apostles.* ICC. Edinburgh: T&T Clark, 1994.

———. *The First Epistle to the Corinthians.* BNTC. Peabody, Mass.: Hendrickson, 1993.

Bauckham, Richard. *The Fate of the Dead: Studies on the Jewish and Christian Apocalypses.* NovTSup 93. Leiden: Brill, 2001.

———. *Jesus and the Eyewitnesses: The Gospels as Eyewitness Testimony.* Grand Rapids: Eerdmans, 2017.

———. "The Relatives of Jesus." *Themelios* 21, no. 2 (1996): 18–21.

Baumgarten, Albert I., ed. *Sacrifice in Religious Experience.* Numen Book Series 93. Leiden: Brill, 2003.

Beale, G. K., and D. A. Carson, eds. *Commentary on the New Testament Use of the Old Testament.* Grand Rapids: Baker Academic, 2007.

Beatrice, Pier Franco. "The 'Gospel according to the Hebrews' in the Apostolic Fathers." *NovT* 48, no. 2 (2006): 147–95.

Bechard, Dean Philip. *Paul outside the Walls: A Study of Luke's Socio-geographical Universalism in Acts 14:8-20.* AnBib 143. Rome: Pontificio Istituto Biblico, 2000.

Bergren, Theodore A. "Plato's 'Myth of Er' and Ezekiel's 'Throne Vision': A Common Paradigm?" *Numen* 64, no. 2–3 (2017): 153–82.

Bernabé, Alberto, Miguel Herrero de Jáuregui, Ana Isabel Jiménez San Cristóbal, and Raquel Martín Hernández, eds. *Redefining Dionysos.* Berlin: de Gruyter, 2013.

Bernardelli, Giovanna Azzali. *Tertulliano, Scorpiace.* Biblioteca Patristica. Florence: Nardini, 1991.

Bernstein, Moshe J. "Angels at the Aqedah: A Study in the Development of a Midrashic Motif." In *Reading and Re-reading Scripture at Qumran*, vol. 1, *Genesis and Its Interpretation.* STDJ 107. Leiden: Brill, 2013.

Bhaumik, Mani. "Is Schrödinger's Cat Alive?" *Quanta* 6, no. 1 (2017): 70–80.

Bickermann, Elias. "Das leere Grab." In *Zur neutestamentlichen Überlieferung von der Auferstehung Jesu*, 272–84. Wege der Forschung 522. Darmstadt: Wissenschaftliche Buchgesellschaft, 1988.

Bildstein, Moshe. *Purity, Community, and Ritual in Early Christian Literature.* Oxford Studies in Abrahamic Religions. Oxford: Oxford University Press, 2017.

Bird, Michael F. *The Gospel of the Lord: How the Early Church Wrote the Story of Jesus.* Grand Rapids: Eerdmans, 2014.

Blacketer, Raymond A. "Word and Sacrament on the Road to Emmaus." *CTJ* 38 (2003): 321–29.

Blackman, Philip. *Mishnayoth: Pointed Hebrew Text, English Translation, Introductions, Notes, Supplement, Appendix, Indexes, Addenda, Corrigenda.* Gateshead, UK: Judaica, 1990.

Bloch, Marc. *The Historian's Craft.* Translated by Peter Putnam. Manchester: Manchester University Press, 1992. From the 1953 ed., a translation of the French original of 1949.

Bloom, Maureen. *Jewish Mysticism and Magic: An Anthropological Perspective.* Routledge Jewish Studies Series. Abingdon: Routledge, 2007.

Blyth, Dougal. "Cicero and Philosophy as Text." *CJ* 106, no. 1 (2010): 71–98.

Bobichon, Philippe. *Justin Martyr: Dialogue avec Tryphon, édition critique.* Paradosis 47/1–2. Fribourg: Academic, 2003.

Boccaccini, Gabriele, and John J. Collins, eds. *The Early Enoch Literature.* Supplements to Journal for the Study of Judaism 12. Leiden: Brill, 2007.

Bockmuehl, Markus. "The Noachide Commandments and New Testament Ethics." In *Jewish Law in Gentile Churches: Halakhah and the Beginning of Christian Public Ethics*, 145–73. Edinburgh: T&T Clark, 2000.

Bollack, Jean. *Dionysos et la tragédie: Le dieu homme dans "Les Bacchantes" d'Euripide.* Paris: Bayard, 2005.

Boman, Thorleif. *Hebrew Thought Compared with Greek.* Translated by J. L. Moreau. Philadelphia: Westminster, 1960.

Bornhäuser, Karl. *Das Wirken des Christus durch Taten und Worte.* BFCT. Gütersloh: Bertelsman, 1921.

Bovon, François. "The Soul's Comeback: Immortality and Resurrection in Early Christianity." *HTR* 103, no. 4 (2010): 387–406.

Bowen, Matthew L. "'They Came and Held Him by the Feet and Worshipped Him': Proskynesis before Jesus in Its Biblical and Ancient Near Eastern Context." *Studies in the Bible and Antiquity* 5 (2013): 63–89.

Bowker, John. "'Merkabah' Visions and the Visions of Paul." *JSS* 16 (1971): 157–73.

———. *The Targums and Rabbinic Literature.* Cambridge: Cambridge University Press, 1969.

Bradshaw, Paul, and Carol Babawi. *The Canons of Hippolytus.* Bramcote, UK: Grove, 1987.

Bratcher, Robert G. "The Meaning of *Sarx* ('Flesh') in Paul's Letters." *BT* 29, no. 2 (1978): 212–18.

Broadbent, Edwin K. *The Gospel of Matthew on the Landscape of Antiquity.* WUNT 378. Tübingen: Mohr Siebeck, 2017.

Brown, Raymond E. *The Gospel according to John (i–xii)*. AB. Garden City, N.Y.: Doubleday, 1966.

———. *The Gospel according to John (xiii–xxi)*. AB 29A. Garden City, N.Y.: Doubleday, 1970.

———. *The Virginal Conception and Bodily Resurrection of Jesus*. London: Chapman, 1973.

Bryan, Christopher. *The Resurrection of the Messiah*. New York: Oxford University Press, 2011.

Bultmann, Rudolf. *Das Evangelium des Johannes*. KEK. Göttingen: Vandenhoeck & Ruprecht, 2011.

———. *A History of the Synoptic Tradition*. Translated by John Marsh. New York: Harper & Row, 1968.

———. *The New Testament and Mythology and Other Basic Writings*. Translated by Schubert M. Ogden. Philadelphia: Fortress, 1984.

Burnett, Joel S. "'Going Down' to Bethel: Elijah and Elisha in the Theological Geography of the Deuteronomistic History." *JBL* 129, no. 2 (2010): 281–97.

Burns, Joshua Ezra. "Essene Sectarianism and Social Differentiation in Judaea after 70 C.E." *HTR* 99, no. 3 (2006): 247–74.

Byassee, Jason. *Praise Seeking Understanding: Reading the Psalms with Augustine*. Grand Rapids: Eerdmans, 2007.

Cabal, Ted. "Defending the Resurrection of Jesus: Yesterday, Today and Forever." *Southern Baptist Journal of Theology* 18, no. 4 (2014): 115–37.

Campbell, Douglas A. *The Rhetoric of Righteousness in Romans 3.21-26*. JSNTSup 65. Sheffield: Sheffield Academic Press, 1992.

Campbell, Joseph. *Flight of the Wild Gander: Explorations in the Mythological Dimension*. Novato, Calif.: New World Library, 2002.

———. *Occidental Mythology: The Masks of God*. New York: Viking Penguin, 1964.

———. *Oriental Mythology: The Masks of God*. New York: Viking Penguin, 1962.

Carnley, Peter. *The Structure of Resurrection Belief*. Oxford: Oxford University Press, 1987.

Carter, Jeffrey, ed. *Understanding Religious Sacrifice: A Reader*. Controversies in Religion. New York: Continuum, 2003.

Catchpole, David. *Resurrection People: Studies in the Resurrection Narratives of the Gospels*. London: Darton, Longman & Todd, 2000.

Cathcart, Kevin, and Robert P. Gordon, eds. and trans. *The Targum of the Minor Prophets*. ArBib 14. Wilmington, Del.: Glazier, 1989.

Charles, R. H. *The Apocrypha and Pseudepigrapha of the Old Testament in English*. Oxford: Clarendon, 1913.

Charlesworth, James H., ed. *The Dead Sea Scrolls: Hebrew, Aramaic, and Greek Texts with English Translations*. Vol. 1, *Rule of the Community and Related Documents*. Tübingen: Mohr, 1994.

———, ed. *The Dead Sea Scrolls: Hebrew, Aramaic, and Greek Texts with English Translations*. Vol. 2, *Damascus Document, War Scroll, and Related Documents*. Tübingen: Mohr, 1995.

———, ed. *The Old Testament Pseudepigrapha*. 2 vols. Garden City, N.Y.: Doubleday, 1983, 1985.

———. *The Pesharim and Qumran History: Chaos or Consensus?* Grand Rapids: Eerdmans, 2006.

Chilton, Bruce. *Abraham's Curse: Child Sacrifice in the Legacies of the West*. New York: Doubleday, 2008.

———, ed. *The Cambridge Companion to the Bible*. 2nd ed. With contributions from Howard Clark Kee, Eric M. Meyers, John Rogerson, Amy-Jill Levine, and Anthony J. Saldarini. Cambridge: Cambridge University Press, 2008.

———. *A Feast of Meanings: Eucharistic Theologies from Jesus through Johannine Circles*. NovTSup 72. Leiden: Brill, 1994.

———. "The Gospel according to John's Rabbi Jesus." *Bulletin for Biblical Research* 25, no. 1 (2015): 39–54.

———. "The Gospel according to Thomas as a Source of Jesus' Teaching." *Gospel Perspectives* 5 (1985): 155–75.

———. *The Isaiah Targum: Introduction, Translation, Apparatus, and Notes*. ArBib 11. Wilmington, Del.: Glazier, 1987.

———. "James and the (Christian) Pharisees." In *When Judaism and Christianity Began: Essays in Memory of Anthony J. Saldarini*, vol. 1, *Christianity in the Beginning*, edited by Alan J. Avery-Peck, Daniel Harrington, and Jacob Neusner, 19–47. Supplements to the Journal for the Study of Judaism 85. Leiden: Brill, 2004.

———. "Jesus, Levitical Purity, and the Development of Primitive Christianity." In *The Book of Leviticus: Composition and Reception*, edited by Rolf Rendtorff and Robert A. Kugler, 358–82. VTSup. Leiden: Brill, 2003.

———. *Mary Magdalene: A Biography*. New York: Doubleday, 2005.

———. "Master/Rabbi." In *Encyclopedia of the Historical Jesus*, edited by Craig A. Evans, 395–99. New York: Routledge, 2008.

———. "'Not to Taste Death': A Jewish, Christian, and Gnostic Usage." In *Studia Biblica 1978: Papers on the Gospels; Sixth International Congress on Biblical Studies*, 2:29–36. JSNTSup 2. Sheffield: JSOT Press, 1980.

———. "One Afterlife of Nickelsburg's Resurrection, Immortality, and Eternal Life." In *George W. E. Nickelsburg in Perspective: An Ongoing Dialogue of Learning*, edited by Jacob Neusner and Alan J. Avery-Peck, 2:315–34. Supplement to the Journal for the Study of Judaism. Leiden: Brill, 2003.

———. *Rabbi Jesus: An Intimate Biography*. New York: Doubleday, 2000.

———. *Rabbi Paul: An Intellectual Biography*. New York: Doubleday, 2004..

———. *Redeeming Time: The Wisdom of Ancient Jewish and Christian Festal Calendars*. Peabody, Mass.: Hendrickson, 2002.

———. "Shebna, Eliakim, and the Promise to Peter." In *The Social World of Formative Christianity and Judaism: Essays in Tribute to Howard Clarke Key*, edited by Jacob Neusner, Peder Borgen, Ernest S. Frerichs, and Richard Horsley, 311–26. Philadelphia: Fortress, 1989.

———. *The Temple of Jesus: His Sacrificial Program within a Cultural History of Sacrifice*. University Park: Pennsylvania State University Press, 1992.

———. "The Transfiguration: Dominical Assurance and Apostolic Vision." *NTS* 27 (1980): 115–24.

———. *Visions of the Apocalypse: Receptions of John's Revelation in Western Imagination*. Waco, Tex.: Baylor University Press, 2013.

Chilton, Bruce (general ed.), with Darrell Bock (associate ed.), Daniel M. Gurtner (ed. for the Pseudepigrapha, Josephus, and Philo), Jacob Neusner (ed. for Rabbinic Literature), and Lawrence H. Schiffman (ed. for the Literature of Qumran) with Daniel Oden. *A Comparative Handbook to the Gospel of Mark: Comparisons with Pseudepigrapha, the Qumran Scrolls, and Rabbinic Literature*. New Testament Gospels in Their Judaic Contexts 1. Leiden: Brill, 2010.

Chilton, Bruce, and Deirdre J. Good. *Studying the New Testament: A Fortress Introduction*. Minneapolis: Fortress, 2011.

Chilton, Bruce, and Jacob Neusner. *Classical Christianity and Rabbinic Judaism: Comparing Theologies*. Grand Rapids: Baker Academic, 2004.

———. *Comparing Spiritualities: Formative Christianity and Judaism on Finding Life and Meeting Death*. Harrisburg, Pa.: Trinity Press International, 2000.

———. *Judaism in the New Testament: Practices and Beliefs*. London: Routledge, 1995.

Cho, Joanne Miyang. "Karl Jaspers' Critique of Rudolf Bultmann and His Turn toward Asia." *Existenz* 5, no. 1 (2010): 11–15.

Chopra, Deepak, with Stuart Hameroff. "The 'Quantum Soul': A Scientific Hypothesis." In *Exploring Frontiers of the Mind-Brain Relationship*, edited by Alexander Moreira-Almeida and Franklin Santana Santos, 79–93. Mindfulness in Behavioral Health. New York: Springer, 2012.

Colish, Marcia L. *The Stoic Tradition from Antiquity to the Early Middle Ages*. Vol. 2, *Stoicism in Christian Latin Thought through the Sixth Century*. Leiden: Brill, 1990.

Collingwood, R. G. *The Idea of History*. Oxford: Clarendon, 1946.

Collins, John J. "The Afterlife in Apocalyptic Literature." In *Judaism in Late Antiquity*, edited by Jacob Neusner, Alan J. Avery-Peck, and Bruce Chilton, 3:119–39. Boston: Brill, 2001.

———. *The Apocalyptic Imagination: An Introduction to the Jewish Matrix of Christianity*. New York: Crossroad, 1998.

———. "Sibylline Oracles: A New Translation and Introduction." In *The Old Testament Pseudepigrapha*, vol. 1, edited by James H. Charlesworth. Garden City, N.Y.: Doubleday, 1983.

Collins, Paul. "Polymorphic Christology: Its Origins and Development in Early Christianity." *JTS* 58, no. 1 (2007): 66–99.

Conzelmann, Hans. *1 Corinthians: A Commentary on the First Epistle to the Corinthians*. Translated by James W. Leitch. Edited by George W. MacRae. References by James W. Dunkly. Hermeneia. Philadelphia: Fortress, 1975.

Costa, Tony. "Paul's Calling as Prophetic Divine Commissioning." In *Christian Origins and Hellenistic Judaism: Social and Literary Contexts for the New Testament*, vol. 2 of *Early Christianity in Its Hellenistic Context*, edited by Stanley E. Porter and Andrew W. Pitts, 203–35. TENTS 10. Leiden: Brill, 2013.

Craig, William Lane. "The Historicity of the Empty Tomb of Jesus." *NTS* 31 (1985): 39–67.

Crichton, Michael. *Timeline*. New York: Knopf, 1999.

Crossan, John Dominic. *The Cross That Spoke: The Origins of the Passion Narrative*. San Francisco: Harper & Row, 1988.

———. "The Dogs Beneath the Cross." In *Jesus: A Revolutionary Biography*, 123–58. San Francisco: HarperSanFrancisco, 1994.

Crossan, John Dominic, and Sarah Sexton Crossan. *Resurrecting Easter: How the West Lost and the East Kept the Original Easter Vision*. New York: HarperOne, 2018.

Crossley, James. "Manufacturing the Resurrection: Locating Some Contemporary Scholarly Arguments." *Neotestamantica* 45, no. 1 (2011): 49–75.

Croy, N. Clayton. *3 Maccabees*. Septuagint Commentary Series. Leiden: Brill, 2006.

Cullmann, Oscar. *Immortalité de l'ame ou réssurection des mort? Le témoignage du Nouveau Testament*. Paris: Delachaux & Niestle, 1956.

Czachesz, István. "Filled with New Wine? Religious Experience and Social Dynamics in the Corinthian Church." In Shantz and Werline, *Experientia, Volume 2*, 71–90.

Czachesz, István, and Tamas Sndor Biro, eds. *Changing Minds: Religion and Cognition through the Ages*. Groningen Studies in Cultural Change 42. Leuven: Peeters, 2012.

Dalley, Stephanie. "The Descent of Ishtar to the Underworld." In *Myths from Mesopotamia: Creation, the Flood, Gilgamesh, and Others*, 154–62. Oxford: Oxford University Press, 1989.

Daly, Brian E. *The Hope of the Early Church: A Handbook of Patristic Eschatology*. Cambridge: Cambridge University Press, 1991.

Damrosch, David. *The Buried Book: The Loss and Rediscovery of the Great "Epic of Gilgamesh."* New York: Holt, 2007.

Davies, Philip R. *In Search of "Ancient Israel": A Study in Biblical Origins*. 2nd ed. Cornerstones. London: T&T Clark, 2015.

Davies, W. D., and Dale Allison. *A Critical and Exegetical Commentary on the Gospel according to Saint Matthew: Commentary on Matthew VIII–XVIII*. ICC. Edinburgh: T&T Clark, 1991.

Davila, James R. *Descenders to the Chariot: The People behind the Hekhalot Literature*. Supplements to the Journal for the Study of Judaism 70. Leiden: Brill 2001.

Davis, Stephen. "Seeing the Risen Jesus." In *The Resurrection: An Interdisciplinary Symposium on the Resurrection of Jesus*, edited by Stephen T. Davis, Daniel Kendall, and Gerald O'Collins, 126–47. Oxford: Oxford University Press, 1997.

Dodd, C. H. "The Appearances of the Risen Christ: An Essay in Form-Criticism of the Gospels." In *More New Testament Studies*, 102–33. Manchester: Manchester University Press, 1968.

Doran, Robert. *2 Maccabees: A Critical Commentary.* Hermeneia. Minneapolis: Fortress, 2012.

D'Oro, Giuseppina. *Collingwood and the Metaphysics of Experience.* London: Routledge, 2002.

du Bois, Page. *Out of Athens: The New Ancient Greeks.* Cambridge, Mass.: Harvard University Press, 2010.

Ebeling, Gerhard. *The Nature of Faith.* Translated by Ronald Gregor Smith. Philadelphia: Fortress, 1961.

Edwards, Dennis. "Divine Action in the Christ Event." In *How God Acts: Creation, Redemption, and Special Divine Action,* 15–34. Minneapolis: Fortress, 2010.

Ehrman, Bart D., ed. *The Apostolic Fathers, Volume II: Epistle of Barnabas, Papias and Quadratus, Epistle to Diognetus, the Shepherd of Hermas.* LCL 25. Cambridge, Mass.: Harvard University Press, 2003.

———. *How Jesus Became God: The Exaltation of a Jewish Preacher from Galilee.* New York: HarperOne, 2014.

Eisenberg, Leonard. "A New Natural Interpretation of the Empty Tomb." *International Journal for the Philosophy of Religion* 80, no. 1 (2016): 133–43.

Elledge, C. D. *Resurrection of the Dead in Early Judaism 200 BCE–CE 200.* Oxford: Oxford University Press, 2017.

Elliott, Barbara A. "Forgiveness Therapy: A Clinical Intervention for Chronic Disease." *Journal of Religion and Health* 50, no. 2 (2011): 240–47.

Elliott, Mark W. "Wisdom of Solomon, Canon and Authority." *Studia Patristica* 63 (2013): 3–16.

Eppstein, Victor. "The Historicity of the Gospel Account of the Cleansing of the Temple." *ZNW* 55 (1964): 42–58.

Epstein, Isidore, ed. *The Babylonian Talmud, Translated into English with Notes, Glossary, and Indices.* London: Soncino, 1961.

Escola, Timo. *Messiah and the Throne: Jewish Merkabah Mysticism and Early Christian Exaltation Discourse.* WUNT 142. Tübingen: Mohr Siebeck, 2001.

Evans, Craig. *From Jesus to Church: The First Christian Generation.* Louisville: Westminster John Knox, 2014.

———. *Jesus and the Ossuaries: What Jewish Burial Practices Reveal about the Beginning of Christianity.* Waco, Tex.: Baylor University Press, 2003.

Everett, Hugh. "The Theory of the Universal Wavefunction" (Ph.D. diss., Princeton University, 1955). In *The Many-Worlds Interpretation of Quantum Mechanics,* edited by Bryce DeWitt and R. Neil Graham. Princeton Series in Physics. Princeton: Princeton University Press, 1973.

Fanti, Giulio, and Roberto Maggiolo. "The Double Superficiality of the Frontal Image of the Turin Shroud." *Journal of Optics A: Pure and Applied Optics* 6 (2004): 491–503.

Fee, Gordon D. *The First Epistle to the Corinthians.* NICNT. Grand Rapids: Eerdmans, 1987.

Fenton, John C. *The Gospel of St Matthew.* Baltimore: Penguin, 1963.

Finel, Irving. *The Ark before Noah: Decoding the Story of the Flood.* New York: Anchor, 2014.

Finley, Thomas. "'Upon This Rock': Matthew 16.18 and the Aramaic Evidence." *AS* 4, no. 2 (2006): 133–51.

Finney, Mark T. *Resurrection, Hell and Afterlife: Body and Soul in Antiquity, Judaism and Early Christianity.* New York: Routledge, 2016.

Fitzmyer, Joseph A. "Aramaic *Kepha'* and Peter's Name in the New Testament." In *To Advance the Gospel: New Testament Studies,* 112–24. New York: Crossroad: 1981.

———. *The Gospel according to Luke I–IX: Introduction, Translation, and Notes.* AB 28. Garden City, N.Y.: Doubleday, 1981.

———. *The Gospel according to Luke X–XXIV: Introduction, Translation, and Notes.* AB 28A. Garden City, N.Y.: Doubleday, 1985.

Fleming, Daniel E., and Sara J. Milstein. *The Buried Foundation of the Gilgamesh Epic: The Akkadian Huwawa Narrative.* Cuneiform Monographs. Leiden: Brill, 2010.

Flesher, Paul, and Bruce Chilton. *The Targums: A Critical Introduction.* Waco, Tex.: Baylor University Press, 2011.

Foster, Paul. *The Gospel of Peter: Introduction, Critical Edition, and Commentary.* TENTS. Leiden: Brill, 2010.

Frankenbury, Nancy K. "Isaac Newton (1643–1727)." In *The Faith of Scientists: In Their Own Words,* 102–21. Princeton: Princeton University Press, 2008.

Frazer, James George. *The Golden Bough: A Study in Magic and Religion.* Part 4, *Adonis Attis Osiris.* New York: St. Martin's, 1990.

Freedman, H., and Maurice Simon, eds. *The Midrash Rabbah.* London: Soncino, 1977.

Friedrich, Rainer. "Dionysos among the Dons: The New Ritualism in Richard Seafords Commentary on the 'Bacchae.'" *Arion: A Journal of Humanities and the Classics* 7, no. 3 (2000): 115–52.

Fuller, Reginald H. *The Formation of the Resurrection Narratives.* New York: Macmillan, 1971.

Fullmer, Paul M. *Resurrection in Mark's Literary-Historical Perspective.* London: T&T Clark/Continuum, 2007.

Gadotti, Alhena. *"Gilgamesh, Enkidu, and the Netherworld" and the Sumerian Gilgamesh Cycle.* Untersuchungen zur Assyriologie und Vorderasiastischen Archäologie 10. Berlin: de Gruyter, 2014.

Gardner, John, John Maier, and Richard A. Henshaw. *Gilgamesh: Translated from the Sîn-legi-unninnî Version.* New York: Vintage, 1985.

Geisler, Norman L. "The Apologetic Significance of the Bodily Resurrection of Jesus." *Bulletin of the Evangelical Philosophical Society* 10 (1987): 15–37.

———. "In Defense of the Resurrection: A Reply to Criticisms." *JETS* 34, no. 2 (1991): 243–61.

Gibbons, Reginald, and Charles Segal. "Bacchae [Bakkhai]." In *The Complete Euripides IV: Bacchae and Other Plays*, edited by Peter Burian and Alan Sjapiro, 199–362. Oxford: Oxford University Press, 2009.

Gilchrist, Roberta. *Glastonbury Abbey: Archaeological Excavations 1904–1979*. Reading: University of Reading, Trustees of Glastonbury Abbey, 2015.

Gillam, Robyn. *Performance and Drama in Ancient Egypt*. London: Duckworth, 2005.

Gillespie, Thomas W. *The First Theologians: A Study in Early Christian Prophecy*. Grand Rapids: Eerdmans, 1994.

Gilmour, S. MacLean. "The Christophany to More Than Five Hundred Brethren." *JBL* 80, no. 3 (1961): 248–52.

Goranson, Stephen. "Nazarenes." In *Anchor Bible Dictionary*, edited by David Noel Freedman et al., 4:1049–50. New York: Doubleday, 1992.

Grappe, Christian. *L'au-delà dans la Bible: Le temporal et le spatial*. Le Monde de la Bible 68. Fribourg: Labor et Fides, 2014.

Grayston, Kenneth. "The Translation of Matthew 28.17." *JSNT* 21 (1984): 105–9.

Green, Joel B. *The Gospel of Luke*. NICNT. Grand Rapids: Eerdmans, 1997.

Greenspahn, Frederick E., ed. *Jewish Mysticism and Kabbalah: New Insights and Scholarship*. Jewish Studies in the 21st Century. New York: New York University Press, 2011.

Guerra, Anthony J. *Romans and the Apologetic Tradition: The Purpose, Genre and Audience of Paul's Letter*. SNTSMS 81. Cambridge: Cambridge University Press, 1994.

Gundry, Robert H. *Matthew: A Commentary on His Handbook for a Mixed Church under Persecution*. Grand Rapids: Eerdmans, 1994.

Haber, Susan. *"They Shall Purify Themselves": Essays on Purity in Early Judaism*. Edited by Adele Reinhartz. EJL 24. Atlanta: Society of Biblical Literature, 2008.

Habermas, Gary R. "Resurrection Research from 1975 to the Present: What Are Critical Scholars Saying?" *Journal for the Study of the Historical Jesus* 3, no. 2 (2005): 135–53.

Haenchen, Ernst. *The Acts of the Apostles: A Commentary*. Translated by Bernard Noble, Gerald Shinn, Hugh Anderson, and R. McL. Wilson. Philadelphia: Westminster, 1971.

Hall, Stuart J., ed. and trans. *Melito of Sardis, Peri Pascha and Fragments*. OECT. Oxford: Clarendon, 1979.

Hameroff, Stuart, and Roger Penrose. "Consciousness in the Universe: A Review of the 'Orch OR' Theory." *Physics of Life Reviews* 11, no. 1 (2014): 39–78.

Haran, Menaham. "Ezekiel, P, and the Priestly School." *VT* 58, no. 2 (2008): 211–17.

Harnack, Adolf von. *Die Verklärungsgeschichte Jesu, der Bericht des Paulus (I. Kor. 15, 3ff) und die beiden Christusvisionen des Petrus*. Sitzungsberichte der Königlich Preussischen Akademie der Wissenschaften zu Berlin. Berlin: Walter de Gruyter, 1922.

Harrington, Daniel J. *The Gospel of Matthew*. SP 1. Collegeville, Minn.: Liturgical, 1991.

Harris, W. Hall. *The Descent of Christ: Ephesians 4:7-11 and Traditional Hebrew Imagery*. Leiden: Brill, 1996.

Hartman, Lars. *"Into the Name of the Lord Jesus": Baptism in the Early Church*. SNTW. Edinburgh: T&T Clark, 1997.

Hays, Harold M. "The Death of the Democratisation of the Afterlife." In *Old Kingdom, New Perspectives: Egyptian Art and Archaeology 2750–2150*, edited by Nigel Strudwick and Helen Strudwick, 115–30. Oxford: Oxbow, 2011.

Hays, Richard B. *Echoes of Scripture in the Gospels*. Waco, Tex.: Baylor University Press, 2016.

———. *Echoes of Scripture in the Letters of Paul*. New Haven: Yale University Press, 1989.

Hedrick, Charles W. "Paul's Conversion/Call: A Comparative Analysis of the Three Reports in Acts." *JBL* 100, no. 3 (1981): 415–32.

Heidel, Alexander. *The Gilgamesh Epic and Old Testament Parallels: A Translation and Interpretation of the Gilgamesh Epic and Related Babylonian and Assyrian Documents*. Chicago: University of Chicago Press, 1963.

Henderson, Timothy P. *The Gospel of Peter and Early Christian Apologetics: Rewriting the Story of Jesus' Death, Burial, and Resurrection*. WUNT 2/301. Tübingen: Mohr Siebeck, 2011.

Hengel, Martin. "Jakobus der Herrenbruder—der erste 'Papst'?" In *Glaube und Eschatologie: Festschrift für Werner Georg Kümmel zum 80. Geburtstag*, edited by E. Grässer and O. Merk, 71–104. Tübingen: Mohr, 1985.

———. *Studies in the Gospel of Mark*. Translated by John Bowden. London: SCM Press, 1985.

Hick, John. *Death and Eternal Life*. New York: Harper & Row, 1976.

Hieke, Thomas. "The Reception of Daniel 7 in the Revelation of John." In *Revelation and the Politics of Apocalyptic Interpretation*, edited by Richard B. Hays and Stefan Alkier, 47–67. Waco, Tex.: Baylor University Press, 2012.

Hilgevoord, Jan, and Jos Uffink. "The Uncertainty Principle." In *The Stanford Encyclopedia of Philosophy*, edited by Edward N. Zaita. Stanford: Metaphysics Research Lab, 2016. Revised July 12, 2016. https://plato.stanford.edu/archives/win2016/entries/qt-uncertainty/.

Hill, David. *New Testament Prophecy*. Atlanta: John Knox, 1979.

Himmelfarb, Martha. *Tours of Hell: An Apocalyptic Form in Jewish and Christian Literature*. Philadelphia: University of Pennsylvania Press, 1983.

Hoffmeier, James K. *Israel in Egypt: The Evidence for the Authenticity of the Exodus Tradition*. New York: Oxford University Press, 1996.

Homer. *Homer: The Odyssey Books 1–12 with an English Translation*. Edited by A. T. Murray. Revised by George E. Dimock. LCL 104. Cambridge, Mass.: Harvard University Press, 1995.

Horner, Robyn. *Jean-Luc Marion: A Theo-logical Introduction*. Farnham, UK: Ashgate, 2005.

Horst, P. W. van der. "Pseudo-Phocylides." In Charlesworth, *Old Testament Pseudepigrapha*, 2:565–73, 582.

Howell, David B. *Matthew's Inclusive Story: A Study in the Narrative Rhetoric of the First Gospel*. JSNTSup 42. Sheffield: Sheffield Academic Press, 1990.

Hughes, Philip Edgcumbe. *The Book of Revelation: A Commentary*. Leicester: InterVarsity, 1990.

Idel, Moshe. *Absorbing Perfections: Kabbalah and Interpretation*. New Haven: Yale University Press, 2002.

———. *Ascensions on High in Jewish Mysticism: Pillars, Lines, Ladders*. Pasts Incorporated, CEU Studies in the Humanities 2. Budapest: Central European University Press, 2005.

Iliffe, Rob. *Priest of Nature: The Religious Worlds of Isaac Newton*. New York: Oxford University Press, 2017.

Incigneri, Brian. *The Gospel to the Romans: The Setting and Rhetoric of Mark's Gospel*. BibInt 65. Leiden: Brill, 2003.

Jacobovici, Simcha, and Charles R. Pellegrino. *The Jesus Family Tomb: The Discovery, the Investigation, and the Evidence That Could Change History*. New York: HarperCollins, 2008.

Janowski, Bernd, and Peter Stuhlmacher, eds. *The Suffering Servant: Isaiah 53 in Jewish and Christian Sources*. Translated by Daniel P. Bailey. Grand Rapids: Eerdmans, 2004.

Jeremias, Joachim. "Artikilloses *Khristos*: Zur Ursprache von 1 Cor 15,3b-5." *ZNW* 57 (1966): 211–15.

Johnson, Luke Timothy. *Prophetic Jesus, Prophetic Church: The Challenge of Luke–Acts to Contemporary Christians*. Grand Rapids: Eerdmans, 2011.

Johnstone, Brian V. "The Resurrection in Phenomenology: Jean-Luc Marion on the 'Saturated Phenomenon Par Excellence.'" *Pacifica* 28, no. 1 (2015): 23–39.

Joseph, Simon J. *Jesus and the Temple: The Crucifixion in its Jewish Context*. SNTSMS 165. Cambridge: Cambridge University Press, 2016.

———. "Jesus in India? Transgressing Social and Religious Boundaries." *JAAR* 80, no. 1 (2012): 161–99.

———. "Redescribing the Resurrection: Beyond the Methodological Impasse?" *Biblical Theology Bulletin* 45, no. 3 (2015): 155–73.

Josephus. *Jewish Antiquities, Books I–IV*. Edited by H. St. J. Thackery. LCL Josephus 4. London: Heinemann, 1930.

———. *Jewish Antiquities, Books IX–XI*. Edited by Ralph Marcus. LCL Josephus 6. London: Heinemann, 1937.

———. *Josephus*. Edited by H. St. J. Thackeray, Ralph Marcus, Allen Wikgren, and Louis H. Feldman. LCL 203, 210, 242, 292, 326, 365, 433, 456, 487, 489, and 490. Cambridge, Mass.: Harvard University Press, 1926–1965.

Kahl, Brigitte. *Galatians Re-imagined: Reading with the Eyes of the Vanquished*. Paul in Critical Contexts. Minneapolis: Fortress, 2010.

Kaku, Michio. *Higher Worlds: A Journey through Creation, Higher Dimensions, and the Future of the Cosmos*. New York: Doubleday, 2004.

Kazen, Thomas. *Jesus and Purity Halakhah: Was Jesus Indifferent to Impurity?* Coniectanea Biblica New Testament Series 38. Stockholm: Almqvist & Wiksell, 2002.

Kelly, Anthony J. *Upward: Faith, Church, and the Ascension of Christ*. Collegeville, Minn.: Liturgical (Michael Glazier), 2014.

Kilgallen, John. *The Stephen Speech: A Literary and Redactional Study of Acts 7,2-53*. AnBib 67. Rome: Biblical Institute Press, 1976.

Kim, Seyoon. *The Origin of Paul's Gospel*. WUNT 2.3. Tübingen: Mohr, 1981.

King, Karen. *What Is Gnosticism?* Cambridge, Mass.: Harvard University Press, 2003.

Klein, Manfred. "Christus ist die Leiche im Keller der Kirche." *Lokalexpress*, September 11, 1996.

Klijn, A. F. J. *Jewish-Christian Gospel Tradition*. Supplements to Vigiliae Christianae 17. Leiden: Brill, 1992.

Kloner, Amos, and Shimon Gibson. "The Talpiot Tomb Reconsidered: The Archaeological Facts." In *The Tomb of Jesus and His Family? Exploring Ancient Jewish Tombs Near Jerusalem's Walls*, edited by James H. Charlesworth, 29–52. Princeton Symposium on Judaism and Christian Origins. Grand Rapids: Eerdmans, 2013.

Knibb, Michael A. *Essays on the Book of Enoch and Other Early Jewish Texts and Traditions*. SVTP 22. Leiden: Brill, 2009.

Knox, John. *The Man Christ Jesus*. Chicago: Willett, Clark, 1941.

Kollmann, Bernd. *Joseph Barnabas: His Life and Legacy*. Translated by Miranda Henry. Collegeville, Minn.: Liturgical, 2004.

———. *Joseph Barnabas: Leben und Wirkungeschichte*. SBS 175. Stuttgart: Verlag Kathlisches Bibelwerk, 1998.

Kovacs, Maureen Gallery. *The Epic of Gilgamesh: Translated, with an Introduction*. Stanford: Stanford University Press, 1989.

Lake, Kirsopp. "The Apostolic Council of Jerusalem." In *The Beginnings of Christianity*, edited by F. J. Foakes Jackson and Kirsopp Lake, 5:195–212. Grand Rapids: Baker, 1979.

———. *The Historical Evidence for the Resurrection of Jesus Christ*. New York: Putnam, 1907.

Lebeau, P. *Le vin nouveau du Royaume: Etude exégétique et patristique sur la Parole eschatologique de Jésus à la Cène*. Paris: Desclée, 1966.

Lehtipuu, Outi. *Debates over the Resurrection of the Dead: Constructing Early Christian Identity*. OECS. Oxford: Oxford University Press, 2015.

Levenson, Jon Douglas. *Resurrection and the Restoration of Israel: The Ultimate Victory of the God of Life*. New Haven: Yale University Press, 2006.

Licona, Michael R. *The Resurrection of Jesus: A New Historiographical Approach.* Downers Grove, Ill.: InterVarsity, 2010.

Liddell, Henry George, and Robert Scott, eds. *A Greek-English Lexicon.* New York: Oxford University Press, 1996.

Lidz, Fritz. "The Little-Known Legend of Jesus in Japan." *Smithsonian Magazine,* January 2013. https://www.smithsonianmag.com/history/the-little-known -legend-of-jesus-in-japan-165354242/.

Lierman, John. *The New Moses: Christian Perceptions of Moses and Israel in the Setting of Jewish Religion.* WUNT 173. Tübingen: Mohr Siebeck, 2004.

Loisy, Alfred. *"The Birth of the Christian Religion" (La naissance du christianisme) and "The Origins of the New Testament" (Les origines du Nouveau Testament).* Translated by L. P. Jacks. New Hyde Park, N.Y.: University Books, 1962.

———. *Les évangiles synoptiques.* Ceffonds: A. Loisy, 1907–1908.

Lowder, Jeffrey Jay. "Historical Evidence and the Empty Tomb Story: A Reply to William Lane Craig." *Journal of Higher Criticism* 8, no. 2 (2001): 251–93.

Lüdemann, Gerd. *The Great Deception: And What Jesus Really Said and Did.* London: SCM Press, 1998.

———. *Jesus' Resurrection, Fact of Figment? A Debate between William Lane Craig & Gerd Lüdemann.* Edited by Paul Copan and Ronald K. Tacelli. Downers Grove, Ill.: InterVarsity, 2000.

———. *The Resurrection of Christ: A Historical Inquiry.* Amherst, N.Y.: Prometheus, 2004.

———. *The Resurrection of Jesus: History, Experience, Theology.* Translated by John Bowden. Minneapolis: Fortress, 1994.

Lüdemann, Gerd, with Alf Özen. *What Really Happened to Jesus? A Historical Approach to the Resurrection.* Translated by John Bowden. Louisville: Westminster John Knox, 1995.

Lüdemann, Gerd, with Tom Hall. *The Acts of the Apostles: What Really Happened in the Earliest Days of the Church.* Amherst, N.Y.: Prometheus, 2005.

MacCormack, Sabine. "Cicero in Late Antiquity." In *The Cambridge Companion to Cicero,* edited by Catherine Steele, 251–305. Cambridge: Cambridge University Press, 2013.

MacDonald, Dennis R. *The Homeric Epics and the Gospel of Mark.* New Haven: Yale University Press, 2000.

Mackinlay, Shane. *Interpreting Excess: Jean-Luc Marion, Saturated Phenomena, and Hermeneutics.* New York: Fordham University Press, 2010.

Macquarrie, John. *The Scope of Demythologizing: Bultmann and His Critics.* New York: Harper & Row, 1966.

Madigan, Kevin J., and Jon D. Levenson. "Who Goes to Sheol—and Who Does Not?" In *Resurrection: The Power of God for Christians and Jews,* 69–80. New Haven: Yale University Press, 2008.

Maier, John, ed. *Gilgamesh: A Reader.* Wauconda, Ill.: Bolchazy-Carducci, 1997.

Malina, Bruce. *On the Genre and Message of Revelation: Star Visions and Sky Journeys.* Peabody, Mass.: Hendrickson, 1995.

Maloney, Linda M. *"All That God Had Done with Them": The Narration of the Works of God in the Early Christian Community as Described in the Acts of the Apostles.* AUSTR 91. New York: Lang, 1991.

Marion, Jean-Luc. *De Surcroît: Études sur les phénomènes saturé.* Paris: Presses universitaires de France, 2001.

———. *In Excess: Studies of Saturated Phenomena.* Translated by Robyn Horner and Vincent Berraud. New York: Fordham University Press, 2002.

———. *Prolegomena to Charity: Perspectives in Continental Philosophy.* Translated by Stephen E. Lewis. New York: Fordham University Press, 2002.

Marsman, Hennie J. *Women in Ugarit and Israel: Their Social and Religious Position in the Context of the Ancient Near East.* OTS 49. Leiden: Brill, 2003.

Martínez, Florentino García, and Eibert J. C. Tigchelaar, eds. *The Dead Sea Scrolls, Study Edition.* Leiden: Brill, 1999.

Martínez, Florentino García, and Julio Trebolle Barrera. *The People of the Dead Sea Scrolls.* Translated by Wilfred G. E. Watson. Leiden: Brill, 1995.

Matson, David Lertis. *Household Conversion Narratives in Acts: Patterns and Interpretation.* JSNTSup 123. Sheffield: Sheffield Academic Press, 1996.

McCrone, Walter C. *Judgement Day for the Turin Shroud.* Chicago: Microscope, 1997.

McGovern, Patrick E. "The Noah Hypothesis." In *Ancient Wine: The Origins of Viniculture,* 16–39. Princeton: Princeton University Press, 2007.

McKay, K. L. "The Use of *hoi de* in Matthew 28.17: A Response to K. Grayston." *JSNT* 24 (1985): 71–72.

Meerson, Michael, and Peter Schäfer, with Yaacov Deutsch, David Grossberg, Avigail Manekin, and Adina Yoffie. *Toledot Yeshu: The Life Story of Jesus.* 2 vols. and database. Tübingen: Mohr Siebeck, 2014.

Mendelsohn, Daniel. *Gender and the City in Euripides' Political Plays.* Oxford: Oxford University Press, 2002.

Meyer, Marvin. *The Gospel of Thomas: The Hidden Sayings of Jesus.* San Francisco: HarperSanFrancisco, 1992.

———. "Making Mary Male: The Categories 'Male' and 'Female' in the Gospel of Thomas." *NTS* 31 (1985): 554–70.

———. *Secret Gospels: Essays on Thomas and the Secret Gospel of Mark.* Harrisburg, Pa.: Trinity, 2003.

Meyers, Eric. "The Jesus Tomb Controversy: An Overview." *NEA* 69, nos. 3/4 (2006): 116–18.

Mezzadri, Bernard. Response to Jean Bollack, *Dionysos et la tragédie: Le dieu homme dans "Les Bacchantes" d'Euripide.* *L'Homme* 187/188 (2008): 541–45.

Michel, Otto. "The Conclusion of Matthew's Gospel: A Contribution to the History of the Easter Message." Translated by Robert Morgan. In *The Interpretation of Matthew,* edited by Graham Stanton, 30–41. IRT 3. London: SPCK, 1983).

Miller, Richard C. *Resurrection and Reception in Early Christianity*. New York: Routledge, 2015.

Mitternacht, Dieter. "Foolish Galatians? A Recipient-Oriented Assessment of Paul's Letter." In *The Galatians Debate: Contemporary Issues in Rhetorical and Historical Interpretation*, edited by Mark D. Nanos, 408–33. Peabody, Mass.: Hendrickson, 2002.

Moffatt, James. *The New Testament: A New Translation*. London: Hodder and Stoughton, 1915.

Moore, Megan Bishop, and Brad E. Kelle. *Biblical History and Israel's Past: The Changing Study of the Bible and History*. Grand Rapids: Eerdmans, 2011.

Morray-Jones, C. R. A. "Paradise Revisited (2 Cor 12:1-12): The Jewish Mystical Background of Paul's Apostolate; Part 1; The Jewish Sources." *HTR* 86, no. 2 (1993): 177–217.

———. "Paradise Revisited (2 Cor 12:1-12): The Jewish Mystical Background of Paul's Apostolate; Part 2; Paul's Heavenly Ascent and Its Significance." *HTR* 86, no. 3 (1993): 265–92.

Most, Glenn W. *Doubting Thomas*. Cambridge, Mass.: Harvard University Press, 2005.

Moule, C. F. D. "Introduction." In *The Significance of the Message of the Resurrection for Faith in Jesus Christ*, edited by C. F. D. Moule, translated by Dorothea M. Barton and R. A. Wilson, 1–11. SBT 8. Naperville, Ill.: Allenson, 1968.

Moyise, Steve. *The Old Testament in the Book of Revelation*. JSNTSup 115. Sheffield: Sheffield Academic Press, 1995.

Mussner, Franz. *Die Auferstehung Jesu*. Biblische Handbibliothek 7. Munich: Kösel, 1969.

Mycoff, David. *The Life of Saint Mary Magdalene and of Her Sister Saint Martha: A Medieval Biography Translated and Annotated*. Cistercian Studies Series 108. Kalamazoo: Cistercian, 1989.

Nancy, Jean-Luc. *Noli me tangere: On the Raising of the Body*. Translated by Sarah Clift, Pascale-Anne Brault, and Michael Naas. New York: Fordham University Press, 2008.

Nasrallah, Laura. "The Acts of the Apostles, Greek Cities, and Hadrian's *Panhellenion*." *JBL* 127, no. 3 (2008): 533–66.

Newman, Carey C. *Paul's Glory-Christology: Tradition and Rhetoric*. NovTSup 69. Leiden: Brill, 1992.

Nickelsburg, George W. E. *1 Enoch 1: A Commentary on the Book of 1 Enoch, Chapters 1–36; 81–108*. Edited by Klaus Baltzer. Hermeneia. Minneapolis: Fortress, 2001.

———. *Resurrection, Immortality, and Eternal Life in Intertestamental Judaism and Early Christianity: Expanded Edition*. HTS 56. Cambridge, Mass.: Harvard University, 2006.

Niebuhr, Richard R. *Resurrection and Historical Reason: A Study of Theological Method*. New York: Scribner's, 1957.

Norwood, Gilbert. "The *Bacchae* and Its Riddle." In *Essays on Euripidean Drama*, 52–73. Berkeley: University of California Press, 1954.

Novak, Michael Anthony. "*The Odes of Solomon* as Apocalyptic Literature." *VC* 66 (2012): 527–50.

Novakovic, Lidija. *Raised from the Dead according to the Scripture: The Role of Israel's Scripture in Early Christian Interpretation of Jesus' Resurrection*. T&T Clark Jewish and Christian Texts Series 12. London: T&T Clark, 2012.

———. *Resurrection: A Guide for the Perplexed*. London: T&T Clark, 2016.

O'Connor, David. *Abydos: Egypt's First Pharaohs and the Cult of Osiris*. New Aspects of Antiquity. London: Thames and Hudson, 2009.

O'Flaherty, Wendy Doniger. *Other Peoples' Myths: The Cave of Echoes*. Chicago: University of Chicago Press, 1988.

O'Neil, John C. Review of *The Resurrection of Jesus*, by Gerd Lüdemann. *Theology* 99 (1996): 154–56.

Oort, Johannes van. *Jerusalem and Babylon: A Study into Augustine's City of God and the Sources of His Doctrine of the Two Cities*. Supplements to Vigiliae Christianae 14. Leiden: Brill, 1991.

Orlov, Andrei A. *The Enoch-Metatron Tradition*. Texts and Studies in Ancient Judaism 107. Tübingen: Mohr-Siebeck, 2005.

Pagels, Elaine. "Ritual in the *Gospel of Philip*." In *The Nag Hammadi Library after Fifty Years: Proceedings of the 1995 Society of Biblical Literature Commemoration*, edited by John D. Turner and Anne McGuire, 280–91. Nag Hammadi and Manichaean Studies 44. Leiden: Brill, 1997.

Palmer, Darryl W. "The Resurrection of Jesus and the Mission of the Church." In *Reconciliation and Hope: New Testament Essays on Atonement and Eschatology*, edited by Robert Banks, 205–23. Grand Rapids: Eerdmans, 1974.

Patterson, Stephen J. *The Gospel of Thomas and Jesus*. Foundations and Facets Reference Series. Sonoma, Calif.: Polebridge, 1993.

Philo. *Philo Volume II*. Edited by F. H. Colson and G. H. Whitaker. LCL 227. Cambridge, Mass.: Harvard University Press, 1991.

———. *Philo Volume VI*. Edited by F. H. Colson. LCL 289. Cambridge, Mass.: Harvard University Press, 1994.

Plato. *The Republic with an English Translation*. Edited by Paul Shorey. LCL Plato 6 Republic 2. London: Heinemann, 1970.

Plutarch. *Drei religionsphilosophische Schriften: Über den Aberglauben, Über die späte Strafe der Gottheit, Über Isis und Osiris*. Edited by Herwig Görgemanns et al. Sammlung Tusculum, Plutarch übersetzt und heraugegeben. Düsseldorf: Artemis & Winkler, 2003.

———. *Plutarch: Moralia*. Vol. 5. Edited by Frank Cole Babbitt. LCL 306. London: Heinemann, 1936.

Popkin, Jim. "I Covered the Rajneesh Cult: Here Is What 'Wild Wild Country' Leaves Out." *Huffington Post*, March 28, 2018. https://www.huffingtonpost.com/entry/cult-wild-wild-country-netflix_us_5ab2b37de4b054d118df49c1.

Porter, Stanley E. *When Paul Met Jesus: How an Idea Got Lost in History*. New York: Cambridge University Press, 2016.

Price, Robert M. *Deconstructing Jesus*. Amherst, N.Y.: Prometheus, 2000.

Pryke, Louise M. *Ishtar*. Gods and Heroes of the Ancient World. London: Routledge, 2017.

Puig i Tàrrech, Armand. "Els sants que ressusciten (Mt 27,51b-53)." In *Estudis de Nou Testament*, 131–69. Collectània Sant Pacià 108. Barcelona: Facultat de Teologia de Catalunya, 2014.

Rabel, Robert J. Review of *The Homeric Epics and the Gospel of Mark*, by Dennis R. MacDonald. *Bryn Mawr Classical Review* 9, no. 16 (2000). http://bmcr.brynmawr.edu/2000/.

Radice, Betty, ed. and trans. *Pliny: Letters, Volume II, Books 8–10, Panegyricus*. LCL 59. Cambridge, Mass.: Harvard University Press, 1969.

Reeves, John C. "Utnapishtim in the Book of Giants?" *JBL* 112, no. 1 (1993): 110–15.

Rennie, Bryan. "Zoroastrianism: The Iranian Roots of Christianity?" *CSSR Bulletin* 36, no. 1 (2007): 3–7.

Robb, John. "Material Culture, Landscapes of Action, and Emergent Causation: A New Model for the Origins of the European Neolithic." *Current Anthropology* 54, no. 6 (2013): 657–83.

Robinson, James M., ed. *The Coptic Gnostic Library: A Complete Edition of the Nag Hammadi Codices*. Leiden: Brill, 2000.

———. "Jesus—From Easter to Valentinus (or to the Apostles Creed)." *JBL* 101 (1982): 5–37.

———, ed. *The Nag Hammadi Library in English*. San Francisco: Harper & Row, 1978.

Robinson, John A. T. "The Shroud and the New Testament." In *La Sindone e la scienza*, edited by P. Coero-Borga, 265–88. Atti del II Congresso Internazionale di Sindonologia. Turin: Paoline, 1979.

Rollston, Holmes, III. "Divine Presence—Causal, Cybernetic, Caring, Cruciform: From Information to Incarnation." In *Incarnation: On the Scope and Depth of Christology*, edited by Niels Henrik Gregersen, 255–87. Minneapolis: Fortress, 2015.

Rosivach, Vincent J. *The System of Public Sacrifice in Fourth-Century Athens*. American Classical Studies 34. Atlanta: Scholars Press, 1994.

Roth, Cecil. "The Cleansing of the Temple and Zechariah XIV.21." *NovT* 4 (1960): 174–81.

Ruthven, Malise. *Fundamentalism: The Search for Meaning*. Oxford: Oxford University Press, 2004.

Santamaría, Marco Antonio. "The Term *Bakkhos* and Dionyos *Bakkhios*." In Bernabé et al., *Redefining Dionysos*, 38–57.

Sawicki, Marianne. *Seeing the Lord: Resurrection and Early Christian Practices*. Minneapolis: Fortress, 1994.

Schaberg, Jane. *The Father, the Son, and the Holy Spirit: The Triadic Phrase in Matt 28:19b.* SBLDS 61. Chico, Calif.: Scholars Press, 1982.

———. *The Resurrection of Mary Magdalene: Legends, Apocrypha, and the Christian Testament.* New York: Continuum, 2002.

Schäfer, Peter, Michael Meerson, and Yaacov Deutsch, eds. *Toledot Yeshu ("The Life Story of Jesus") Revisited: A Princeton Conference.* Tübingen: Mohr Siebeck, 2007.

Schenke, Hans-Martin. *Das Philippus-Evanglium (Nag-Hammadi-Codex II, 3).* TU 143. Berlin: Akademie, 1997.

Schneemelcher, Wilhelm. "The Acts of Peter." In *New Testament Apocrypha*, edited by Edgar Hennecke and Wilhelm Schneemelcher, translated by R. McL. Wilson, 2:259–322. Philadelphia: Westminster, 1964.

Schneider, Tammi J. *An Introduction to Ancient Mesopotamian Religion.* Grand Rapids: Eerdmans, 2011.

Schofield, Alison, and James C. VanderKam. "Were the Hasmoneans Zadokites?" *JBL* 124, no. 1 (2005): 73–87.

Schonfield, Hugh J. *The Passover Plot: New Light on the History of Jesus.* New York: Geis Associates, 1965.

Schöpflin, Karin. "The Revivification of the Dry Bones: Ezekiel 37:1-14." In *The Human Body in Death and Resurrection*, edited by Tobias Nicklas, Friedrich V. Reiterer, and Joseph Verheyden, 67–85. Deuterocanonical and Cognate Literature, Yearbook 2009. Berlin: Walter de Gruyter, 2009.

Seaford, Richard, ed. *Euripides: Bacchae, with an Introduction, Translation and Commentary.* Warminster, UK: Aris & Phillips, 1996.

Sedley, David. *Creationism and Its Critics in Antiquity.* Sather Classical Lectures 66. Berkeley: University of California Press, 2007.

Segal, Alan F. *Life after Death: A History of the Afterlife in the Religions of the West.* New York: Doubleday, 2004.

———. "The Resurrection: Faith or History." In *The Resurrection of Jesus: John Dominic Crossan and N. T. Wright in Dialogue*, edited by Robert B. Stewart, 121–38. Minneapolis: Fortress, 2006.

Setzer, Claudia. *Resurrection of the Body in Early Judaism and Early Christianity: Doctrine, Community, and Self-Definition.* Boston: Brill Academic, 2004.

Shaked, Shaul. "Eschatology i: In Zoroastrianism and Zoroastrian Influence." *Encyclopedia Iranica* 7, no. 6 (1996): 565–69.

Shantz, Colleen. *The Neurobiology of the Apostle's Life and Thought.* New York: Cambridge University Press, 2009.

———. "Opening the Black Box: New Prospects for Analyzing Religious Experience." In Shantz and Werline, *Experientia, Volume 2*, 1–15.

Shantz, Colleen, and Rodney A. Werline, eds. *Experientia, Volume 2: Linking Text and Experience.* Atlanta: Society of Biblical Literature, 2012.

Shapiro, Robert. "The Mystical Bone of Resurrection." *Radiology* 163, no. 3 (1987): 718.

Sheehan, Thomas. "*Kehre* and *Ereignis*: A Prolegomenon to *Introduction to Metaphysics*." In *A Companion to Heidegger's Introduction to Metaphysics*, edited by Richard Polt and Gregory Fried, 3–16. New Haven: Yale University Press, 2001.

Sleeper, C. Freeman. "Pentecost and Resurrection." *JBL* 84, no. 4 (1965): 389–99.

Smail, Daniel Lord, and Andrew Shryock. "Body." In *Deep History: The Architecture of Past and Present*. Berkeley: University of California Press, 2011.

Smelik, K. A. D. "The Witch of Endore: 1 Samuel 28 in Rabbinic and Christian Exegesis till 800 A.D." *VC* 33, no. 2 (1979): 160–76.

Smith, Daniel A. *Revisiting the Empty Tomb: The Early History of Easter*. Minneapolis: Fortress, 2010.

Smith, George. "The Chaldean Account of the Deluge." *Transactions of the Society of Biblical Archaeology* 2 (1873): 213–34.

Smith, James K. A. "Liberating Religion from Theology: Marion and Heidegger on the Possibility of a Phenomenology of Religion." *International Journal for Philosophy of Religion* 46, no. 1 (1999): 17–33.

Smith, Mark. *Following Osiris: Perspectives on the Osirian Afterlife from Our Millennia*. Oxford: Oxford University Press, 2017.

Söding, T. "Erscheingung, Vergebung und Sendung: Joh 21 als Zeugnis entwickelten Osterglaubens." In *Resurrection in the New Testament: Festschrift J. Lambrecht*, edited by Reimund Bieringer, Veronica Koperski, and B. Lataire, 207–32. BETL 165. Leuven: Leuven University Press, 2002.

Standhartinger, Angela. "'What Women Were Accustomed to Do for the Dead Beloved by Them' ('Gospel of Peter' 12.50): Traces of Laments and Mourning Rituals in Early Easter, Passion, and Lord's Supper Traditions." *JBL* 129, no. 3 (2010): 559–74.

Stauffer, Ethelbert. *Jesus and His Story*. Translated by R. Winston and C. Winston. New York: Knopf, 1960.

———. *New Testament Theology*. Translated by John Marsh. New York: Macmillan, 1955.

Steinhart, Eric. "The Revision Theory of Resurrection." *RelS* 44, no. 1 (2008): 63–81.

Stendahl, Krister. *Paul among Jews and Gentiles and Other Essays*. Philadelphia: Fortress, 1976.

Stoops, Robert F., Jr. "The *Acts of Peter* in Intertextual Context." In *The Apocryphal Acts of the Apostles in Intertextual Perspectives*, edited by Robert F. Stoops Jr., 57–86. Semeia 80. Atlanta: Scholars Press, 1997.

Stordalen, Terje. *Echoes of Eden: Genesis 2–3 and Symbolism of the Eden Garden in Biblical Hebrew Literature*. CBET 25. Leuven: Peeters, 2000.

Tabor, James D., and Simcha Jacobovici. *The Jesus Discovery: The Archaeological Find that Reveals the Birth of Christianity*. New York: Simon and Schuster, 2012.

Taylor, John H. *Death and Afterlife in Ancient Egypt*. London: British Museum Company; Chicago: University of Chicago Press, 2001.

Thayer, H. S. "The Myth of Er." *History of Philosophy Quarterly* 5, no. 4 (1988): 369–84.

Thiselton, Anthony C. *The First Epistle to the Corinthians: A Commentary on the Greek Text.* NIGTC. Carlisle, UK: Paternoster; Grand Rapids: Eerdmans, 2000.

———. "Realized Eschatology at Corinth." *NTS* 24 (1978): 510–26.

Thomas, Christine M. *The Acts of Peter, Gospel Literature, and the Ancient Novel: Rewriting the Past.* New York: Oxford University Press, 2003.

Tibbs, Clint. *Religious Experience of the Pneuma: Communication with the Spirit World in 1 Corinthians 12 and 14.* WUNT 2/230. Tübingen: Mohr Siebeck, 2007.

Tigay, Jeffrey H. *The Evolution of the Gilgamesh Epic.* Philadelphia: University of Pennsylvania Press, 1982.

Tomes, Roger. "Why Did Paul Get His Hair Cut? (Acts 18.18; 21.23-24)." In *Luke's Literary Achievement: Collected Essays,* edited by C. M. Tuckett, 188–97. JSNT-Sup 116. Sheffield: Sheffield Academic Press, 1995.

Torre, Emilio Suárez de la. "Apollo and Dionysos: Intersections." In Bernabé et al., *Redefining Dionysos,* 58–81.

Traunecker, Claude. *The Gods of Egypt.* Translated by David Lorton. Ithaca: Cornell University Press, 2001.

Trocmé, Etienne. *Le livre des Actes et l'histoire.* Paris: Presses Universitaires de France, 1957.

Tune, Anders S. "Quantum Theory and the Resurrection of Jesus." *Dialog* 43, no. 3 (2004): 166–76.

Twomey, Jay. Review of *Noli me tangere: On the Raising of the Body,* by Jean-Luc Nancy. *Bible and Critical Theory* 6, no. 2 (2010): 52.1–52.3.

Van Minnen, Peter. "The Akhmîm *Gospel of Peter.*" In *Das Evangelium nach Petrus: Text, Kontexte, Intertexte,* edited by Thomas J. Kraus and Tobias Nicklas, 53–60. TUGAL 158. Berlin: de Gruyter, 2007.

VanderKam, James C. *The Book of Jubilees: A Critical Edition.* CSCO 510. Scriptores Aethiopici 87. Peters: Louvain, 1989.

———. *The Meaning of the Dead Sea Scrolls: Their Significance for Understanding the Bible, Judaism, Jesus, and Christianity.* San Francisco: HarperSanFrancisco, 2002.

Vinzent, Markus. *Der Ursprung des Apostolikums im Urteil der kritischen Forschung.* Forschungen zur Kirchen- und Dogmengeschichte 89. Göttingen: Vandenoeck & Ruprcht, 2006.

Viviano, Benedict T. *The Kingdom of God in History.* Eugene, Ore.: Wipf and Stock, 1988.

Ward, Graham. "Transcorporality: The Ontological Scandal." *Bulletin of the John Rylands Library* 80, no. 3 (1998): 235–52.

Ware, James. "Paul's Understanding of the Resurrection in 1 Corinthians 15:36-54." *JBL* 133, no. 4 (2014): 809–35.

Way, Arthur S., ed. *Euripides with an English Translation.* Vol. 3. LCL 11. London: Heinemann, 1924.

Webb, Robert L. "'Apocalyptic': Observations on a Slippery Term." *JNES* 49, no. 2 (1990): 115–26.

Wedderburn, A. J. M. *Baptism and Resurrection: Studies in Pauline Theology against Its Graeco-Roman Background.* WUNT 44. Tübingen: Mohr Siebeck, 1987.

Weiss, Konrad. "*Pous.*" In *Theological Dictionary of the New Testament,* edited by Gerhard Friedrich, translated by Geoffrey W. Bromiley, 624–31. Grand Rapids: Eerdmans, 1968.

Wenham, David. *The Rediscovery of Jesus' Eschatological Discourse.* Gospel Perspectives 4. Sheffield: JSOT Press, 1984.

West, M. L. *The Orphic Poems.* Oxford: Clarendon, 1998.

Wilkinson, Toby A. H. *Early Dynastic Egypt.* London: Routledge, 1999.

Wilson, Walter T. *Healing in the Gospel of Matthew: Reflections on Method and Ministry.* Minneapolis: Fortress, 2014.

Winkler, John J., and Froma I. Zeitlin, eds. *Nothing to Do with Dionysos? Athenian Drama in Its Social Context.* Princeton: Princeton University Press, 1990.

Wittkowsky, Vadim. "'Pagane' Zitate im Neuen Testament." *NovT* 51, no. 2 (2009): 107–26.

Wojciechowski, M. "Le naziréat et la Passion (Mc 14,25a; 15:23)." *Biblica* 65 (1984): 94–96.

Wolfson, Elliot R. *Through a Speculum That Shines: Vision and Imagination in Medieval Jewish Mysticism.* Princeton: Princeton University Press, 1994.

———. *Language, Eros, Being: Kabbalistic Hermeneutics and Poetic Imagination.* New York: Fordham University Press, 2007.

Wolkstein, Diane, and Samuel Noah Kramer. *Inanna, Queen of Heaven and Earth: Her Stories and Hymns from Sumer.* New York: Harper & Row, 1983.

Wright, N. T. "Resurrection Faith." *Christian Century,* December 18–31, 2002, 28–31.

———. *The Resurrection of the Son of God.* Christian Origins and the Question of God 3. London: SPCK; Minneapolis: Fortress, 2003.

———. *What Saint Paul Really Said: Was Paul of Tarsus the Real Founder of Christianity?* Grand Rapids: Eerdmans, 1997.

Yamauchi, Edwin M. "Tammuz and the Bible." *JBL* 84, no. 3 (1965): 283–90.

Ziolkowski, Theodore. *Gilgamesh among Us: Modern Encounters with the Ancient Epic.* Ithaca: Cornell University Press, 2012.

Index of Terms

Joppa, 116, 158, 186
"just one," 161, 196

Kêpha', 78–81, 87–89, 99–100,
111–12, 157, 190, 206, 207, 226n20,
227n23, 232n23; *see also* Peter (and
Simon Peter)
Khristos, 71, 74, 113, 124, 167

Lucius of Cyrene, 160

maat, 18
Maccabeus, Judas, 46, 51, 53
mainades, 22
Manaen, 160
martyrdom, 46, 53, 55, 62, 80, 94,
130, 163, 227n26, 231n15
Mary Magdalene, 2, 5, 88–90, 108,
133, 136, 143–44, 146–47, 149–51,
155–56, 166–69, 170–76, 179–80,
182–83, 185, 195, 200, 207, 246n43,
251n31
Merkhabah or chariot, 35–37, 39, 41,
60, 260n46
mishnah, Mishnah, 52, 55, 100, 102,
111, 114, 206, 223n31, 238n34
"More than Five Hundred," the, 5, 78,
82, 112–14, 117, 146, 235n2, 236n9
Moses, 16, 36, 41–44, 55, 76, 79,
104–5, 108, 114–15, 119, 125–28,
142–43, 180, 186
Mysteries, 21, 24

Nazarênos, 141, 144, 244n24
Nazirite, 128–29, 130–32, 141,
144–45, 156, 193, 195, 239n38,
244n24
Noah, 11, 29, 114, 128, 212n2, 216n2,
236n10
nous, 74, 76, 119, 150

Obadiah (officer of Ahab), 36–37
Osiris, 9, 15–22, 26, 29–30, 32, 35, 28,
41, 44, 204, 213n6, 213n9, 213n14,
215n32

parousia, 86, 135, 139, 140, 173, 176,
182–83, 193, 207
Paul, 1, 3–5, 44, 68–88, 112, 116–22,
127–28, 132–33, 140, 142–43, 145,
150–51, 155–62, 182–84, 190–92,
200, 205–7, 209, 218n25, 223n1,
224n6, 225n12, 225n15, 225n16,
226n18, 226n19, 226n21, 228n33,
236n5, 236n9, 237n18, 239n41,
242n14, 243n21, 245n31, 247n54,
247n2, 248n3, 248n6, 248n8,
248n9, 249n12, 249n13, 251n28,
251n31, 254n10, 255n17, 257n25,
263n67
Pentecost, 95, 112–17, 119–20, 176,
192, 206, 207, 235n2, 235n4, 236n7,
237n18
Pentheus, 23–24
Peter (and Simon Peter), 2, 5, 70,
79, 81, 87, 88–90, 92–99, 104–6,
111–14, 116–18, 120, 123–26, 130,
137, 140–41, 147–50, 155, 158–59,
165–66, 168–69, 172, 174, 176,
180–83, 188, 192, 200, 226n22,
229n5, 230n6, 230n9, 230n12,
231n14, 231n15, 231n17, 233n32,
237n18, 237n21, 240n43, 240n45,
244n24, 246n43; *see also Kêpha'*
Pharisees, 52, 55, 64, 122, 125, 136,
137, 140, 254n10
Philip, 120, 124, 166, 167, 168, 195,
240n43
Pilate, 136, 137, 141
Plain of Oblivion, 40
Plato, 39, 44, 59, 64, 218n21, 219n27;
"The Vision of Er" in the *Republic*,
39, 41–44, 50–51, 59
Pompey, 47
prophecy, 6, 33–34, 38, 48, 84, 92,
106, 115, 120–21, 129, 151, 157,
163–64, 168, 208, 219n4, 225n15,
234n40, 251n28
Psukhê, 72–74

Toledoth Jesu, 148, 180
transfiguration, the, 43, 103–4, 156,
    186, 189, 190, 234n39
Twelve, the, 5, 78, 81–82, 90, 92, 96,
    99–107, 109, 111, 112, 114, 155–56,
    176, 182–83, 190, 192, 200, 206–7,
    230n6, 230n7, 231n14, 234n42

Uruk, 11–14
Utnapishtim, 9, 11–15, 21, 26, 29,
    32–33, 35–36, 41, 44, 215n32

vision, 6, 25, 36, 38, 39, 40–44, 49–51,
    58–59, 61, 83, 84, 104, 108, 111,
    114, 124, 131, 141, 144–46, 148–51,
    157–66, 168–69, 171–73, 175, 179,
    182, 186, 189, 192, 195, 205, 207,

208, 219n4, 230n9, 240n45, 246n43,
    248n8, 249n13, 257n25, 261n55

Wisdom of Solomon, 42–43, 62, 64,
    84, 159, 218n25

"The Younger Avesta," 50

Zadok, 47, 50, 221n11
Zechariah, 41, 48, 84, 129, 135, 164,
    186, 194, 241n3
Ziusudra, 12
Zoroastrianism, 50, 219n5

Index of Passages

Old Testament Apocrypha and Pseudepigrapha

New Testament Apocrypha and Pseudepigrapha